Final Cut Pro X

Making the Transition

Larry Jordan

To Jane,
who makes everything I do possible.

Final Cut Pro X: Making the Transition

Larry Jordan

Peachpit Press
1249 Eighth Street
Berkeley, CA 94710
(510) 524-2178
Fax: (510) 524-2221

Find us on the Web at www.peachpit.com
To report errors, please send a note to errata@peachpit.com
Peachpit is a division of Pearson Education

Senior Editor: Karyn Johnson
Copy Editors: Kimberly Wimpsett and Jacqueline Aaron
Production Editor: Danielle Foster
Proofreader: Elizabeth Welch
Composition: Danielle Foster
Indexer: Valerie Perry
Interior Design: Danielle Foster
Cover Design: Aren Straiger

Notice of Rights

Notice of Liability

Trademarks

ISBN-13: 978-0-321-81126-4
ISBN-10: 0-321-81126-7

9 8 7 6 5 4 3 2 1

Printed and bound in the United States of America

CONTENTS

Welcome viii

1 **Preparing for Final Cut Pro X** 1

Getting Your System Ready to Edit 2

Why Use an Editing Workflow? 8

Summary 14

2 **Get Started Editing** 15

Learning About Events and Projects 16

Starting Final Cut Pro X 18

Touring the Interface 19

Creating a New Event 25

Importing Media 27

Creating a New Project 30

Creating a Simple Edit 32

Summary 37

Keyboard Shortcuts 38

3 **Managing Events, Projects, and Shortcuts** 39

All About Events 40

All About Projects 48

Creating Keyboard Shortcuts 60

Summary 63

Keyboard Shortcuts 64

4 Managing Media 65

Overview 66

Naming Media Folders 68

Importing Media 71

Special Cases 89

Summary 96

Keyboard Shortcuts 96

5 Organizing Clips: Ratings, Keywords, and Extended Metadata 97

Displaying Events and Clips 98

Working the Ratings 103

Keying in on Keywords 106

Managing Metadata 113

Summary 115

Keyboard Shortcuts 116

6 Editing 117

The Editing Process 118

The Editing and Playback Preferences 119

Editing Techniques 122

Summary 138

Keyboard Shortcuts 139

7 Organizing Your Edit 141

Making Selections 142

Using Markers and To-Dos 142

Copy and Paste Options 146

The Magnetic Timeline 147

The Magic of Compound Clips 148

A Grab Bag of Tools 152

Roles 156

The Timeline Index 159

Summary 163

Keyboard Shortcuts 163

8 **Trimming Your Edit** 165
Getting Ready to Trim 166
Setting the Scene 169
The Precision Editor 170
Twelve Trimming Techniques 174
Introducing the Trim Tool 175
Summary 182
Keyboard Shortcuts 183

9 **Audio** 185
Audio Basics 186
Audio in Final Cut Pro X 187
Introducing the Inspector 191
Audio Techniques 192
Special Situations for Audio 200
Mixing 204
Explaining Keyframes 207
Summary 209
Keyboard Shortcuts 210

10 **Transitions** 211
Transitions Overview 212
Transition Basics 217
Advanced Transitions 220
Transition Inspector 223
Transition Browser 224
Summary 228
Keyboard Shortcuts 228

11 **Titles and Text** 229
Title Basics 230
Modifying Titles 232
Displaying Action and Title Safe 235
Finding and Replacing Text 236

Specific Title Examples 237
Summary 240
Keyboard Shortcuts 240

12 Built-in Effects 241
Effects Basics 242
Transform Effects 243
Animate Using Keyframes 247
Trim, Crop, and Ken Burns 251
Distort, or Corner Pinning 257
Image Stabilization 258
Rolling Shutter 259
Spatial Conform 260
Compositing 262
Special Case: Use Compound Clips for Effects 266
Summary 268
Keyboard Shortcuts 268

13 Themes and Generators 269
Themes 270
Generators 271
Adjusting a Generator in Motion 275
Summary 276

14 Keying 277
Planning a Key 278
Creating a Luma Key 279
Creating a Chroma Key 281
Adding a Mask 288
Summary 290
Keyboard Shortcuts 290

15 **Retiming** **291**

The Basics of Retiming 292

Hold Frames 292

Constant Speed Changes 296

Variable Speed Changes 298

Other Speed Effects 300

Summary 301

Keyboard Shortcuts 301

16 **Color Correction** **303**

Color Correction Basics 304

Color Looks 304

Color Correction with the Enhancement Menu 305

How to Read the Video Scopes 307

Adjusting Grayscale and Color 310

Using Masks for Color Correction 318

Summary 320

Keyboard Shortcuts 320

17 **Sharing and Exporting** **321**

Overview of the Output Process 322

Exporting a High-Quality Master File 323

Exporting Roles 324

Other Options in the Share Menu 329

Summary 332

Keyboard Shortcuts 332

Index **333**

● NOTE

Please register your book at **http://www.peachpit.com/register** for two bonus chapters: The Visual Effects Cookbook and the Audio Effects Cookbook.

WELCOME

Final Cut Pro X was born amid controversy.

And that is a shame, because if you ignore the trauma surrounding its birth, there's a lot of exciting new technology, power, and ease of use hiding under the hood.

That got me thinking about writing this book.

When you decide to move to Final Cut Pro X, you are also deciding to make a transition—a transition from the system you were using to this new system. For some, that transition is easy. For others, it's difficult. In all cases, it helps to have a guide to show you the way.

That's the purpose of this book—to ease your transition into Final Cut Pro X.

Who This Book Is For

Knowledge is knowing "how" to do something. Wisdom is knowing "why." It is my hope that this book contains both. This book is for anyone interested in editing video using Final Cut Pro X.

This book is designed to help you learn the new software from beginning to end; I'll start with getting you and your system ready and wrap up with exporting.

Best of all, you don't need to be an editing genius or technical geek to understand this book. Some editing experience is expected (this is a "transition" book, after all) but the first two chapters help you get organized and explain the basics so you can get started immediately. Then, once you're up and running with the new software, I'll spend the rest of the book walking you through the whole application in detail so you can make it fly.

In fact, if you browse around the book, you'll discover lots of little tips and tricks scattered throughout. I love these—there's nothing like a good shortcut to brighten my day!

What This Book Covers

When I first saw Final Cut Pro X, my initial thought was, "This is way too different for me to learn." This was chiefly because I knew earlier versions of Final Cut so well, and this version appeared to be so different. However, after spending time studying it and writing this book, I realized that there is a lot of power under the hood, and learning this version of Final Cut is a lot easier if you get started the right way. That's my goal: I want to save you hours of figuring it out on your own so you can become productive immediately.

I've been writing about Final Cut Studio for ten years in books, magazines, newsletters, and the Web. My free monthly newsletter—now in its seventh year—is the oldest and most widely read publication on Final Cut Pro in the world (*www.larryjordan.biz/newsletter*). It reaches tens of thousands of readers worldwide each month.

I got my start in this industry more than 35 years ago as a producer and director. I've worked in local television and the networks, principally doing live broadcasts, drama, and special events. I'm a member of the Directors Guild of America and the Producers Guild of America. This is the sixth book I've written on editing software (five on Final Cut Pro and one on Adobe Production Premium). I'm an Apple Certified trainer in digital media and travel the world doing seminars and training, helping editors become better at their craft.

I was one of the few people outside of Apple to see a preview of this new version of Final Cut several months before it was released. I realized then that this software would revolutionize the way we think about video editing.

In talking with hundreds of editors after FCP X was launched, I realized that a lot of them are looking for guidance in how to make the transition to the new software. Gone were many of the terms and functions they had become used to; they've been replaced with a new interface and a new way of thinking about editing.

This transition to Final Cut Pro X is difficult for many Final Cut Pro 7 editors because there is a lot to "unlearn." On the other hand, after working with this awhile, much of the new interface becomes intuitive, though it's different from what they've used before.

Video editing is part of the process of visual storytelling. Editing a film starts with planning, as you'll learn in Chapter 1. This process flows from planning to production to editing and final delivery. Final Cut Pro X is one stop along that continuum. It is at the core of the editing/postproduction process.

I'm a firm believer that, as a teacher, I need to do more than simply tell you which buttons to push. I need to explain the "why" as well as the "how." I need to do more than tell you that a hammer is used to pound nails. I need to illustrate how you use that hammer to build a house, when to use other tools, and show how that hammer fits into the whole process of house building.

In other words, one of my goals is to put Final Cut Pro X in the context of the larger world of visual storytelling and not simply say, "Click here and, poof, magic happens!" Knowing where to click is good. Knowing *why* to click is even better.

Late-Breaking News

Just as this book was going to press, Apple updated Final Cut Pro X to version 10.0.1. So, I went back and rewrote most of these chapters to reflect the new features. Where possible, I've also flagged which features are part of this new release. For anyone considering the 10.0.1 upgrade, I strongly recommend you get it, especially because it is free.

Effects Cookbooks Available for Download

One of the challenges in writing a book is that it is easy to run out of pages before I run out of ideas. That's the case here.

I have created two additional chapters—the Visual Effects Cookbook and the Audio Effects Cookbook—which are available in PDF form as a free download, once you register your book at *http://www.peachpit.com/register.*

These two chapters provide step-by-step instructions on how to create almost two dozen clip effects—from simple picture-in-picture techniques to sophisticated audio filters and processing.

This is just a partial list of what's available in these two chapters:

- Adding, adjusting, disabling, resetting, and removing clip effects
- Animating a blur and adding title text
- Creating a vignette
- Adding lighting effects
- Creating a color mask

- Using Audio Enhancements
- Matching audio between clips
- Creating an audio effect
- Warming up a voice
- Using the Limiter effect to boost and smooth out audio levels

There are a lot of cool techniques and insider tips you can use in your own effects. Register your book and download your copies of these useful bonus chapters today.

Where the Images Came From

One of the hardest challenges in creating a book is finding the right media to use to illustrate the concepts I am trying to teach. This makes me especially grateful to the following people for allowing me to use their images:

For the interview footage of Dr. Vint Cerf, I want to thank both Dr. Cerf and Alcatel/Lucent. This interview was recorded in 2004 for Alcatel/Lucent as Dr. Cerf was getting ready to deliver a speech at Van Nuys High School, in Van Nuys, California, about the importance of education and staying in school. Visit the Alcatel/Lucent website at *www.alcatel-lucent.com*.

I'm grateful to Pond5 for sharing some of their vast collection of royalty-free images. This is but a small sampling of what is available at *www.pond5.com*.

The dramatic footage in Chapter 6 comes from John Putch and his movie *Route 30, Too!* John has graciously shared a number of scenes from his film to help me illustrate the challenges of editing dramatic work. Learn more at *www.route30trilogy.com*.

Since I am a huge train fan, I want to thank Fran and Miles Hale of Model Railroad Builders for the stunning model train layout video. Frankly, I was having so much fun watching the trains roll past, I almost didn't get this book written. Visit their website at *www.franandmileshale.com*.

I've been using snowboarding footage from the great folks at Standard Films for all of my books. In fact, it's the same footage. Don't mess with success! I'm grateful to Mike Hatchett for allowing me to continue to use this footage. Visit their website at *www.standardfilms.com*.

I am also grateful for clips from Michael Shaw, Resmine Atis, and Tom Centeno.

Finally, I want to thank SmartSound Software, Inc., for access to their music library. I've been a fan and user of SmartSound since 1997 and happily recommend them to anyone looking to build a library of great production music. Learn more at *www.smartsound.com*.

● **NOTE** How I Do My Screen Captures

While the Mac has a built-in screen capture utility (Shift+Command+3 captures the entire screen and Shift+Command+4 displays a cursor so you can capture a portion of the screen), I prefer the flexibility and options of Ambrosia Software's SnapZ Pro X. All the screenshots in this book were captured with SnapZ Pro X.

Special People to Thank

Writing a book is the effort of one person. Publishing a book takes a team.

I'd like to thank Karyn Johnson and the folks at Peachpit Press for inviting me to write this book. This is the fifth book I've done for Peachpit, and they make the process easy (well, as easy as writing a book can be, which is rarely easy).

An incredible team of very talented folks here at my company, Larry Jordan & Associates, Inc., including Debbie Price, Laura Peters, Mina Qubaisi, and Cirina Catania for keeping things running when I was busy writing. I count on them more than I can possibly express. Patrick Saxon for his help with some of the initial drafts and Noë Gold for his in-depth review of all the chapters.

Jacqueline Aaron and Kim Wimpsett, two copy editors who strove mightily to make sure my grammar, syntax, and punctuation were coherent. To an amazing compositor, Danielle Foster, who continually delighted me with her ability to balance great design with squeezing as many words on the page as would beautifully fit.

Katie Fredeen for the illustrations (below and in Chapter 1). I only wish there was room to print more of them.

A team of experts to help me better understand the technology, including Philip Hodgetts, Greg Clark, and hundreds of editors who took the time to e-mail me their questions and thoughts about the new software.

Finally, special thanks go to members of the Apple Final Cut Pro team: Richard Townhill, Steve Bayes, Luke Tristam, and Jud Coplan for answering innumerable questions and helping me better understand this new application.

Still, I hasten to add that though I've had a lot of help, the responsibility of writing this book is mine, as are any (ideally few) mistakes that might still be lurking inside.

One Last Thought

Producing good-quality, interesting video is not for the faint of heart. The reason we got into this bizarre, competitive, deadline-driven business was that we like to tell stories. Visual stories. Stories with passion, movement, and characters people want to care about.

Final Cut Pro X is a tool that helps us tell those stories—faster, better, and more easily than any other editing software. It has been a fascinating process learning this software and sharing it with you.

Whether you edit video as a hobby or as a profession, powerful stories create profound results. Video can change the world—for good or bad. It can increase understanding or build barriers. Final Cut Pro X gives us the power, but how we use it is up to us.

Thanks, and edit well.

PREPARING FOR FINAL CUT PRO X

This first chapter focuses on getting organized for editing and thinking about your workflow. A *workflow* is simply a fancy word for the process you follow to get something done. The better your planning and workflow, the more successful the outcome.

This chapter has two sections: getting your system ready for editing and then getting *you* ready for editing in Final Cut Pro X.

Getting Your System Ready to Edit

Since specifications change faster than I can update this book, the best place to go to learn the technical requirements for the latest version of Final Cut Pro X is the Apple website, at *www.apple.com/finalcutpro/specs/*.

Just to amplify what Apple has written, FCP X will use all the memory you have on your system. I recommend you install 8 GB of RAM, if your hardware supports that much. FCP X will use even more than that, but the improvement in speed may not be sufficiently offset by the cost of more RAM.

FCP X supports multiple processors. In fact, if you have a choice, more processors running at a slower speed will yield better performance than fewer processors running faster. (Weird, but true.)

NOTE New Feature—GPU-acceleration

New with version 10.0.1, Apple harnessed the power of the graphics processing unit (GPU) to accelerate exports, in addition to supporting real-time playback. If you own a Mac Pro and are creating lots of projects that you need to export and post quickly, investing in a fast GPU is a good idea.

FCP X requires a minimum of Mac OS X 10.6.8 (and the new, full-screen editing option requires upgrading to Lion). You do not need to upgrade to Lion to run FCP X, though as Lion matures, upgrading your FCP X system will be a good idea.

The big issue with video editing is media storage. Over the course of your editing career, you will spend far more money buying storage hardware than computer gear. Far more.

So, I want to spend a little time, right at the beginning, making sure your system is ready to edit video problem-free.

It Isn't the Amount of the Storage; It's the Speed

Video editing requires two things: vast storage and fast data transfers between the computer and the hard disk.

The storage part we pretty much understand. The more gigabytes (GB) or terabytes (TB) your hard disk holds, the better. A terabyte is just a ridiculously vast amount of storage—a *trillion* times bigger than a single byte. (I find it truly depressing that my media seems to fill a terabyte of storage in virtually no time at all.)

A TB Isn't Really a TB

With OS X 10.6, Apple changed the way it calculates storage. In "the old days," a megabyte contained 1,024 KB, while a gigabyte contained 1,024 MB. For engineers and the hard disk of your computer, it still does. But to simplify the lives of computer users, Apple changed how it displays these numbers. Now, a megabyte contains only 1,000 KB, while a gigabyte contains 1,000 MB. Your files are perfectly safe, but the sizes will seem to vary depending upon which version of the OS is reporting the size of the file. This new method will make your files seem slightly bigger.

Table 1.1 illustrates a few common video formats. The middle column shows how much storage one hour of media will require. The right column indicates the sustained speed (the *data transfer rate*) required for continuous, smooth playback of a single stream of media.

TABLE 1.1 Hard Disk Storage and Data Rate Requirements*

Video Format	Store One Hour of Media	Data Transfer Rate
DV (NTSC or PAL)	13 GB	3.75 MB/second
HDV	13 GB	3.75 MB/second
AVCHD (Native)	Up to 11 GB	3.0 MB/second
(H)DSLR—also called H.264	18 GB	About 5 MB/second
XDCAM EX	19 GB	5.2 MB/second
DVCPROHD	51 GB	14 MB/second
AVC-Intra 100	51 GB	14 MB/second
ProRes Proxy for HD	20 GB	5.6 MB/second
ProRes 422 for HD	66 GB	18.1 MB/second
R3D (Native)	137 GB	38 MB/second

* Note: HD file sizes vary depending upon image size and frame rate. These numbers are based on shooting 1080i/60 HD. Lower frame rates, or smaller images, will result in smaller files. Optimizing media in FCP X converts long-GOP media from its native file format to ProRes 422. An hour of stereo, 16-bit, 48 kHz audio requires about 650 MB, which is included in these numbers.

Table 1.1 is helpful for two reasons. First, it provides the ability to estimate how much storage your project is going to require. Second, it illustrates that different video formats require different speeds from your hard disk.

Planning Your Storage

The reason these storage sizes are so important is that for many video formats, FCP X gives you the option to "optimize" your media. In general, this is a good thing, because it provides better performance and improved image quality for effects. However, optimizing your long-GOP media means that Final Cut Pro will convert it (a process called *transcoding*) from its native format (the format shot by the camera) to ProRes 422. This transcoding process means that your storage requirements will increase.

For example, one hour of AVCHD media will take about 11 GB to store, plus another 66 GB when it is transcoded into ProRes 422. This transcoding is not bad; in fact, I recommend it. However, it does mean your hard disks will fill up more quickly than you might expect.

● **NOTE** But Doesn't Transcoding Take Time?

Yes, but you won't notice. One of the real advantages to FCP X is that all this transcoding, rendering, importing, and file handling happens in the background. While you are busy working on your project, FCP is busy behind the scenes processing media.

Another option in FCP X is to copy your media into a central storage location that Final Cut Pro tracks. For new editors, this is an excellent idea, because you don't need to worry about keeping track of all your media.

However, this also increases your storage requirements.

Again, in the example, an hour of AVCHD stored on your hard disk takes 11 GB to store. First, FCP X copies it to the Final Cut Events folder. This takes another 11 GB. Then, FCP X transcodes it into ProRes 422. This takes another 66 GB. So, when FCP X is done, your media files have been backed up and transcoded, while your file storage has jumped from 11 GB to 88 GB. One of the benefits of this system, though, is that you now have three copies of your media. So, if something gets accidently deleted, you have backups you can use to restore the missing file.

A little later in this chapter, I'll explain a system that you can use for storing and naming media—either from videotape or from media cards.

In any case, however, media takes a *lot* of storage space!

Adding More Storage

Although it is technically possible to edit video using only one drive (your boot, or start-up, drive), it is not a wise idea to do so. This is because your boot drive has many, many, many calls on its attentions: the operating system, Final Cut Pro, any background applications, all background processes, and then—dead last in priority—playing media.

The problem with this is that unless media plays smoothly, second after second and minute after minute, the rest of the editing system is useless.

By adding a second drive, specifically for media storage, not only do you provide a lot more storage for your media but you significantly improve the performance of your system by allowing your boot disk to concentrate on serving the needs of the operating system and Final Cut Pro X, while the second drive concentrates on storing and playing all media.

How Many Drives Do I Need?

Um, three, actually. The first one is your boot drive. This holds the operating system and all your applications. The second is the media drive used by Final Cut Pro X. The third drive is the backup drive for tapeless media. If you are shooting on videotape, you don't need this drive. But, if you are shooting tapeless, it is a *really* good idea to store camera source files on a hard drive separate from the drive you store your media for editing. Just in case.

I use the phrase *second drive*, and most of the time, this drive will be external to your computer. However, for Mac Pro systems, a second drive can be an internal drive.

An internal drive on a Mac Pro will be faster than an external single drive connected via USB or FireWire 400. Recent FireWire 800 drives will be about as fast as an internal single Mac Pro drive.

How You Connect Your Drives Matters

I strongly recommend against using USB-connected drives because they are consistently too slow on Macs to support reliable video editing. FireWire 800, iSCSI, or Thunderbolt-connected drives are much better. Because Mac Pros allow plug-in cards, they also support data connections such as eSATA, mini-SAS, and Fibre Channel, which are all plenty fast for video editing. However, over time, I suspect Thunderbolt will become the connection protocol of choice, provided your hardware supports it.

Internal drives are cheaper than external drives. However, if something goes wrong with an internal drive, you lose access to your computer while you get the drive fixed. I recommend using external drives for your storage, even for Mac Pros.

Adding a second drive to your system is a wise investment and, with the prices of hard drives falling daily, not that expensive, either.

Sad Truths About FireWire

FireWire is a great connection protocol for hard drives. But it has several weaknesses: First, the more hard drives you attach via FireWire, the slower they go. The limit is about five drives before you start to notice significant speed slowdowns. Second, connecting both a FireWire 400 drive and a FireWire 800 drive slows the FireWire 800 drive down to just a little faster than FireWire 400 speeds. Third, the fuller a hard drive becomes, the slower it goes. When it is totally full, it stops; it won't play back or record anything. Try to keep at least 20 percent free space, or more, on all hard drives.

Why Not Use the Network?

Well, with the initial release of Final Cut Pro X, you couldn't use the network. But the 10.0.1 update fixed that. This new upgrade added support for Xsan, Apple's file-sharing system. These network features should work with any network file server provided the data transfer rate is fast enough from the server to the local computer to support media file transfers and provided the server supports user permissions and record locking, which OS X Server does.

● **NOTE** How Fast Does My Network Need to Be?

Pretty darn fast. Apple recommends networks connected via Fibre Channel. At a minimum, you need Gigabit Ethernet. It all depends upon the video format you are using and how many users are on the network. The higher the data rate required by your media—see Table 1.1—the faster your network needs to be to support it.

Shared media on a server has always been supported by FCP X.

With the new release, now Projects and Events can also be stored on a server. Media can be accessed by multiple users at the same time; however, Project and Event folders can be accessed by only one person at a time. In other words, multiple editors can now share the same Project; however, only one editor can be in that Project at the same time. FCP X provides a simple menu choice allowing editors to move Events and Projects into, or out of, the app as necessary.

For non-network setups, a second drive will still be necessary.

To RAID or Not to RAID?

RAIDs (Redundant Array of Inexpensive Drives/Devices/Disks—there's a lot of debate on which is the correct word for the letter *D*) are the fastest, largest, and best storage systems for editing video. They are also the most expensive.

A RAID combines the speed and storage of multiple hard drives into a unit that connects via a single cable to your computer. There are many types of RAIDs, the most common of which are illustrated in **Table 1.2**.

My recommendation is that if you are going to invest in a RAID, buy a RAID 5. They are worth the money and the peace of mind.

How you connect your RAID to your computer, just like connecting a hard drive, has a significant impact on the speed you'll get from the system. **Table 1.3** illustrates this. My recommendation is to use the fastest connection protocol your hardware supports.

TABLE 1.2 RAID Configurations

RAID Type	Benefits	Limitations
RAID 0	Inexpensive, fast. Requires minimum of two drives.	No data redundancy. If you lose one drive, you lose all your data.
RAID 1	Inexpensive. Data is mirrored (copied) to both drives. Requires minimum of two drives.	Slow. Total storage is limited to the smaller of the two drives in the system. Generally used on set to capture data from camera cards.
RAID 5	Very fast. If you lose one drive, your data is safe. These require a minimum of three drives but generally contain four to eight drives in the system.	More expensive. If you lose *two* drives at once, you lose all your data.
RAID 6	Fast, though not as fast as a RAID 5. Data is double-redundant. If you lose two drives at the same time, your data is safe.	More expensive.
RAID 50	Very, very fast. Combines benefits of RAID 0 with RAID 5. Data is safe if a hard drive fails. These generally contain eight to sixteen drives in the system.	Expensive. Generally used when really high performance is required.

TABLE 1.3 Connecting Hard Drives to Mac Computers

RAID Connection Protocol	Average Transfer Speed
USB or FireWire 400	Don't use for a RAID
FireWire 800	85–90 MB/second
iSCSI	100–105 MB/second
eSATA	Up to 400 MB/second
mini-SAS	Up to 700 MB/second
Thunderbolt	Up to 1.25 GB/second

I recommend you connect three drives to your system: one for the operating system, one for Final Cut Pro's media files, and one as your source media backup drive.

When it comes to your projects, buying more storage is a whole lot cheaper than going back to reshoot.

Don't Put Your Hard Drives on the Shelf

Looking to store media for a long time? Don't put your hard drives on the shelf! When a hard drive is powered off and stored on a shelf, a process called *bit flux* causes the data stored to "evaporate." After just a year or two, chunks of data that you thought was safe are gone.

Hard drives are great when they are plugged in and spinning. They are perfect for short-term video editing and storage. However, they are not perfect for long-term storage. Just giving you a heads-up. (My current recommendation for long-term archiving is LTO tape.)

Why Use an Editing Workflow?

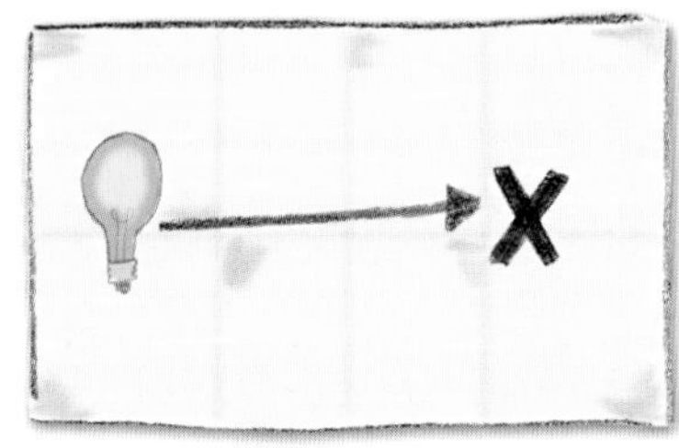

Well, the short answer is that a workflow keeps you organized and minimizes distractions. More importantly, as you turn to video editing to make a living, having a consistent, efficient workflow makes the difference between earning a living and losing your shirt.

As editors, all we have to sell is our time and our creativity. The more efficient we are with our time, the more projects we can tackle and the more money we can make. Or putting it another way, wasting time costs *us* money.

A workflow answers this key question: What should I be doing *right now* to be as efficient as possible? In thinking about this, I created a 12-step workflow for Final Cut Pro X that divides into two big sections: creating the story and polishing the story.

When you're creating your story, the first thing you need to do is get organized and plan what you want to do. Then, gather your media into one spot, build your story in the Timeline, organize your story, and trim it.

Once you've completed the story part, you fine-tune it. You add transitions, add text and effects, polish the audio (*audio repair and mixing*), and adjust the color (*color correction and grading*). Then you export or share the finished project. At the end, and most importantly, you need to archive the project, because you don't want to have it cluttering up your system forever. So, you have to figure out a way to store it for the long term.

Let's take a closer look at these 12 steps, because this whole book is organized around this concept.

Step 1: Plan Twice, Cut Once

The first step is to plan. When I tell this to new editors, their faces fall, because the very first thing they want to do is get in and start cutting. Wrong. You have to think about the story you want to tell first.

You need to know your story and how to interpret it for your audience. Then, again, who *is* your audience? What do they expect? Who needs to see and approve your edits? What media or other files do you need? What footage will be shot? What footage do you need to buy? What footage do you need to create? What's your budget? What are your exact deliverables? What's your deadline? How much storage do you need? Do you need to buy any special gear or software? Who provides final approvals?

Take a deep breath at the beginning, and think through your whole process. Planning makes your life a whole lot easier, because you'll discover it's much simpler to solve a problem by avoiding it than trying to dig yourself out of that unexpected hole you just fell into.

This current chapter covers the initial planning process.

Step 2: Get Organized

The second step is to get organized. Figure out where you are going to store media. What are you going to name files and folders? Make sure you have enough storage. Copy the camera files from any card or external device to a locally attached hard drive or RAID. And remember, be sure to create backups.

In Final Cut Pro X, media, Event, render, and Project files can be stored either on a local hard disk, a RAID, or on a network server.

Personally, I'm of the "old school" and organize my files and folders in the Finder before starting editing. It helps me to think through the process. However, by default, Final Cut Pro X is designed to automatically organize your files for you by copying media from wherever it is stored in your system into the Event folder for editing.

Chapters 2 and 3 focus on getting organized.

Step 3: Import (and Track) Every Byte

The third step is to gather your media so you can edit it. Import your media directly from your camera, from a camera folder on your hard drive, or from an attached media device such as a card reader or a camera. Although you need to capture media stored on videotape directly from the camera in real time, for tapeless media you have more choices. My *strong* recommendation is that you copy tapeless media to a folder on your hard drive before you import. Then, import from that folder.

Final Cut Pro X does not support video capture from tape using timecode to determine the Start and End of a clip (the In and the Out). It only supports video streamed in real time from tape. Basically, you push the play button on your tape deck, and Final Cut Pro captures whatever audio and video flows in.

After you've imported your media, you need to label it so you can keep track of it. To do this, you'll add ratings, keywords, and metadata. Properly filing your clips at the beginning makes them much easier to find later.

Chapter 4 discusses importing and managing media. Chapter 5 shows you how to use ratings, keywords, and metadata to track your media.

Step 4: Build Your Story

The fourth step is to build your story. When you plan, every show is perfect. Then, reality hits.

Your first pass through an edit should not be to make it perfect. Just get the pieces roughed in (which is why it is called a *rough cut*) so you can see what's there, see what's missing, and start to figure out where you need to go.

Building a story means previewing your clips, deciding which shot you want to use, selecting the portion of the shot you want to use, editing it to the Timeline, and then repeating over and over and over until your story is complete. Don't be too fussy at this point. The goal is to quickly create an edit of your story and then refine it until you either get it perfect or run out of time. And don't worry—you'll *always* run out of time. That's why being efficient is so important.

When you're looking at video of a past family event, you generally don't really want to edit it because each frame brings back too many memories. You look and say, "Wow, I remember that day" or "Oh, look how small they used to be!"

But for the rest of us who don't know your family and don't have that backstory, watching home movies is about the most mind-numbing thing I can imagine. Oftentimes, our family events don't contain compelling content. Editing removes the dull parts so the audience gets interested in the characters and the story.

Chapter 6 illustrates how to edit your clips into a rough cut, and Chapter 9 amplifies this with specific techniques for audio.

Step 5: Organize Your Story

Once you have your story built, then you organize it. Where does your story actually begin? You'll want to shuffle the clips. Delete the clips you don't need. Add clips. Keep polishing the material until you get your story the way you want. The initial process of editing is the process of refining your story by making sure you have the right clips in the right order.

Chapter 7 shows how to select, organize, and delete clips in the Timeline; how to work with placeholders and gaps; how to use markers and To-Dos; and how to find things; plus an extended discussion of the new Roles feature.

Step 6: Trim Your Story

Trimming is the process of adjusting where two clips touch and ultimately makes the difference between an amateur movie and a professional one.

Trimming adjusts where two clips touch to smooth the transition between two clips. You want one shot to flow so seamlessly into the next shot so that they don't even look edited. Sometimes I'll spend a half hour making the perfect edit between two shots. It can look so good and flow so smoothly that no one notices all the hard work that was put into it.

Chapter 8 walks through all the trimming techniques in FCP X.

Step 7: Add Transitions

Once you have these first six steps done, your story is complete. The next six steps allow you to polish the story, principally by adding effects.

The seventh step is to add transitions. There are three types of transitions: cuts, dissolves, and wipes. You use cuts the most, dissolves second most, and wipes only when you're forced, because wipes are most cool when they're rarely used. Also, don't spend time adding transitions until you have the order of your shots pretty much figured out.

Because you and I both know what's going to happen.

You're going to add this really cool transition. And you're going to spend five or ten minutes tweaking it and making it exactly right. Then, you realize the first shot is not necessary. You delete the first shot. You've just wasted ten minutes putting that transition in. These are ten minutes you really can't afford to waste.

Add transitions only after your shots are pretty much in the order you want.

Chapter 10 presents the different transition options in Final Cut Pro.

Step 8: Add Text and Other Effects

Effects will soak up every available minute of your time for any project, because you can tweak them forever. So, I recommend you start adding effects only *after* your story is complete, because there's nothing worse than having your story half-edited, with great effects, and running out of time to edit the rest.

Just like there are three types of transitions, there are also three broad categories of effects. These are text effects, built-in effects, and clip effects. This book will discuss all of them.

Starting with Chapter 11, you'll see a lot more about effects and learn how to incorporate them into your projects.

Step 9: Polish the Audio

Now, it's not really called *audio polish*. Instead, editors call it *audio editing and mixing*, but I'm trying to stay with this polish analogy we've got going on here. When the story is complete and your effects are done, that's the time to finish your audio.

Don't get too hung up adjusting audio until you have all your shots in the right order and trimmed. The process of polishing your audio is doing things such as adding sound effects, adding music, adding filters, and setting audio levels.

The general rule of thumb is that you do your final audio mix after all of your editing is done, after all of your trimming is done, and after most of your effects are done. In other words, when the picture is locked.

Final Cut Pro can create both stereo and 5.1 surround audio mixes, which gives you plenty of room to make your project sound great.

Chapters 9 turns up the volume on audio.

Step 10: Color Correct and Grade

The tenth step is to create that final "look" for your project. When everything else is done, you create the final look for your project by adjusting the color of your clips. Now, this final color step has two parts. First is correcting for color problems. Overexposure, underexposure, when the camera is not white balanced...that kind of thing. And the second is to create a color grade or color look. Final Cut Pro X can do both.

In high-end productions, the audio mix and color grading both occur at the same time, using two different teams, and then both are integrated back into the final project for output. Final Cut Pro allows you to do both in the same application.

Chapter 16 highlights how to do color correction.

Step 11: Share Your Project

The second-to-last step is to export, what Apple calls *sharing*. To create your finished project, you share it.

Sharing is fast and easy and works with existing presets. Export creates a master file of your project, which you can then compress later. If you're in a hurry to get something up to the Web, sharing is the best option. It's faster and easier. Use exporting to create a high-quality master file or to save a still frame from your project.

Just as a note, Final Cut Pro X does not support outputting to tape, just outputting to a file. To output to tape, you would need to use hardware and software from companies such as AJA, Blackmagic Design, or Matrox.

Chapter 17 shows what you need to know about sharing or exporting your final project.

Step 12: Archive Your Project

The last step on any project is to archive it.

Archiving is the process of collecting all your assets and preserving them for the long term. Final Cut Pro X makes the process of collecting assets for final archiving easy. *How* you decide to archive them is up to you, though my current recommendation is LTO-5 tape.

LTO tape requires buying more gear, but it's a lot more secure than long-term storage on a hard disk.

The whole reason behind creating a workflow is that it helps you be both creative and efficient, by focusing on the task you need to do right now. It helps you minimize spinning your wheels and wasting time.

This book is organized around these 12 steps. When you're organized with a workflow, you can focus on the art and craft of storytelling, while Final Cut Pro X watches over the technical side of editing your video.

Summary

Time spent thinking about your project and getting organized is never wasted—even if you take only a few minutes to organize your thoughts.

But I also know you are anxious to get started. So, here's the deal. The next chapter provides a quick guide to show you *how* to use Final Cut Pro X in the editing process. Then, the next four chapters go into far more detail so you can understand the *why* behind the process.

If you can't wait to start, read Chapter 2 and then jump to Chapter 6. If you want to get your questions answered and really understand what Final Cut Pro is doing, start reading Chapter 3.

Or, you can just continue reading the whole book—there's a lot to learn, regardless of which choice you make.

In any case, our planning is over—let's get to work.

GET STARTED EDITING

I know you're in a hurry to get started. That's what this chapter is about. It introduces the interface, defines several key concepts, and covers the process of creating a new Event, creating a new Project, and making a simple edit. I'll show you how to set system preferences, and, at the end, I'll present some essential keyboard shortcuts and how to create new ones.

There's a lot to learn, but the purpose of this chapter is to give you a sufficient overview to help you start editing quickly. Later chapters will go into all these subjects in much more detail.

Learning About Events and Projects

Making the transition into Final Cut Pro X requires learning new concepts. Two of them are Events and Projects. An *Event* is a collection of media files. A *Project* is how you want those media files edited together.

The power of Final Cut Pro X is that both Events and Projects are stored in two separate databases, and both databases are stored in different locations. Any piece of media is now instantly available to any project. Unlike working with Final Cut Pro 7, you don't run into problems from using too many clips. No more relinking offline media. No more importing media into a project before you can even start editing. That was the old way of doing things; welcome to the new world of Final Cut Pro X.

The databases make all the difference. The Final Cut Events folder contains all the media and metadata captured from a camera, imported from a card, or imported from the Finder. And this includes metadata that is autogenerated by Final Cut Pro X. Inside the Final Cut Events folder are individual folders for each new Event you create.

Events can be shared between Projects, can be merged into a single Event, can be moved from one disk to another, and can even be deleted, all from within Final Cut Pro X. By default, the Final Cut Events folder is stored on your boot disk in the [Home directory] > Movies folder. But you can easily choose to store it on a different drive, which is something I strongly recommend.

You can use FCP X to move Events, you can use the Finder, or (my personal favorite) you can use a separate utility to move and organize your Events.

In the initial release of FCP X, Events and Projects could be stored only on locally attached storage, either an internal drive, an external drive, or a RAID. However, with the release of FCP X version 10.0.1, full Xsan support is now available. This new release allows storing media, Events, and Projects on network devices. Media can be shared simultaneously by multiple editors. While Events and Projects can be shared between editors, only one editor can use an Event or Project at a time. FCP X provides a simple menu choice allowing editors to move Events and Projects into, or out of, the app.

Final Cut Pro is managing all this information using databases. The power of a database means that Final Cut Pro can organize your files faster and better than the Finder can. To help in that organization, media can either be copied or be linked to the Events folder. Linking *points* to the file, similar to the way that Final Cut Pro 7, or Final Cut Express 4, works. Copying *duplicates* the file and moves the copy into the Events folder.

More on Events

An Event is a collection of media. All the media related to a single Event is stored in an Events folder. All your Events folders are stored in the Final Cut Events folder. While you can have only one Final Cut Events folder per hard drive, you can have an unlimited number of Event folders stored inside the Final Cut Events folder.

In general, although you can use the Finder to move Event folders in and out of the Final Cut Events folder, don't move the Final Cut Events folder itself or the individual files inside a single Events folder. Even more importantly, don't rename the Final Cut Events folder or anything in it.

The Final Cut Pro default is to copy all media files into an Events folder. For new users, the default setting of copy is probably the best choice. However, if you're an experienced editor, linking more closely resembles how Final Cut Pro 7 works with media. Linking also avoids duplicating media, which reduces your storage needs.

My recommendation is to store all Events and Projects on a second hard drive. This consolidates all your media files in one place. (I'll show you how to do this in Chapter 3.) You can create a Final Cut Events folder for each hard drive or RAID attached to your computer. However, you're allowed only one Final Cut Events folder per drive.

The Final Cut Projects folder is another database, this one containing edit instructions along with render files, waveforms, thumbnails, and other supporting files for your Projects. Just as Events are stored in the Final Cut Events folder, Projects are stored in the Final Cut Projects folder. Each Final Cut Projects folder can store an unlimited number of individual Projects. Each Project contains exactly one sequence, which is different from Final Cut Pro 7 where you could have an unlimited number of sequences in one Project. There is no practical limit to the number of clips, layers, or duration of a Project.

Projects are associated with one specific Event but can use media from multiple Events. One of the nice things is that using media in more than one Project does not duplicate media.

By default, the Final Cut Projects folder is also stored on your boot drive in the [Home directory] > Movies folder. As with Events, you can change Project locations using Final Cut Pro X, which I also recommend you do. I'll explain how to do this in Chapter 3.

NOTE What's the Boot Drive?

The boot drive is a technical term that describes the hard disk that holds your Applications folder and operating system. Unless you've changed the name of the drive, it's called Macintosh HD, and if you display hard drives on your desktop, it is generally displayed in the top-right corner of your Desktop.

This drive is the main workhorse for your operating system and applications, but for performance reasons, the boot drive is not the best place to store either the Final Cut Events folder or the Final Cut Projects folder. Instead, I recommend you use an attached second drive, either an internal or external device.

Don't rename anything in the Final Cut Projects folder. And, as with the Final Cut Events folder, you can have only one Final Cut Projects folder per drive. These two folders can both be stored on the same drive, or they can be stored on different drives. The Final Cut Events folder will almost always require more storage space than the Final Cut Projects folder.

Starting Final Cut Pro X

You can start Final Cut Pro X in three ways:

- Double-click the FCP X icon in the Applications folder of your hard disk.
- Click the FCP X icon in the Dock.
- Click the Final Cut Pro X icon in the Launchpad (requires Mac OS X 10.7).

You used to open Final Cut Pro by double-clicking any project file. But, since projects are now stored in a database, that option is no longer available. (A fast way to open the Applications folder is to press Shift+Command+A.)

What Happened to Final Cut Studio (3)?

If you installed Final Cut Pro X on a system that already had Final Cut Studio (3) installed, FCP X created a new folder called Final Cut Studio and moved all your old applications into that folder. These older applications all still work, but features such as round-tripping and Compressor droplets will break until you change some settings.

To fix Compressor droplets, simply open the earlier version of Compressor in the Final Cut Studio folder and resave your droplets. Resaving fixes that problem.

To get FCP 7 to round-trip properly with other Studio (3) applications, open FCP 7. Choose Final Cut Studio > System Preferences > External Editors.

Figure 2.1 shows my settings. This will make round-tripping work again for Photoshop, Motion, and Soundtrack Pro.

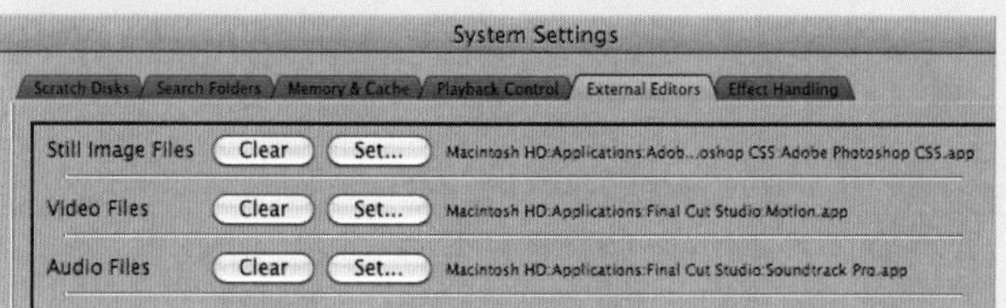

FIGURE 2.1
Once FCP X is installed, you need to change the External Editors settings in Final Cut Pro 7 to get round-tripping working again.

Touring the Interface

Final Cut Pro X has one window with three visible sections (**Figure 2.2**). In the upper left is the Event Library and Event Browser, which are where media is stored, organized, and previewed.

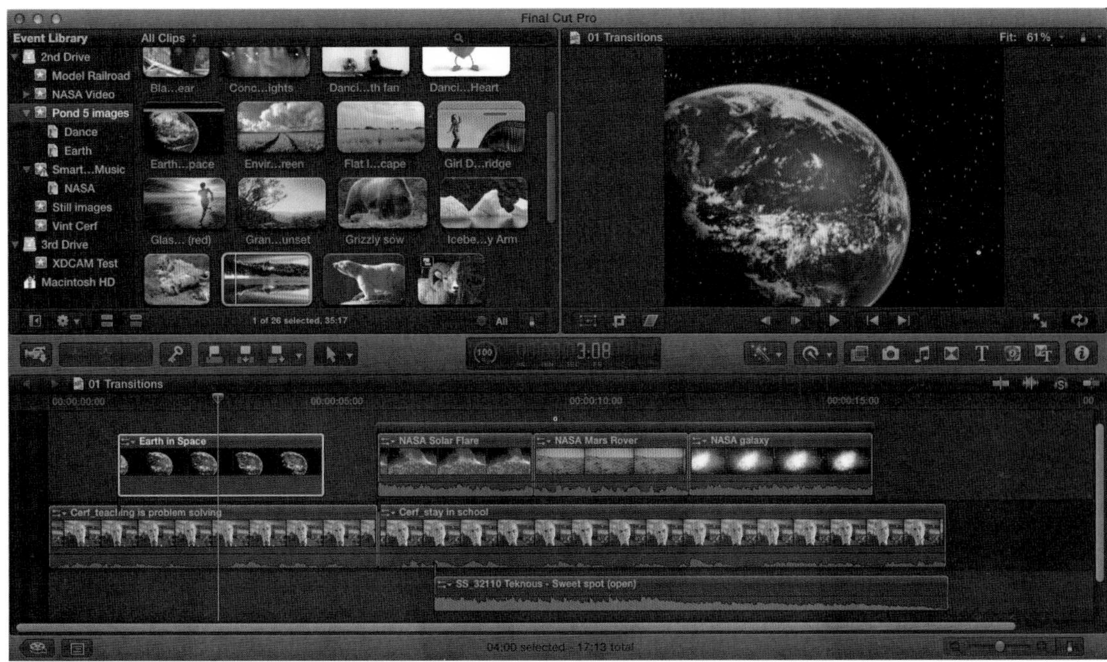

FIGURE 2.2
The Final Cut Pro X interface.

The Viewer is in the upper right. This is a context-sensitive window that displays whatever is the selected clip.

The Timeline covers the entire lower half of the interface. This is where you build your edits. Think of the Timeline as the architectural view of your edit, while the Viewer is a photograph of the finished building.

There are also several hidden areas to the interface: Inspector, Color Board, Video Scopes, Effects Browsers, and Import windows.

An area that is not hidden is the bar running horizontally across the middle of the interface. This is called the toolbar and is an area where you can quickly access many of the tools within FCP X.

A new feature in FCP X is the skimmer. (Keyboard shortcut: S.) This turns your cursor into an instant playback device. When skimming is on, you instantly see whatever clip is under your cursor in the Viewer. You don't even need to press the mouse button. The gray button to the right of the video skimmer turns audio skimming on or off (**Figure 2.3**). Video skimming is on by default, while audio skimming is turned off.

● **NOTE** Colors Mean Something

If an icon is blue, that feature, such as skimming, is turned on. If the icon is gray, that feature is turned off. Blue is used throughout the application to indicate that something is turned on, or enabled.

FIGURE 2.3
The skimmer can be turned on or off using this button.

NOTE Here's a Cool Skimmer Feature

When skimming audio, the audio is pitch-shifted, which means no matter how fast or slow you move the skimmer, the audio pitch remains constant.

FCP X offers two ways to view a clip: You can roll over it with the skimmer, or you can select the clip, press the spacebar, and play it. When we play a clip, the vertical line with the small triangle on the top, the playhead, shows what part of a clip, or the Timeline, is playing. (Oh, you stop playback by pressing spacebar again.) FCP also supports gestures, such as swipes, but we won't be covering them in this book.

The Viewer

The Viewer, that large image in the upper-right corner, provides a wealth of controls for media playback and manipulation. This context-sensitive window displays whatever clip is under either the skimmer or the playhead.

The Fit button at the top of the Viewer controls the scaling of the image in the Viewer. Until you get into effects, this is best left in the Fit position (**Figure 2.4**). You can also press Command+[plus key] or Command+[minus key] to zoom into or out of an image. My favorite keyboard shortcut is Shift+Z, which fits the image into the frame.

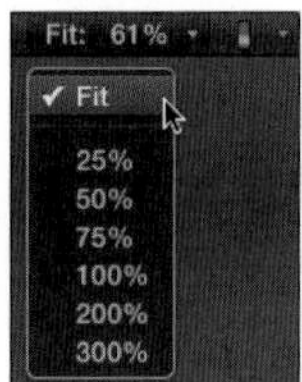

FIGURE 2.4
The Scale pop-up menu adjusts the scale of the image in the Viewer; this affects only the display, not the actual image size.

TIP A Quick Way to Go Full-Screen

There's also a fast keyboard shortcut to play your video full-screen. Press Shift+Command+F. To get back, press Escape.

The Viewer playback buttons control, well, play back (**Figure 2.5**). From left to right, these are "Go back one frame," "Go forward one frame," Play, "Go to previous edit," and "Go to next edit." While these are very nice and all, I never use them. I use keyboard shortcuts instead. The keyboard equivalents are left arrow, right arrow, spacebar, up arrow, and down arrow—in that order.

The two buttons shown in **Figure 2.6** provide additional playback control. The left button displays your video full-screen (press Escape to return to the normal interface). The right button toggles loop playback. When this is on—in other words, blue—the Timeline, or selected range within the Timeline, repeats continuously until you stop playback.

FIGURE 2.5
The Viewer playback controls.

FIGURE 2.6
The left button plays the Viewer image full-screen. The right button loops playback from start to end over and over.

> **New with Lion**
>
> With one exception, running FCP X in Mac OS X 10.6 is the same as running it in Lion (10.7). The one exception is that Mac OS X 10.7 offers a full-screen mode for editing. This allows you to use every square inch of your monitor for editing, as well as playback.

Event Library and Event Browser

That brings us to the Event Library and the Event Browser (**Figure 2.7**). The Event Library, on the left, lists all the hard drives that are attached (and turned on) to the computer. In this example, the 2nd Drive has Event media on it, while the 3rd Drive and Active Production, at the bottom, are not used for Events at all. Notice that there are no Events listed for either of them.

The Event Browser, on the right, displays all the clips in the Event folder that is selected in the Event Library. (You can select multiple Events in the Event Library.)

Once you've selected an Event folder, you can hide the Event Library to free up some screen real estate. Click this button in the lower-left corner of the Event window to toggle the display of the Event Library (**Figure 2.8**). (Keyboard shortcut: Shift+Command+1.)

The Event Browser allows you to browse individual clips. When you skim a clip, you have the option of displaying additional information about the clip.

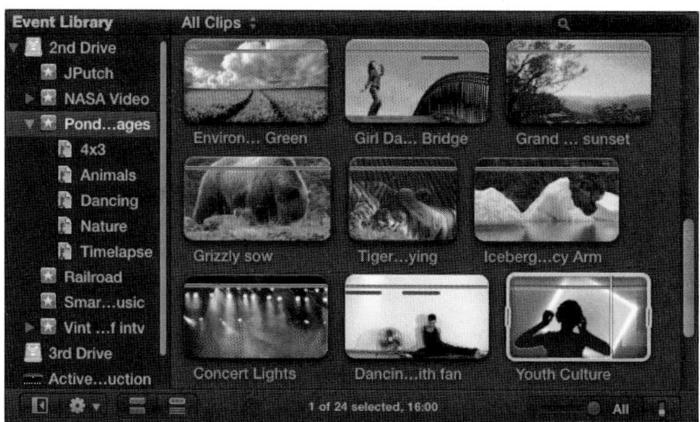

FIGURE 2.7
The Event Library, left, and Event Browser. These store and display all media.

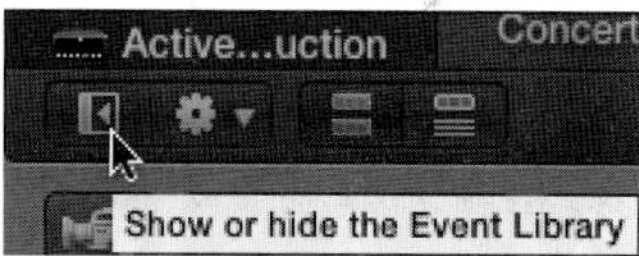

FIGURE 2.8
This button toggles the display of the Event.

FIGURE 2.9
You can turn on skimmer info by pressing Control+Y.

For example, in **Figure 2.9**, the small info box tells you the name of the clip, the keywords assigned to the clip, and the timecode position of the skimmer. This skimmer info box can be turned on and off either with a menu choice or with a keyboard shortcut. To toggle this on or off, choose View > Show Skimmer Info. It is off by default. (Keyboard shortcut: Control+Y.)

The Toolbar

FIGURE 2.10
The Dashboard displays the timecode associated with a clip or the Timeline.

Speaking of timecode, you can also see timecode in the Dashboard; it's part of the toolbar in the center of the display (**Figure 2.10**). The Dashboard contains three elements, from left to right: the background task status, current timecode, and audio meters. Background tasks include importing, rendering, transcoding, and exporting. To open the Background Tasks window, click the percentage clock on the left. (Keyboard shortcut: Command+9.)

This Dashboard actually has some very cool things about it. For instance, if you want to jump to a specific time in the Timeline, make sure nothing is selected, then click the timecode numbers once and type the time you want to jump to. For instance, type **500**, and the playhead jumps to exactly five seconds and no frames from the start of your Timeline. Or type **1..** (note the two periods after the one), and it jumps to exactly one minute, no seconds, and no frames. (The period is the same as entering two zeros.) You don't even have to figure out the math. Typing **99** is the same as typing **3:09** (assuming your project runs at 30 frames per second). Or, typing **45** is the same as typing **1:15**, again assuming the project is at 30 fps.

Excuse Me...What's Timecode?

Timecode is a numbering system that uniquely identifies each frame of video. Rather than simply start at 1 and count up, you number video in increments of time: Hours : Minutes : Seconds : Frames.

Hours, minutes, and seconds you already understand. A *frame* is a portion of a second, based upon the frame rate of the video your camera shoots. Common frame rates include 24, 25, 29.97, 50, and 60 frames per second (fps).

Timecode gives you the ability to label every frame with a unique number (for that clip), and because it is based on time, you can use it in your editing process. Just to confuse you and to give teachers trick questions for tests—*not* that I have ever done this myself!—there are two types of timecode: drop frame and non-drop frame. These terms refer to dropping timecode numbers used to identify frames and *not* to dropping frames of video, which it does not do.

You can even move in increments which I call "timecode offsets." To move back 20 frames, type **-20**. You don't need to click anywhere; just type. Negative numbers move the playhead backward (to the left). Positive numbers move right. For instance, type **+200** to move two seconds to the right.

Continuing our tour of the interface, the toolbar in the middle, which houses the Dashboard, has two other button groups. To the right are the Effects Browsers, with the far-right button opening the Inspector. On the left are editing and keyword buttons, which are covered in this chapter and the next.

The Timeline

Below the toolbar is the Project Timeline (**Figure 2.11**). The Timeline is where you build your projects. This window has four sections in it and two sets of buttons at the bottom.

FIGURE 2.11 The Project Timeline. There is one Timeline per Project.

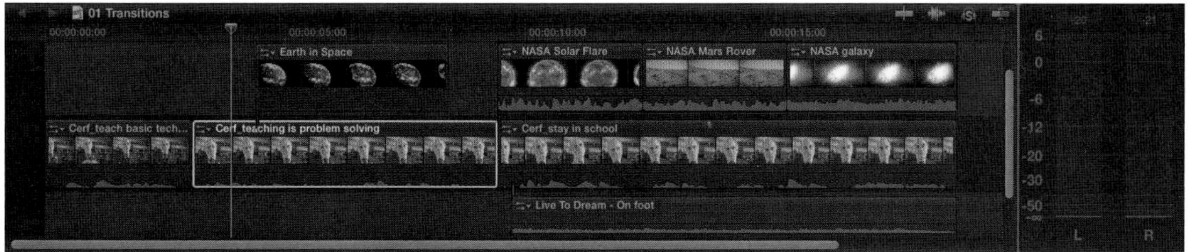

The slider in the lower right controls the horizontal scale of the clips in a project; however, I prefer to use the keyboard shortcuts of Shift+Z, Command+[plus key], or Command+[minus key] to scale the Timeline to fit, zoom in, or zoom out, respectively.

The Switch controls the contents of thumbnails, sets the vertical height of clips, and toggles on or off connection display (**Figure 2.12**). Click one of the six icons to set the Timeline thumbnails to display from audio only, to a mix of audio and video, to video only. The far-right icon displays what I call "lozenges," which is very useful for seeing your Timeline in miniature.

FIGURE 2.12 The slider controls the horizontal scale of Timeline clips. The Switch controls the display of clips in the Timeline.

These two buttons on the lower left of the Timeline opens two more Timeline windows (**Figure 2.13**). The left button opens the Project Library; you can also press Command+0, which is a collection of all your projects, grouped by the hard disk they are stored on, and the right button displays the Timeline Index.

FIGURE 2.13 Located in the lower-left corner of the Timeline, the left button displays the Project Library, and the right button displays the Timeline Index.

The Timeline Index is a list of all the clips, transitions, keywords, markers, and To-Dos in the currently active Timeline (**Figure 2.14**). This is a very cool feature that allows you to quickly navigate, search, hide, or delete elements within the Timeline. This becomes increasingly useful as your project size increases.

FIGURE 2.14
The Timeline Index is new with Final Cut Pro X.

FIGURE 2.15
The Project Library stores all Projects. Only one Project can be open at a time.

▲ **TIP** The Problem with Folders

The idea of storing projects in folders is a good one. The only problem is that when you drag a project into a folder to store it, FCP X often does not scroll the Library window as you drag the clip.

This makes placing projects in folders really, really tricky.

▲ **TIP** The Number-One Interface Rule

That reminds me that the number-one interface rule for Final Cut Pro X is this: "Select something, and do something to it." This may not be as deep as "I think; therefore I am." But inevitably you're going to ask "How do I do X?" And the answer is: Select something, and do something to it.

Just watch. I'll prove this to you.

The Project Library

The Project Library is where you store and manage all your projects (**Figure 2.15**). Projects are sorted alphabetically, by hard disk. There is no limit to the number of projects you can access inside Final Cut Pro X. All projects are stored inside the Final Cut Projects folder on your hard disk, where each project has its own folder.

When you are in the Project Library, three buttons appear in the lower-left corner. The left button toggles you into, or out of, the Project Library. The middle button creates a new project. And the right button creates a new folder, or *bin* as they were called in FCP 7, in which you can store projects.

There are other interface elements:

- Tool palette
- Keyword editor
- Inspector
- Color Boards
- Video Scopes
- Import windows
- and tons of contextual menus (these are what appear when you right-click something)

But, for now, that's enough of an orientation to get you started. Also, as you are discovering, there are a plethora of keyboard shortcuts. At the end of each chapter, I'll summarize some of the more important ones that I discuss during the chapter.

There is a ton of control here that's hidden until you need it. Final Cut Pro invites an attitude of "What happens if I click this?" There is far more to the interface than appears at first glance. Virtually everything is clickable.

So, give yourself permission to click stuff, and watch what happens.

Creating a New Event

In this section, you'll learn a simple way to create a new Event. In the next section, you'll see how to create a new Project. Chapter 3 goes into Events and Projects in detail; this is just to get you started.

Although you can start by first creating a new project, it's generally easier to start by creating a new Event, importing media into it, and then creating the Project. This is because Projects must be linked to Events. So, creating the Event first simplifies the process.

Events store media. Media files can be video, audio, or still images. Files can be imported from cameras, hard drives, media cards, or other applications, such as iMovie and iPhoto. By default, the Events folder is stored in the Home directory of your boot drive. However, I recommend that all Events be stored on a second drive. Storing media on a second drive provides better performance and, potentially, greater storage. But, frankly, the real reason is speed.

The Basic Steps

The *fastest* way to create a new Event is to choose File > New Event (or press Option+N). However, a much *better* way is to first select the hard drive where you want to store the event in the Event Library and then create the new Event. (If the Event Library is hidden, press Shift+Command+1 to display it.) Selecting the hard drive first allows you to control where the new Event will be created and your media stored.

For instance, the drive 2nd Drive RAID was selected for the location of a new Event. Then, choose File > New Event (or press Option+N).

The new Event now appears under the name of your hard disk, and the hard disk has a little right-pointing triangle next to it (**Figure 2.16**). I call these *twirl-downs*—indicating that there are Events stored on that hard disk.

By default, this Event is named New Event followed by today's date. While you can rename an Event at any time, I like renaming a new Event as soon as I create it. This way, I know what it is supposed to contain. So, I'm going to call this Model Railroads. (If you can't enter text, select the Event and press the Enter key, or just click to select the name.)

● **NOTE** Definition Reminder—Event

An Event is a collection of media files that are stored inside your computer—specifically an Events folder in the Final Cut Events folder. You can import media from a wide variety of sources.

● **NOTE** Where Does FCP X Store Stuff?

Final Cut Pro X stores everything in two folders: Final Cut Events and Final Cut Projects. These two folders can be stored in your Home directory (the default), on any locally attached hard drive or RAID, or, with the 10.0.1 update, on a server. Also, each of these folders can be stored on different drives.

Each Event is stored in its own folder inside the Final Cut Events folder. Likewise, each Project is stored in its own folder inside the Final Cut Projects folder.

FIGURE 2.16 Select the hard disk to hold the new Event, and then press Option+N to create a new Event. A new Event is assigned a default name with today's date.

Using Two Computer Monitors

● **NOTE** Can Final Cut Pro Output to a Video Monitor?

Not at this point—Apple says this feature will be coming in the near future. Final Cut Pro is designed to output video to a computer monitor. For best results, use a computer monitor that supports ColorSync to provide a consistent color display from initial capture through to final output.

Although Final Cut Pro looks great on a single monitor, you can really expand your view of a Project using two computer monitors.

When you have a second computer monitor attached to your system, two new menu items become available in the Window menu.

Window > Show Events on Second Display: This moves the Event Library and Event Browser to the second monitor.

Window > Show Viewer on Second Display: This moves the Viewer and related controls to the second monitor.

Window > Revert to Original Layout: This is available for both single- and dual-monitor displays and is a fast way to return to the default window layout, where all elements are contained in a single window on the main computer display.

Figure 2.17 shows what the main window looks like, with Events moved to the second window.

● **NOTE** Can You Change the Layout?

Yes, but not the way in which you expect. You can't move windows or tabs, but you can resize elements. Put your cursor on the dividing line between two elements, for example, between the Event Browser and the Viewer, and drag. As you drag, you can resize both windows. To return to the original layout, choose Window > Revert to Original Layout.

FIGURE 2.17 The main monitor display, when Events are moved to a second monitor.

And **Figure 2.18** shows how the main window looks when the Viewer is displayed on a second monitor.

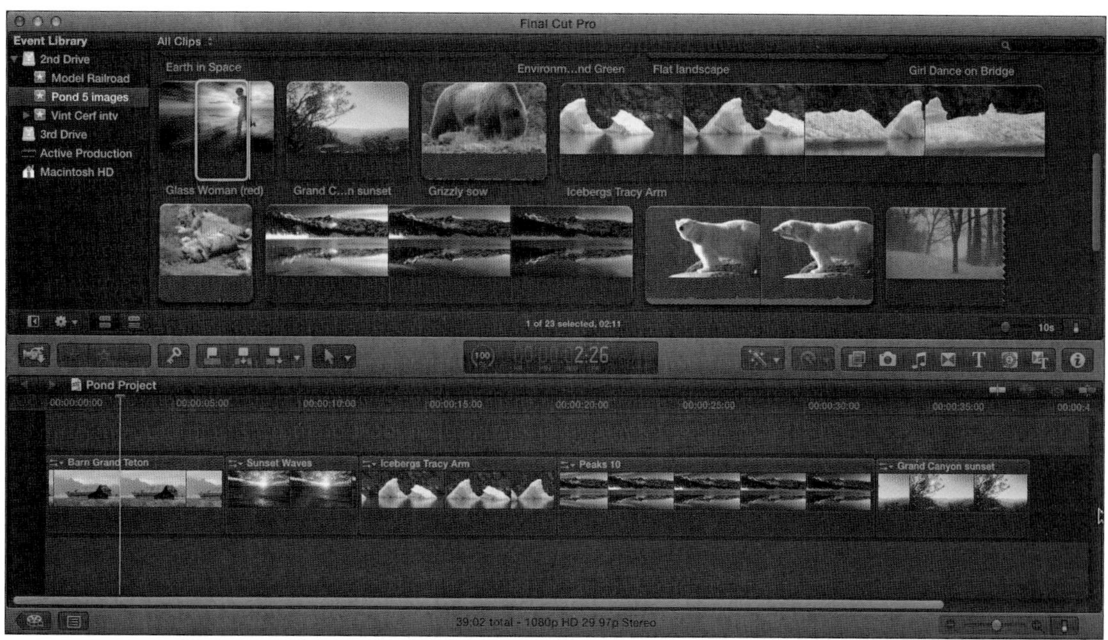

FIGURE 2.18
The main monitor display, when the Viewer is moved to a second monitor.

▲ TIP Here's a Tip to Make Your Monitor Look Great

While it is beyond the scope of this book to provide step-by-step instructions, to get the best results from your second monitor, be sure to calibrate it using System Preferences > Display > Color.

Importing Media

Since Events store media, let's import some media into that Event before creating a new Project. (Chapters 3 and 4 cover this in detail, so you'll just import a few files to get started.)

There are three broad categories of media you can import into Final Cut Pro:

- Files imported directly from a camera or memory card
- Files imported from a folder on your hard disk
- Files imported from iMovie

The difference between these three categories is whether the files need to be converted to play on your computer. If QuickTime can play the file, then it is converted, and all you need to do is import it. If QuickTime can't play the file, you'll need to read Chapter 3 to learn how to bring the file into FCP X.

For now, you'll simply import a few files stored in a folder on your computer. Since QuickTime can play these files, all we need to do is import them.

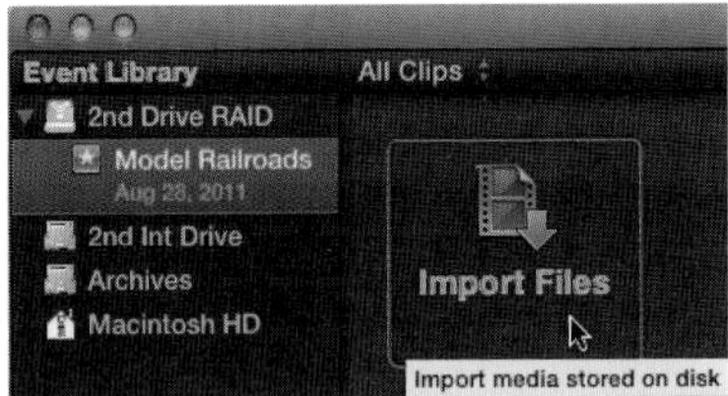

FIGURE 2.19
Click this icon to import files from your hard disk.

1. There are several ways to import files. The easiest, provided you haven't imported any media yet, is to click the Import Files icon in the center of the Event Browser (**Figure 2.19**).

   However, if you, or someone you know, has already imported media into this system, that Import Files icon will no longer be displayed, in which case you can either choose File > Import > Files or press Shift+Command+I.

   This opens the Import Files dialog. I'll go into more detail on importing in Chapter 4. For now, I'll just keep it simple.

2. In the Import Files dialog, select the hard drive containing the files you want to import, and then select the files you want to import.

   As with all Mac applications, there are different ways to select files. You can click a single file to select it, click the first file, and then Shift-click the last file to select a range of files, or you can hold the Command key and select whatever files you click. (Holding the Command key and clicking is also called *selecting an arbitrary number of files*.)

   You can also select the folder containing the files, in which case Final Cut Pro X will bring in all the files contained in the folder. (If one of the files is a format that FCP X doesn't support, Final Cut Pro will pop up a warning about that incompatible file but import everything else.)

3. Once you have your files selected, it's time to decide how you want Final Cut Pro to import them. In this case, I want to bring in some model railroad footage (thanks, Miles, for sharing these!). So, I select the folder that contains the files I want. FCP will bring in the entire contents of the folder automatically.

   However, the choices at the bottom of this dialog have been known to scare small children (**Figure 2.20**). Again, Chapter 4 talks about this in detail, so here are the settings I'm currently recommending.

4. For now, just copy these settings and click Import.

   Almost instantly, small icons of all your files appear in the Event Browser. The Event Browser displays the contents of a single Event (**Figure 2.21**).

So, just to repeat, the Event Library displays all your Events. The Event Browser displays all the clips associated with a single Event. When you select an Event in the Event Library, its contents are immediately displayed in the Event Browser.

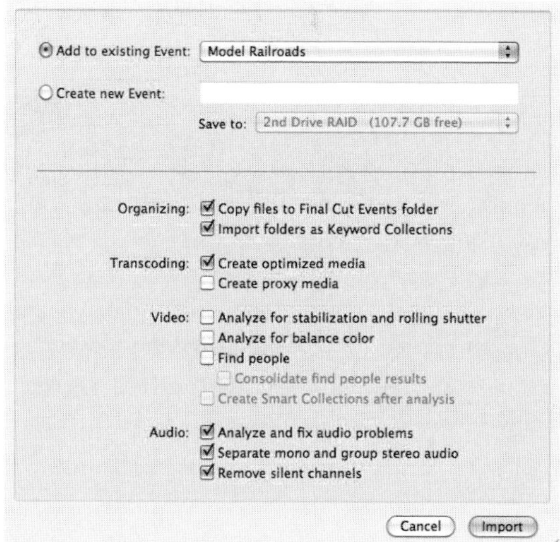

FIGURE 2.20
This is the bottom half of the standard import file picker window, where you set import settings.

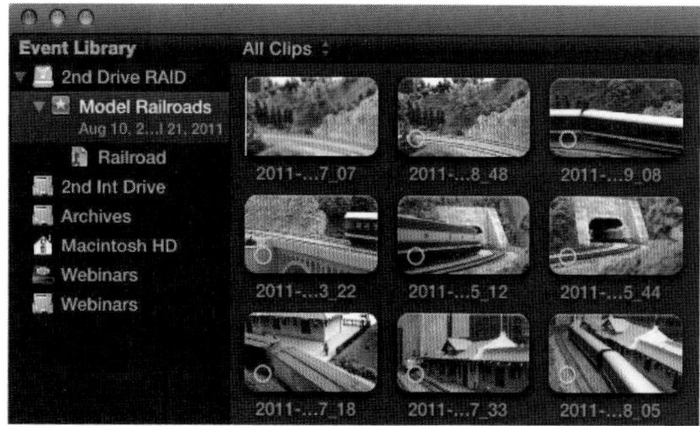

FIGURE 2.21
The Event Library (left) and Event Browser (right) that shows the clips you just imported.

Although the contents of the Event are displayed immediately, behind the scenes Final Cut Pro is doing a lot of work. In the past, you needed to wait for FCP to finish before you could start working, but the new version delegates all these housekeeping chores to what's called *background processing*.

What's in the Background?

Final Cut Pro X harnesses all the power and speed of the latest hardware to get work done faster. Tasks such as importing, rendering, analyzing, and converting are now done in the background.

This speed is why computer geeks get so excited with terms like *64-bit memory addressing*, *multiprocessor support*, and *GPU processing*. I'd explain these to you, but, frankly, I'd rather spend my time telling stories and editing. Suffice it to say that these are all good things.

By the way, running in the background doesn't mean faster; it just means something is out of the way. This is because a foreground application always takes priority over the background. If the foreground app needs something the background uses, the background waits until the foreground is done. However, most of the time, speed is much less the issue than our ability to continue editing while this background process is completing.

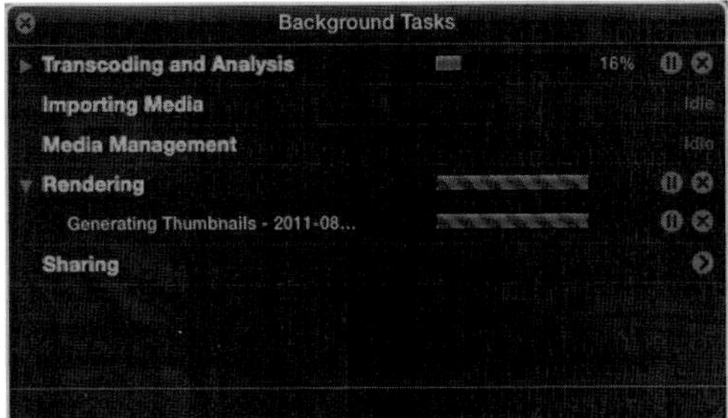

FIGURE 2.22
The Background Tasks window shows all active background tasks.

In the center of the screen is the Dashboard. On the left side is a small clock icon. This is your gateway into discovering what Final Cut Pro is doing in the background. Click the small clock face once, and the Background Task window appears (**Figure 2.22**).

This window shows all the different tasks that Final Cut Pro is running in the background. In this case, FCP is busily calculating thumbnails, which are the small icons that show what your clips look like; importing the files; analyzing them for color problems; and converting them into optimized media. This means faster renders, improved effects, and faster exports.

Now that you've imported some files, we can move to the third step, which is creating a new Project.

Creating a New Project

Just as you need to select a hard drive to hold Events, you also need to select a hard drive to store Projects. By default, FCP X puts Projects in the Home directory of your boot drive.

Just as FCP needs a place to display all your Events, it also needs a place to display all your Projects. And that place is called the Project Library. You can see it on the left side of the Timeline. If it is hiding, press Command+0 to display it.

Select the hard disk you want to use to store your Projects; in this example, I selected 2nd Int Drive. Remember, when creating either Events or Projects, select the hard drive *first*, and then create the new Event or Project.

1. Just as with Events, there are multiple ways to create a new Project. The easiest, provided you haven't created any Projects yet, is to click the Create Project icon in the center of where the Timeline will be. Or, if someone has already created a project, which means this icon is no longer visible, you can choose File > New Project or press Command+N.

   You can also take advantage of a contextual menu. I would not normally tell you this now, but I would be really embarrassed if you heard about this from a "friend" first, so here goes.

   Right-click the name of the hard disk where you want to create a new Event or Project. A contextual menu appears (**Figure 2.23**). These puppies are scattered everywhere in this program. Choose New Event, or New Project from the contextual menu, and you are good to go.

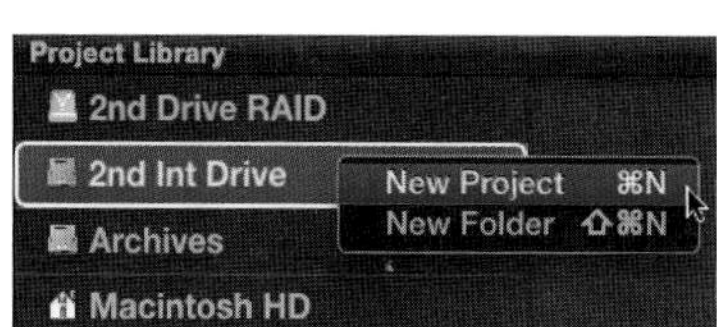

FIGURE 2.23
Right-click an object to display a contextual menu, such as the name of a hard disk in the Project Library to create a new Project. (You can do the same thing to create a new Event in the Event Browser.)

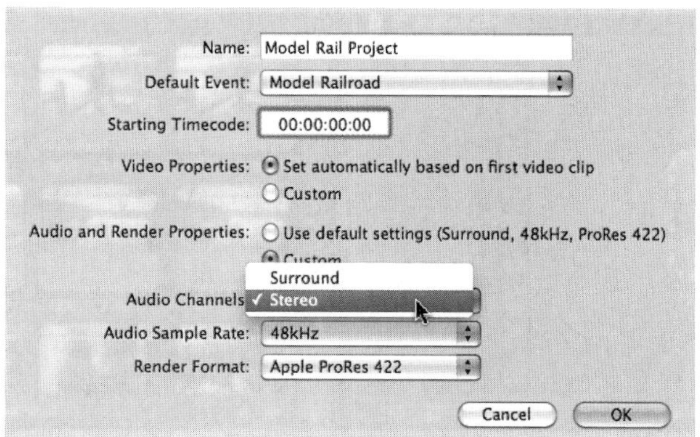

FIGURE 2.24
Always name a new Project and link it to an Event. The ability to set starting timecode is a new feature in FCP X 10.0.1. The default audio setting creates a surround mix.

2. However you decide to create a new Project, the new Project dialog appears. At the top of the dialog, give your Project a name (**Figure 2.24**). I recommend you use something that makes sense to you, rather than a cryptic code. In this case, I called it Model Rail Project.
3. All Projects must be linked to an Event—remember, both Events and Projects are, ultimately, databases—so I set the default event to our Model Railroad footage. You can actually use footage from any Event in any Project. This window also allows you to change the starting timecode of a Project; I'll talk more about this in Chapter 3.
4. The two radio buttons at the bottom need a short comment. The top one is set correctly for most projects. For now, leave it alone. However, the bottom set of preferences can lead to confusion, and while the default can't be changed, the setting can. Click the Custom radio button for Audio and Render Properties and change the default audio setting from Surround (six tracks of audio) to Stereo.

And that's it! You are now ready to edit.

● **NOTE** FCP Remembers Current Audio Setting

Although it is nice that FCP X supports surround sound, most Projects will be stereo. It would be good if Apple supplied a default for this setting, but it doesn't. However, Final Cut Pro remembers the current audio setting so that when you create a new Project, and change the Audio and Render Properties radio button to Custom, FCP X will remember the audio setting according to the last new project you created.

How Many Projects and How Many Sequences?

Unlike Final Cut Pro 7 and Final Cut Express, Final Cut Pro X allows only one *sequence*, or edited collection of clips, per Project. (This is not completely true, because you can get around this using compound clips; however, it is true enough for right now.)

However, there is no limit, aside from hard disk storage space, on the number of Projects you can access within FCP X, the clips inside a Project, or the length of a Project. Plus, all Projects are always available.

Um, We Haven't Saved Anything...!

Not to worry. Final Cut Pro X saves everything, all the time. As soon as you make a change, Final Cut Pro saves it. This means that if you have a crash, all your work, up to the instant before the crash, is saved.

This is both great news and, um, a bit tricky. It's great news, because now you don't need to worry about saving your projects or Events or media or anything. Saving is automatic. It's a bit tricky because sometimes you don't want to save the changes you are making.

In the next chapter, you'll learn how to duplicate a Project. Duplication is the best way to keep a copy of the current state of your Project, without worrying about whether unwanted saves are making changes that you don't expect.

Creating a Simple Edit

Your media is stored in a new Event, and you have a new Project ready to go.

The time has come to create a simple edit. In this case, you'll create a very simple scene where Miles Hale is showing how to build a piece of railroad scenery. Then, you'll add a connected clip, what some editors would call *B-roll*, that illustrates what the scenery looks like when he is done.

Here's the editing process:

1. Preview a clip to decide whether you want to use it.
2. Mark the clip with a Start point and an End point (also called *In* and *Out*).
3. Edit the clip to the Project Timeline to add it to your story.
4. Adjust the audio level so you can hear it properly.
5. Repeat until your story is complete.

Previewing the Clip

In general, it is easiest to build your entire story for content; this is called *creating the radio script*. Then, go back and add the pictures that illustrate your story, using connecting clips. Then, go back a third time to add transitions, titles, and effects.

What you discover in going back over the same material is that you find ways to improve it by adding new clips, adjusting or removing existing clips, and rethinking the order of how all your clips fit together. Just like practicing a speech makes it better, reviewing your edits improves the final project.

There is no one perfect way to edit anything—which can be both a joy and a frustration. Every story is different. But, like any good story you tell to your friends, the more you practice and polish it, the better it gets.

1. Double-click the name of a Project in the Project Library to open it in the Timeline.

   Clips that you can select for this Project are displayed in the Event Browser (**Figure 2.25**). Meet Miles Hale, of Model Railroad Builders. He is showing you how to construct scenery for a model train layout.

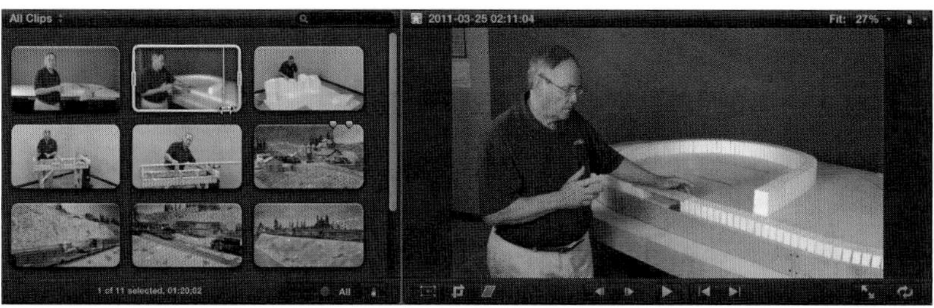

FIGURE 2.25 The Event Browser, left, allows you to quickly look over all your clips; the Viewer, right, allows you to see one clip in more detail.

2. To preview a clip, either move the skimmer across the clip to watch it in high speed or click the skimmer at the beginning of the clip (which sets the position of the playhead) and press the spacebar to play the clip in real time.

   Either way, you watch the clip in the large Viewer window on the right and listen to it on your speakers.

Marking Start and End Points

Once you decide what your first clip will be, follow these steps:

1. Click the clip to select it.
2. Drag the left edge of the yellow box to the right (**Figure 2.26**). This sets a selection that will determine the Start (In) and the End (Out) of a clip. (The Start is on the left, and the End is on the right.)

   As you drag, you'll see the shot change in the Viewer. The small numbers you see changing along the left edge of the yellow rectangle you are dragging is the timecode (the frame identifier) that represents the timecode address of the current frame under the yellow boundary that you are setting as the Start.

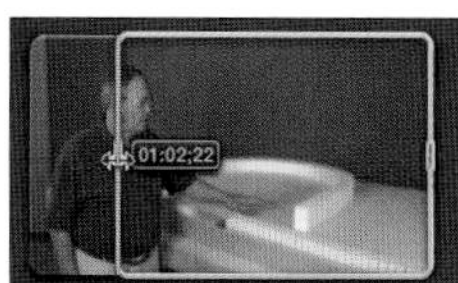

FIGURE 2.26 Click a clip to display the yellow boundary. Drag the left edge to set the Start, and drag the right edge to set the End.

3. Once you have the In, um, I mean the Start set, do the same thing with the right edge of the clip—drag it to the left until you find the frame where you want the clip to end. This sets the End of the shot you will edit to the Timeline.

This process of setting the Start and the End is often called *marking a clip*. The keyboard shortcut to set the Start is I, and to set the End it is O. This marked area is also called the *selected range*.

What's with This "In" and "Out" Business?

Traditionally, editors have called the beginning of a clip they want to edit the *In* and the end of a clip they want to edit the *Out*. This terminology goes back to the very early days of silent film editing in the early 1900s.

In FCP X, Apple decided to modernize the terminology, so the In is now called the *Start*, and the Out is now called the *End*. As an, ahem, old editor, I'm having some problems adapting to the new terms. So, I will use both. They mean the same thing, and they both use the same keyboard shortcuts: I to set the In, or Start, and O to set the Out, or End.

Editing the Clip to the Project Timeline

Next up is editing the marked clip.

Click the Append edit button (or press E) to edit the selected range of a clip into the Project Timeline (**Figure 2.27**). The Project Timeline is almost always just called the Timeline, mainly because, by definition, the Timeline can contain only one Project.

Instantly, the clip you selected in the Event Browser appears at the beginning of the Timeline, and the playhead jumps to the end of the clip.

This process of editing continues in this same manner—preview a clip, set the Start, set the End, and edit to the Timeline (**Figure 2.28**).

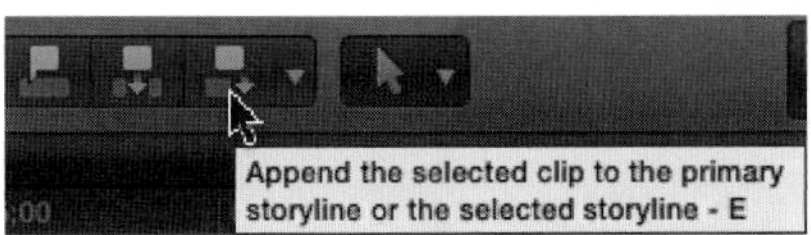

FIGURE 2.27
Click the Append edit button to edit the selected clip to the end of the Timeline.

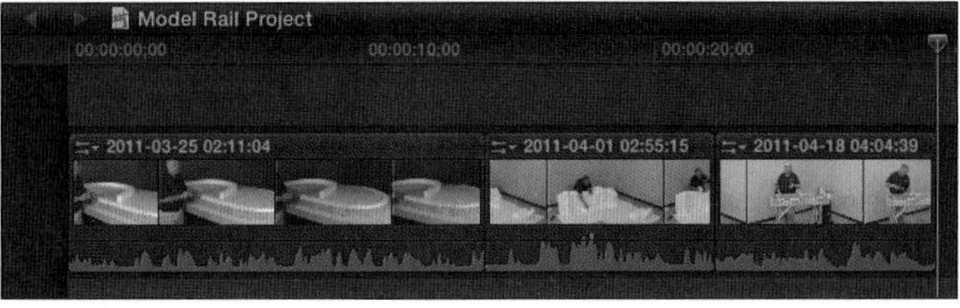

FIGURE 2.28
Three clips edited to the end of the Timeline—note that the playhead is at the end of the three clips.

Adjusting the Audio

In this example, I have three different clips edited into the Timeline. Generally, for documentary, news, or nonfiction work, I edit all the clips that have audio (also called *sound bites*) into the Timeline to make a complete story. Then, I go back and add pictures and other elements to make it look pretty. But I focus my initial edit on getting the story told in the best way possible before I worry about images, titles, or effects.

Notice in the Dashboard there are two very small audio meters. This allows you to see what your audio levels look like. However, they are darn near impossible to see. Click the small audio meters in the Dashboard once, and the large audio meters appear (**Figure 2.29**). (You can resize these meters by dragging the left edge to the left or right.)

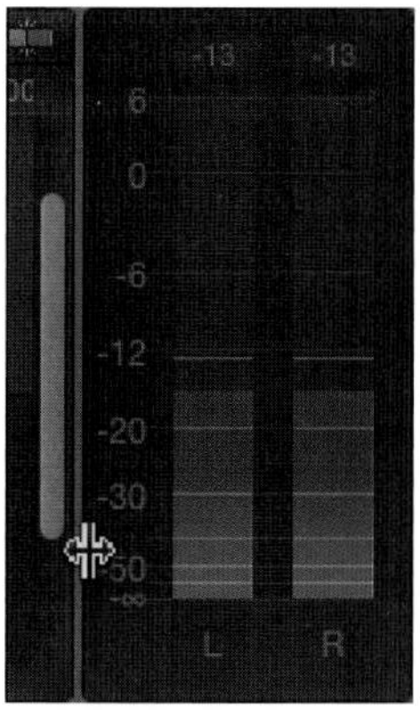

FIGURE 2.29 The larger audio meters; drag the left edge to resize them.

I *love* the size of these new meters; they're much better than anything we had in Final Cut Pro 7. I also really, really like that you can resize them.

The Number-One Audio Rule

I will mention this more than once, but it is really, really important. The number-one audio rule is that your levels, the volume, of your Project must never exceed 0 dB. Not once, not ever, not even for a little bit.

When you export or share your Project and the audio levels exceed 0 dB, your audio will distort. This sounds like clicking or scraping and is fingernails-on-the-blackboard annoying, and there is not a technology on the planet that can fix it.

Audio levels that are too loud are very, very bad. You have been warned.

To adjust your audio levels, drag the black volume lines near the bottom of each clip (also called *black rubber bands*) up to make the audio louder or down to make the audio softer (**Figure 2.30**). You should be able to clearly hear what they are saying without driving your audio levels over 0 dB as measured on the audio meters. (Chapter 9 covers audio in more detail.)

FIGURE 2.30 Drag the black horizontal line in the audio portion of the clip to adjust audio volume.

Wait a Minute! I Can Drag This Rubber-Band Thingy Over 0 dB!

Yes! There are two ways to measure audio: relative levels and absolute levels.

The audio meters measure the absolute level of your audio. Absolute levels are what we care about when we don't want our audio to distort.

Clips use relative levels that refer to the volume of your audio compared to the level at which it was recorded. So, when you drag the black volume line up, you are increasing the level compared to what it was when the clip was recorded. Dragging the black line down makes the clip softer than the level at which it was recorded.

Using Shortcuts for Faster Editing

Now that you have a few clips edited to the Timeline, here are some shortcuts that can be helpful.

- To preview an edit, put your playhead, or skimmer, near what you want to preview and press Shift+?—this backs the playhead up a few seconds and then plays for the next several seconds before resetting the playhead position. This allows you to determine whether the edit makes sense. (Chapter 8 covers *trimming*, which is the process of adjusting where two clips touch.)
- If you want to move vertically within the Timeline, you can use the scroll wheel on your mouse or drag vertically on your trackpad.
- To display the Viewer full-screen so you can watch your story unfold, press Shift+Command+F. To return to the interface, press Esc.
- To add a dissolve between two clips, click where the two clips touch (**Figure 2.31**). This turns the edge of one of the clips yellow. (If an edge turns red, you may not be able to add a transition. This is covered in more detail in Chapter 8.) By the way, it doesn't make a difference which edge changes color. All you are doing is selecting the edit point (the place where two clips touch) so that Final Cut Pro knows where to apply the transition.
- To add the transition, press Command+T. There are more than 100 transitions you can add to your Projects. However, this keyboard shortcut applies the most popular: a one-second cross-dissolve. (Chapter 10 covers transitions in detail.)

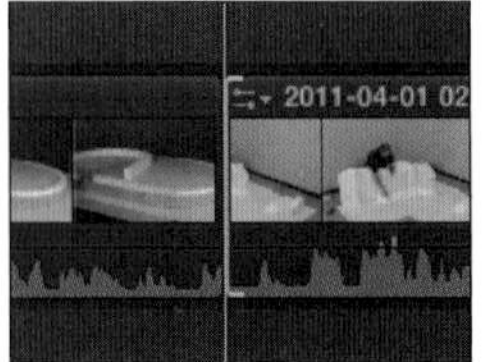

FIGURE 2.31 Select an edit point, where two clips touch, and one edge highlights with a yellow bar.

Creating B-roll

B-roll, *cutaways*, and *inserts* are all words that describe images that illustrate what the person on camera is talking about or doing (**Figure 2.32**). For example, if you interview an astronomer, B-roll would be video of the stars. In this book, I'll use the term *B-roll* to refer to the wide variety of ways you can illustrate what someone is speaking about.

In this case, you want to add some B-roll that shows a train rolling through the scenery that Miles is constructing. You do this using a connected clip.

As with any clip, find the clip you want to use in the Event Browser, and add a Start and an End (In and Out).

FIGURE 2.32 B-roll are pictures that illustrate a piece of dialogue or interview.

Then, unlike editing a clip into the primary storyline, you need to tell Final Cut Pro where this connected clip should start (**Figure 2.33**). You have two options:

- If skimming is active, the position of the skimmer determines the Start point of the clip in the Timeline.
- If skimming is inactive or if the skimmer is not in the Timeline area of the interface, the playhead determines the Start of the connected clip.

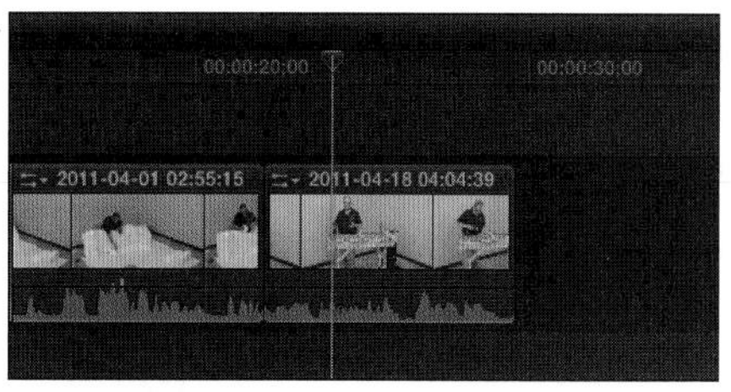

FIGURE 2.33
Position the playhead in the Timeline where you want the B-roll clip to start.

In this case, I'm using the playhead to set the position in the middle of the last clip.

Click the Connected Edit icon (or press Q), and the selected clip in the Event Browser is connected to the primary storyline at the position of the playhead (**Figure 2.34**).

FIGURE 2.34
Click the Connected Edit button, or press Q, to edit the clip into the Timeline as a connected clip.

Notice that, by default, if a connected clip is video, it's placed above the primary storyline. If it's audio, it's placed below the primary storyline (**Figure 2.35**).

If you look really carefully, at the very start of a connected clip (and a connected storyline, for that matter), you'll see a small hook connecting the clip into the clip in the primary storyline. This connection is, by default, at the first frame of the connected clip, and it always hooks into the primary storyline. This is how each clip on the primary storyline knows what clips are connected to it.

FIGURE 2.35
A connected clip is attached to the primary storyline. In this case it's video so it's placed above the primary storyline.

What you've just done is typical of many editing projects where you have someone on camera talking and then illustrate what he is talking about using B-roll. You'll follow this same workflow hundreds of times in your projects.

Summary

Sometimes you just want to get started—and that's where this chapter can help. You now know how to create a new Event, create a new Project, and perform a simple edit. Now it's time to go beyond a superficial overview and get into the details of how, and why, the software works.

The hardest part of any journey is the first step. You now have a basic understanding of the interface and the key concepts behind Final Cut Pro X. The rest of this book guides you in the adventure of exploring the application and learning how to put its power to work for you.

At the end of each chapter, I'll provide a list of the keyboard shortcuts that are relevant to the chapter. Here's the list for this chapter on the next page.

Keyboard Shortcuts

Finder Shortcut	What It Does
Shift+Command+A	Open the Applications folder
Shift+Command+U	Open the Utilities folder
Option+Command+D	Show/hide the Dock
Final Cut Pro Shortcut	**What It Does**
Option+N	Create new event
Shift+Command+1	Display/hide Event Library
Shift+Command+I	Import files from computer
Command+N	Create new project
Command+0	Show/hide Project Library
Shift+Command+F	Display Viewer full-screen
Shift+Command+8	Toggle display of audio meters
S	Toggle skimmer on or off
Shift+S	Toggle audio skimming on/off
E	Perform an append edit
Shift+?	Preview around the playhead
Q	Perform a connected edit
Command+T	Apply the default transition
Shift+Z	Fit existing Project into Timeline or display one thumbnail per clip in the Event Browser, whichever is selected
Command+[plus]	Zoom into selected window, either Timeline or Viewer
Command+[minus]	Zoom out of selected window, either Timeline or Viewer
Command+H	Hide Final Cut Pro X
Command+Q	Quit Final Cut Pro

3

MANAGING EVENTS, PROJECTS, AND SHORTCUTS

As you make the transition to Final Cut Pro X, it's important to understand two things in order to use the software effectively.

You were introduced to them in the previous chapter: Events and Projects. But there are still a lot of unanswered questions. For instance, how can you move, copy, rearrange, or delete Events? What about doing the same for Projects? Can you customize keyboard shortcuts? In fact, where do you find keyboard shortcuts?

In this chapter, I'll answer those questions, as well as illustrate a step-by-step process you can use to create your own customized keyboard shortcuts and shortcut groups.

All About Events

An *Event* is a collection of media. Generally, the media is all related to a similar subject, but, truthfully, that isn't necessary. Just like a drawer will hold whatever you throw into it, an Event will store whatever media you give it. The benefit of an Event over a drawer is that the Event is stored in a database, which makes keeping track of what's in it a lot easier than just tossing stuff in a drawer.

Most of the time, an Event will contain media related to a single production, visual theme, or shooting date.

What's in a Name?

The word *Event* is used in a variety of ways in Final Cut Pro X. Let me define how I'm using it here:

Event: This is a collection of media, video, audio, and/or stills, listed in the Event Library and stored in the Final Cut Events folder on a hard disk.

Event Library: Inside Final Cut Pro X, this is a list of all the different Events and hard disks that Final Cut can access.

Event Browser: Inside Final Cut Pro X, this displays all the clips for a single Event, selected in the Event Library.

Final Cut Events folder: In the Finder, this is the "master" folder stored on one hard disk that contains individual Event folders. There is only one Final Cut Events folder per hard disk connected to your computer.

Event folder: This is a single folder, stored inside the Final Cut Events folder on your hard disk, that contains all the media, and the database, related to a single Event. There is no limit to the number of Event folders that can be stored inside a single Final Cut Events folder.

Media: This is what's stored inside an Events folder. This can be video, audio, or stills.

▲ TIP Events Are Always on Top

The Final Cut Events folder is always stored at the root, or top, level of a hard disk. You can't put this folder inside another folder.

You can have only one Final Cut Events folder per hard disk. However, you can have a separate Final Cut Events folder on each hard disk. One Final Cut Events folder holds an unlimited number of specific Event folders, and each Event can hold an unlimited number of clips.

Events are stored in the Final Cut Events folder (**Figure 3.1**). By default, this is in the Home directory of your boot drive. (That's the drive that also holds your Applications folder.) But you can choose to store this folder at the root level of your boot drive or any other hard drive, RAID, or server that is attached to your computer and turned on.

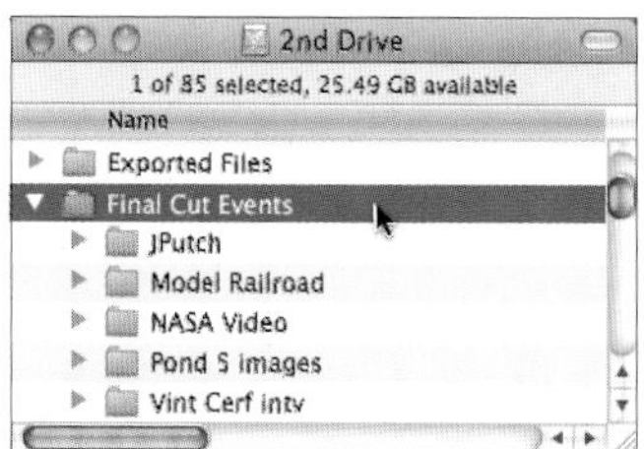

FIGURE 3.1
Media is stored in Event folders that are stored in the Final Cut Events folder.

FIGURE 3.2
To prevent an Event from appearing in FCP X, move it into a folder you create called Final Cut Events Not in Use.

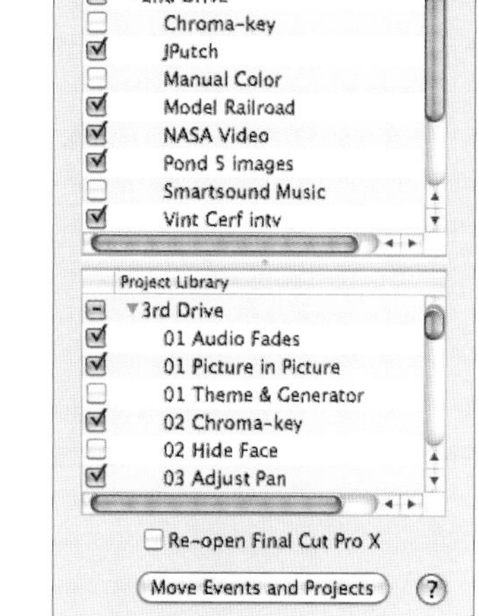

FIGURE 3.3
Event Manager X is a very helpful utility for managing FCP X Events and Projects.

In fact, as you learned in the previous chapter, I strongly recommend storing this folder on an attached hard disk.

The key phrase is "attached to...and turned on." Final Cut Pro X expects to have access to all Events and all Projects all the time.

This can be a real problem if you are doing work for different clients. You don't want one client seeing media or projects from a second client. While you could rename the Event inside Final Cut, the media is still available and could be displayed accidentally. A better approach is to use the Finder for two simple workarounds outside of Final Cut: the simple way and the cool way.

The simple way is as follows:

1. Quit Final Cut Pro X.
2. Create a second folder to store all the Events you don't want to use on the same drive as the Final Cut Pro Events folder.

   For example, in **Figure 3.2**, I created a folder called Final Cut Events Not in Use.
3. Then, using the Finder, drag any Events that you want to remove from the Event Library in FCP X from the Final Cut Events folder into the Final Cut Events Not in Use folder.

   This does not delete any media, but it does make that media unavailable to Final Cut Pro, or any project that uses that media.

It's simple, and it works fine. But it's kinda boring.

A very cool, and inexpensive, alternative is a program called Event Manager X, published by Intelligent Assistance (*www.intelligentassistance.com*) (**Figure 3.3**). This simple utility tracks all your Events and Projects across all your hard disks and makes them active, or inactive, to Final Cut Pro.

> **NOTE** Critical Note for Moving Folders
>
> Always quit Final Cut Pro before moving folders.
>
> Always drag the entire Event folder from one location to another. Never drag individual files from the folder.

Additionally, it tracks Events and Projects for hard disks that are not currently connected or turned on. This allows you to see where you stored files, without needing to keep all your hard disks running at the same time. There's also a very neat Find utility to help you find the Project or Event you want to work on.

The ideal solution is to have Final Cut Pro handle all Event and Project management. But, until it does, Event Manager X fills the bill. I used it constantly in writing this book, plus in my training and editing with FCP X.

Media Management Tips

Although you can use the Finder to move Events around, it is not a good idea to use the Finder to manage the individual elements within each Events folder. Because all these elements are being tracked in a database, if you start moving stuff manually, the database is going to lose track of it.

For this reason, don't rename any files inside the Events folder. Don't move elements from one Events folder to another. And don't rename any folders.

Event Management

The Event Library inside Final Cut Pro X lists all the Events stored on all hard disks that are currently connected to your computer. And the Event Browser displays all the media contained by a single Event selected in the Event Library.

The previous chapter showed how to create an Event by first selecting the hard drive where you want to store the Event and then choosing File > New Event (or pressing Option+N).

Now, let me show you how to use the Event Library to copy an Event to a different hard disk, move an Event to a different hard disk, merge two Events into a single Event, and delete an Event. Then, we'll use the Event Browser to rename a clip and to delete a clip.

NOTE One Events Folder per Hard Disk

Remember, since you can have only one Final Cut Events folder per hard disk, Final Cut doesn't allow you to copy an Event to the same hard disk upon which that Event is already stored.

Copy an Event

To copy an Event to another hard disk, select the Event name in the Event Library, and then choose File > Duplicate Event or press Command+D.

This displays the Duplicate Event dialog. Within this menu, you can give the Event a new name (it can be the same as, or different from, the existing Event) and pick a hard disk where you want the Event stored. There's no need to pick a folder within that hard disk, because Events are always stored in the Final Cut Events folder at the top level of the selected hard disk.

Pick the location you want the Event copied to, and click OK.

That's the dull, boring way to duplicate an Event. It works fine, but it isn't sexy. Here's the *secret* way to duplicate an Event: Drag the name of the Event from the Event Library to the name of the hard disk in the Event Library where you want to copy the Event.

Poof! The Duplicate dialog instantly appears. Much cooler.

The best part of this is, because of the power of background processing, Final Cut Pro X allows you to view, edit, trim, or play clips that you are currently copying while the copying is still going on! So, you don't have to wait for the copy to finish before you get back to work.

Move an Event

The difference between copying an Event and moving an Event is that when you copy you have media in more than one place. When you move, all the media packs up and leaves its old location and takes up residence in the new. (I have fun picturing all these files with feet moving from one hard disk to another....)

To move an Event, select the Event in the Event Library, and then choose File > Move Event. (There isn't a keyboard shortcut for this option.)

In the resulting dialog, choose the hard disk where you want to move the Event (**Figure 3.4**). You'll notice, when you do this, that the hard disk where the Event is currently stored is not listed. This is because it doesn't make any sense to move the Event to the same location where it already is. So, FCP removes that option.

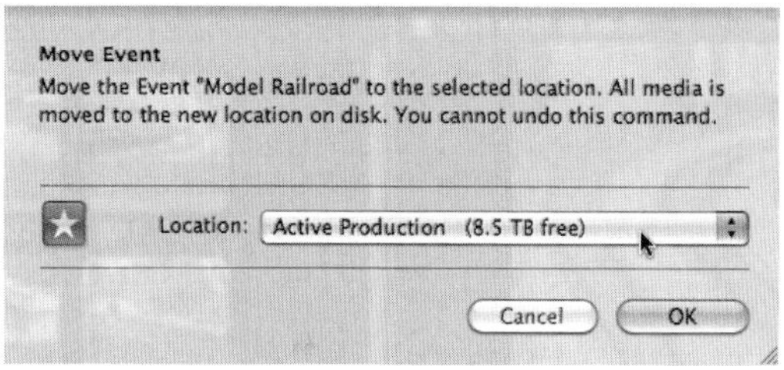

Move Event
Move the Event "Model Railroad" to the selected location. All media is moved to the new location on disk. You cannot undo this command.
Location: Active Production (8.5 TB free)
Cancel OK

FIGURE 3.4
This dialog allows moving an Event from one hard drive to another.

Yawn...another nice technique, but wouldn't it be neat if there were a secret way to do this, too? Don't tell anyone, but there is: Hold down the Command key and drag the name of the Event you want to move from the Event Library to the name of the hard disk where you want to move the Event. The Move dialog then appears. Cool—and it's faster than going to the File menu.

Organize the Media for an Event

It sounds as if you are throwing a massive party. But, nope, you are just collecting all your media in one spot.

As you'll learn in the next chapter, when you import media, you have the option of copying it into the Event folder or pointing to its current location. The benefit of pointing is that you save disk space. The benefit to copying is that all your media is in one spot, which makes managing it a lot easier.

New in FCP X 10.0.1

Apple added Xsan and network support to Final Cut Pro X with the 10.0.1 release. Now, media, Events, and Projects can all be stored on network devices (**Figure 3.5**). This allows sharing media between multiple editors. And it also means that Events and Projects can be accessed by multiple editors; however, only one editor can be in the same Event or Project at a time.

FIGURE 3.5
The latest version of FCP X allows storing media, Events, and Projects on a network device.

To simplify the process of adding or removing SAN locations, Apple added two new menu choices in the File menu: Add SAN Location and Remove SAN Location. Although this feature is specifically designed for Xsan, it should work for any server-based production system with fast bandwidth between the server and the computer and for any server that supports permissions and record locking, such as OS X Server.

If you decide to simply point to the existing location of your media during import and then change your mind later, selecting File > Organize Event Files will copy all your media from wherever it is to the appropriate Event folder inside Final Cut Events.

This is especially helpful if you have media scattered across multiple drives and want to consolidate it all into one folder.

To move files from outside the Event folder into the Event folder, select the Event you want to organize in the Event Library, and then choose File > Organize Event Files. (Remember, don't use the Finder to move files into an Event folder.)

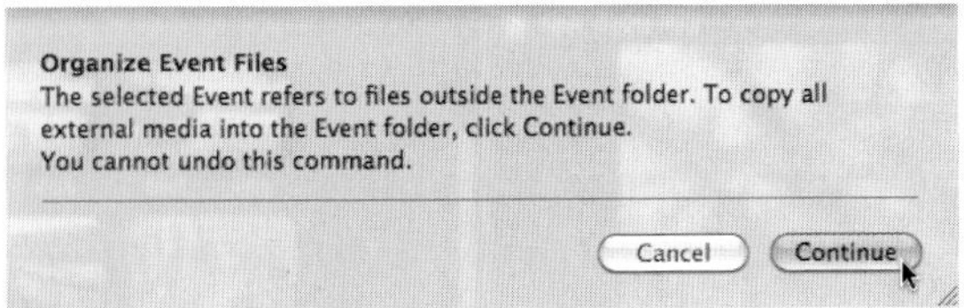

FIGURE 3.6
Organizing is very helpful when media is scattered across multiple hard disks.

The Organize Event Files dialog appears, reminding you that it will copy all media from outside the Event folder into the Event folder (**Figure 3.6**).

Note the key word *copy*. It is not moving your original files; it's merely making a copy of them. This is a safe way to gather your media together, but it also means that your storage requirements are going to increase because now you have two copies of your files: one in the original location and a copy in the Events folder.

Musing on Media

Media files are huge. In fact, they are beyond huge. They can often be gigantic. Other applications, such as Word or Quicken, store all your data in a single file. FCP doesn't do this. It "points" to wherever your media is stored on your hard disk.

The benefits to this are that Project files stay very small, because the size of your media doesn't affect the size of your Project. However, the disadvantage of this system is that if you start moving media files around or change the name of a file or folder, you'll break the link. This is the key benefit to having FCP X copy your media files into the Event folder—it prevents broken links, which would prevent your media from playing inside your Project.

● **NOTE** On Copying

For those of us raised before digital devices became omnipresent, copying something always meant a decrease in quality. Today, when dealing with media files, you can copy the same file as many times as you want without degrading quality. So, don't worry about making multiple copies of the same file. When you compare them, they will all look, and be, identical.

Merge Two, or More, Events

Sometimes, Projects get so big that the media can't be contained on a single hard disk. Or, perhaps, you have several small hard disks and finally have the money to buy a RAID big enough to store everything. What you need to do now is merge the media from more than one Event so that everything gets gathered together in one place.

That's what the Merge Events menu is all about: getting everything together so you can take it on the road.

For Merge Events to work, you must select more than one Event folder, before choosing File > Merge Events. Those folders can be stored either on the same hard drive or on multiple hard drives (**Figure 3.7**).

In this example, I have two Events filled with Model Railroad footage. One is on the 2nd Drive, and the other is on the 3rd Drive. Both Events are selected. However, this option also works if both Events are stored on the same hard drive. The key is to select all the Events you want to merge prior to selecting the menu.

When the menu is selected, the Merge Events dialog appears, asking you to give the newly merged file a name and pick the location where you want all these different files gathered together.

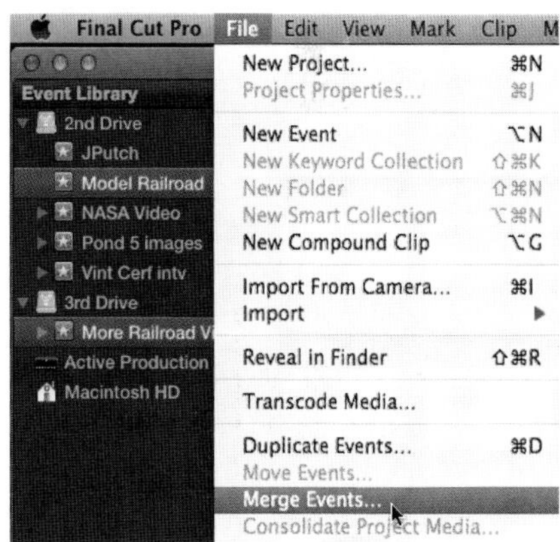

FIGURE 3.7
Notice the two selected Event folders on two different hard drives. Select the folders *before* choosing File > Merge Events.

Merging Is a Great Way to Consolidate Files

Merging your Events is a great way to consolidate them from multiple hard drives, as well as move them from a linked location into a single location. Unlike organizing, which *copies* your files, merging *moves* your files. This saves on storage space. Plus, if you have a bunch of linked files, merging moves them from where they were to the new Event folder that you selected in the Merge dialog.

A caution, though: If you are using the same file in multiple Projects, FCP will update all necessary internal links during the merge so none of your projects loses track of the file. However, if you are linking to those files from other applications, such as Final Cut Pro 7 or After Effects, those other applications don't have any way to know what FCP X is doing, which means the links in those applications will break.

Delete Event Render Files

When a clip is analyzed or has effects applied to it in the Event Browser, Final Cut creates render files for that clip. These render files take up space, which, after a while, you may want to get back.

(There are actually two sets of render files: one for the Event and one for the Project. This section talks about Event render files; I'll cover Project render files in a few pages. In general, Project render files will take more space.)

To delete render files associated with an Event, select the name of the Event in the Event Library and choose File > Delete Event Render Files.

Select the choice that's most appropriate:

- You can delete render files that are not being used by any Project.
- You can delete all render files associated with this Event.

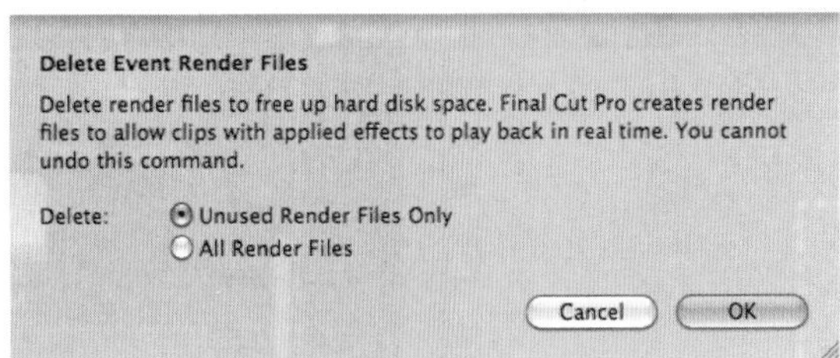

FIGURE 3.8
Delete render files only when projects are complete.

The good news is that if you delete too many render files, Final Cut will just re-create the ones it needs in the background while you go about the process of editing your project (**Figure 3.8**).

Trash an Event

You can also move an event to the Trash. This is not the same as deleting the Event, but it's pretty darn close. Moving an Event to the Trash allows you to change your mind and bring the files back before they are permanently erased either using Undo (Command+Z) or using the Finder to go into the Trash and drag the files back into the Final Cut Events folder.

What Does Trashing Actually Mean?

Trashing an Event immediately removes an Event from the Event Library so that it and all the media it contains are no longer available inside Final Cut Pro X.

At the same time, the entire Event folder stored inside Final Cut Events is moved to the Trash. This includes the Event database for this event and all original media, plus all Event render files, optimized media, proxy media, and analysis files.

In a word, everything.

You can get all this back by either selecting Undo or dragging it out of the Trash. Once you empty the Trash, though, everything in this Event is permanently gone. As a note, however, if you linked to media for an Event, trashing the Event will trash the links but not the media stored elsewhere on your hard disk to which those links point.

There are three options to trash a no-longer-needed Event:

- Right-click the name of the Event in the Event Library and select Move to Trash.
- Select the name of the Event and press Command+Delete.
- Select the name of the Event you want to delete and choose File > Move to Trash.

Whichever one you pick, the Event is immediately removed from the Event Library and moved to the Trash (**Figure 3.9**).

If you switch out of Final Cut and look inside the Trash, you'll see the entire Event folder and all its contents. If you change your mind, drag the folder out of the Trash and back into the Final Cut Events folder. If you really do want it gone, just empty the Trash.

Most of the time, after you create an Event and import your media, you won't need to do much with your Events except use them to organize your media. But, when you need to do more, now you know how.

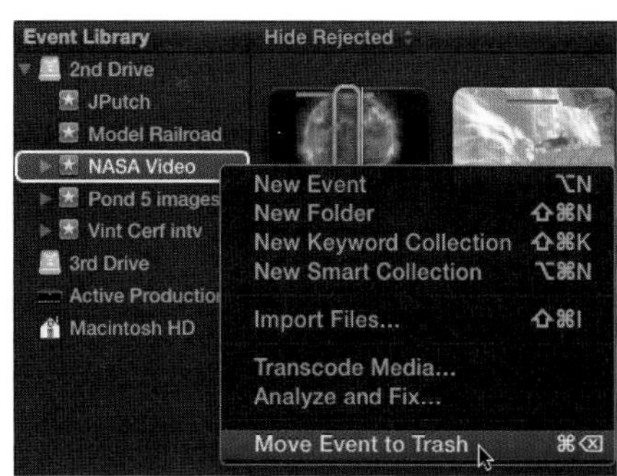

FIGURE 3.9
Trashing Events moves files to the Trash, which allows recovering an inadvertently trashed file, if necessary, by pulling it out of the Trash.

Can I Delete All My Events? What If I Need to Hide an Event?

No, you can't delete all your Events. If you try to delete the last Event in the Event Library, you'll get the warning shown in **Figure 3.10**. You can delete all your Projects, but you must have at least one Event, even if there is no media in it.

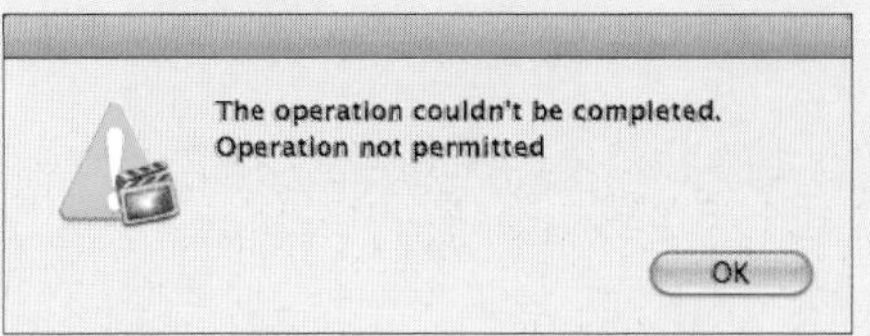

FIGURE 3.10
There must always be at least one FCP X Event, even if it is empty.

Let's say you have media from a client that you cannot allow anyone else to see, yet you have a different client coming in to do some editing with you. What do you do?

You can solve this, but you need to use the Finder.

First, always quit FCP X. Then, in the Finder, go to the Final Cut Events folder that contains the Event you want to hide and drag the Event folder for that Event somewhere else. (Dragging a folder from one location on a hard drive to another location on the same hard drive moves all files.) In my case, I create a folder called Final Cut Events Not in Use, and any Event that I want to hide I store there. This makes an Event invisible to FCP X.

All About Projects

Like Events, Projects are tracked using a database and stored in a master folder. The Project folder is called Final Cut Projects. Inside this master folder is a folder for each individual Project. Inside each Project folder is the database for that Project, along with render files and other technical elements that FCP X needs for its own purposes.

This Project database is new with FCP X and provides a solid foundation upon which to build your edit. Because both Events and Projects use databases for tracking their elements, managing Projects is very similar to managing Events.

In this section, I will show you all the different ways you can manage a Project, from creation to archiving.

There are three elements to the Timeline:

- Project Library (Keyboard shortcut: Command+0)
- Timeline Index (Keyboard shortcut: Shift+Command+2)
- Timeline (Keyboard shortcut: Command+0)

The Project Library, like the Event Library, is a list of all the different Projects you've created in Final Cut Pro X (**Figure 3.11**). Like Events, all Projects are always online, but only one Project can be loaded to the Timeline at any given time.

FIGURE 3.11
This is the Project Library, displaying five different Projects.

While there is no limit to the number of Projects you can create, each Project can contain only one *sequence*, or collection of clips. You can work around this limitation either by using compound clips, which we will talk about in Chapter 5, or by duplicating Projects, which I'll talk about shortly. According to Apple, there is no limit to the number of clips that can be edited into a Project.

Create a New Project

Before you create a new Project, select the hard disk where you want the project stored (**Figure 3.12**). (This is exactly the same process you go through when creating a new Event to make sure the Event is stored on the correct hard drive.)

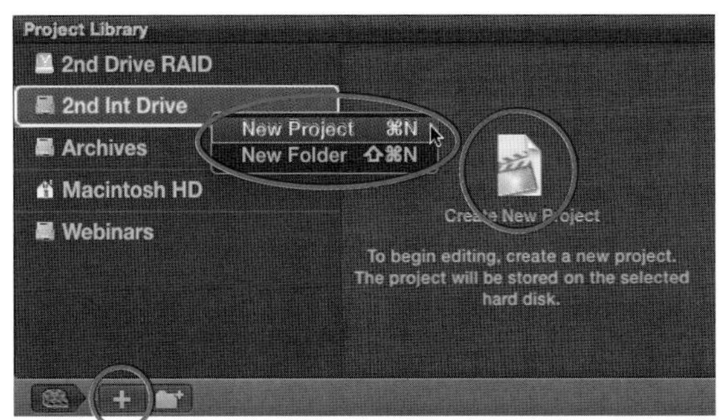

FIGURE 3.12
There are several ways to create a new Project—clicking one of the highlighted icons or pressing Command+N.

Once you have the hard drive selected, there are five (yup, *five*!) ways to create a new Project:

- Right-click inside the Project Library and choose New Project.
- Choose File > New Project.
- Press Command+N.

- Click the + (plus) key at the bottom of the Project Library.
- If you are running FCP X for the first time, click the New Project icon.

Whichever option you select, the New Project dialog appears (**Figure 3.13**). Give your project a name and select the Event that you want to link it to.

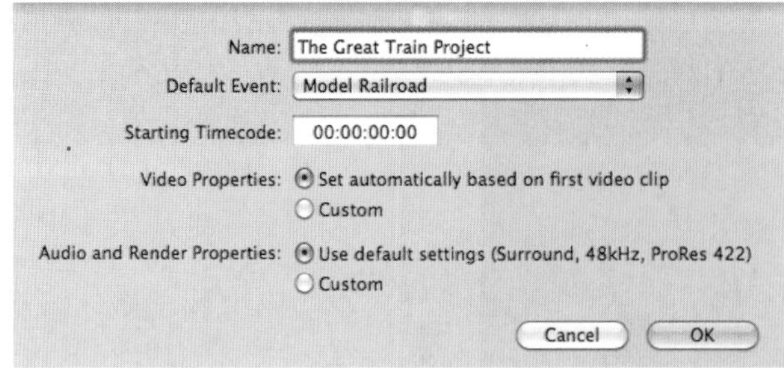

FIGURE 3.13 This is the standard New Project dialog from version 10.0.1.

NOTE Linking Projects to Events

Databases need connections. Because both the Event and the Project use databases for tracking their elements, Final Cut Pro X requires that the Project database be linked to an Event. This simply ensures that all the database connections are properly maintained. Once this initial link is established, which you do when you create the Project, you never need to worry about it again. And, even though you've linked to one Event, you can use media from any Event. (See the "Changing the Event Reference Simplifies Sharing Projects" section.)

After you link your Project to an Event, you still have three more choices to make:

- New with version 10.0.1 is the ability to specify the starting timecode. Virtually all professional projects in North America start at 01:00:00:00. However, if you and your clients don't care about timecode, you can leave the default setting at 00:00:00:00.
- Set the video properties for the Project.
- Set the audio and render settings.

When Can I Change Timecode?

Anytime you want. At the beginning, middle, or end of a Project. Also, you can change between drop and non-drop timecode whenever you want.

To change any of these settings later, choose File > Project Properties. (I will illustrate this a bit later in this chapter.) And, just so you know, I generally change the timecode to 01:00:00:00 for my projects. However, for this book, I left it at the default setting to keep things simple.

There's no preference setting that allows setting a default timecode value.

As a general rule, I use the default setting for the top radio button: "Set automatically based on first video clip." This works similarly to Final Cut Pro 7 and Express, where the Timeline will autoconfigure itself based upon the first clip you edit into the Project. Since FCP X edits most video formats natively, this will be a good option for most projects (**Figure 3.14**).

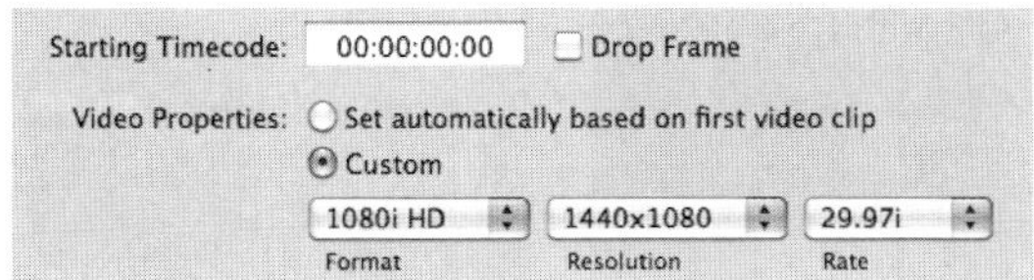

FIGURE 3.14
Video properties can be customized for each project.

If, on the other hand, you need to create a Project to meet specific technical settings, you can configure them here by selecting the Custom radio button and setting the Format, Resolution, and Rate pop-up menus.

When Is Interlacing a Good Thing?

Um, never, actually. Interlacing consists of those thin, horizontal lines radiating off all moving objects in the frame (**Figure 3.15**).

FIGURE 3.15
Interlacing consists of thin, horizontal lines radiating sideways from moving objects.

It is always preferable to shoot and edit progressive rather than interlaced. Interlaced video, where each frame is divided into two fields composed of all the even lines in the image, followed by all the odd lines, was invented at the dawn of television. It worked great for CRT TV sets, but it looks terrible on computer monitors. When you watch interlaced video on a computer, thin horizontal lines radiate out from all moving objects. (Interlaced formats are indicated by a small *i* after the frame size, as in 1080i.)

Progressive video, on the other hand, shoots the entire image at once. (Film does too, for that matter.) So, when you watch progressive video on either a CRT TV or your computer monitor, it looks great.

If you are given the choice to shoot either progressive or interlaced, shoot progressive. The ideal image size is 1080p (where the *p* stands for progressive), because this format can be easily converted into any other format.

If you are going to the Web, my recommendation is to shoot 720p. File sizes are smaller, and many cameras support this format. At this point, 720 images are the standard HD video display size when playing back video on the Web.

The second radio button, though, hides a trap (**Figure 3.16**). By default, it mixes your audio to a surround (5.1) mix. This means that whenever you export your project, you are exporting six audio tracks.

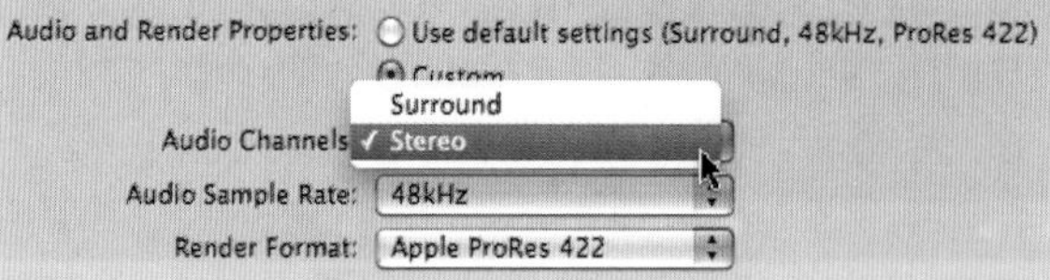

FIGURE 3.16
In almost all cases, you should change the audio setting from Surround to Stereo.

Perhaps in the future everyone wants to hear our audio in surround format. But, since most of us just need a stereo mix, exporting in surround means that you are exporting two audio tracks with audio and four empty audio tracks. This wastes space and extends download time.

Since this cannot be controlled by a preference setting, I make a point to reset this in the pop-up menu to Stereo whenever I create a new Project.

The other two settings for 48 kHz audio and render files using ProRes 422 are both fine, and I leave them alone.

Click OK, and your new Project is created and opened in the Timeline, ready to edit. (I promise, we will get to this...in Chapter 5.)

How Do I Work with Multiformat Media?

If you're unsure of the final distribution format for your video, the most important decision you can make before creating your project is choosing your Project's frame rate. It's easy to change the format and the frame *size* of your Project at any time, but changing the frame *rate* can cause all the edit points in your project to shift in time.

Video format, frame size, and frame rate are all set in the Project Properties window, when you create a new Project.

My recommendation is to decide the frame rate based on one of two criteria:

- What frame rate are you supposed to deliver to the client?
- If the client has no preference, set the frame rate based upon the frame rate of the majority of your source video.

Personally, I shoot just about everything I post to the Web at 60 fps. If I lived in a PAL country, I'd shoot 50 fps.

Duplicate Projects

One of the strengths of FCP X is also a weakness: It is *always* saving your Project files. This means that as soon as you make a change, Final Cut immediately saves it. No more losing files because of a power failure or system crash.

This is great news...except that when you open a Project to review what's in it, if you make any changes to the Project, they are immediately saved to the file.

Duplicating projects allows you to protect a copy of your Project from accidental changes. It also makes it easy to save incremental edits, in case you need to go back in time.

There are three ways you can duplicate a Project (**Figure 3.17**):

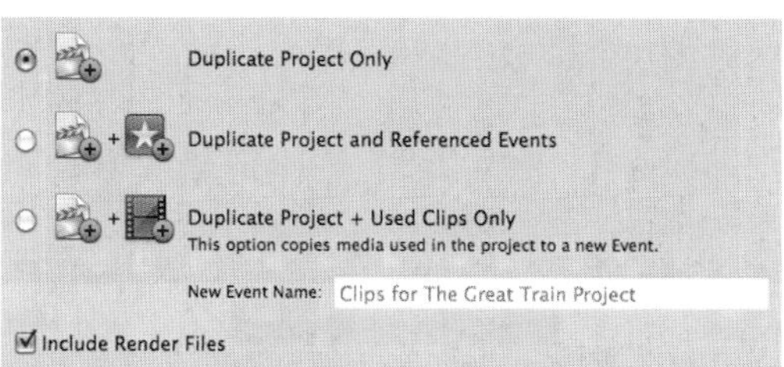

FIGURE 3.17 The three options for duplicating a project.

Duplicate Project Only. This is a great way to make a protection copy of your Project. It requires the least amount of additional hard disk space and can be processed quickly. In virtually every case when duplicating just the Project file, I recommend not duplicating render files; FCP can re-create them if it needs them.

Duplicate Project and Referenced Events. This duplicates the Project file, all Events referenced by the Project file, and all of the media in the referenced Events. In other words, it duplicates darn near everything. This is the best choice when you need to make an archive of a Project where you want to keep as much source material as possible. Again, I recommend against duplicating render files, just to save space, because FCP will re-create them if it needs them.

Duplicate Project and Used Clips Only. This duplicates the Project file and only the media files that are used within that Project. However, for Timeline clips, Final Cut duplicates the entire clip that's stored on your hard drive, not just the media used in the Timeline. So, while you don't need to worry about specifying handles, your storage requirements will be higher because entire media clips are being duplicated, not just the portion used in the Timeline.

With that as background, the actual process of duplicating a Project is easy; do one of the following:

- Select the Project and choose File > Duplicate.
- Select the Project and press Command+D.
- Right-click the name of a Project and select Duplicate Project.

NOTE What's a Handle?

Handles are extra video before the Start (In) of a clip and after the End (Out). Handles are generally necessary when trimming a clip or adding transitions. We'll talk more about handles in Chapter 8.

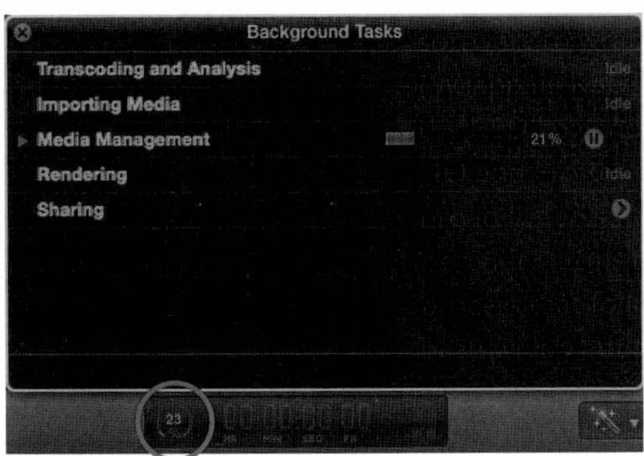

FIGURE 3.18
The Background Tasks window monitors background activity, allowing you to pause or cancel it.

Whichever you choose, the Duplicate Project dialog opens allowing you to give your new project a name and specify what you want to duplicate. (As a note, uncheck Include Render Files to save hard disk space.)

When you have the settings to your liking, click OK.

Like most media tasks in Final Cut Pro, duplicating projects runs in the background. This means you can immediately get back to editing while Final Cut Pro is busy duplicating everything.

To check the status of any background task, click the small "clock" face in the Dashboard, or press Command+9. This opens the Background Tasks window (**Figure 3.18**). The window provides a summary of all background tasks. To get more detail, twirl down one of the right-pointing triangles on the left side of the window.

Two Fast Ways to Get Things Moving

Want to *copy* a Project from one hard disk to another? In the Project Library, drag it from where it is to the name of the hard disk you want to copy it to. This will duplicate the Project to another hard drive.

Want to *move* a Project from one hard disk to another? In the Project Library, press the Command key while dragging a Project from where it is to the name of the hard drive where you want it to go. This will move the Project, and all related files, from one hard drive to another.

Organize Multiple Projects Using Folders

Once you have a lot of Projects created—especially if you have lots of versions of the same Project—grouping them into folders can make your life a lot easier.

To create a new folder for storing Projects, go to the Project Library (Command+0), select the hard disk where you want the folder to appear, and then do one of the following:

- Choose File > New Folder.
- Press Shift+Command+N.
- Click the New Folder icon at the bottom-left corner of the Project Library.
- Right-click the name of the hard disk and select New Folder.
- Right-click the name of the Project and select New Folder.

Whew! There are a lot of ways to do the same thing. Whichever option you choose creates a new folder (surprisingly named New Folder) and indents it under the name of the hard disk.

- To move a Project into the folder, just drag it in. To move the Project out of a folder, drag the Project out of the folder and on top of the name of the hard disk.
- To hide the Projects inside a folder, click the twirl arrow (the right-pointing triangle next to the name of the folder).
- To reveal the Projects inside a folder, click the twirl arrow.
- To delete a folder, either right-click the name of the folder and select Move Folder to Trash or press Command+Delete.

A Note on the Delete Key

There are two Delete keys on a full-size keyboard. In fact, they are both there on a laptop, too, but one of them is hidden (**Figure 3.19**).

FIGURE 3.19
Be sure you know which Delete key to use. In general, use the big one.

Whenever I refer to the Delete key, I am *always* referring to the big Delete key, which is two keys straight up from the Return key. The small delete key, often labeled Del, is just to the left of the End key. (On laptops, you can access this key by pressing the Fn+Delete keys.

This Del key is programmed differently from the Delete key. So, just to avoid confusion, unless I say otherwise, I will always be referring to the big Delete key in this book.

Share Projects with Event Reference

As you discovered in Chapter 2, projects are connected to the media of a specific Event. Most of the time, one editor works with one Event. However, there's a special way to connect media, called an *Event reference*, that allows you to connect to similar media stored in a different place.

An example of this, say, is an editor and a producer who want to send Project files back and forth, without also sharing media.

An Event reference is the ability to take a Project and point it to media in a different Event. What you are doing is changing the media that is connected to a Project by changing the Event reference.

Say you have an editor and a producer who are in different locations. The editor sends the producer the media, Event folder, and Project folder to start the project.

The producer makes changes to the Event for their own organizational needs—say adding keywords, changing clip names in the Event Browser, and flagging clips as Rejected using ratings. (I'll explain all of this in the next chapter.) But they are not changing the media itself.

Then, the producer sends just the Project folder back to the editor. The original Event folder and media remain with the editor. A copy of the Event folder and media are now also with the producer—and the producer's Event folder contains those revised keywords and ratings. If the editor were to open the Project sent to her by the producer, all the clips would be offline, because the Project is still linked to the Event folder on the producer's system.

FIGURE 3.20
Modify Event References allows changing the Event connected to a Project by pointing to a different Event folder.

Instead, the editor copies the Project folder to her local system in the Final Cut Projects folder. Opening Final Cut Pro X, she selects the Project in the Project Library, without opening it in the Timeline.

With the Project selected, the editor chooses File > Project Properties (or presses Command+J). She clicks Modify Event Reference and navigates to the Event folder stored locally on her system (**Figure 3.20**). The editor's Project now connects to this local media, rather than the media on the producer's system.

Both the producer and the editor have their copy of the Event folder and media stored locally. Changing Event References allows repointing a Project from one Event folder to another.

This is a very robust use of the media management in FCP X because it easily allows changing the Event that is referenced by a Project.

Archive Projects and Media by Consolidating

As you move from videotape to tapeless media, the problems of archiving become increasingly challenging. Gone are the days of storing your final masters on tape. Now, you need to figure out how to store digital files for the long term.

This is the short answer: Never use hard disks for long-term storage, especially if they are unplugged. After a few years, your data will slowly disappear from the surface of the hard drive, in a process called *bit flux*.

This is the longer answer: We haven't figured out the best way to store digital assets for the longer term. However, the best option, today, is a form of magnetic tape called LTO. As of the time I write this, the current version of LTO is version 5, abbreviated as LTO-5.

This provides the best combination of long-term storage—about 25 years per tape, the same as videotape—reasonable price, and full support for Macintosh systems. It is beyond the scope of this book to go into detail on LTO archiving; however, if you want to keep your projects and media for longer than a year or two, you need to find a way to move them off your hard disks and onto something much more permanent.

That being said, the best way to archive the elements of a Project is to use the Duplicate Project and referenced Events option we just talked about. (I still wouldn't duplicate render files, though.)

The best way to archive a completed Project is to export it as a QuickTime movie (Share > Export Media). While there is a large debate within the professional archiving community on the best codecs to use for archiving for extremely long periods of time, exporting your files using your Project settings should be fine for the next 5 to 15 years.

To get ready to archive a Project, especially large Projects, you should consider consolidation. As Projects get bigger, they start to spill over onto multiple hard disks. This makes the process of archiving much more complex, especially if files are being pulled from a variety of different Events, each on different hard disks.

NOTE Consolidation Isn't Always Necessary

Consolidation is necessary only if your media is stored on multiple hard disks. If all your media is stored on one drive, Consolidate Project Media will be grayed out.

That's where Project consolidation can help.

What consolidating a Project does is gather all the media used in a single Project from multiple hard disks and puts it all in one spot.

To consolidate a Project, select the Project name in the Project Library and choose Consolidate Project Media (**Figure 3.21**).

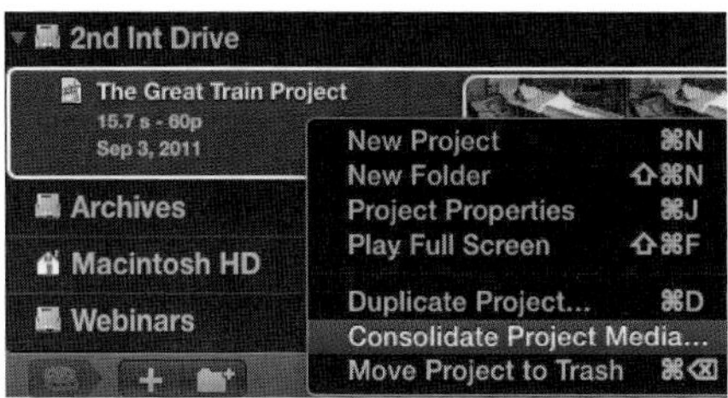

FIGURE 3.21 A fast way to consolidate the media for a Project is to pick it from the contextual menu.

The Consolidation dialog provides three choices:

- Copy Referenced Events
- Move Referenced Events
- Copy Used Clips Only

● **NOTE**
Give Yourself Room

If you are consolidating a Project, move your Project to a hard disk with enough room to hold all your consolidated media. Consolidated media is stored on the same hard disk as your Project.

Copy Referenced Events. This is the best choice when you are still using the media in other projects or other applications. This makes a copy of all Events referenced by your Project, and all the clips stored in those Events, and stores them at the location of your Project. The only disadvantage of copying is that it requires more disk space to store the duplicated files.

Move Referenced Events. This is the best choice for media related to a single project where you want to get it off the drives it is on and put it in one spot. This is the best choice as well when you are adding a new, larger hard drive, or RAID, to your system and want to move files from the older drives to the newer and bigger drive. This moves all Events, and the media they contain, from the old location to a new location.

Copy Used Clips Only. This copies just the media you are using in your Project. However, it copies the entire media file, not just the portion used in your Timeline. This is the best option when you want to save hard disk space at the new consolidation location. This also gives you the option to name the new Event.

Another Way to Archive

Final Cut Pro allows you to create a *camera archive* for both tape and tapeless media. I explain how this works in Chapter 4, so let me just give you a summary here.

Camera archives are backup copies of your existing media. You can back up tape or tapeless media. You can create archives as a stream directly from the camera or by copying files already on the hard disk.

Camera archives provide a browsable "near-line" archive of media that you can view in the Import from Camera window, without first having to import it into Final Cut Pro. Because this is generally used as a backup to your existing media, make a point to store it on a different hard disk than the one(s) you are using for editing. Both Chapter 4 and the Final Cut Pro user manual go into this in more detail.

Delete Project Render Files

Just as Events have render files for effects applied to clips in the Event Browser, Projects have render files. And, in most cases, the Project render files will take more space.

In general, never delete render files for a Project you are currently working on. However, when the Project is complete, you can delete render files to save hard disk space. To do so, open the Project Library (Command+0) and select the Project with the render files you want to delete. Choose File > Delete Project Render Files.

Select the option that best applies to your Project:

- **Delete Unused Render Files Only:** This deletes files not used by the current Project.
- **Delete All Render Files:** This deletes all render files associated with that Project.

For those who worry about making mistakes, if you make the wrong choice and delete too many render files, Final Cut will simply rebuild the render files it needs in the background as you continue your editing.

Trash a Project

When the time comes to send your Project to the big digital archive in the sky, you need to know how to delete a Project.

By now, you should know the drill:

1. Go to the Project Library.
2. Select the Project you want to delete.
3. Press Command+Delete, or right-click the Project name and select Move Project to Trash.
4. Then, when the time comes, empty the Trash.

If you change your mind prior to emptying the Trash and need to resuscitate your Project, switch to the Finder, drag it out of the Trash, and move it into any available Final Cut Projects folder.

What If You Need to Hide a Project?

Because all projects are always available, this could cause a problem if you need to keep a project confidential and unseen by other clients. What do you do?

You can solve this two ways: in FCP or in the Finder. In Final Cut, you can hide Projects in folders. Or, to use the Finder, you follow a procedure similar to what you did to hide an Event:

1. Quit FCP X. This keeps Final Cut from getting confused when a Project disappears.
2. In the Finder, go to the Final Cut Projects folder that contains the Project you want to hide and drag the Project folder for that Project somewhere else on the same hard disk. (Dragging a folder from one location on a hard drive to another location on the same hard drive moves all files.)
3. In my case, I create a folder called Final Cut Projects Not in Use on the same hard disk that holds my Final Cut Projects folder and any Projects that I want to hide I store there. This makes a Project invisible to FCP X.

Creating Keyboard Shortcuts

I don't really know where to talk about keyboard shortcuts, so here is as good a place as any. Apple has totally reengineered the interface for creating keyboard shortcuts. You'll find it in Final Cut Pro > Commands.

The Command Editor window opens (**Figure 3.22**). The top half of the Editor displays the layout of the keyboard currently connected to your computer, while the bottom half displays a variety of lists of keyboard shortcuts. This lower half displays all menu items, whether or not there is a keyboard shortcut associated with it.

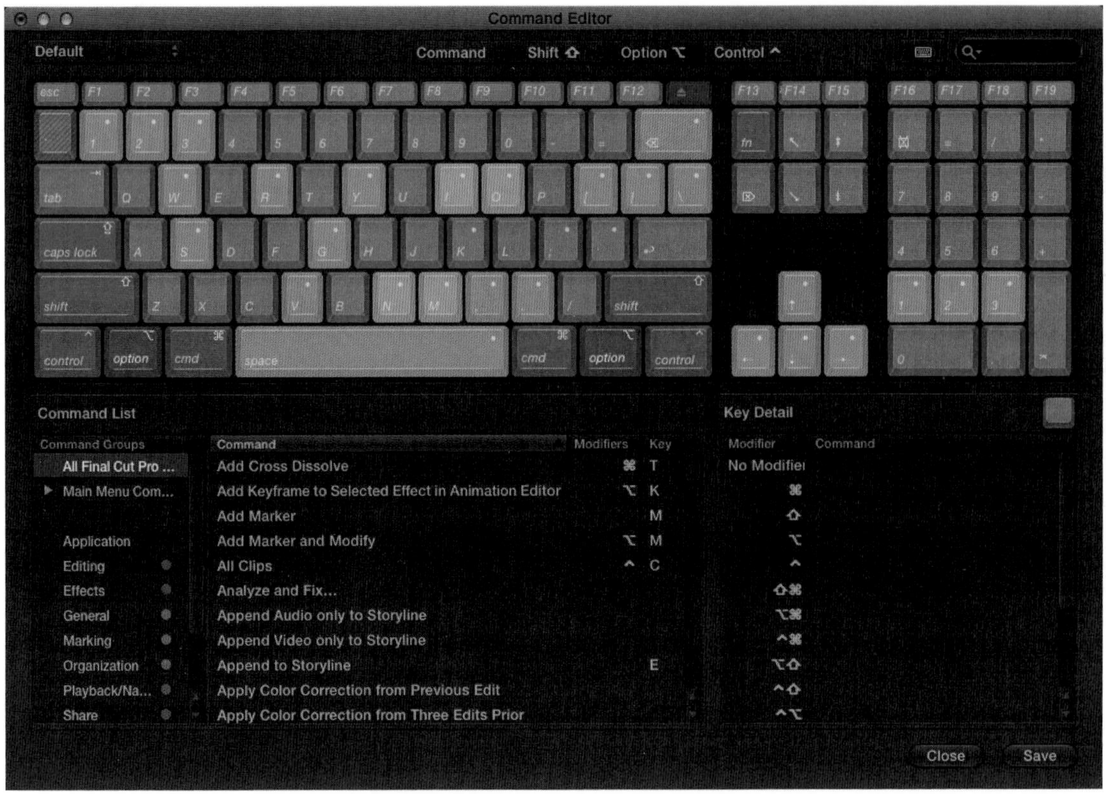

FIGURE 3.22 How you change keyboard shortcuts has been totally redesigned for FCP X.

Keyboard shortcuts are stored in groups. The default keyboard group is called Default (I kid you not) and can't be modified. As you will learn in the next few pages, creating new keyboard shortcuts and shortcut groups is very easy.

For instance, click the word *Editing* in the Command List in the lower left of this window. All the keyboard shortcuts that relate to editing are displayed in the middle Command window. Notice that all the keys that have editing keyboard shortcuts assigned to them glow with a light blue color. (I must admit, this is pretty cool!)

Another way to find related keyboard shortcuts is using the Search box in the top-right corner. For example, in Figure 3.23, I had typed **Zoom**. All the menu commands that relate to zooming are displayed in the Commands window at the bottom.

FIGURE 3.23 Enter text in the Search box in the top right to find all commands related to a search entry. Then, highlight all keys related to that search by clicking the small "keyboard" button just to the left of the Search text box.

Let's create our own keyboard shortcut and see how this new interface works. I've decided to create a shortcut for Modify > Analyze and Fix. Let's see first whether it has a shortcut.

1. We *could* go up to the Modify menu and check to see whether a shortcut is assigned to Analyze and Fix, but that's the boring and obvious route. Instead, go back to the Search text box in the top-right corner and type **Analyze**.
2. Only two menu commands refer to analyzing. And Analyze and Fix doesn't have a keyboard shortcut assigned to it.

   The easiest way to see whether a key is available to use as a keyboard shortcut is to click it. In this case, I'll click the letter *A*, which is what I want to use for the shortcut.

▲ **TIP** Keyboard Highlight button

See that small box to the left of the Search text entry in the top-right corner? That's called the Keyboard Highlight button. Click it, and all the keys that have keyboard shortcuts assigned to them for all the commands listed in the Commands window will glow with color. Another very neat trick.

3. In the Key Detail pane, all the different key combinations linked to a specific keyboard key are displayed, along with any assigned keyboard shortcuts (**Figure 3.24**). My first choice, Control+A, is not available since it is being used to toggle the display of Audio Animation. While I could easily replace this shortcut with a new one, I'll be polite and use a different combination. Shift+A is available; there's no shortcut next to those symbols.

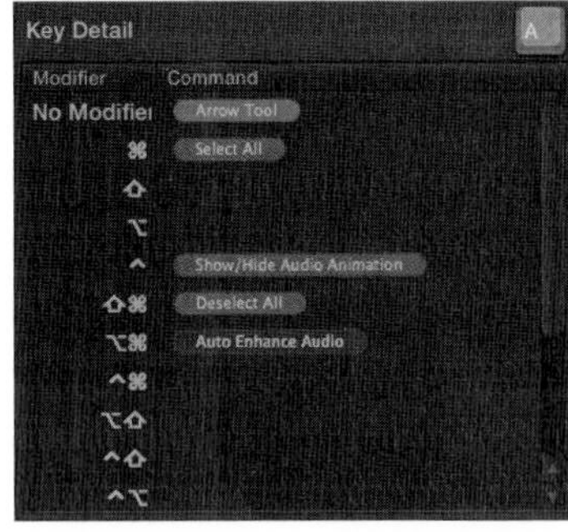

FIGURE 3.24 The Key Detail pane, on the right, shows every combination of shortcuts linked to a specific keyboard key.

4. At the top of the screen are buttons for the four modifier keys: Command, Shift, Option, and Control. I click Shift, which makes the button go slightly darker, indicating that I want to use the Shift modifier for this shortcut.

   As soon as I click Shift, all the keys that have shortcuts assigned to them using Shift as a modifier glow with color. Fortunately, the letter *A* is gray, meaning it is available (**Figure 3.25**).

FIGURE 3.25 All keys that have shortcuts assigned to them with that modifier glow with color. Available keys stay gray. Notice the Shift button at the top is dark.

5. Grab the Analyze and Fix command from the Commands list at the bottom, and drag it up to the letter *A* and drop it on the key.

6. A warning appears, indicating that you can't modify Apple's default keyboard shortcut set. Since you want to create a new set, click Make Copy.

7. Give the new shortcut set a name you're likely to remember...um, ah! I chose Larry's Keyboard Shortcuts. Then click OK.

   Look back down to the Key List, and there's the new shortcut, listed next to Shift+A!

8. Click the Default pop-up menu in the top-left corner to see the newly created keyboard shortcut set listed at the bottom (**Figure 3.26**).

9. Click Save at the bottom-right corner of the window to save all your newly created keyboard shortcuts and sets. There's no limit to how many shortcuts you can create or how many sets you can use.

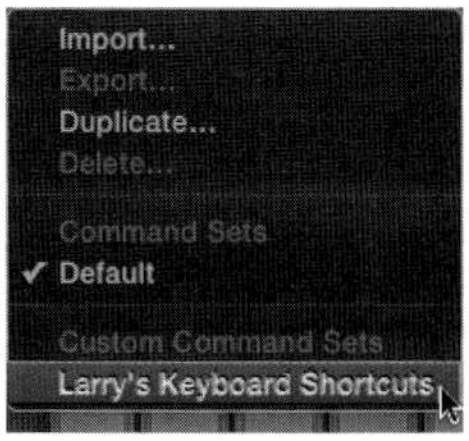

FIGURE 3.26 Also, the new command set is listed in the pop-up menu in the top-left corner.

What makes all these different sets even easier to use is that you only need to go to Final Cut Pro > Commands and select the set you want to use from that initial menu, rather than needing to reopen the Command Editor to change sets.

Summary

Whew! A huge amount of territory was covered in this chapter. And a lot of it was pretty heavy lifting. Fortunately, once you understand how Events and Projects work, they become almost second nature, and you'll only need to refer to this chapter for the cool keyboard shortcuts that you can create to go even faster.

As you make the transition into Final Cut Pro X, Events and Projects are two of the new concepts that you really need to understand to make the most of this software.

There are two other significantly new concepts still to go, and each has its own chapter: working with media and working with keywords. Both are new, and I'll cover media next.

Keyboard Shortcuts

Shortcut	What It Does
Option+N	Create new Event
Shift+Command+1	Toggle the display of the Event Library on or off
Option+Command+1	Display Event Browser in Filmstrip view
Option+Command+2	Display Event Browser in List view
Command+N	Create new Project
Command+0	Toggle between Project Library and Timeline
Shift+Command+2	Toggle the display of the Timeline Index on or off
Command-drag	Move the Event or Project being dragged
Shift+Command+N	Create new Project folder
Command+Delete	Move the selected item to the Trash
Option+Command+K	Display keyboard shortcut Command Editor
Command+[comma]	Open the FCP Preferences window
Command+9	Display background tasks

4

MANAGING MEDIA

All editing software tries to make working with media as easy as possible. Final Cut Pro X is no different in this respect. But, what *is* different is *how* it manages media. Unlike any other editing system, FCP X is designed from the ground up to work with *tapeless* media, which is media recorded to cards and hard disks, not videotape. Working tapeless requires changing how you think about media and changing how your editing system works with media.

Managing this media is what this chapter is all about.

Overview

Apple's goal with Final Cut Pro X was to create a rock-solid, single-user media workflow that helps editors avoid losing media. To do this, Apple consolidated the Import, Log and Capture, and Log and Transfer screens used in Final Cut Pro 7 into a single interface. Apple also provided three media options:

- You can edit media natively in its original camera format.
- You can optimize media by converting it into ProRes 422 for faster performance and potentially better image quality.
- You can create small *proxy* files to reduce the file size of media, while still retaining optimum performance with good image quality.

Final Cut Pro X supports importing from a file-based camera via a card, from a hard disk, or from a folder on your hard disk. It supports importing either stills or video from a DSLR or (H)DSLR camera, a tape-based camera or deck connected via FireWire, an iMovie project, an iMovie Event Library, files stored on your hard drives, and a camera archive created from tape or tapeless media.

This chapter explains how to organize your files before you even import them, how to set import preferences, how and why to optimize and analyze media, the different ways you can import media, how to import iMovie projects and media, how to size and import still images, and how to create a camera archive for both tape and tapeless media.

● **NOTE** A Really Important Website

Before you start shooting, be sure your camera and video format work with Final Cut Pro X. To do this, visit Apple's FCP X website at http://help.apple.com/finalcutpro/cameras/. This site lists all supported cameras and devices. It is always better to discover problems with your gear before you shoot, rather than afterward.

Keep in mind that many video formats require driver updates from camera vendors before they can be used in Final Cut Pro X. So, be sure to confirm compatibility before beginning any project. Final Cut Pro X does not currently support direct capture from videotape using timecode or RS-422 to control playback, and it doesn't "hide" media; all Event folders are always available.

Organize and Name Media

New users often make two common errors when working with tapeless media:

- They import directly from the memory card to Final Cut.
- They copy only some of the files from the card to their hard disk and then try to import them.

Both of these choices lead to catastrophe. Here's the one rule you need to remember: Always either create a disk image of your camera card or copy the *entire* contents of your camera card to a folder on your hard disk. My recommendation is to create a folder and copy your card into that folder.

It is impossible to overstress the importance of this rule. Follow it, and everything works great. Try to get fancy and outthink the system, and you'll always end up with problems.

Copy Your Media

When you edit video, you're working with two sets of files:

- **Source media:** This is the media you shoot in your camera. These are your master files.
- **Edit media:** This is the media you edit with. Sometimes these are the same files. Sometimes they aren't.

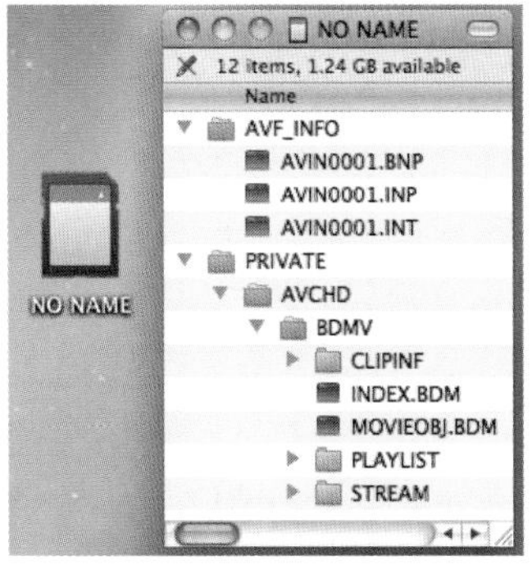

FIGURE 4.1
This shows a typical memory card mounted on the Desktop, along with its folder structure.

This section illustrates a system you can use to copy, organize, and name the source files you shoot. **Figure 4.1** shows the contents of a typical memory card opened in the Finder after media has been recorded to it—lots of weirdly named files and folders.

Here's the problem. In production, you record images from your camera to a card. You copy the card to a hard disk and then you *erase the card(!)* so you can use it again in production. (That word—*erase*—just sends chills down my back!)

For production, you need a fast, reliable, and easy-to-implement system that guarantees all data is transferred from the card to a hard disk. For postproduction, you need a system that assures that you can easily find all the media from that production.

Well, there are three parts to the solution. First, you want to be sure you are copying the correct files. Second, you want to copy the files safely and accurately to folders on at least one hard disk. And third, you want to organize and name the folders properly so you can associate them with the correct Project and find them when you need them.

You have two options here: Create a disk image of the card that you can store and access later, or copy the entire card to a folder on your hard drive. Both options support backups. Both options work. My preference, though, is copying the card to a folder. The key is to do it right.

Always select the *entire* contents of the card and copy the *entire* contents of the card to a single folder on your hard disk. You copy one entire card to one folder. Never, ever copy just a portion of the card. It will always lead to disaster. Always copy everything on the card—files, folders, locked files, everything. Final Cut knows what to do with all these files, even if they don't make sense to you.

And—even though you can—never import files directly from the card. Always copy the files to a folder on your hard disk first and then import them from that folder.

Why? If you import from the card and then erase the card, you don't have any backups. If, for some reason, the file you imported gets corrupted or lost or

NOTE Why All the Weird Files?

The reason there are so many weird files is that the contents of this card are far from a QuickTime movie. When FCP imports a file from a card, it takes all the different elements from all those different folders and builds it into a single QuickTime file. However, constructing that QuickTime movie does not mean it is changing the video format, just the structure of the files.

NOTE Is This Really That Important?

Yes! I can't tell you how many e-mails I get from editors trying to figure out how to salvage a shoot because they thought they needed to copy only a few files. Make your life simple and sleep well at night—copy the entire card to a single folder on your hard drive. One folder per card.

NOTE But, What If You Need to Save Hard Disk Space?

Look, let's get real for a second. How much time, effort, money, pain, and aggravation did it take to get your video shot? Which costs more—re-shooting or buying a new hard disk?

Storage is dirt cheap compared to the costs of even a simple production. Don't be penny-wise and pound-foolish. If you need it, buy more storage.

erased, you've lost that particular shot permanently. There's no way to get it back. You *always* want to make a backup because these folders become your camera masters. In fact, I recommend always making at least one backup of all media shot during production before you leave the set that day. That way, you know you have multiple copies of all the media of that day's shoot.

A Great Backup Utility

When on set, speed and file safety are paramount. I recommend copying files on set to a RAID. Either a RAID 1 or a RAID 5 system automatically creates what's called *data redundancy*. It duplicates your data so that if one of the hard drives inside that RAID dies, your data is still safe.

The speed of your hard disk or your RAID is much less important than data redundancy, because you're simply copying from the camera or the card, most generally from a very, very slow USB device. And it's not unusual to copy files to more than one hard disk at a time. If you're going to be doing a lot of tapeless work, there's a good utility that makes working with tapeless media a lot easier. It's published by Imagine Products, and it's called Shotput Pro (*www.imagineproducts.com*).

Naming Media Folders

The next step is to name your folders. With tapeless media, you don't name files; you name folders. Final Cut Pro X can use this folder name as a keyword to help you find that media in the future. Naming is critical because files that you can't find, or can't associate with a Project, are useless.

One Method

Whenever I start a new Project, I create a project code so I can easily track elements related to this Project. For example, let's say I have Just a Moment Productions as a client. They give me a new Project, the second one I've done for them. Before I do anything else, I create a project code (**Figure 4.2**).

FIGURE 4.2 Here's the naming convention I use for tapeless media folders. The project code is the first four characters: two letters for the client followed by two numbers for the job.

This code consists of two letters and two numbers: JM is the two-letter client code for Just a Moment Productions, and 02 indicates this is the second job I've done for that client. Then I use that project code at the beginning of all filenames for materials created for that Project.

All my Photoshop files start with that project code; so do graphics files, Final Cut Pro Project names, Motion projects, After Effects comps, voice-over recordings, everything. That way, if I ever need to find a file, I simply search for the project code, and every filename that starts with that project code shows up.

Folder naming for tapeless media builds on this project code. Remember, use one card per folder and a folder for every card you shoot. These folders become your camera master files from here on out. Organizing them now makes all the difference. Here's how I name the folders.

I start with the project code, then the date I shot the card, the camera (i.e., A, B, or C), and the card number. In Figure 4.2, JM02 is the project code, 110928 is the date I shot the card, A is the camera, and it's the third card I shot that day from that camera.

(Note that the date format is year, month, date. This allows the folder to sort alphabetically and chronologically at the same time.)

These source files are the original camera masters before Final Cut Pro copies them into the Events folder. I store all my source media folders on a separate hard drive from my editing files. Source files are not stored in the Events folder.

Figure 4.3 shows how I organize my source media folders on the hard disk. On the second drive, I created a folder called Source Media. Inside Source Media is a folder for each client. Inside each client folder is a folder for every Project. Inside the project folder is a folder for every card. (I've color-coded the levels to make them easier to see, but these colors are totally optional on your part.)

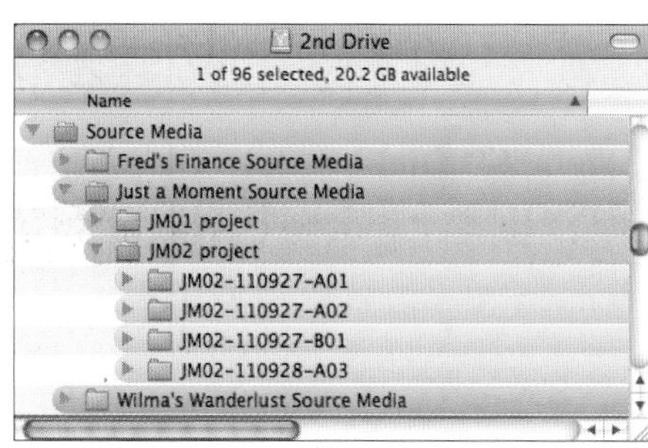

FIGURE 4.3
This is how I organize my folders for tapeless media—by client, project, and card.

There are several good things about this system:

- It is easy to implement and understand.
- You can see at a glance what client, date, and camera is inside each folder.
- When it comes time to import, Final Cut Pro X can easily extract the shots you need for edit.
- Final Cut Pro will track the folder name as part of the metadata associated with every clip from that folder, so finding the original media again in the future is trivial.

NOTE What If You Want to Archive Your Cards?

One way to do this is to make a disk image of the card by choosing Utilities > Disk Utility. A disk image copies the entire contents of the card into a single file on your hard disk, which is easy to archive. Even better, because all the different files are stored in a single file, nothing gets lost.

NOTE Are Camera Archives Only for Tape-Based Media?

No. Camera archives can be used for tape, or tapeless, media. It is also a great way to gather all the media from a project and store it in one spot. You will learn more later in this chapter or by reading the FCP X Help files.

When working with tapeless media, copy one card into one folder. Final Cut Pro will then take the contents of that folder and import the shots you need from it. Spend a little time thinking about how you want your files organized and named before you start shooting, because what you're creating with those folders are your camera master files. Make sure you have enough storage on set. Make backups during production. Create and name your folders in an organized fashion. And keep your source files separate from your editing files just in case.

Once that's done, you are ready to import your files and start editing.

FCP X Has a Simpler Way

The benefit to making disk images or copying memory cards the way I just outlined is that you can do it on set, without using FCP X. This way, you are making an exact copy of the files as they exist on the memory card.

However, Final Cut Pro X has another way to do this, called a *camera archive*. As you would expect, an archive is a collection of data. Creating a camera archive makes it easy to make a copy of your memory cards. You'll see how this works later in this chapter.

The point I want to make now is that the difference between copying the card manually and using FCP X to make a copy is in the end result. Manually copying files from the card to a folder makes a complete copy of exactly the same files that are on the card. This new folder can be read by any application that knows how to read the contents of a memory card: FCP X, FCP 7, Adobe, Avid...you get the idea.

The limitation of this method is that you no longer have a single file to watch—you need to keep track of the entire folder. And if any of the contents of the folder get lost, there is a very good chance you won't be able to access the media inside the folder.

What FCP X does is create a single file, which you name, stored in a single folder called Final Cut Camera Archives on whatever hard disk you want. The important point here is that Final Cut Pro transfers all of the media from the card into a single file on your hard disk that is *readable only by FCP X*.

The advantages are that, because all the contents are sealed into this one file, it is easy to manage and there is no risk of individual files getting lost. The disadvantage is that the only application that can read this file is FCP X. Note that FCP is not applying any data or video compression to the file. The file you create on your hard disk is the same size as the data stored on the card.

I am always leery of storing media in a format that can be read by only one application—even from large companies like Apple. My recommendation is to copy your files manually, from the card to a folder on your hard disk as discussed earlier. This can be done easily on set, without requiring the use of Final Cut Pro X. Additionally, other applications are able to read the contents of this folder.

Finally, you can use utility software, such as Shotput Pro, to copy the files to multiple hard disks at the same time. However, if you prefer simplicity and security to flexibility, a camera archive is hard to beat.

Importing Media

Importing is the process of making Final Cut Pro X aware that media files exist. Sometimes, this process involves converting the files from a camera format into something that FCP X can read. Other times, you just need to point to a file to let Final Cut Pro know that it is there. Additionally, FCP X can optimize (convert) files into a format that renders and exports faster, or it can create proxy files to allow you to reduce the file size of your media so you can edit it on smaller systems.

In all cases, FCP X is not actually importing anything. It is just creating a *pointer*, a path, that tells it where the media file it should use for editing is located. No media files are actually copied into your Project.

One of the good things about FCP X is that when Apple created it, it made much of the import process run in the background. "Background" means that you can be doing one thing while Final Cut Pro is importing, analyzing, and processing all your files. This means you don't have to wait for FCP to finish importing before you can start editing. In fact, you can start viewing and editing files almost immediately, even though they are still importing.

What's even cooler is you can monitor all this background activity—I'm a big fan of blinking lights and charts and graphs. I'll show you how to monitor your background tasks shortly, when you actually have some imported media to monitor.

Even better, Apple has added a bunch of options that are handled during import that can save you time later. Those options are controlled from Final Cut Pro's preferences. Let me start the discussion of importing by looking at these preference settings. Then, I'll show you how to import a wide variety of media.

Set Import Preferences in the Import Window

My goals for this section are to explain how Final Cut Pro decides where to store media, to describe the settings in the Import Preferences window, and to provide recommended settings for your importing. Final Cut Pro X also makes it easy to change, or verify, import preferences before importing media.

There are three preference windows in Final Cut Pro: Editing, Playback, and Import. For this chapter, you'll look at the Import preferences. I'll discuss the other two in Chapter 6.

There are two ways to open Final Cut Pro's preference window:

- Press Command+[comma].
- Choose Final Cut Pro > Preferences.

● NOTE Final Cut Pro X Is Nondestructive

In spite of what it seems as you are editing, Final Cut Pro is not making any changes to the media files you have stored on your hard disk. No matter what you do inside FCP X, the media files on your hard disk are safe. This is a very reassuring thing to know—nothing you do inside Final Cut Pro will harm your media. Even when you ask Final Cut Pro to delete media, it only moves it to the Trash. You still have the opportunity to recover it from the Trash, if you moved it there by mistake.

● NOTE Where Does Media Get Stored?

Good question, and from the previous chapter, you already know the answer. Media used for editing is copied into the Events folder or FCP points to its current location on your hard disk. You control which of these options FCP follows, based upon how you set preferences inside FCP X.

The preference window opens (**Figure 4.4**). Click the Import icon. (In this example, the checkboxes also indicate my recommended import preferences.)

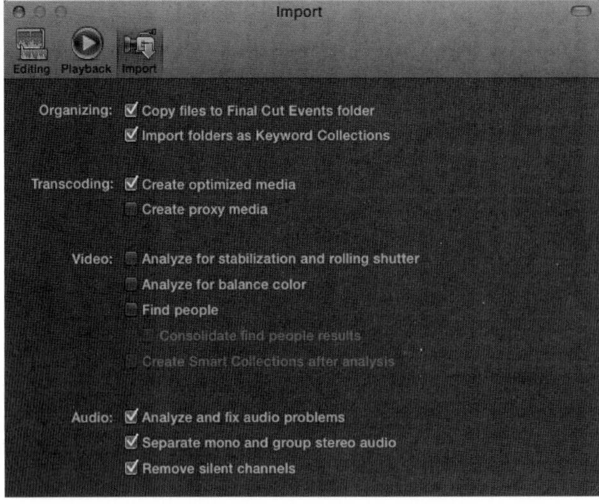

FIGURE 4.4 This screen sets preferences for importing media.

The Import window has four sections: Organizing, Transcoding, Video, and Audio. (*Transcoding* is a technical term that simply means converting. Transcoding a file means converting a file from one format to another.) Let's take a look at what each of these settings means.

Organizing

The Organizing section of the Import window contains the following:

- **Copy files.** If "Copy files to Final Cut Events folder" is checked, FCP will copy your media file from wherever it is into the Events folder. This is the best way to consolidate all your media files into one location. The downside is that, because you are duplicating files, your storage needs will increase. Checking this option does not move the original file.

  If you are someone who is very organized and knows where all your files are, you can *uncheck* this box. If, on the other hand, you have better things to do than organize and track all your files, then *check* this box. There is no impact on performance regardless of how you check this box. All file copying happens in the background. (More on that later.)

- **Import folders.** Keywords are one of the powerful tools that Final Cut uses to help you find files. Depending upon how you select your files, when this option is checked, FCP will assign the name of the folder that contains the source media as a keyword for each of the imported clips.

In my case, I generally have both of these checked.

How Does Importing Folders Really Work?

It's a bit confusing, so here's an example. **Figure 4.5** shows a folder (Larry01) that contains a file and another folder (Larry02), which also contains a file and another folder (Larry03). This third folder also contains a file.

When I choose File > Import > Files and select the folder (Larry01) that contains all these different files and folders, FCP X will import the files and assign keywords, which are the folder names, to the file. Notice that Import folders as Keyword Collections is checked (**Figure 4.6**).

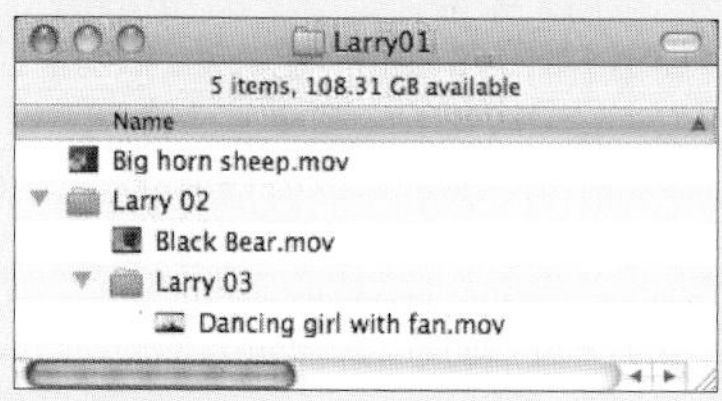

FIGURE 4.5
Note the organization of files and folders.

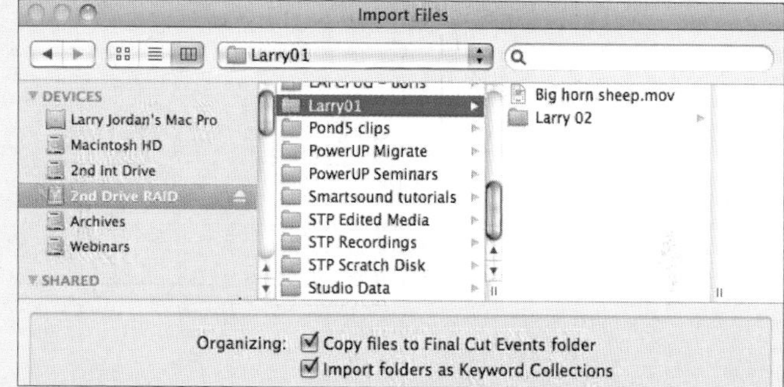

FIGURE 4.6
Folder names as keywords are imported only if a folder, not a specific file, is selected for import.

In this example, the Larry01 keyword was assigned to all the files. The Larry02 keyword was assigned to the two files contained inside the Larry 02 folder (one was in the Larry02 folder, and the other file was in the Larry03 folder). The Larry03 keyword was assigned to the single file contained inside the Larry03 folder (**Figure 4.7**).

FIGURE 4.7
When the containing folder is selected, all folder names are imported as keywords.

continues on next page

How Does Importing Folders Really Work? (*continued*)

However, if I don't select the folder, but instead select the file(s) inside the folder, no keywords are assigned. In this example, I'm selecting the file contained in the Larry03 folder itself, without selecting any folders (**Figure 4.8**).

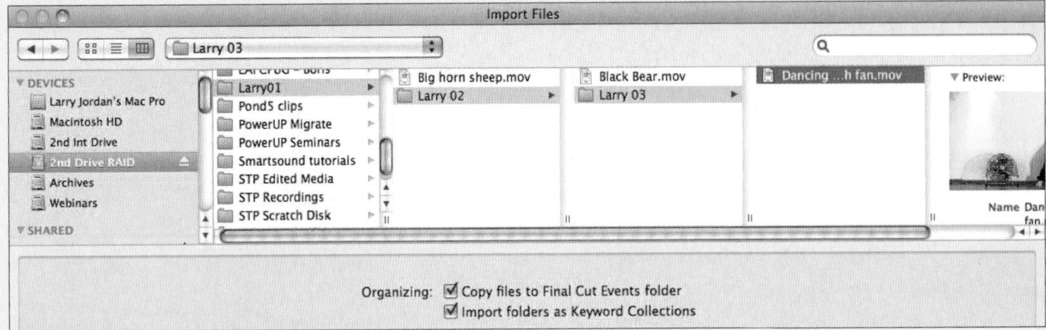

FIGURE 4.8
However, when a file, not a folder, is selected, no keywords are created.

Now, notice that no keywords were imported, even though the same import option was checked, because you selected the files, not the folder that contained the files (**Figure 4.9**).

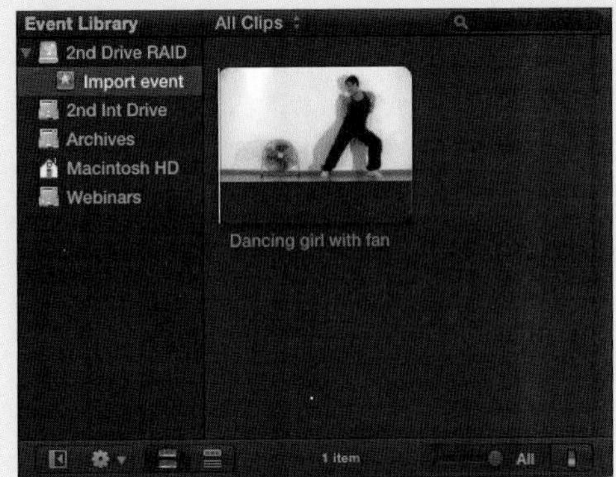

FIGURE 4.9
No keywords are applied to the clips.

Transcoding

Apple makes a big deal out of the fact that FCP X edits files in the camera's native format. This is, in general, a good thing. However, some video formats, because of their complexity, take longer to calculate effects and export than others. Also, some video formats are better for color correction than others.

To solve this problem, Apple provides the option of transcoding (converting) media from one format into another; specifically, ProRes 422. While this is an excellent codec, if you wanted to change to a different format, you can't.

You can transcode files in two ways:

- **Optimize media:** Some files are compressed using long-GOP formats such as MPEG-2 and MPEG-4 files. While FCP can edit these formats natively, it works better when they are "optimized." Optimizing converts these files into ProRes 422. Optimized files provide faster renders, potentially higher image quality for effects, and faster exports. The downside is larger file sizes—generally about four times bigger than the native camera files. Optimizing simply means that FCP is creating a high-quality ProRes 422 file from your source camera media.
- **Proxy media:** Creating proxy media creates another copy of your media using ProRes Proxy. This version of ProRes is optimized for small file sizes. Proxy files are about the same file size as the camera native files.

Codecs and Formats

To be stored on a computer, video needs to be converted from the light our eyes see into the 1s and 0s of binary storage used by the computer. This conversion is done mathematically, using instructions found in a codec (COmpressor/DECompressor). Different codecs are optimized for different tasks. For instance, HDV and AVCHD are optimized to create small files but sacrifice some image quality. HDCAM and ProRes are optimized for high image quality but don't create small files.

(*File size* refers to the storage requirements of media on your hard disk. Changing file size has *no* impact on the size of your image, though changing the size of your image will often affect file size.)

There is no perfect codec that creates impossibly small files with incredibly high quality. There are always trade-offs. That's why Apple provided the option of optimizing your files. This converts them into a format known for high image quality (ProRes 422), fast render times, and the ability to handle effects well, but with the downside of requiring more storage space because ProRes requires larger file sizes. The term video *codec* and video *format* are often used interchangeably, even though they aren't the same, really.

If both Optimize and Proxy are checked, then you'll end up with three versions of your files: the camera master, the optimized file, and the proxy file. If Copy Files is also checked, you'll end up with a fourth version, which is a copy of your camera source file stored in the Events folder. (Like I said earlier, storage is cheap; be sure you have lots.)

What happens if you don't create either optimized or proxy media during import? No problem; FCP will edit the video in its native format; plus, you can transcode it later, if you so choose.

Select the Event you want to optimize or create proxies for. Then, choose File > Transcode media. Check the appropriate checkboxes, and click OK. Final Cut Pro will create all necessary files in the background and store them in the Event folder.

Accessing Proxy Media

The reason proxy media exists is to allow you to edit without having to tote massive hard disks around with you. For example, you can use a laptop and a small attached FireWire drive. Here's how you get the proxy media from your main edit system.

In the Finder, locate the Final Cut Events folder that contains your Event. The proxy files will be inside it (**Figure 4.10**).

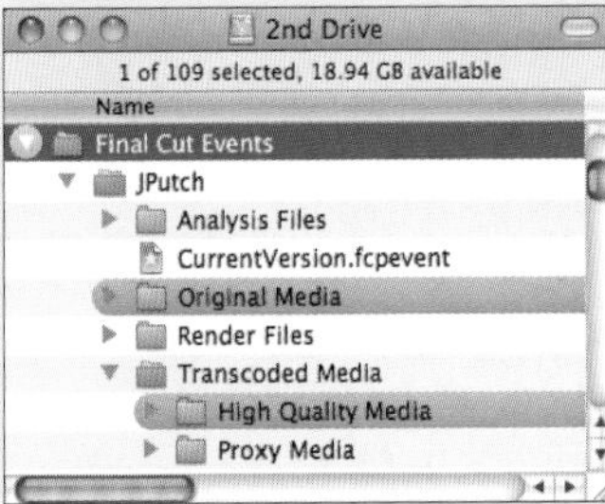

FIGURE 4.10
Proxy media is stored in the Transcoded Media folder inside the Event folder.

Copy the entire Event folder to the smaller hard disk you want to travel with. If the folder is too big to copy, copy everything in the folder, *except* original media and, inside the Transcoded folder, high-quality media. In some cases, one, or both, of those folders may not exist. Don't worry if they are not there.

The only issue will be if you add new media on the laptop. If so, you'll need to copy the original media and the proxy media from the laptop to the Event folder on the main system when you move your files back.

Video

The Video section analyzes your video for problems and suggests possible repairs. The nice thing about this feature is that while it suggests ways to repair your media, you can accept, reject, or modify the suggestions. The only downside to this analysis is that it can take a *loooonngg* time. Yes, it runs in the background, but background processing means you need to leave both your computer and FCP running while FCP processes your files.

Here are your choices:

- **Analyze for stabilization and rolling shutter:** This option looks at handheld footage for shaky camera moves or DSLR footage for rolling shutter problems (see Chapter 12). This process can take a long time and generate *very* large render files. My suggestion is to leave this off and manually analyze the clips you need to correct later.
- **Analyze for balance color:** This looks at your images to see whether there is a color cast (the shot is blue or orange). If there is, FCP can automatically fix it. The automatic correction actually does a pretty good job. Again, however, the analysis takes a long time. I recommend manually analyzing clips that need color correction to save time. Chapter 16 explains how color correction works.
- **Find people:** This analyzes your shot to see how many people are in the frame. This is *not* facial recognition, at least not yet. Instead, the program determines whether there are one, two, three, or more people in the frame. And, it determines whether the shot is a close-up, medium shot, or wide shot.

In theory, this is a neat trick. In practice, I've found it to be inaccurate and time-consuming. For now, I don't use it. If you experience problems using this feature, Apple is interested. Upload samples of footage that return inaccurate results and report them to *www.apple.com/feedback/finalcutpro.html.*

Audio

Audio analysis, unlike video analysis, is very fast. I generally like what FCP is suggesting for audio repairs, and when I don't, I can override its suggestions. For this reason, I recommend leaving all three of these settings on.

- **Analyze and fix audio problems:** This examines a clip for hum, distortion, and noise. If it finds any, it applies filters to remove it. I'll show you how this works in the Chapter 9.
- **Separate mono and group stereo audio:** Many people mistakenly think that because they want their ultimate mix to be stereo they need to record everything in stereo. For music and sound effects, this is a good idea. For interviews, it is not. Interviews should be recorded where each voice is on its own channel and the audio is imported as dual-channel mono. This option is here to make sure audio imports properly. Again, I recommend you check this.

NOTE Changing Preference Settings

Changing import preferences has no effect on any media that has already been imported.

- **Remove silent channels:** Sometimes, audio gets exported with too many channels, for example when a stereo pair is exported as a six-channel surround clip. This option prevents importing audio channels that are silent.

Again, I suggest checking all three of these options. When you are done setting your preferences, simply close the window, and FCP saves them automatically.

Importing 101

There are two types of files you need to import:

- Files from a camera that need to be converted into something Final Cut Pro can play
- Files already playable that are stored somewhere on a hard disk

There's a third option, which is importing files from an iMovie project, but that is simply a special case of the second option.

So, how do you decide whether you need to import from a camera or a file? Easy. Try it. If it works, you guessed right. If not, try the other option. If that's a bit too *laissez-faire* for you, think of it this way. If you can open the file in QuickTime, you import the *file*. If you can't, you import the *camera*.

You import from camera when you are importing directly from a camera card, from a camera card transferred to your hard disk, or from videotape. The rest of the time, you import from a file. Here are some specific examples.

What About R3D Files?

Until RED updates its import plug-in, you can use its free REDCINE-X software to wrap R3D files in QuickTime to edit in Final Cut Pro X. (Wrapping R3D files in QuickTime is the same process that FCP 7 used with the RED Log and Transfer plug-in.) Most editors prefer working with ProRes HQ and ProRes 4444 for R3D files, and those files are accepted by most broadcasters and studios. In addition, you can use the RED ROCKET card or render farms to accelerate the transcoding of RED RAW to ProRes—a process that follows the traditional dailies workflow of Hollywood and has been widely adopted on professional productions.

Importing from a File-Based Camera

There are two main types of cameras: those that record to videotape and those that record tapeless. However, videotape is no longer the wave of the future; tapeless media is. So, we will start by looking at importing tapeless media.

Tapeless media has two main categories: cameras that record to memory cards (of which there is a large variety) and those that record to hard disks. However, hard disks generally record video files that don't need conversion; they can be played straight from the hard disk. This section talks about media recorded to memory cards.

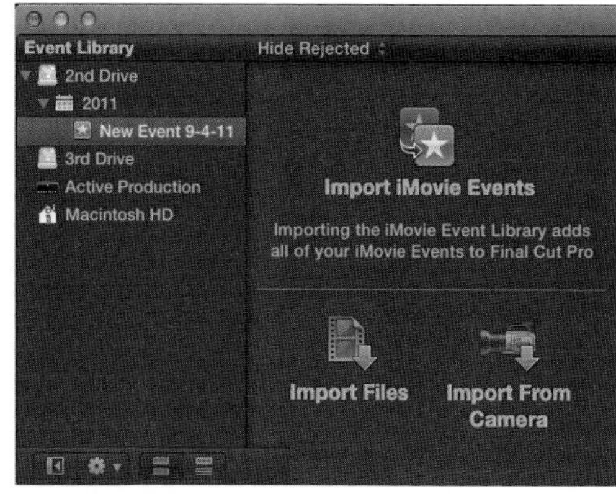

FIGURE 4.11
There are a variety of ways to create a new Event—however, these three icons show up only the very first time you run FCP X.

The Basic Steps

1. If this is the first time you've started Final Cut Pro X, you'll see the screen in **Figure 4.11**. However, after you create your first event, you'll never see this screen again.
2. As you have come to expect, there are multiple ways to import from a camera:
   - Choose File > Import from Camera.
   - Press Command+I.
   - Click the Camera icon on the extreme left edge of the toolbar (**Figure 4.12**).

   Whichever you select, the Camera Import window opens (**Figure 4.13**). In the top-left corner is a list of all the drives attached to your system. If you have connected your camera or plugged in your memory card to the computer, it will show up here.
3. If, on the other hand, you copied your media to your hard disk before importing it, as I recommend, then you'll need to do one extra step. To import files from a card you've copied to your hard drive, you will need to open an archive.

FIGURE 4.12
To import files from a camera or a memory card, click this Import from Camera icon.

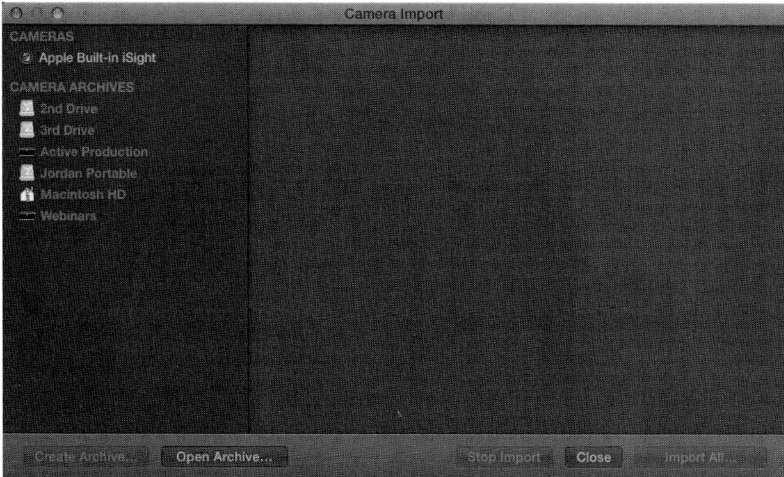

FIGURE 4.13
This is the Camera Import window—with no files loaded.

Opening an Archive

FIGURE 4.14 If a memory card is plugged into your computer, it will show up in this list—for example, the card NO NAME.

Remember that camera archive we talked about earlier? Well, to Apple, an archive is a collection of media still in its camera-native format (as opposed to a folder of QuickTime files). If you copied your media files into a folder on your hard disk, you open that folder by opening an archive. You can also create archives from either a memory card or a tape-based camera, which I'll talk about in a few pages.

If the memory card is plugged into your computer, it will show up at the top of your list of drives in the top-left corner. In **Figure 4.14**, the memory card NO NAME is displayed, and the files it contains are displayed in the large window to the right.

If you copied the files to your hard disk first, click Open Archive in the lower-left corner. A standard file picker window shows up. Navigate to where you stored the media you copied from the camera and select the folder. You don't need to select the files in it. Once you select the folder and click OK, the images from this archive are displayed in the large window to the right.

Whichever option you choose, all the files in the selected device or folder are now displayed on the right side of the window (**Figure 4.15**).

FIGURE 4.15 This is what an opened camera archive looks like.

The purpose of this window is to allow you to review all your clips and to decide which ones you want to import into FCP so you can edit them. The large image at the top right allows you to preview a clip. The small images at the lower right allow you to quickly scroll through all the clips in that archive or device.

● **NOTE** Your Source Media Is Safe

Regardless of what you decide, all your source images will remain on your hard disk. Nothing you do in this window will affect your source media.

As you would expect, this portion of the Camera Import window allows you to play a clip. The buttons across the bottom, from left to right, allow you to do the following:

- Move left one frame at a time
- Move right one frame at a time
- Play from the beginning to the end of a clip (or from the start to the finish; more on that in a minute)
- Play, or stop, a clip
- Jump to the beginning, or start, of a clip (these are not the same thing)
- Jump to the end of a clip (and *end* has two different meanings)

Oh, and that small twisty thing on the far right? Click it, and when you play something, it will repeat, over and over and over...until you stop playback.

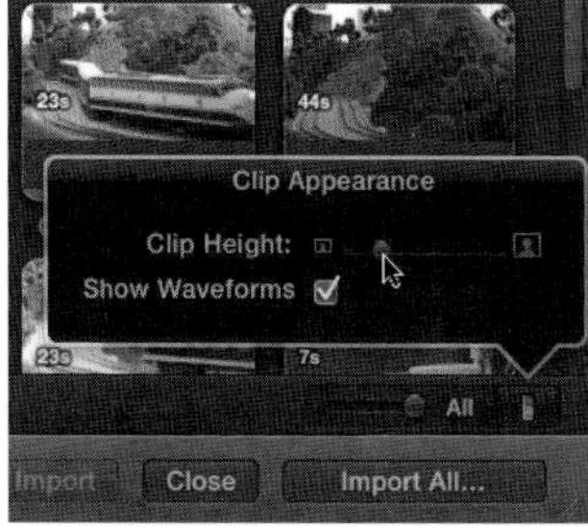

FIGURE 4.16
The Switch allows adjusting the height of the thumbnails and whether the audio waveforms will be displayed.

The small pictures, also called *thumbnails*, show all the clips stored in that archive. Click the Switch in the lower-right corner to adjust the size of these thumbnails and to turn the display of audio waveforms (a picture of the sound of your audio) on or off (**Figure 4.16**). I generally tend to work with small thumbnails, but this is absolutely a matter of personal preference, because Final Cut doesn't care what the thumbnail size is.

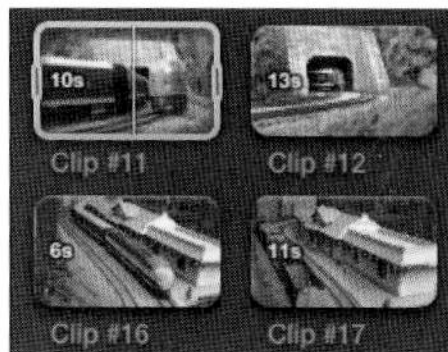

FIGURE 4.17
Click a clip to select it—notice the yellow border indicating the portion of the clip that's selected.

Selecting and Marking Clips

To select a single clip to import, click it. The yellow box around the clip indicates the portion of the clip that is selected (**Figure 4.17**).

To select a group of clips, select the first clip you want to import; then, while holding down the Shift key, select the last one. All the clips in between are selected as well.

To select any arbitrary group of clips, hold the Command key down while clicking. Whatever you click will be selected, but the clips around it will not (**Figure 4.18**).

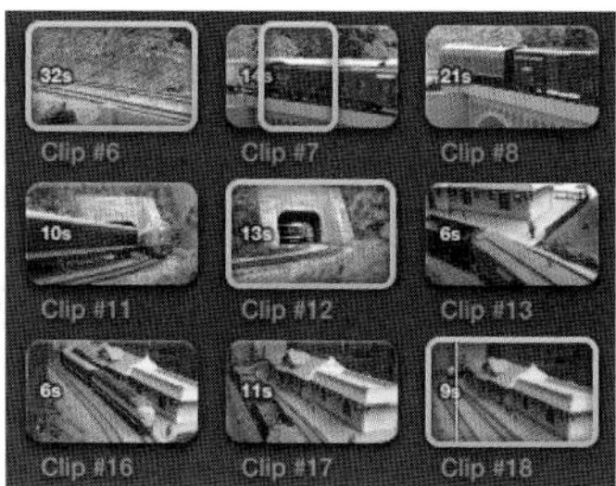

FIGURE 4.18
You can select a portion of one clip or multiple clips using either the Shift or Command key. One clip with a range and three other whole clips are selected here.

While you might think that being able to select just the clips you want is pretty darn neat, the real magic happens when you realize you can select just a portion of a clip. This is called *marking a clip* or *setting a clip range*. This is a real power tool, because you don't want to clutter up your Event Browser with clips you'll never use or waste time skipping over portions of clips you don't need.

NOTE How Accurate Should This Marking Be?

Not really very accurate. I've been editing for more than 30 years, and I've learned that bringing in a little more media than you think you need is always a good idea. So, I try to be close but never precise—not on importing. Precision is reserved for the editing process, which, I promise, I am going to cover. But you need to import the media first.

NOTE You Can Always Change Your Mind

There is no limit to the number of clips you import or how many times you can go back to the same archive to grab more clips. If you are not sure you need a clip, you can leave it alone until you are ready to use it. This is why I like copying all my cards to folders on the hard disk. Once that card is erased, I can't go back to it to recapture more media. This is also a good reason why backups are so important.

There are several ways to mark the Start and End (or In and Out) of a clip:

- Click with the skimmer where you want the shot to start and *drag* until you reach the end of the portion you want. The yellow box indicates the Start and End of your clip.
- Click the skimmer before the portion you want and press the spacebar to play the playhead in the clip. When you reach the spot you want to start, press I. Continue playing until you reach the spot where you want the clip to end and press O.
- Hover the skimmer over the frame (that is what an individual image within a clip is called) that you want to mark as the Start and press I. Hover over the end of the portion you want to import and press O.
- Click the playhead where you want the shot to start and choose Mark > Set Selection Start. Go to the end of the shot and choose Mark > Set Selection End.
- To select an entire clip, click it; or, if you've already set marks (the Start or End), press X.

In other words, there are lots of options. And, for the power user, all these marks can be set in real time, during playback, or by precisely positioning the skimmer or playhead. Your choice. They all work.

There is one problem with all of this, and it is so obvious that I'm expecting it to get fixed in the next update to the software. If you set an In and an Out for a clip and then click another clip to select it, when you go back to the first clip, it's forgotten the In and the Out.

In every other editing system on the planet, clips remember their In and Out until you change them. I expect that will happen with clips in Final Cut Pro X as well. It just hasn't happened yet. A corollary to this "not remembering the In and Out" problem is that you can import only one clip with a range at a time, though you can easily import as many whole clips as you want.

Importing a Clip

Let's try a specific example. **Figure 4.19** shows two clips—one with a selected range and one where the entire clip is selected. I've decided I want to import these two clips so I can use them for my edit.

1. When all the clips you want to import are selected, click Import Selected in the lower-right corner. You can import as many times and as many clips as you want. You can even return later and import more. No rush.

   Final Cut instantly displays the import dialog (**Figure 4.20**). The settings in this dialog are based upon the preference settings you created at the beginning of this chapter. Displaying this window now allows you to change your settings, should you want to.

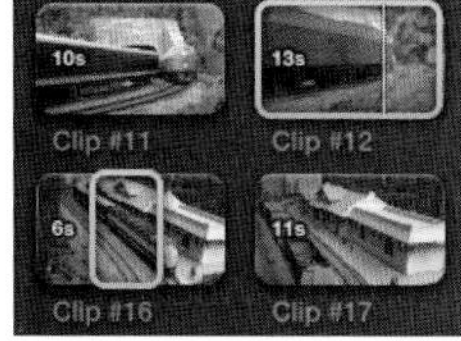

FIGURE 4.19
Both an entire clip and a range within a single clip are selected.

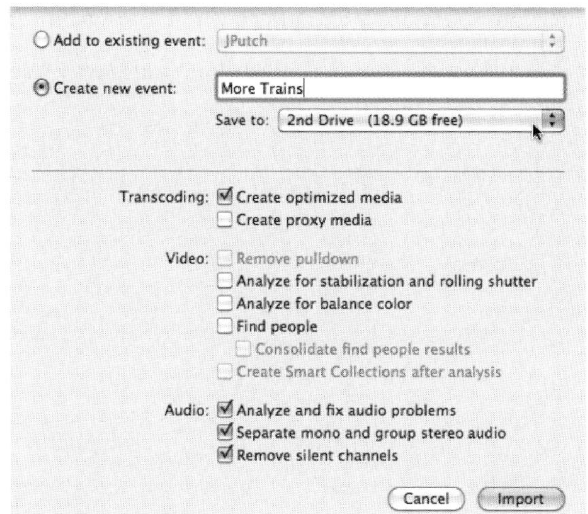

FIGURE 4.20
Every time you import, you are able to change your import settings. The Import preferences determine the default settings, but you can change these at any time.

● **NOTE**
Hide Imported Clips

Also, in the future, when you return to this archive, click the Hide Imported Clips checkbox at the bottom, and all those marked portions will be made invisible so only those clips you haven't imported yet are displayed.

● **NOTE** **New Feature: The Camera SDK**

With version 10.0.1, Apple released a camera software development kit (SDK) so that camera manufacturers can add support for FCP X at the same time they release a new camera.

2. Look at the top of the dialog. For the purpose of this example, I created an existing Event called JPutch. I could import this train footage into that Event—except John has given me some excellent dramatic footage that you'll see in the editing section, so these train clips should be put somewhere else.

   Instead, I created a new Event, in this window, during import. This just goes to show, again, that there are multiple ways to do the same thing. In the previous chapter, I talked about creating new Events first. Now, you discover that you can create a new Event during import. However, to do it, you *must* create an Event to store media. My new Event is called More Trains and is stored on the second drive. (Remember, try really, really hard not to store media on your boot drive, especially if you are going to optimize it.) I discussed these import settings earlier in this chapter, except for "Remove pulldown." This feature is used for 24-frames-per-second film transferred to videotape.

3. Once you are happy with your import settings, click Import, and FCP leaps into action and imports your clips.

   The Camera Import window stays open, but notice at the bottom of each clip, or portion of a clip, that you imported, a pale salmon-colored line (some would call this orange) appears (**Figure 4.21**). That indicates the portion of the clip that was imported. This is a great visual aid to remind you which shots were imported and which weren't.

4. When you are done importing, click Close (it's next to Import Selected), and you'll discover your clips are already loaded into the Event Browser for that Event, ready for editing.

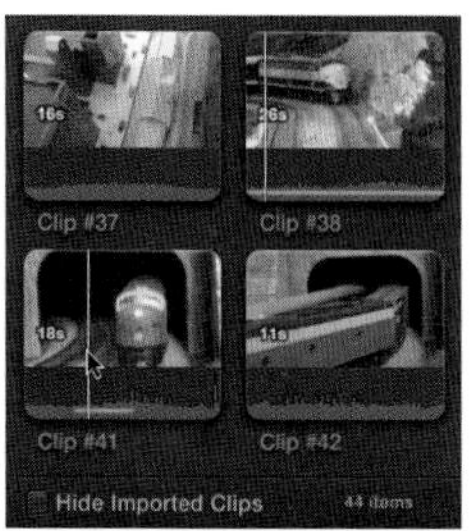

FIGURE 4.21
The orange bar, at the bottom, indicates the portion of the clip that was imported.

Monitoring and Changing Background Tasks

However, while the process of importing clips is both fast and easy, behind the scenes there's still a lot of work being done. And this shows the power of Final Cut Pro X, because in the past, you would need to wait until all the finding, transcoding, and importing tasks were complete. Not so today. Today, Final Cut Pro X processes all that in the background.

Definition: Background

Something running in the background means that your computer is busy doing something without needing any input, or assistance, from you. Printing happens in the background; you don't need to wait for the printer to finish before you do other work. Video compression also runs in the background. Many of Final Cut Pro's heavy-duty calculations such as importing, rendering, or exporting happen in the background.

FCP is very busy with all this processing, but you can still review clips, make edits, and play projects without worrying about all the background work that's going on.

As a note, however, tasks that run in the background tend to run slower because if the foreground application needs the computer to do something, the background application is momentarily paused while the computer devotes itself to meeting that need. Those delays are generally not excessive. I'm just letting you know.

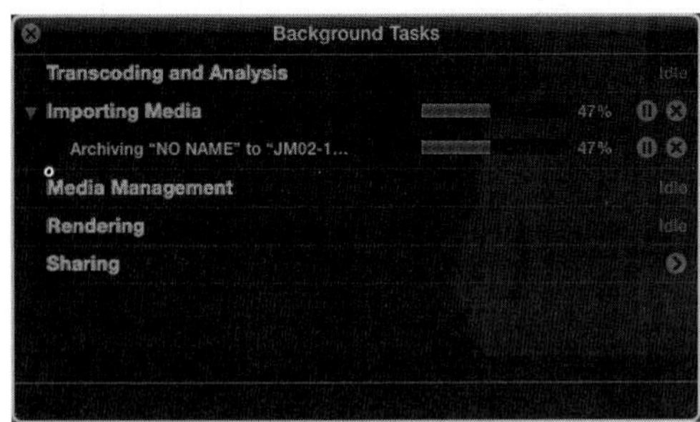

FIGURE 4.22
The Background Tasks window displays all the activities FCP is running behind the scenes.

One of the neat features in FCP X—mainly because I'm a fan of blinking lights and charts and graphs—is the Background Tasks window. To open the Background Tasks window, click inside the "clock face" on the left side of the Dashboard in the middle toolbar of Final Cut Pro X. (You can also display this task window by pressing Command+9 or choosing Window > Background Tasks.) This opens the Background Tasks window, which displays the status of all actively running tasks (**Figure 4.22**). In this case, it shows that FCP is 47 percent done importing the media clips selected earlier.

This Background Tasks window can be very useful when running Final Cut Pro. You can reference it to check the status of importing, analyzing clips, transcoding from one format to another, rendering transitions and effects, and exporting.

Importing from a Tape-Based Camera

Wow! That included a lot of steps. The good news is that once you understand how importing works—and you spent a lot of time going over all the steps in the previous section—these other options are just slight variations on the same theme.

Let's turn our attention to capturing from videotape. Here, Final Cut Pro X has some significant limitations. It can capture only from videotape cameras or decks that are attached via FireWire. Companies such as AJA, Blackmagic Design, and Matrox are working on ways to capture using other videotape protocols. New products are expected about the same time this book is published, so visit these companies to see what their latest gear can do.

However, assuming you *do* have a FireWire deck or camera, here's what you need to know to capture clips from it.

1. Connect your FireWire camera or deck to the computer. Turn it on and load a tape. (You can also use this process for capturing from a live camera, but this example assumes you are using tape.)
2. Open Final Cut Pro, select an Event you want to use to store the media, and click the Import from Camera icon (or press Command+I) (**Figure 4.23**).

   In the top-left corner of the Camera Import window, the name of the camera or deck will be listed.
3. In the Camera Import window, you'll see an image from your tape, along with the word *Pause*, indicating the tape is not running (**Figure 4.24**). Unlike earlier versions of Final Cut Pro, you cannot set Ins or Outs when capturing from tape. (In FCP 7 terms, FCP X uses Capture Now when importing from tape.) So, to capture a shot or an entire tape, rewind the tape using either the controls on the camera or deck or the controls at the bottom of the Preview window to rewind the tape until it is a few seconds before the start of the shot you want.

FIGURE 4.23 Here's an example of a DV videotape deck (Sony DSR-11) attached to the computer via FireWire.

FIGURE 4.24 This is the Camera Import window. Notice the text displays at the top.

4. Click the Import button at the bottom.

   Just as you saw in Figure 4.20, when importing tapeless media, the Import dialog appears, allowing you to configure how you want the clips imported. "Create optimized media" is grayed out because this video format (DV) is already optimized and does not need conversion to ProRes.

5. When you are happy with the settings, click Import.

   If the tape does not start playing, push the Play button on your camera or deck. Final Cut Pro will start capturing the images directly to your hard disk, storing them in the Event you selected before opening this window (**Figure 4.25**).

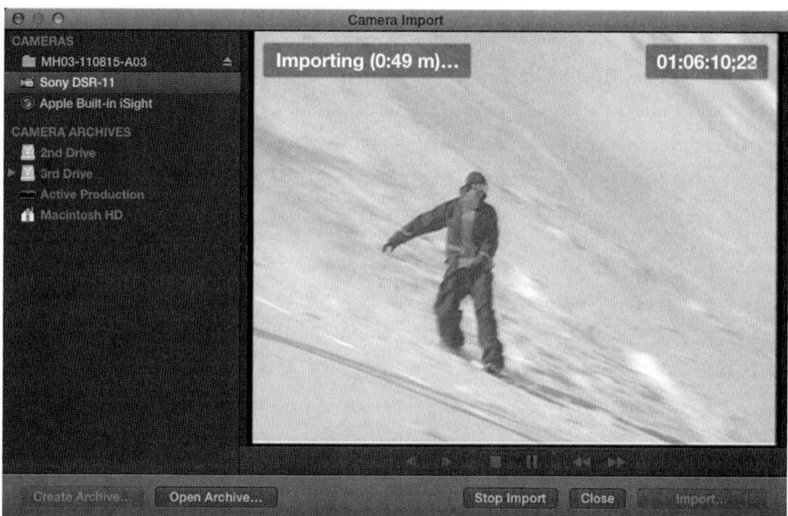

FIGURE 4.25 Notice the monitoring display at the top of the screen during tape playback.

6. The import status at the top displays the shot being captured, the amount of time currently captured to disk (top left), and the timecode on the tape at that moment during playback (top right). When you want to stop the capture, either click the Stop Import button at the bottom or simply stop the camera or deck.

   Although the Camera Import window remains open, the captured clip is instantly displayed in the Event Browser for the selected Event.

7. Repeat this process until all the shots you need are captured from tape.

NOTE What About Timecode Breaks?

When capturing from videotape, it is essential that timecode remain continuous. If there are timecode breaks on the tape, FCP X will capture each section on the tape, between breaks, as a separate clip. You will probably lose about three seconds of media before and after each break.

Creating a Camera Archive

Camera archives, which were mentioned earlier in this chapter, are also a way to easily digitize entire videotapes so you can store them on your hard disk until you are ready to use them. The benefit of this process is that videotape only has a shelf life of 20 to 25 years. FCP X makes it easy to digitize your historical tapes before they get too old to capture.

What Final Cut Pro does is transfer all the clips from your tape into a single master file stored on your hard disk. This is basically a straight-through transfer. Final Cut Pro is not recompressing these files; it is simply bundling them into a single package to make them easier to label, store, and move around.

Archiving is not importing. Archiving copies the media from a videotape to a file on your computer. The images are not imported into Final Cut Pro. All files are stored on the hard disk you specify, in a Final Cut Camera Archives folder.

Here's how this works:

1. As you did in the previous section, connect your camera or deck and turn it on. Load a tape and start Final Cut Pro X.
2. Click the Import from Camera icon, or press Command+I.
3. In the Camera Import window, select your camera or deck from the list at the top left (refer back to Figure 4.24).
4. Click the Create Archive button in the lower-left corner of the Camera import window (**Figure 4.26**).
5. Name the archive. Since this is a collection of all the shots on the tape, you are not naming individual shots; rather, you are naming the entire collection. Since I number all my tapes, I make a point to include the tape number as part of the filename.
6. Choose the hard drive where you want the archive stored, and click OK.

   FCP automatically rewinds the tape to the beginning and shifts into capture mode. As the tape plays from beginning to end, FCP stores all the media from the tape into the archive and displays the status of this transfer process at the top of the image (**Figure 4.27**).
7. Just like importing from tapeless media, Final Cut Pro captures your media from tape in the background as well. If you need to stop the transfer at any time, click the Stop button in the lower right or simply stop the tape. FCP asks whether you want to keep what has already been captured or discard everything. When the end of the tape is reached, FCP closes the transfer and saves the file.
8. You can see this archive by opening the hard disk that you specified as the location and opening the Final Cut Camera Archives folder. Additional archives can also be stored in this folder; there's no limit—aside from storage space—to the number of archives you can create and store.

● **NOTE** What Can I Archive?

You can archive media stored on videotape and accessed through a FireWire connection. You can archive media stored on memory cards or other tapeless formats. You can also archive media stored on a memory card. However, you can't archive video from a live camera, such as the iSight; a live video stream; or media stored in an Event.

● **NOTE** How Much Space Do You Need for an Archive?

In general, an hour of DV media takes 13 GB to store. This storage size is true for both NTSC and PAL DV video. (By the way, an hour of HDV media also requires 13 GB to store.) In other words, the archive takes the same amount of space to store your media as it would if you captured it directly to your hard disk as a media file.

FIGURE 4.26
Click Create Archive to create a new camera archive.

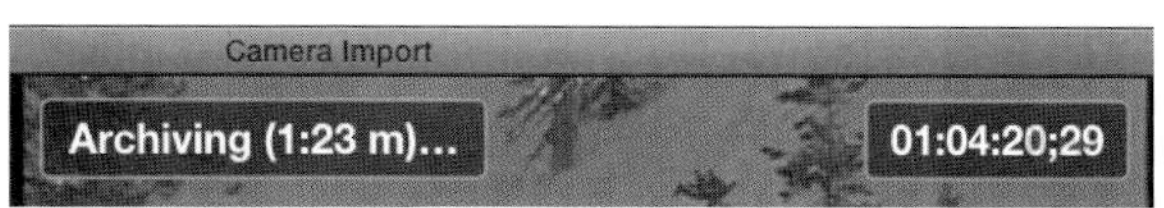

FIGURE 4.27
During the archive process, Final Cut Pro displays a constantly updated status.

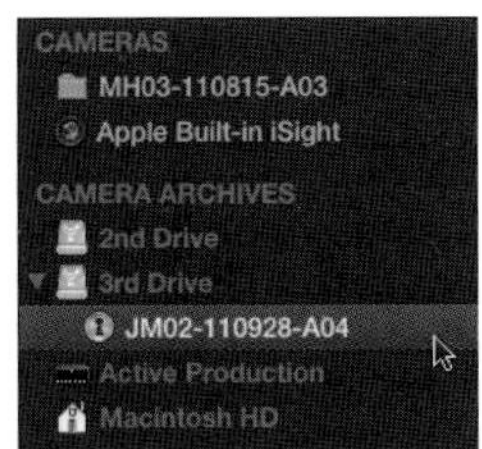

FIGURE 4.28 Archives can be mounted at any time, providing "near-line" access to your media.

You can now handle this archive as another other file. Move it, back it up, copy it, or archive to disc or tape—all using the Finder (**Figure 4.28**).

9. Once an archive is created, you can review it at any time and import clips from it. Simply highlight the archive from the list of drives in the top-left window. All the shots from the archive are displayed on the right, the same as for a memory card.
10. Select what you want to import: a portion of a shot, an entire shot, or a collection of shots; this is identical to what you did in the section on importing tapeless media.
11. To close an archive, click the eject icon on the right side of the archive name. This does *not* affect the file on your hard disk; it just closes the images so they are not displayed in the Camera Import window.

Camera archives are a great way to preserve video assets on tape before time runs out and the tape dies.

Importing Files

After the complexity of importing tapeless files from memory cards or importing from videotape, the process of importing QuickTime movies, or other computer-based media files, is very easy. Importing files is the way you generally import audio files and still images, as well as existing QuickTime movies.

1. Select the Event where you want the imported media stored. (Or, create a new Event. The key is you need to select the Event before importing the media.)
2. Then, do one of the following:
   - Right-click the Event and select Import Files (**Figure 4.29**).
   - Press Shift+Command+I.
   - Choose File > Import > Files.
   - Click the Import Files icon, if this is your first time running FCP X.

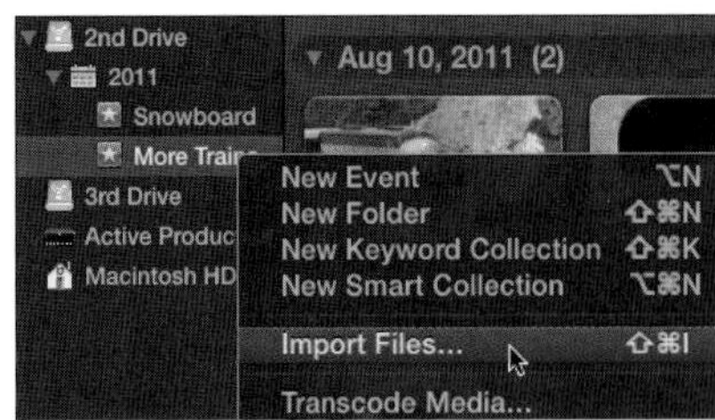

FIGURE 4.29 A fast way to import files is to right-click the Event you want to import into.

3. The standard Import Files dialog appears. By now, you should know to select the files you want to import, set the preference settings the way you want, and click Import. Even when you select an Event as the destination of an import, you can change the Event in the Import Files dialog or even create a new Event for the files. Changing your mind at the last minute is absolutely OK.

As usual, Final Cut Pro charges into action, importing your files and doing any necessary file management in the background. What is especially cool about this process is that, even though FCP is importing the media, you can start viewing and editing that same media into your Timeline!

Apple has done a great job of making the file import process fast and efficient.

Special Cases

Here are some special cases of importing media that require a different approach.

Importing iMovie Projects and Events

Final Cut Pro X finally fulfills a long-held dream of iMovie users that there be some way to get their iMovie Projects and Events into Final Cut Pro. And, in fact, it is very easy.

If all you need is access to your iMovie media, import the iMovie Event Library. This brings in all your iMovie media, allowing you to reedit it using the full power of Final Cut Pro X. Or, if you want to bring in your iMovie Project, you can do that as well.

Here's how these both work:

1. To import an iMovie Project, choose File > Import > iMovie Project.
2. Navigate to where your project is stored; typically, this is in the Movies folder in the Home directory of your hard disk. Then click Import.
3. By now, you are an old hand at navigating the Import Files dialog. Once you import your files, the project will open and all associated iMovie Events and media are loaded into the Event Library.

To import all your iMovie media, choose File > Import > iMovie Event Library. This loads all the media that you captured in iMovie into Final Cut Pro.

● **NOTE** Does Final Cut Pro X Import Earlier Final Cut Pro Projects?

No. At the launch of FCP X, Apple said it is not possible for FCP X to import FCP 7 or 6 projects. However, I expect that problem will get solved, at least to some degree, before this book gets published, probably by a third-party developer.

Using Photos Browser or Music and Sound Browser

Built into Final Cut Pro X is access to your iPhoto, Aperture, and iTunes libraries. This means you can easily access any image, or sound they contain, without even going to the process of importing.

Here's how.

The Browsers—for images and effects—are all located on the right side of the bar running across the middle of the FCP X interface (**Figure 4.30**).

FIGURE 4.30
Click this icon to display the contents of your iPhoto or Aperture library.

FIGURE 4.31
Click this icon to display the contents of the Music and Sound Browser, including your iTunes library.

Click the icon for the Photos Browser, and it opens to display images from your iPhoto or Aperture library. These images are always available to you for every Project. You don't need to import them. Whenever you want to use one of these images, simply drag it from the Browser onto the Timeline. You don't need to move it to the Event Browser first.

To open the Music and Sound Browser, click the icon with the musical note on it (**Figure 4.31**). This opens your iTunes library. In addition to iTunes, if you downloaded the extra material from Apple after you purchased FCP X, you also have access to thousands of sound effects and music cues—all royalty free and stored in this Browser.

Again, like the Photos Browser, you don't need to import these files. If you find one you like, simply drag it from the Browser into the Timeline. (I'll show you how to do that when I cover editing, in a couple of chapters.)

NOTE Why Do You Call It an (H)DSLR Camera?

The term (H)DSLR is used to denote DSLR cameras that also shoot HD video. Since not all DSLR cameras shoot video, this makes it convenient to just talk about the cameras that do. You can find out whether your camera is supported by FCP X by visiting *http://help.apple.com/finalcutpro/cameras/*.

Importing from an (H)DSLR Camera

(H)DSLR cameras shoot a video format called H.264. This is a very compressed, and mathematically challenging, video format. H.264 is a good format for shooting, it is an excellent format for distribution on the Web, but it is not a good format for editing.

Still images can be directly imported into Final Cut Pro—see the "Dealing with Still Images" section to come—or you can import them into Aperture or iPhoto. Then use the Photos Browser to import them into Final Cut Pro.

Video files are imported directly from the DCIM folder created by the camera, which you need to copy from the camera card into a folder on your hard disk or from a disk image of the card. Don't use Import from Camera; use Import > Files.

DSLR audio and video files, which are often separate, can be synchronized using Clip > Synchronize Clips. And syncing does not affect source files, only the clips in the Event Browser.

Since audio files are imported using File > Import > Files, you don't need to cover that process again.

To import (H)DSLR footage, choose File > Import > Files. Navigate to where you stored the contents of the (H)DSLR card on your hard disk. In this example, I'm about to import some files shot by Chuck Spaulding. Notice that the DCIM folder is selected but not the contents of the folder (**Figure 4.32**). If you select a folder, FCP understands that you want to bring in the contents of the folder.

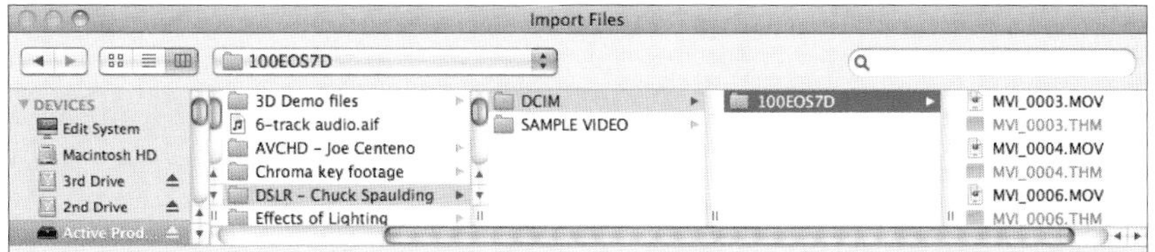

FIGURE 4.32 Importing media from an (H)DSLR camera involves navigating to where the actual media is stored, ideally in a folder on your hard disk.

When importing (H)DSLR footage, be sure to check "Create Optimized media" as part of the Import dialog. While FCP can, and will, edit H.264 video natively, you'll get faster renders, higher-quality effects, and faster exports by optimizing. The only downside is that the optimized files take more space to store.

Once you have your preference settings to your satisfaction, click Import. An error dialog may pop up saying that FCP can't import all the files in this folder, specifically, those ending with .THM (**Figure 4.33**). This is OK. When you import files directly from the DCIM folder, you may notice that there are both .MOV and .THM files. Just select everything in the folder.

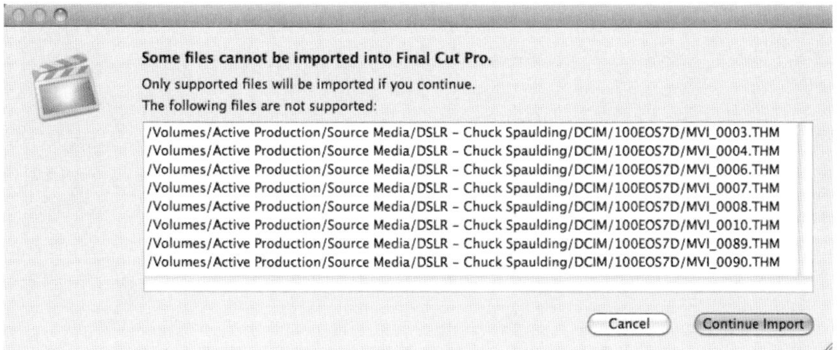

FIGURE 4.33 Don't panic. This message simply means that FCP could not import all the files it found in that folder.

Click OK, and Final Cut Pro will import just the .MOV files and ignore the .THMs. This is much faster than just selecting each movie file individually. You are taking a shortcut so that only the .MOV files are imported.

Sync Double-System Audio

Because the audio recording capability on almost all (H)DSLR cameras is really poor, you often record audio using a "double-system": The camera records video and a digital audio recorder records audio.

Now, you need to get them in sync. This means during production you need to create a sync point. A *sync point* is a common point of reference between multiple cameras or between audio and video. Professional movies always use clapper slates. However, you can use a pair of clapping hands, dropping brick, or anything else that has a rapid movement coming to a quick stop and making a sharp noise.

You find the point in the video where the movement stops and the same point in the audio where the noise is made. That point is your *sync point*, the point that is the same for both audio and video.

Clips are always synced well before the start of action in a shot. So, once you have the sync point set, you still need to set a Start and End (In and Out) for your shot before you edit it to the Timeline. Final Cut provides built-in syncing capability, based upon the following:

- Matching markers
- Matching timecode
- File creation date
- Audio content

FIGURE 4.34
Notice how both audio (green) and video (picture) clips are selected and both have a blue marker set at the top of the clip, which marks the sync point.

FIGURE 4.35
This is the symbol in the top left corner of the synced clip.

Most of the time, the production team will use a clapper slate to mark the start of a shot for both audio and video. So, I'll show how to sync two clips using markers that you set to match the position where the clapper slaps down.

To create a marker, put the skimmer or playhead on the frame of the video clip that marks the sync point of a shot, and press M. That blue shape at the top of the clip is a marker. (I'll talk more about markers in Chapter 7.)

Do the same for the audio clip. Put a marker at the sync point by positioning the skimmer or playhead at the exact point where the audio matches the video, and press M.

Select the video clip you want to sync; then, while holding the Command key, select the audio clip. With both clips selected, choose Clip > Synchronize Clips or press Option+Command+G (**Figure 4.34**).

This creates a new, synchronized clip in the Event Browser with a little sync icon in the top-left corner (**Figure 4.35**). Remember to use this clip, not the two source clips, when the time comes to edit.

Dragging Files in from the Desktop

You can even import files by dragging them in from the Desktop. There are only two places you can drag clips from the Desktop: onto the *name* of an Event in the Event Library or into the Timeline.

To import a file by dragging, grab the title bar of Final Cut Pro and drag it to the side so you can see the image, or images, you want to import on the Desktop. Notice when you drag a clip from the Desktop to an Event, a white ring appears around the name of the Event. This tells you where your media will be stored. You can also drag directly into the Timeline. I discuss the Timeline in detail starting in Chapter 5 and continuing for the rest of the book.

● **NOTE**
FAQ: Dragging Clips

When you drag files from the Desktop, you don't get the Import dialog you saw earlier. Instead, the clips are immediately imported using the current Import preference settings.

Dealing with Still Images

I've saved this section for last because it causes more confusion than any other. Apple has simplified the process of importing, sizing, saving, and exporting still images. Final Cut Pro works best with bitmapped images, like those taken with a digital still camera or created inside Photoshop, and it supports a wide variety of image formats, though some formats provide higher quality than others.

With the latest version of Final Cut Pro, there does not seem to be a practical limit on image dimensions within Final Cut Pro. If you choose the Import preference to optimize media, images without transparency (called an *alpha channel*), are converted to JPEG, while those that do contain an alpha channel are converted to PNG. If you don't choose to optimize media, still images are imported in their native format. PSDs (Photoshop documents) import with all layers flattened but with transparency information retained.

Images are measured in total pixels across by total pixels down, not by dots per inch (DPI). DPI is a printer reference and doesn't apply to video. Also, you always want to create your images using square pixel dimensions.

● **NOTE** **Can You Import a Layered Photoshop File?**

Yes and no. Yes, it will import. However, Final Cut Pro will convert it to a PNG file and collapse all the layers into a single layer. Any alpha channel data (transparency) in the file will be retained. So, yes to Photoshop; no to layers. However, Motion 5 can import Photoshop files and retain their layers, and Motion projects can be saved or exported to work with Final Cut Pro X.

Moving on Stills

If you want to do moves on an image while retaining the highest image quality, create the image to be larger than the frame size. Image quality is degraded if you scale an image larger than 100 percent. And for images, PNG or TIFF formats will yield better image quality than JPEG or JPG formats.

In the past, Final Cut Pro would choke if you imported an image greater than 4,000 pixels on a side. In my testing for this book, I imported an image that was 10,000 pixels on a side and FCP had no problem with it.

If your still image is larger or smaller than the video frame, then the image will import correctly. However, if your still image is exactly the size of the video frame, then you need to size it using specific dimensions in order for the image geometry to be correct after import. The problem of image sizing is caused by the fact that video uses rectangles to describe image pixels, while computers use square pixels. And this difference has caused ulcers in the industry for years.

By default, stills import with a duration of four seconds. Here's how to modify the default duration for an imported still image:

1. Choose Final Cut Pro > Preferences (or type Command+[comma]) and click the Editing preference icon at the top.
2. Toward the lower portion of this screen is the default duration assigned to imported still images. It's four seconds by default, but you can change it to anything. The decimal point after the four is not frames but hundredths of a second. So, if you wanted your stills to import at three-and-a-half seconds, enter **00:00:03.50**.
3. Close the preference window to accept your changes.
4. Import the files you need using File > Import > Files and select the files you want to bring in.

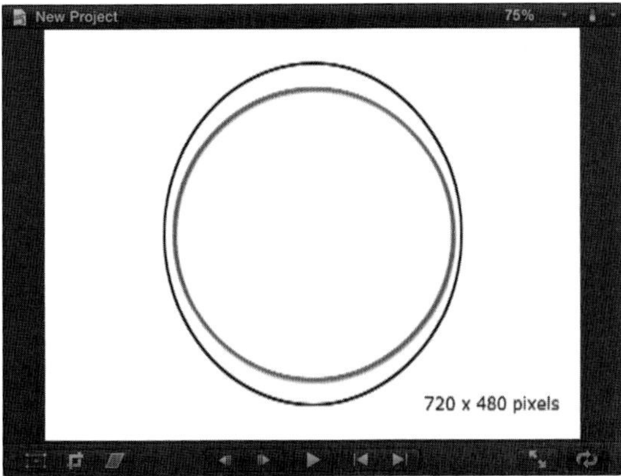

FIGURE 4.36
Importing still images drives all of us nuts. Here's the problem you often have with trying to get imported still images to look correct.

You remember I mentioned earlier that when images were the same size as the frame, you have problems? Well, **Figure 4.36** illustrates that.

As you may know, NTSC DV video is 720 pixels across by 480 pixels high. These pixel dimensions are the same, surprisingly, for both 4:3 and 16:9 video. (While the pixel *count* does not change, the pixel *shape* does!) These *aspect ratio* issues exist in NTSC, PAL, and many HD video formats, but the numbers are different.

In Figure 4.36, the black circle was created in Photoshop using square pixel dimensions and imported into FCP, where it got squished. The red circle is generated in FCP and is a perfect circle.

The reason for this is the differences in aspect ratio between the computer and video. Video uses rectangles for its default pixel shape, while the computer uses squares. You'll see a solution for this in **Table 4.1**.

However, when you properly size graphics in Photoshop before importing into FCP, circles come in as circles and squares look like squares (**Figure 4.37**).

Table 4.1 provides dimensions you can use to determine how to size your graphics. The left column indicates the video format. The middle column indicates the size you should create if you want the entire image to completely fill the frame, without doing any moves on the image. The right column indicates the size you should create if you want the image to completely fill the frame *and* you want to do moves on the image, which is also called the "Ken Burns Effect" (see Chapter 12).

You'll be working with stills throughout this book. Chapter 6 shows how to edit and size them to fit the frame, while Chapter 12 illustrates how to do moves on stills. Chapter 15 explains how to export stills for use in other applications.

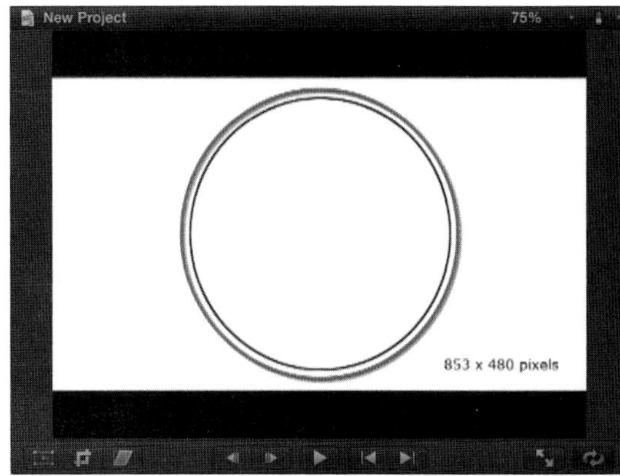

FIGURE 4.37
This is what your images look like when you do it right! Whew!

TABLE 4.1 Creating the Right Sizes for Still Images*

Video Format	Fill the Frame	Fill the Frame and Move Around
NTSC DV 4:3	720 x 540	1800 x 1350
NTSC DV 16:9	852 x 480	2130 x 1200
PAL 4:3	768 x 576	1920 x 1440
PAL 16:9	1024 x 576	2560 x 1440
720 HD	1280 x 720	3200 x 1800
1080 HD	1920 x 1080	4800 x 2700
2K	2048 x 1024	5120 x 2560
4K	4096 x 2048	8192 x 4096

* All images should be created at 72 dpi, because video just pays attention to the total pixels across and down. Only printers use DPI. Also, save files as PNG or TIFF to retain the highest quality.

New Feature! XML Import

New with version 10.0.1 is the ability to import XML, an interchange language that lets applications share data. The process is simple. Once another application has created an XML file, choose File > Import > XML and find the file you want to import. Pick a hard disk to store the data from the Storage Location pop-up menu and click Import. That's it. What you do with that data depends upon where it comes from, and that varies by application.

Summary

This is the longest chapter in the book, because getting media into FCP is essential if you are going to edit it. You must understand the process well so your clips look as good as they can. Fortunately, once you grasp the process, FCP makes it truly efficient, and you'll be importing clips in no time.

There's one more chapter to go before you start editing: working with ratings and keywords. You can't edit your projects if you can't find the clips you need.

The good news is that after the next chapter, all the prep work is done, and you get to spend time with the fun stuff—editing your projects and making them look great!

Keyboard Shortcuts

Shortcut	What It Does
Command+[comma]	Open FCP Preferences window
Option+N	Create new Event
Command+N	Create new Project
Command+I	Import from camera
Shift+Command+I	Import from file
Option+Command+G	Sync audio and video clips
Command+9	Display Background Tasks window
Command+click	Select any combination of clips
I	Set the Start (In) of a clip
Shift+I	Jump playhead to the Start (In) of clip
Option+I	Delete the Start (In)
O	Set the End (Out) of a clip
Shift+O	Jump playhead to the End (Out) of clip
Option+O	Delete the End (Out)
X	Mark the entire duration of a clip
Option+X	Delete the Start and End of a clip
Command+D	Select Desktop in any file picker dialog

ORGANIZING CLIPS: RATINGS, KEYWORDS, AND EXTENDED METADATA

Metadata bores most people to tears. That's a shame, because if you think of metadata as labels, it becomes a whole lot more interesting. This chapter looks at all the different ways you can label your clips so you can find them again in the future—ratings, keywords, and extended metadata.

Ratings are the easiest—fast, simple, but limited in scope. Keywords provide a great balance between depth of features and ease of use. Metadata allows you to label and track just about any conceivable data element associated with your clips, with one problem: You can search only a little bit of it.

Displaying Events and Clips

Before you look at applying labels to your clips, I want to show you a couple secrets buried at the left of the toolbar. For example, these buttons control how Events and clips are displayed in the Event Library and Event Browser (**Figure 5.1**).

FIGURE 5.1 The three buttons to the right control how media is sorted and displayed in the Event Library and Event Browser.

From the left, they are as follows:

- Toggle display of Event Library (Shift+Command+1)
- Control display of Events in Event Library (the Gear icon)
- Display clips in Event Browser as thumbnails (the Blue button in Figure 5.1)
- Display clips in Event Browser as a list

It is these right three buttons that I want to focus on for a page or two.

Click the gear icon to change how Events are displayed in the Event Library. For example, when Group Events by Disk is checked, the hard drives attached to your computer are displayed, along with the Events stored in them (**Figure 5.2**). When this option is unchecked, only the Event names are displayed.

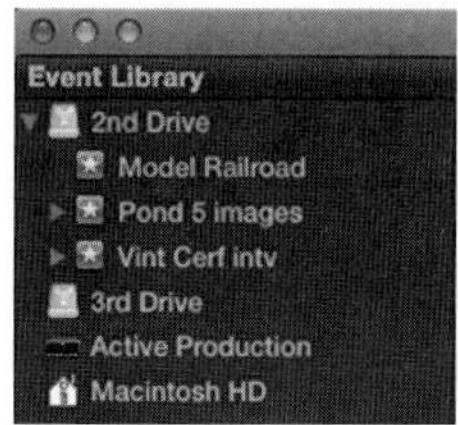

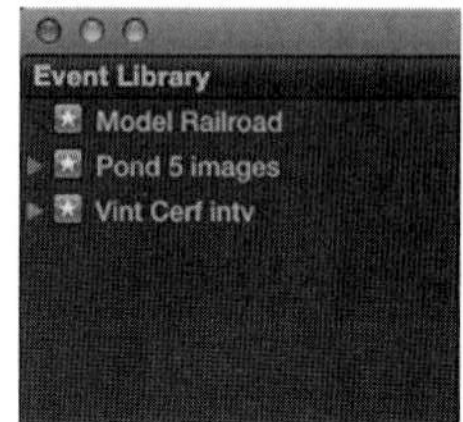

FIGURE 5.2 Checking Group Events by Disk (left) displays hard disk names (center); unchecking it does not (right).

Within Group Events by Date, you can also select to display the year the Event was shot (**Figure 5.3**). If Group Events by Year and Month is checked, FCP displays both the year and the month of the Event.

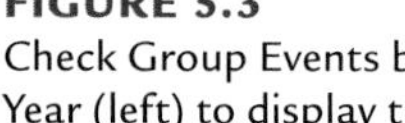

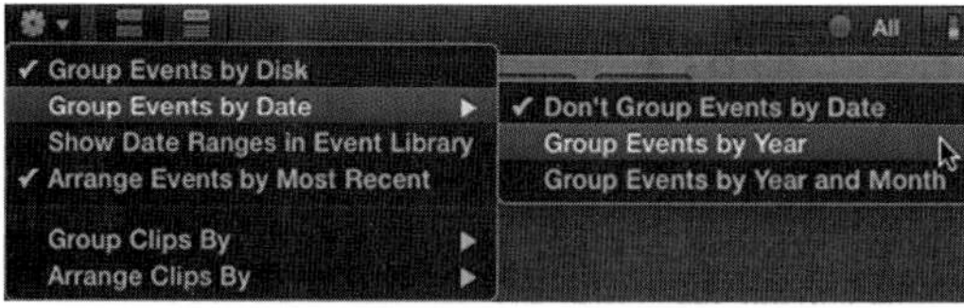

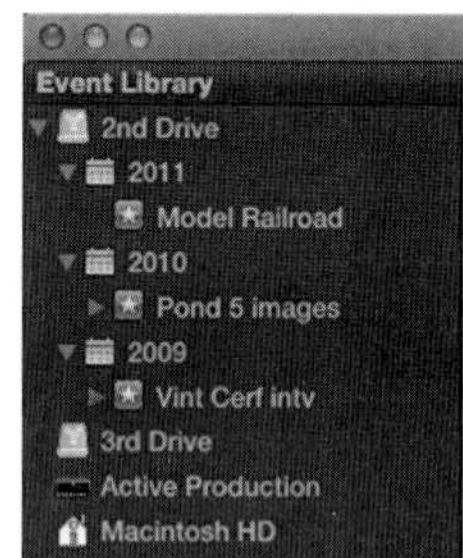

FIGURE 5.3 Check Group Events by Year (left) to display the year the media for that Event was shot (right).

New Version: Apple Adds XML Import/Export

With the release of FCP X 10.0.1, Apple provided the ability to export and import XML. XML is the interchange language of applications. From XML you can derive EDLs, OMFs, AAFs, and all the other acronyms you need to move files from one place to another.

However, there's still a problem—XML is like language; there are variations. That means before we, as editors, can take advantage of this, developers need to work with it first.

XML is the critical first step to allowing you to share files between different applications and to unlock the world of third-party plug-ins. Now, it's up to the developers to work their magic.

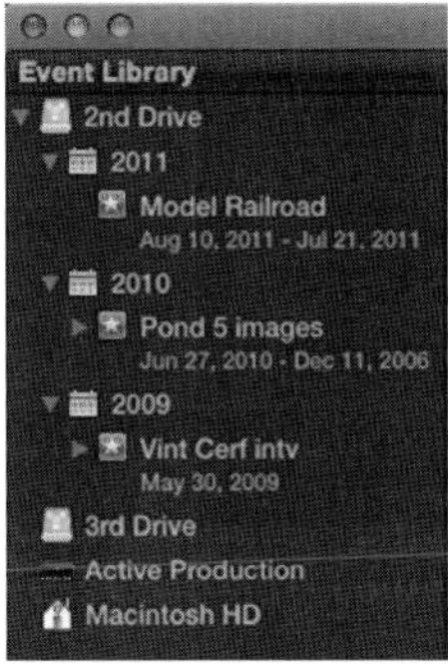

FIGURE 5.4 When Show Date Ranges in Event Library is checked (left), the image on the right is the result.

When Show Date Ranges in Event Library is checked, the range of dates represented by the clips in that Event are displayed below the Event name (**Figure 5.4**).

When Arrange Events by Most Recent is checked, Events are displayed with the most recent event sorted to the top. When this is unchecked and the date display is turned on, Events are displayed in chronological order. If the date display is turned off, Events are displayed in alphabetical order, regardless of how this choice is set.

The bottom two menu choices affect the Event Browser; the top four affect the Event Library:

- **Group Clips By:** This controls how clips are displayed in the Event Browser (to the right of the Event Library). For example, in **Figure 5.5**, the clips are grouped by Reel (or card). New with version 10.0.1, you can also group clips by Role. (See Chapter 7.)
- **Arrange clips By:** This determines the sort order of clips in the Event Browser. Options include sorting by filename, take number, duration, or creation date.

● **NOTE** Not All Dates Are Real

When using date display with videotape, the date is the date the video was captured, not the date it was shot. For existing QuickTime movies, there may not be a date at all. This date option is most useful when working with tapeless media that was imported directly from the card or camera by Final Cut Pro.

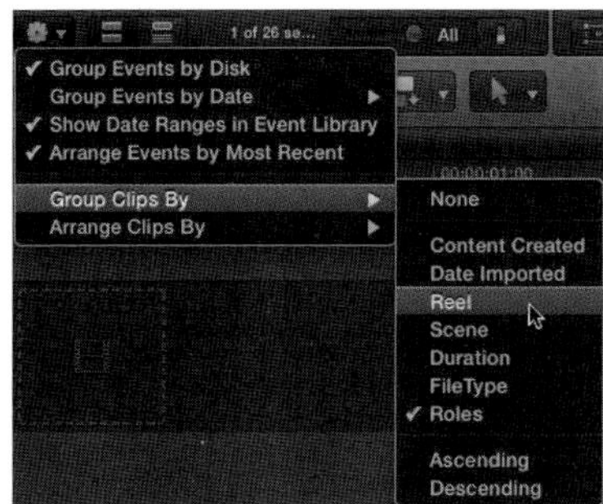

FIGURE 5.5
When Group Clips By and Reel is checked (left), images are categorized by reel name in the Event Browser (right).

● **NOTE** Can You Hide the Clip Names?

Yes. The names of clips displayed in the Event Browser can be hidden easily. Choose Clip > Hide Clip Names (or press Option+Shift+N). Hiding clip names is useful when the names are not meaningful or you want to reduce on-screen clutter. To bring the names back, press Option+Shift+N again, or choose Clip > Show Clip Names.

Immediately to the right of the gear icon are two buttons that further determine how clips are displayed in the Event Browser. Click the left button to display clips in Filmstrip view (**Figure 5.6**). On the next page, I'll show you how to change the size of those filmstrips.

Click the right button, and clips are displayed in List view. Only one thumbnail is displayed—the clip that's selected in the list (**Figure 5.7**).

Like the Browser in FCP 7 or Final Cut Express, this list gives you access to essential information about each clip:

- Filename
- Starting timecode for the entire clip (this does not change when you set an In)
- Ending timecode for the entire clip (this does not change when you set an Out)
- Clip duration of the entire clip (this does not change if you set an In or Out)
- The date the clip was created

FIGURE 5.6
Clicking the Filmstrip button (it's blue because it is currently active) displays Event Browser clips as filmstrips.

FIGURE 5.7
List view (the blue icon) displays key information about each clip. Only one clip thumbnail is displayed at a time.

- A searchable note you can add to the clip (double-click the Notes field to make an entry) (**Figure 5.8**). Notes can also be added in the Timeline Index and the Info tab of the Inspector.

FIGURE 5.8 Notes are useful places to comment about a clip. Notes can be added in List view, the Inspector, or the Timeline Index.

NOTE Skimmer Trick

As long as we are talking about hidden features, here's a cool trick with the skimmer. Hover the skimmer over any clip in the Event Browser and press Control+Y. (You can press Control+Y any time; this is just more dramatic!)

By the way, the thumbnail above the list shows the highlighted clip using three images: the starting frame, the middle frame, and the ending frame. Also like Final Cut Pro 7 and Final Cut Express, if you right-click any of the column headers, a list with additional clip information is displayed. To show a particular column, check it. To hide a column, uncheck it (**Figure 5.9**).

Immediately above whatever clip the skimmer is hovering over, a small text display appears with the name of the clip and the timecode of the current position of the skimmer (**Figure 5.10**). This is especially useful when the clips are very small and you can't read filenames. (As you skim, timecode is also displayed in the Dashboard in the center of the toolbar.)

One more thing and I'll wrap up this section. In the lower-right corner of the Event Browser, when the Event Browser is in Thumbnail view, is...the Switch (**Figure 5.11**).

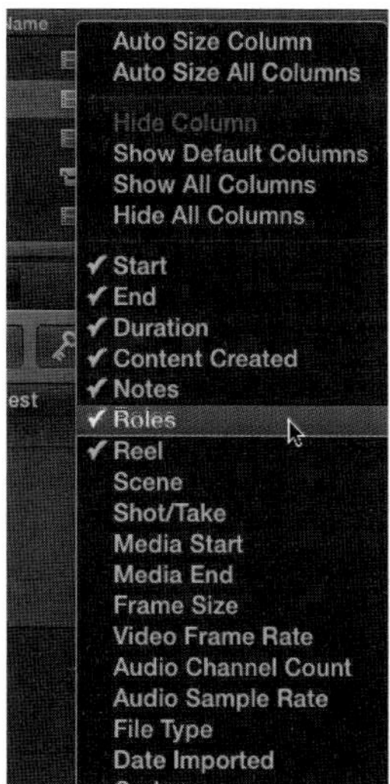

FIGURE 5.9 Right-click any list column header to reveal additional columns of information.

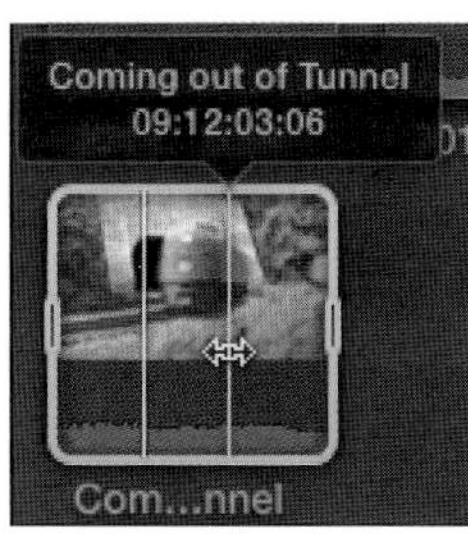

FIGURE 5.10 To display, or disable, additional skimmer info, press Control+Y.

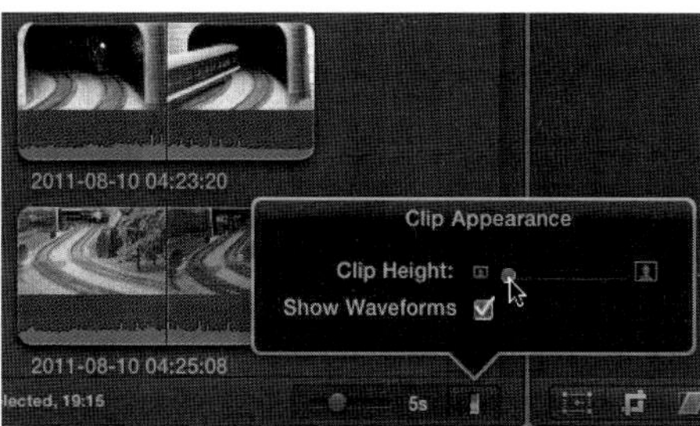

FIGURE 5.11 The Switch, in the lower-right corner of the Event Browser, determines clip height and whether audio waveforms are displayed.

A Digression on Timecode

Timecode is a number, a "label," that uniquely identifies every frame of video. It also uniquely identifies every frame in your project (**Figure 5.12**).

Timecode is generally expressed as four pairs of numbers, moving from left to right:

- Hours (using either a 12-hour or 24-hour clock)
- Minutes
- Seconds
- Frames

FCP X adds one more setting: *subframes*, or 1/80th of a frame

You can control how time is displayed with FCP X by choosing Final Cut Pro > Preferences (press Command+[comma]) and going to the Editing tab (**Figure 5.13**). I almost always use the default setting of HH:MM:SS:FF.

- **HH:MM:SS:FF:** Hours/minutes/seconds/frames is the default timecode setting.
- **HH:MM:SS:FF + subframes:** This allows much more accuracy in audio editing.
- **Frames:** This is often used in animation and heavy effects work.
- **Seconds:** This displays the total seconds and hundredths of a second, of your project.

Although timecode is expressed as time, it does not necessarily—and in fact rarely does—correspond to the time of day of the day you shot the video. It can, if the camera is set to record timecode that way, but it is never safe to assume this.

FIGURE 5.12
Timecode is essential to all editing and is displayed in the Dashboard.

FIGURE 5.13
Timecode preferences are set in the Editing tab.

continues on next page

A Digression on Timecode (*continued*)

Every video clip has timecode associated with it. In fact, QuickTime movies can have up to three tracks of timecode, each of which can be different! However, Final Cut Pro works hard to mask timecode for editors who don't want to worry about it, while making it available to editors who can't live without it.

When you are playing or skimming a clip in the Event Browser, the Dashboard shows the timecode of the source clip. When you are playing a Project in the Timeline, the Dashboard shows the timecode of the Project. At this point, there is no way to display the timecode of the source clip once it has been edited into the Timeline.

There are many, many different techniques that use timecode, and I'll be illustrating them throughout the rest of this book.

Click the Switch (Figure 5.11) , and use the top slider to control the size of the thumbnails. Click Show Waveforms, and you can see the audio waveforms attached to each clip. (A *waveform* is the visual representation of the volume of the sound associated with a clip.)

Just to the left of the Switch is a horizontal slider. Move this to determine how many thumbnails to display for each clip. Slide it all the way to the right—to All—and you display one thumbnail per clip. This shows the most clips in the least amount of space. Slide it left, and you see more thumbnails per clip. In this example, 5s means that it is displaying a thumbnail for every five seconds of a clip.

When you zoom into a clip, notice that the side edges of the clip appear torn. This means there is more of the clip displayed on the thumbnail above (torn on the left) or below (torn on the right). You don't need to display the Switch in order to adjust the duration between thumbnails.

Working the Ratings

Ratings are a fast and easy way to apply some basic selection criteria (um, labels) to a portion of a clip, an entire clip, or a group of clips. There are, essentially, three ratings:

- Favorite rating (green star)
- No ratings (clear star)
- Rejected rating (red "X")

To apply a Favorite rating, select a clip, a group of clips, or a portion of a single clip and click the green star (or press F). The selected portion of each clip is marked with a green line across the top (**Figure 5.14**).

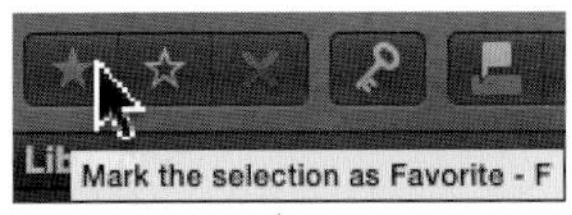

FIGURE 5.14
Select a clip, click the green Favorite star, and a green bar appears at the top of all selected clips, or ranges. Rejected clips display a red bar.

To apply a Rejected rating, select a clip, a group of clips, or a portion of a single clip, and click the red X (or press Delete). A red bar appears across the top of the rejected clip, or the portion of the clip, that was selected. *Rejected*, however, is a relative term. You aren't actually doing anything with the clip except applying this label. You can edit rejected clips as easily as you would any other clip. However, the benefit to this label will become more obvious in a second.

To remove either a Favorite or Rejected rating, select the clip, or clips, containing the rating you want to remove and click the white star (or press U). All ratings associated with those clips are removed. (Removing ratings, by the way, does not remove any analysis or keywords that are applied to any of these clips.)

The real benefit to using ratings comes in when you want to find clips. For instance, in **Figure 5.15**, notice the three clips across the top. The first clip has a Favorite bar across the entire clip, the second has a Favorite bar across only a portion of the clip, while the third clip has a red rejection bar.

Notice, also, the *All Clips* text at the top. This is the hidden button to the Filters pop-up menu. When you click All Clips, a pop-up menu appears. By default, this Filters menu, as Apple calls it, displays all the clips in that Event (**Figure 5.16**).

Note the keyboard shortcuts next to each Find option. For example, you can hide all the rejected clips in this display by choosing Hide Rejected (or pressing Control+H). The benefit to using this filter is that the clips are still there, unlike a clip that you delete. To reveal all the rejected clips, select All Clips.

This same filtering process works for Favorites. Choose the Favorites filter (press Control+F), and all the Favorite clips from that Event, or all selected Events, are displayed in the Browser.

Or, find just the Rejected clips by selecting Rejected.

FIGURE 5.15
Ratings have color codes: green for favorites and red for rejected.

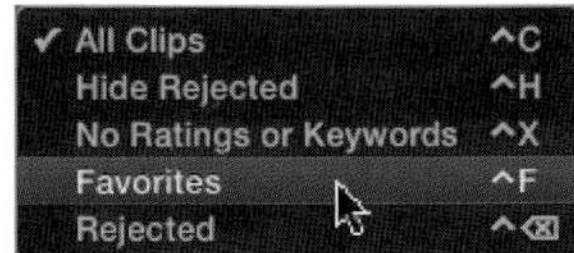

FIGURE 5.16
All Clips allows fast filtering of clips to display all Favorites or hide all Rejected.

Another cool thing about ratings is that you can use them to find Favorites in multiple Events (**Figure 5.17**).

You find all clips that don't have a rating or a keyword applied by selecting No Ratings or Keywords, or by pressing Control+X.

In the Event Library, select all the Events you want to search. Then, in the Filters pop-up menu, select Favorites (or Rejected or No Ratings...you get the idea). All the Favorite clips, or clip regions, from all the selected Events are displayed in the Event Browser, sorted by Event. Cool!

There's also a hidden feature to using List view with ratings in the Event Browser. (The List View button is just above the red *X*—see Figure 5.7.) Click the List View icon to display clips in the Event Browser as a list.

Those clips that have a small, right-pointing arrow next to the name have either a rating or a keyword applied to them. Click the arrow to display the rating or keyword. In this case, two clips have Favorite ratings, and one clip has a Rejected rating. Even more useful, click the name of the rating, in other words, Favorite, to select the portion of the clip that has the rating applied to it (**Figure 5.18**).

The thing I like most about ratings is that they are fast and simple to use. However, they don't deal with complexity at all. To label and find clips based upon multiple criteria, you need keywords. We'll look at those next.

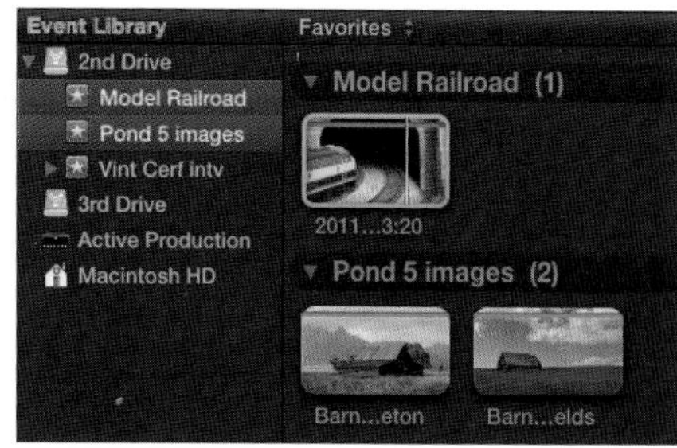

FIGURE 5.17
You can even filter for ratings across multiple selected Events.

FIGURE 5.18
Twirl-down arrows to the left of clip names indicate clips with either ratings or keywords.

A Workaround for Finding Start and End Points

As mentioned in Chapter 2, one of the limitations of the current version of FCP X is that a clip does not remember the Start and End (In or Out) points that are applied to it, if you deselect the clip. A simple workaround to this is to apply a Favorite rating to the selected area of the clip. You can easily reselect that Start and End point by displaying clips in List view in the Event Browser and then clicking the Favorite rating displayed under that clip. The Start and End (or In and Out) are instantly remarked and ready for editing.

Keying in on Keywords

● **NOTE** Where Is All This Stuff Stored?

Ratings and keywords are stored in the Event database. Metadata elements are placed in the media file during import. However, metadata that is added after import, or custom metadata fields, are not stored in the media file but in the Event database.

● **NOTE** So, What's a Keyframe?

A keyframe is a point of change during playback. It is the basic building block of animation—which you will get to in the second half of this book. (By the way, you always use keyframes in pairs, just in case you were curious.)

Keywords, like keyframes, have an intimidating air about them. But, really, the concepts behind both are very simple, though their power is profound. A *keyword* is simply a label that you apply to a portion of a clip, an entire clip, or a range of clips that allows you to categorize it and search for it.

Keywords allow you to label clips with a variety of categories and find clips based on any or all of these categories. Now, you can quickly zero in on exactly the clips you want from a pool of potentially thousands of clips. In FCP X, Apple has simplified the process of assigning, modifying, and finding keywords.

There are two types of keywords within Final Cut: automatic keywords and manual keywords:

- **Automatic keywords:** These are applied during import or analysis. For example, keywords are applied indicating the video format, or image size, or when you analyze a clip for excessive shake or to determine how many people are in the shot.
- **Manual keywords:** These are applied by you and can represent anything. For example, typical keywords might be the scene number, an actor's name, the location, the costumes, whether it's a good or bad take—in other words, manual keywords generally relate to the visual or audio content of a shot that can't be figured out automatically by the computer.

Adding and Deleting Keywords with the Keyword Editor

To add a keyword, go to the Event Browser and select the portion of a clip, a clip, or a group of clips, where you want to add keywords. Then, click the Key icon in the middle of the interface (**Figure 5.19**).

This opens the Keyword editor. This window is where you add and remove keywords from clips. It also allows you to assign keyboard shortcuts to keywords (**Figure 5.20**).

FIGURE 5.19
Click the Key icon to display the Keyword editor.

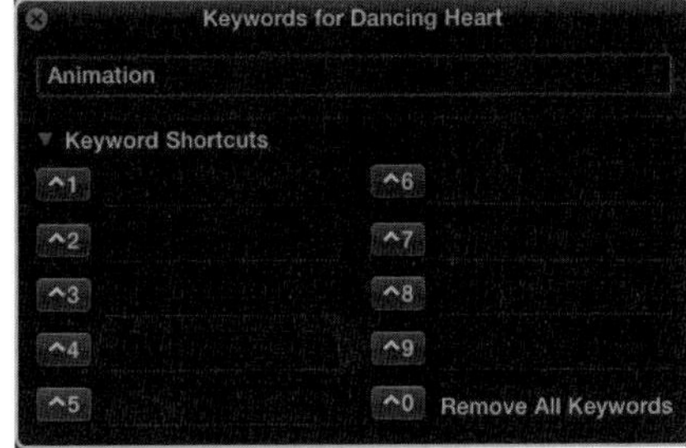

FIGURE 5.20
This is an empty Keyword editor, where keywords can be added to clips.

To add a keyword to a selected clip (and in this section, using the word *clip* also means "portion of a clip or group of clips"—I just get tired of writing the same phrase over and over), type the keyword in the top data entry box.

FIGURE 5.21
A keyword, *Animation*, being added to a clip. Note the blue bar added at the top.

In this case, I entered **Animation** for a clip that features a dancing heart.

When you finish typing the word, all the selected clips animate, showing the keyword being placed inside them (**Figure 5.21**). Also, as soon as a keyword is applied to a clip, a blue bar appears near the top of the selected portion of the image. This is the visual indicator that at least one keyword has been applied to a clip.

To remove a single keyword, select the clip (or portion of a clip...you get the idea) in the Event Browser; then, in the Keyword editor, delete the word from the top line of the Editor (**Figure 5.22**).

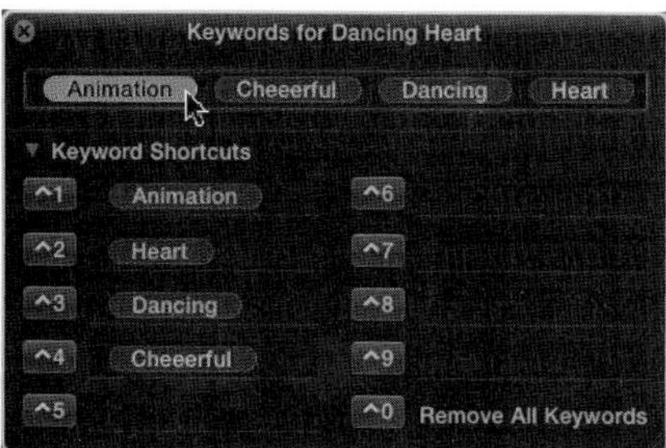

FIGURE 5.22
To remove a keyword, select a clip(s), delete the word in the Keyword editor (left), and watch the explosion (right).

In this example, with four keywords to this clip, I highlighted *Animation* and deleted it. The deleted animation explodes inside the dancing heart clip.

If you want to remove all the keywords in a clip, click the ^0 button just to the left of Remove All Keywords at the bottom of this window, or, even easier, press Control+0.

The Keyword editor makes it easy to automate the process of adding keywords. Here, for example, I have four keywords added in the window which were filled in as I entered keywords.

- **To add a new keyword,** without applying it to a clip, type it directly in the text box next to a number.
- **To delete a keyword,** without removing it from a clip, highlight the text next to a number and press Delete.
- **To change a keyword,** without changing it in the clip, select the text next to a number and type over it.
- **To apply any of these keywords to a selected clip,** either click the button to the left of the text or type the keyboard shortcut. (The thingy that looks like a roof is the symbol for the Control key.)

The Keyword editor does not have to be open for the keyboard shortcuts next to the text to work. The shortcuts are always available.

NOTE Can You Apply Keywords to an Entire Event?

No...and yes. You can't select an Event in the Event Library and apply a keyword to the entire Event. However, you can select all the clips in the Event Browser and then apply a keyword to the selected clips. Also, analysis keywords and the folder that contains the media files can be applied as keywords during import.

Viewing Keywords

There are many different places to view the keywords associated with a clip:

- In the Event Browser, you can use the skimmer to display keywords. Press Control+Y to turn on skimmer info. Keywords are displayed in the Info window.
- Also in the Event Browser, display clips in List view and twirl down the arrow to display all ratings and keywords associated with a clip. (To display clips as a list, click the blue button displayed in the lower-left corner of **Figure 5.23**.)

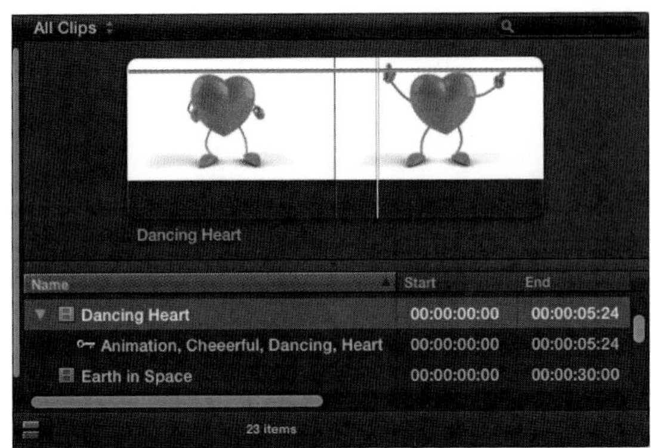

FIGURE 5.23 The List view in the Event Browser displays all the keywords applied to each clip.

Two Quick Keyword Renaming Tricks

Tip #1: A fast way to apply an existing keyword to multiple clips is to select all the clips you want to apply the keyword to and drag them on top of the keyword in the Event Library. This also adds those clips to that Keyword Collection (**Figure 5.24**).

FIGURE 5.24 Drag clips on top of a keyword to quickly add that keyword to those clips.

Tip #2: A fast way to rename a keyword is to select it in the Event Library and enter the new name. All clips with the old name are instantly updated to the new name.

- Keywords are also displayed in the Event Library either as a Keyword Collection or as a Smart Collection (**Figure 5.25**). A Keyword Collection is a list of all the clips containing that keyword. (A *Smart Collection* is a saved dynamic search, which I will discuss shortly.) To see the clips that contain a specific keyword, click the keyword in the Event Library.

  To see all the clips that contain more than one keyword, use the Command key to select all the keywords you want to review, and all the clips that contain at least one of the selected keywords will be displayed. (Folks who understand logic call this an "Or" search—a clip will be displayed if it contains "either this keyword *or* that keyword.")

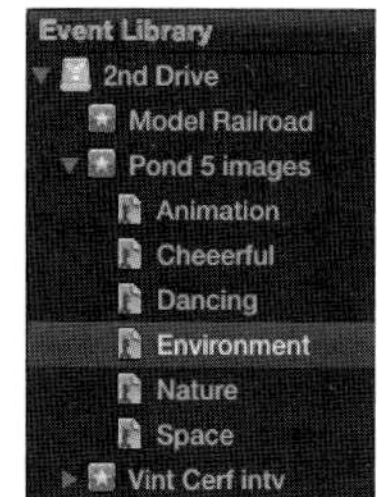

FIGURE 5.25
All keywords contained in an Event are displayed under each Event as a Keyword Collection.

Find Clips Using Keywords

Clicking the name of a Keyword Collection is a fast way to find clips using keywords. But there is far more you can do with keywords to find what you need.

First, you can find clips using the Event Library and Keyword Collections.You can also use the Search box in the top-right corner of the Event Browser. Type in the text you are searching for, and all relevant clips will be selected (**Figure 5.26**).

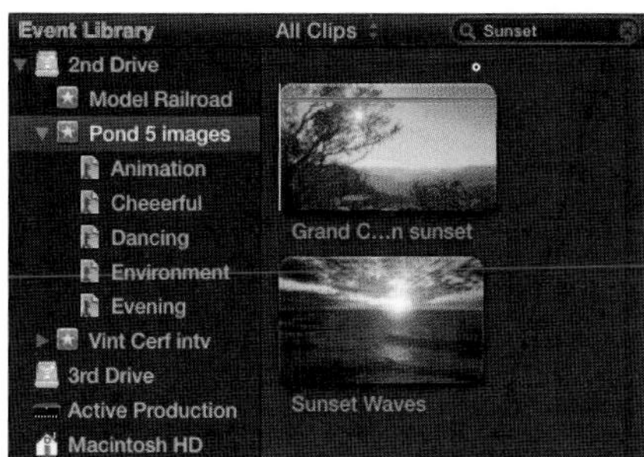

FIGURE 5.26
Use the Search box in the top-right corner of the Event Browser to locate clips by filename.

▲ TIP The Reset Button

By the way, if you want to cancel a search or clear the Search box, click the small, gray X in a circle on the right side of the Search box. (Apple calls this the Reset button.)

● NOTE Can You Find Keywords in the Timeline?

Yes, using the Timeline Index (press Shift+Command+2), you can search and display all keywords associated with clips in the Timeline. I'll talk more about this in Chapter 7.

By default, this text box looks for filenames. In this example, entering the word **Sunset** displays all clips that contain the word *Sunset* in the filename. However, you can refine this further by selecting a Keyword Collection (or, as you'll see a bit later, a Smart Collection) in the Event Library and then entering a word in the Search box. For example, click the Keyword Collection Environment and display all clips that contain the word *Sunset* in their filename *and* contain the Environment keyword.

Creating, Modifying, and Deleting Smart Collections

The real power of keywords appears when you use them in combination, which leads me into talking about Smart Collections. Look at Figure 5.26 again. See that small magnifying glass on the left side of the Search box? That little icon opens a whole new world of search possibilities: the Filter window. When you enter text into the Search box, what you are *really* doing is entering a search into the default setting of the Filter window (**Figure 5.27**).

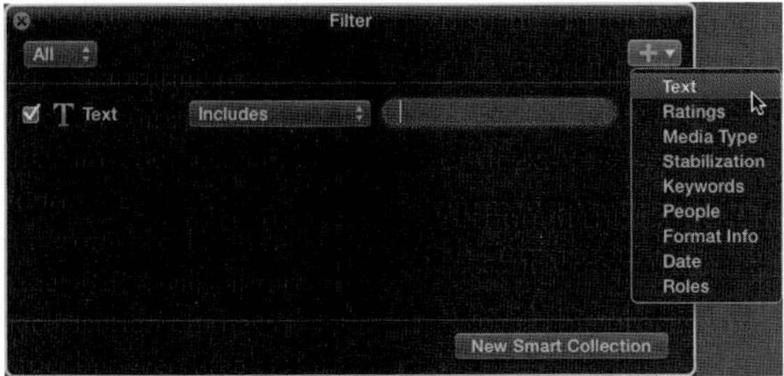

FIGURE 5.27
Click the magnifying glass to reveal the Filter window, which provides much more extensive search capabilities.

FIGURE 5.28
A typical search would be for clips containing specific keywords.

The Filter window allows you to create searches based on a wide variety of criteria: Text in a filename, Ratings, Media type, Image stabilization, Keywords, People, Format info, Date, and Roles.

First, the Filter window allows you to combine as many of these different search types into one search as you want, which is why it is more powerful than just a single Keyword Collection. Second, the Filter window allows you to save this search as a Smart Collection so that as new clips get added to the Event that match the criteria of the search, the clips automatically show up as part of the collection, without having to formally add them to the collection or change the search to include them.

Click the plus button (it's called the Add Rule pop-up menu) and add **Keywords**. A second set of criteria is displayed, showing all the available keywords. Uncheck the keywords you don't want to search for. In this example, you are just searching for clips that contain the keywords *Environment* and *Evening* (**Figure 5.28**).

The search is updated dynamically. As soon as you change a setting, all the clips that meet the revised search criteria are displayed. You don't need to approve the search or even exit the Filter window. This allows you to instantly see whether you are finding the clips you need.

You can even search across multiple Events and multiple hard disks. For instance, in **Figure 5.29**, I selected the 2nd Drive, which means I am searching across all Events contained on this drive. (Select more than one hard drive if you want to search across multiple drives.)

I turned off the Text search—notice the Activate checkbox on the left is unchecked. This is important, because if Text is turned on and blank, you'll get weird search results.

I checked just the keyword I wanted to search on, *Tunnel*. (You can search on multiple keywords; just check the ones you want to search on.)

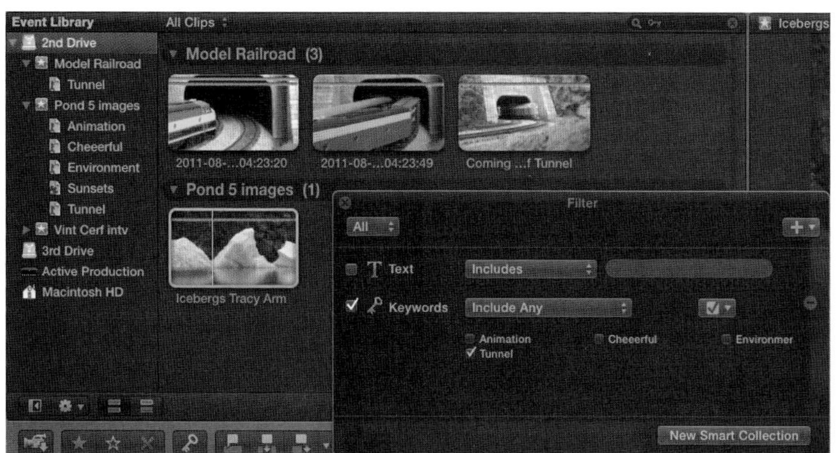

FIGURE 5.29 As media libraries get bigger, searching on multiple criteria becomes even more useful.

Instantly, the four clips that have the keyword *Tunnel* applied to them appear in the Event Browser. (Also, if you have eagle eyes, a small blue key appears in the Search box at the top—yes, it is virtually impossible to see—which indicates a keyword search is in place.)

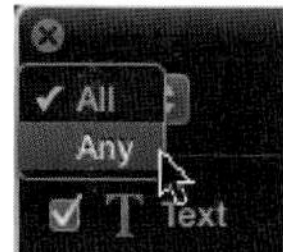

FIGURE 5.30 To further refine a search, Boolean "and" and "or" can be added.

To cancel the search so you can see all your clips again, click the small *X* in a circle at the right side of the Search text window.

By default, Final Cut Pro displays only the clips that match *all* the selection criteria in the Filter window. This is called an "And" result. If you want to search for all the clips that meet *any single* one of these search criteria, change And to Any in the Filter window (**Figure 5.30**). Now, any clip that meets at least one of these criteria will be displayed.

"And" is more exclusive, displaying fewer clips. "Any" is broader, displaying more clips. If you want to delete a search you've entered, click the red minus (-) in a circle. (Apple calls this the Remove button.) It's to the right of any added search criteria.

● **NOTE** Help! I Can't Find My Clips!

If all, or most, of your clips have disappeared when you were not expecting them to disappear, it's probably because you have a search in place that you forgot about. Click the Reset button in the Search box to cancel any searches to get your clips back.

Let's take a look at some of the different search criteria you can enter in the Filter window:

- **Media types** allows you to display files that contain specific media, such as audio or video.
- **Ratings** shows clips that have ratings, Favorite or Rejected, assigned to them.
- **People** displays those shots that Final Cut Pro has identified as containing people, for example, a close-up, two-shot, or wide shot. Note that, like keyframes, all the selection options for people are represented by checkboxes.
- **Stabilization** shows clips that FCP has flagged as containing excessive shake. (This option does not include clips flagged as having rolling shutter problems.)
- **Format** allows you to search for clips using a wide variety of technical criteria (**Figure 5.31**).

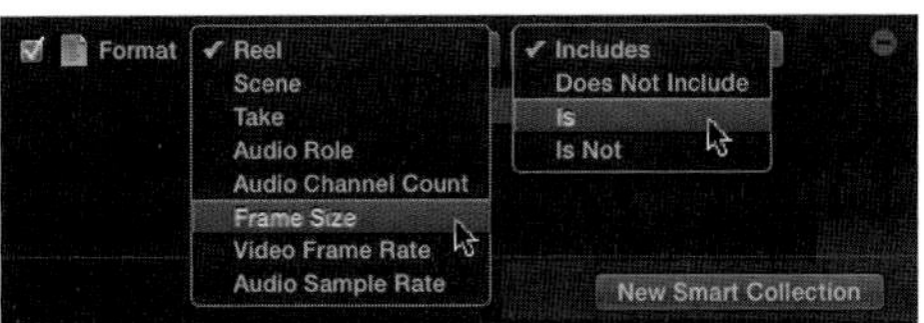

FIGURE 5.31
Formats allows you search on a wide variety of technical criteria.

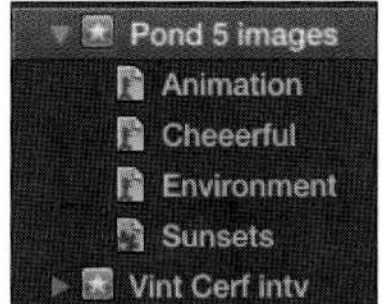

FIGURE 5.32
The three icons of the Event Library: Event, Smart Collection, and Keyword Collection.

▲ TIP Keywords Are Not Text

Remember, text searches look at the text associated with a clip—specifically, the filename, plus any notes or markers attached to the clip. Keywords are separate from text and won't appear in a simple text search.

● NOTE This Won't Work

You can't add a clip to a Smart Collection by dragging it on top of the Smart Collection in the Event Library. This works for Keyword Collections but not Smart Collections.

- **Date** shows clips based upon a range of dates compared to when they were either created or imported.
- **Roles** shows clips based upon the Roles (a new feature in 10.0.1) assigned to each clip.

Many searches are simple; others get quite complex. However, whether a search is simple or detailed, it can speed finding clips by saving the search so you can easily reuse it.

Saved searches are called *Smart Collections*. To convert a search to a Smart Collection, click the New Smart Collection button at the bottom of the Filter window. The Smart Collection is immediately saved and displayed under the selected Event. **Figure 5.32** illustrates the three different icons in the Event Library:

- **Event.** This is the icon next to Vint Cert intv or Pond 5 images.
- **Keyword Collection.** This is the icon next to Animation or Cheerful.
- **Smart Collection.** This is the icon next to Sunsets.

As you start adding more and more keywords, keeping them organized becomes a real challenge. Just as you use folders in the Finder to organize your files, you can use folders in the Event Library to organize both Keyword and Smart Collections.

To create a new folder, do one of the following:

- Select File > New folder.
- Press Shift+Command+N.
- Right-click an Event name and select New Folder.

Moving Collections into a folder is easy—just drag them in.

● NOTE What Can a Folder Store?

Unlike Final Cut Pro 7 or Final Cut Express, folders in the Event Library of FCP X store keywords. You can't use folders to hold Events or clips.

Event Browser Line Colors

The Event Browser uses a series of lines and colors to indicate properties associated with a clip. **Table 5.1** shows what the colors mean.

TABLE 5.1 Event Browser Line Colors

Color	Meaning
Green	Marked as a Favorite
Red	Marked as Rejected
Blue	Keywords applied by you
Purple	Analysis keywords applied

Managing Metadata

In addition to Ratings and Keywords, there is a whole new section of extended metadata that's included but hidden in Final Cut Pro X. There are hundreds of metadata fields just two mouse clicks away.

However, I'm just going to touch on this extended metadata here because, unlike Ratings or Keywords, most of the metadata inside Final Cut is not easily searched. While you can enter data in some of these fields, modify data, and even add custom data fields and views, most of the information contained in the metadata files can't be searched or exported. In the short term, this metadata is principally of interest to developers, which is why XML import and export is so important.

The Info Inspector

To see this extended metadata that Final Cut Pro is storing, select a clip in the Event Browser and then click the Inspector icon, or press Command+4 (**Figure 5.33**). You can also select clips in the Timeline and view them in the Inspector. The Inspector is a part of the interface you'll learn more about in Chapter 9. For now, just know it is central to all FCP's effects.

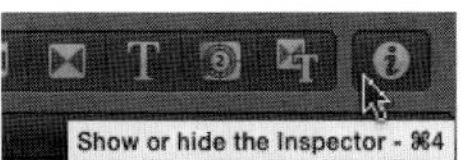

FIGURE 5.33 Click the Inspector icon (Command+4) to view metadata.

In earlier versions of Final Cut (both Pro and Express), you made changes to clips and effects in the Timeline or in the various tabs of the Viewer. In FCP X, all those changes are centralized in the Inspector. Starting with Chapter 9, working with the Inspector will be an essential part of the editing process. For now, though, I just want to introduce this part of the interface as it regards metadata.

When you click the Inspector icon, the Inspector window opens. Depending upon what you have selected, a variety of text tabs appear at the top of the Inspector. In this example, there are three: Video, Audio, and Info.

Click the Info tab at the top, and the metadata window opens (**Figure 5.34**).

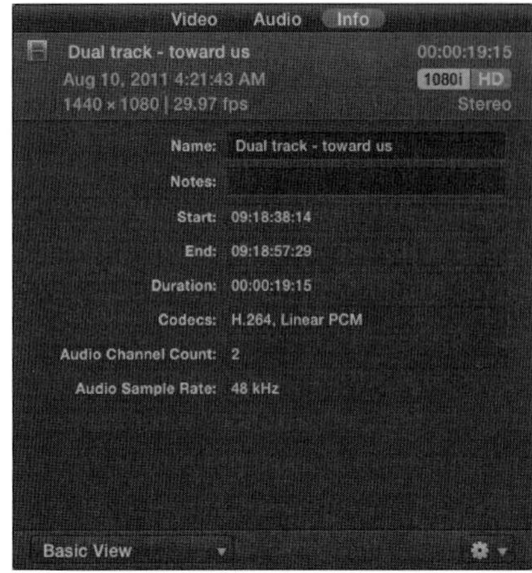

FIGURE 5.34 The Basic view of metadata, accessed using the Info tab.

This is the Basic view of the metadata associated with the clip. It includes things like clip title, the Notes field from the List view in the Event Browser, the clip start and end timecode, and the general codec and audio info.

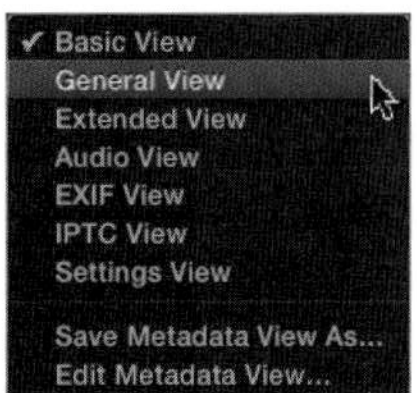

FIGURE 5.35 Click Basic View in the lower-left corner of the Info tab to reveal more view options, and then click General View.

In the lower-left corner is a hidden button. Click Basic View, and a new menu choice appears. These view options allow you to see more and more of the metadata that is actually being tracked for this clip. For instance, watch what happens when you select General View (**Figure 5.35**).

The amount of information displayed expands significantly! In fact, there's so much of it, you need to scroll down to see all of it. As you'll discover, each time you choose a new view, more, and more, and more(!) metadata is revealed. You can add new metadata fields, create new views of your metadata, and save custom metadata views.

In the lower-right corner is a gear menu, which Apple calls the Action menu. Click it, and an interesting option appears: Show File Status (**Figure 5.36**).

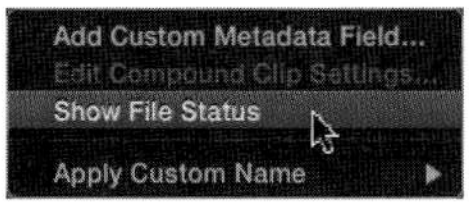

FIGURE 5.36 The gear menu allows reviewing file status.

The File Status window adds a very interesting collection of data to the bottom of whatever metadata view you are looking at (**Figure 5.37**). This new data shows where the source file is stored on your hard disk, which Events are storing the clip, which Projects the clip is used in, and whether the file has been optimized or converted to a proxy file. This also allows you to reestablish links between Projects and Events.

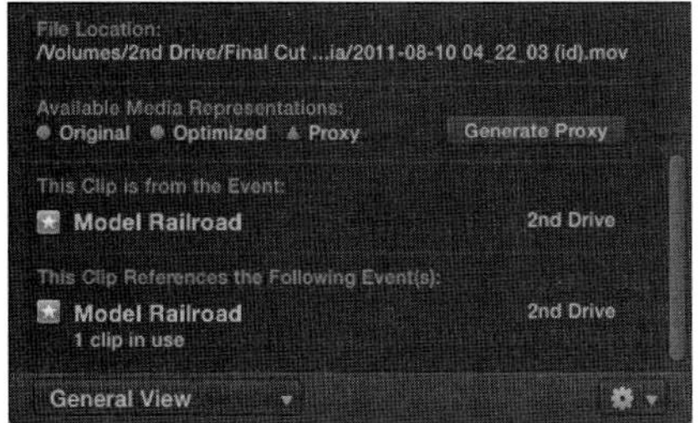

FIGURE 5.37 File Status shows where clips are used or stored, and whether optimized or proxy files exist.

Just as XML was the underlying framework that made Final Cut Pro 7 such an industrial workhorse, the extensive metadata that is modified, tracked, and, ultimately, imported and exported with Final Cut Pro X will unlock new applications and utilities that will provide capabilities that you can only begin to imagine now.

Summary

In the past, you would track your clips by filename, by the folder they were stored in, or if you were feeling really creative, by a color label. However, in FCP X, you have a lot more tools to label, track, and find exactly the clip you need when you need it. This ability to search for clips, especially between multiple Events and multiple hard disks, makes working with very large projects, with truly large collections of clips, much more manageable.

Keywords will become critical to managing large libraries of tapeless media.

Keyboard Shortcuts

Shortcut	What It Does
Shift+Command+1	Toggle display of Event Library
Control+Y	Toggle display of skimmer info
Option+Shift+N	Toggle display of clip names in Event Browser
F	Mark selected area as a Favorite
Delete	Mark selected area as Rejected
U	Remove Favorite or Rejected rating from selected clip(s)
Control+F	Display all Favorite clips
Control+Delete	Display all Rejected clips
Control+X	Display all clips with neither Ratings nor Keywords
Control+C	Display all clips, ignoring ratings
Control+0	Delete all keywords in selected clip(s)
Shift+Command+2	Display Timeline Index
Command+F	Open Filter (Find) window
Control+1 through 9	Add a keyword assigned to that keyboard shortcut
Shift+Command+K	Create New Keyword Collection
Option+Command+N	Create new Smart Collection
Shift+Command+N	Create new folder
Command+4	Toggle Inspector open/closed
Option+Shift+N	Show/Hide Event Browser clip names

6

EDITING

It seems like all we've been doing so far is getting ready. That's important, to be sure, but it's nothing to write home about. Now the fun part starts... editing. *Editing* is the process of deciding how to combine all the different media at your disposal to tell a compelling story. And *story* is the key word here. Never lose sight of the reason you are editing—you are telling a story. Ideally, it's a story someone else wants to watch.

Here's the key point: In the initial edit, edit your clips as quickly as you can into the Timeline. Don't worry about perfection—that's why it's called a *rough* cut. It isn't until you see what you *actually* have to work with that you can start making meaningful decisions about how to best tell your story.

Final Cut Pro X introduces new concepts, and new technology, that makes telling your stories faster, easier, and more flexible than ever.

The Editing Process

As you've seen, you need to understand some new concepts as you make the transition into Final Cut Pro X. In Chapter 3, you learned about Events and Projects. In Chapter 5, you learned about keywords. Now, when it comes to editing, you need to understand storylines. And in Final Cut Pro X there are two types of storylines: primary storylines and connected storylines.

The simplest definition is that a *storyline* is a collection of clips contained on the Timeline. These clips can consist of video, audio, or still images. The *primary storyline* is the main collection of clips inside your project. There is only one primary storyline per project. (In Final Cut Pro 7 terms, the primary storyline is similar to tracks V1, A1, and A2—except that Final Cut Pro X doesn't use tracks.) However, you can have an unlimited number of connected storylines.

No Tracks?

No. Final Cut Pro X is called a *trackless* editor, which means you can connect clips to the primary storyline without worrying about the vertical position of a clip. This lack of tracks is one of the more disorienting new features of FCP X for experienced editors.

New with the 10.0.1 update, Apple added *Roles*. Roles are metadata tags that allows you to group clips by function. For example, all the dialog clips, effects, and titles can be quickly located and displayed. I cover Roles in more detail in Chapter 7; however, for now, it is enough to know that Roles allow you to group, highlight, hide, and export clips in groups.

● **NOTE**
On Connected

I keep using the word connected. That's because whenever you edit a clip into the Timeline, it has to be connected to something. It is either part of the primary storyline or connected to it.

Connected storylines, which are also just called *storylines*, connect to the primary storyline. These additional storylines are used for B-roll (images that illustrate what the person on camera is talking about), sound effects, still images, titles, background plates, and so on. Generally, though not always, a connected storyline contains multiple clips.

There are also *connected clips*, which are just single clips connected to the primary storyline. You first met a connected clip in your simple edit in Chapter 2.

The benefits to this connection, as you'll see in future chapters, is that whenever you move a clip in the primary storyline, all clips connected to that clip will move with it. This vastly reduces the risk of getting clips or Projects out of sync by moving some clips but not all of them.

In Chapter 2, you learned how to do a simple edit. In this chapter, you'll learn how to use all the editing power that Final Cut Pro X provides.

Defining Direction

The Timeline flows from the left to the right. The beginning of your Project is on the left, and the end is on the right. Because of this "flow," you can use a water analogy to define where you are, or where you are going, in the Timeline.

For example, the terms *move up*, *move left*, *move earlier*, and *move upstream* all mean the same thing—you are moving toward the beginning of the Timeline. The terms *move down*, *move right*, *move later*, and *move downstream* also all mean the same thing—you are moving toward the end of the Timeline.

The *outgoing* clip is the one on the left, because you are near the Out, or the End, of that clip. The *incoming* clip is the one on the right, because you are near the In, or the Start, of the clip.

The Editing and Playback Preferences

Before you start editing, though, you need to tweak two preference panes. The first time you went to preferences, in Chapter 3, you set your import settings. Now, you need to adjust how FCP X handles editing and playback.

Editing Preferences

Choose Final Cut Pro > Preferences (or press Command+[comma]) to open the preferences window (**Figure 6.1**).

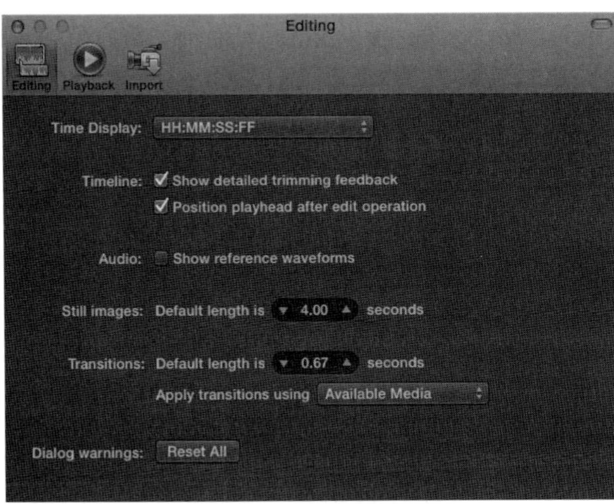

FIGURE 6.1 This is the Editing preferences window. The settings displayed are how I have my Editing preferences set.

Time Display allows you to set the time format displayed in the Dashboard in the center of the toolbar as you move the skimmer or the playhead (**Figure 6.2**). You can set it to the following:

FIGURE 6.2
There are four different timecode display options.

- **Timecode,** which is best for video editing.
- **Timecode, plus subframes,** which is best for audio editing. A subframe is 1/80th of a video frame.
- **Frames,** which is best for animation and some film.
- **Seconds,** which is best for short projects of less than a minute.

Show detailed trimming feedback makes trimming clips a lot easier by displaying the clips you are trimming in the Viewer. The default is off; I recommend turning this on and will demonstrate it in Chapter 8.

Position playhead after edit operation moves the playhead from wherever it is to the end of a clip when you edit that clip into the Timeline.

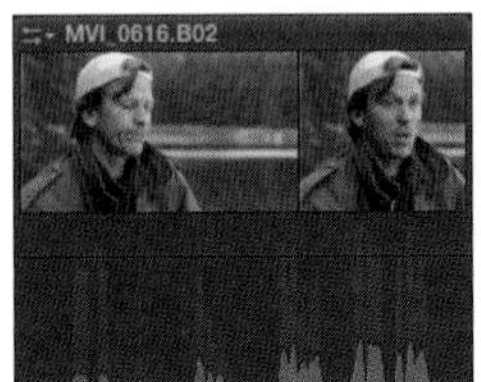

FIGURE 6.3
Reference waveforms allow you to see audio levels as though the audio were normalized. This is display-only and doesn't affect editing.

Show reference waveforms displays a "ghost image" in your audio waveforms that shows the waveform volume as if it were normalized (**Figure 6.3**). If you are always dealing with very soft clips, this can make viewing your audio waveforms much easier, because it accentuates the level changes. If your audio is already loud, turning this on won't make any difference. This is a display-only function and does not affect the audio levels themselves.

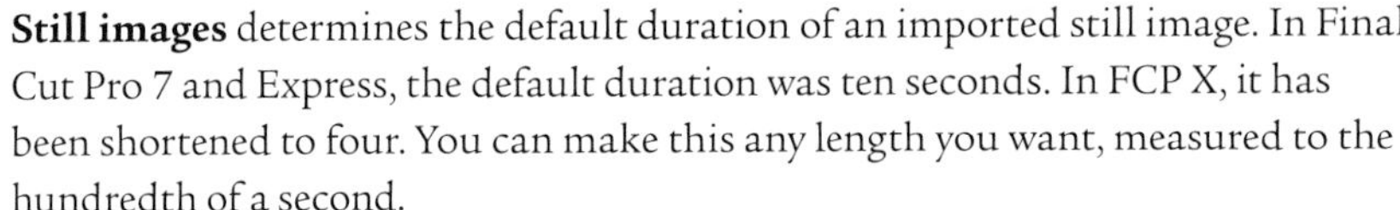

Still images determines the default duration of an imported still image. In Final Cut Pro 7 and Express, the default duration was ten seconds. In FCP X, it has been shortened to four. You can make this any length you want, measured to the hundredth of a second.

Transitions determines the duration of the default transition—a cross dissolve. In FCP X, Apple decided to display all time values as seconds and hundredths of a second, rather than frames. Given all the different frame rates currently in HD—something like eight and growing—this makes sense. However, I miss entering my frame values. (By the way, a 20-frame dissolve, which is my favorite duration for 30 fps video, is 0.67 seconds—just in case you want to know.)

Apply transitions using has two choices: Full Overlap and Available Media. To apply a transition to an edit point, you need extra media (called *handles*) before the Start and after the End. The reason is that during a dissolve, for example, you need to see both the outgoing and incoming clips. You need video from both clips for the duration of the dissolve. (Chapter 10 covers this in more detail.)

Well, what happens if you don't have the video handles for the transition?

- **Full Overlap** means that Final Cut Pro will pull up (move left) the downstream clip (the incoming clip) to create enough overlap for the transition to be applied. The good news is that this works great at making sure your transitions all work. The bad news is that this will shorten your downstream clip by the duration of the transition, which may, or may not, cause problems with your content.

- **Available Media** is the traditional behavior of clips you saw in Final Cut Pro 7. To apply a transition, FCP needs at least four frames of overlapping video. If there are not four frames of handles, FCP won't apply the transition. If there are more than four frames but fewer than the duration you want to apply, FCP will adjust the duration of the transition to match the number of handles available.

This setting applies only to transitions, and the default setting is Available Media.

Playback Preferences

The final preference pane you need to visit controls playback (**Figure 6.4**). Most of the default settings are fine.

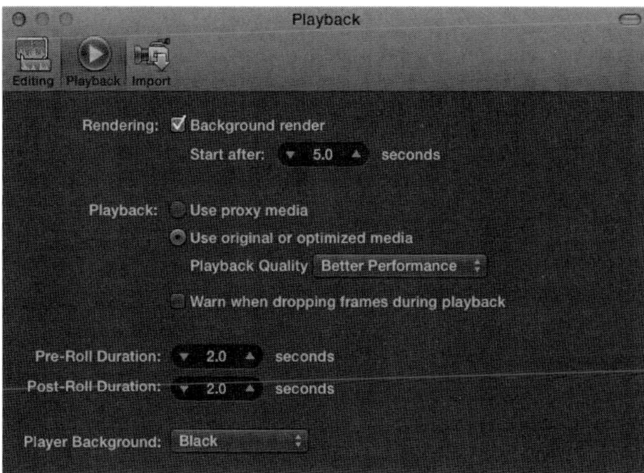

FIGURE 6.4 This is the third of three preference windows: Playback.

Rendering allows you to turn on, or off, background rendering when the system is idle and to determine how long FCP waits before starting a background render. Most of the time I have background rendering turned on. The only time I turn it off is when I am doing a live streaming event—like a webinar—using Final Cut Pro. Because background rendering is so processor-intensive, I turn off background processing for my event to make sure I have enough CPU power to make the live event flow smoothly. The rest of the time, I leave this on.

Playback allows you to switch between displaying proxy clips, optimized clips, and original clips. This is a toggle switch—you can select proxies, optimized clips, or originals. You can change the Timeline display at any time; however, you can display only one format at a time.

Warn when dropping frames during playback tells you when you are dropping frames, and I *always* want to know when I am dropping frames. Dropping frames is a good indicator that your hard disk is not fast enough to keep up with playback. The best way to fix this error is to get a faster hard disk or connect it using a faster protocol. This is one of those errors that can screw up your project. If you are laying off to tape, turning this on is essential. If you are exporting your media, turning this on is helpful.

Pre-Roll Duration and **Post-Roll Duration** determine the amount of time to play before and after a selection when looping playback or auditioning clips.

Player Background determines the color of the Viewer when previewing effects but does not affect output. The Viewer background is always black when outputting.

Now that your preferences are set, it's time, finally, to start editing.

Editing Techniques

Thanks to John Putch and his *Route 30, Too!* film. I'll use some real scenes to illustrate how to edit dramatic footage.

Append Edit

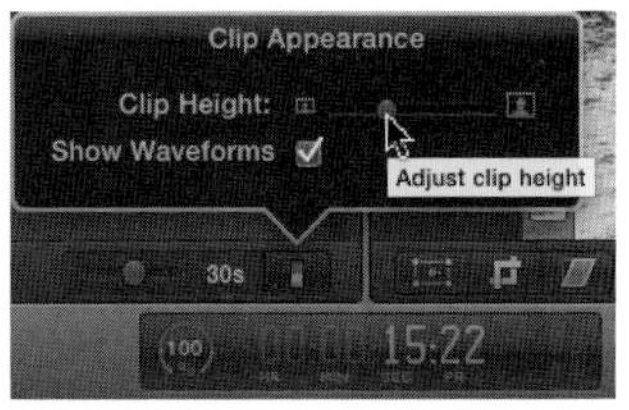

FIGURE 6.5
Click the Switch to set clip height and display waveforms in the Event Browser.

FIGURE 6.6
My favorite keyboard shortcut is also a button—which toggles "snapping."

Let's start by looking at the basic building block of editing in FCP X: the append edit. An append edit takes the selected clip, or range within a clip, and edits it to the end of the Timeline, regardless of the position of the playhead or the skimmer.

So that you can see clips better in the Event Browser, click the Switch in the lower-right corner and adjust the size of the clips to your satisfaction. If you want to see more of the clip, grab the slider just to the left of the Switch and drag it (**Figure 6.5**).

Also, be sure Show Waveforms is turned on so that you can see the audio associated with each clip. Notice that waveforms are embedded at the bottom of the video clip. This makes it easy to quickly see both the audio and the video for a clip.

The All option means that you are seeing the entire clip as a single thumbnail. As you drag the slider more to the left, the thumbnails expand to show more of the clip; say a thumbnail every minute, or one every ten seconds. To keep my screenshots small, I generally set this to All.

Also, I've found it very useful to turn snapping on for editing and then turn it off for trimming (**Figure 6.6**). In this case, since you are editing, I'll turn snapping on. To do this, do one of the following:

- Click the Snapping button in the top-right corner of the Timeline.
- Press N (for "snnnnnnnnnapping"). This is a toggle that turns snapping either off or on. Me? I almost always use the keyboard shortcut.

This scene contains seven clips: Two men walk from the field to the doorway of a barn, where a conversation takes place. The shots are displayed in clip name order, not shot order. If you were to number the clips in this image in shot order, it would be: 1, 3, 4a, 4b, 5a, 5b, 2 (**Figure 6.7**).

FIGURE 6.7 These are the clips we'll be working with for this short scene.

So, let's set the Start and End for the first clip. In Chapter 2, you learned that you can drag the selection boundaries for a clip to set the Start and End. While this works, it often is not accurate or fast enough.

Here are other ways to set the Start, also called the In, of a clip:

- If the skimmer is active, move the skimmer where you want the shot to start, and press I.
- If the skimmer is not active, move the playhead where you want the shot to start, and press I.
- Drag the left side of the selected clip boundary.
- Select the clip in the Event Browser; then, click the Dashboard to switch it to "timecode jump" mode, and enter the starting timecode of your shot. You don't need to enter punctuation—for example, to move the playhead to 51:20, simply enter **5120** and press the Enter key.
- Using the J-K-L keys, play the playhead and press I where you want the shot to start. This allows you to set the Start in real time during playback.
- Play the clip and press I where you want the shot to start.

Just as there are multiple ways to set the Start, there are also multiple ways to set the End:

- With the skimmer active, move the skimmer where you want the shot to end, and press O.
- With the skimmer inactive, move the playhead where you want the shot to end, and press O.
- Drag the right side of the selected clip boundary.
- With the clip selected and a Start set, choose Modify > Change Duration (or press Control+D) and change the duration of the clip.

- Select the Dashboard, enter the timecode you want for the Out, press the Enter key, and then press O.
- Using the J-K-L keys, play the playhead and press O where you want the shot to end. This allows you to set the End in real time during playback.
- Play the clip and press O where you want the shot to end.

However you decide to do it, set an In and an Out for your first clip. **Figure 6.8**, for example, shows the selected clip with the Start and End marked and the clip visible in the Viewer.

FIGURE 6.8
This is the first clip in the Viewer and what it looks like in the Event Browser.

▲ **TIP** Psst... Wanna Play a Clip from Start to End?

Piece of cake. Press /.

Just as there are several ways to mark a clip, there are several ways to perform an append edit:

- Click the append edit button in the toolbar (**Figure 6.9**).
- Press E.
- Choose Edit > Append to Storyline.
- Drag the clip from the Event Browser to the Timeline.

The clip is automatically edited from the Event Browser to the end of the Timeline, regardless of the position of the playhead or the skimmer.

Let's do this again. Using one of the techniques outlined earlier, set the Start and the End for a second clip (**Figure 6.10**). Then, press E, or use another method, to append the clip from the Event Browser to the Timeline.

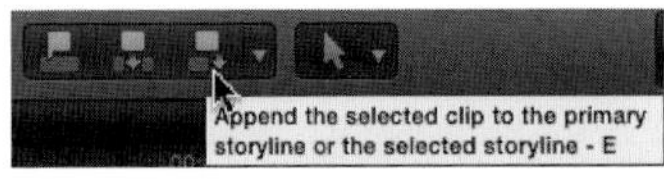

FIGURE 6.9
Click this button to make an append edit. Shortly, you'll be using the keyboard shortcut: E.

FIGURE 6.10
The yellow border indicates the selected range of the next clip to be edited to the Timeline.

Something Different

Unlike earlier versions of Final Cut, FCP X bundles both the audio and video elements into a single clip. Apple says it did this because it wanted to prevent clips going "out of sync," which means the audio and video are playing at different times. This creates the weird illusion where the actor's lips are moving but the wrong sounds are coming out.

This unified clip approach simplifies editing—until the time comes to do audio-only edits or transitions. I'll talk about audio-only editing later in this chapter and transitions in Chapter 10. Also, Chapter 9 is devoted to special techniques you can use when working with audio.

NOTE Hey! What About Those Storylines?

By default, an append edit is applied to the primary storyline. However, if you want to append a clip to a connected storyline, click the dark gray bar above the connected storyline to select it before clicking the append edit button or pressing E.

This technique does not work with connected clips. I'll explain how to create and edit to connected storylines later in this chapter.

To preview the edit point, use the up and down arrow keys to jump the playhead between two clips. Note that this always lands the playhead on the starting frame of the clip to the right (the incoming clip). Then, press Shift+?.

This is a very cool shortcut, where the playhead backs up a few seconds before the edit point, plays through the edit point, and then, after a few seconds of playing past the edit point, resets itself to its original position in the Timeline.

Hmmm...you go from a shot of the two men in the field to them walking up to the barn. This feels awkward; what you need is a transition shot between these two shots. And doing that requires an Insert edit.

Insert Edit

An insert edit places a clip between two clips at the position of the playhead. If the playhead is between two shots, the new clip is inserted between those two shots. If the playhead is in the middle of a clip, an insert edit breaks the clip into two pieces and inserts the clip between those two pieces. An insert edit always changes the duration of a Project.

FIGURE 6.11 You need this transition shot to get the men from the field to the barn. Notice the In and Out are already selected.

In **Figure 6.11**, for instance, you have a transition shot of the men walking out of the field and heading toward the barn. This will smooth the transition nicely between the field shots and the barn shots.

Notice, also, that the clip is already marked—the Start and the End are set. Since I discussed marking a clip as part of the previous edit, you don't need to repeat the process here. However you decide to mark your clip, do so now.

FIGURE 6.12
Click this button to perform an Insert edit, or press W.

FIGURE 6.13
To make a video-only edit, select that option from the small arrow to the right of the edit buttons.

When the clip is marked and the playhead is where you want the new shot to go, there are three ways to insert the new shot (**Figure 6.12**):

- Click the Insert button.
- Press W.
- Choose Edit > Insert.

The new shot is inserted into the Timeline at the position of the playhead.

With all edits, but especially for inserts, you have another option to consider: What part of the media do you want to edit to the Timeline? You can edit the audio and video, the video only, or the audio only.

There are three ways to control what media from a clip edits to the Timeline (**Figure 6.13**):

- Choose Edit > Source Media, and then pick one of the three options.
- Click the small downward-pointing arrow just to the right of the append edit button and select one of the three options.
- Use one of the three keyboard shortcuts:
  - **Option+1**: Edit video and audio
  - **Option+2**: Edit video-only
  - **Option+3**: Edit audio-only

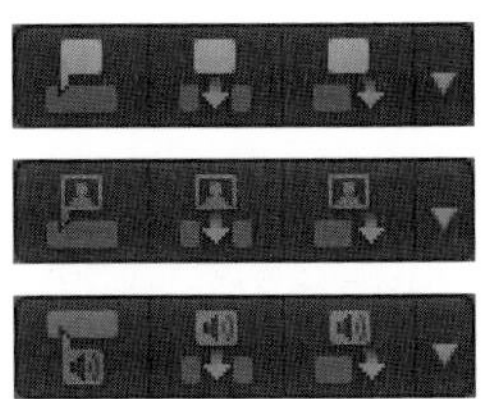

FIGURE 6.14
Different icons mean different functions: audio and video (top), video only (middle), and audio only (bottom).

Whether you choose from the menu or use the keyboard shortcuts, the option you choose remains in effect until you change it.

There's a visual indicator that shows special edit settings are in effect. Take a look at the different color icons in **Figure 6.14**):

- **White boxes:** Audio and video is being edited.
- **Blue icon:** Video only is being edited.
- **Green icon:** Audio only is being edited.

Now that you have the three action shots edited, it's time to cut to a dialog shot (**Figure 6.15**). The process is the same: preview the clip, set the Start, set the End, and edit the shot to the Timeline. Since this is the last shot in the short piece, you can use an append edit and press E. You have now created a four-shot project.

FIGURE 6.15 Here's the last shot in the sequence.

Special Case: Insert into a Range

There's a special case of the insert edit where you can insert a clip into a range in the Timeline. The range can be contained entirely in one clip or span more than one clip. Here's how this works.

1. From the Tool palette, select the Range tool (or press R) (**Figure 6.16**).
2. In the Timeline, drag the Range tool to select the area you want to replace with a new shot (**Figure 6.17**). In this example, I'm selecting the end of the second shot and the beginning of the third shot; ranges can be within a single shot or span between clips.
3. In the Event Browser, mark the clip (this means to select the clip and set the Start and End) you want to edit into this range. In this example, I'm picking a very yellow clip so you'll be able to see the new clip in the Timeline very clearly.
4. Click the Insert button, or press W.

The new clip is edited into the selected range of the Timeline (**Figure 6.18**). But, and this is very important, notice that it *inserted* the clip into the range. The second half of the second clip was pushed down to the right, as were all the downstream clips. No media is lost with an Insert edit.

● **NOTE** Hey! What About Those Storylines (Um, Again)?

By default, an insert edit is applied to the primary storyline. However, if you want to insert a clip to a connected storyline, click the dark-gray bar above the connected storyline to select it, and then position the skimmer (or the playhead) where you want the clip inserted before clicking the Insert button or pressing W. This technique does not work with connected clips.

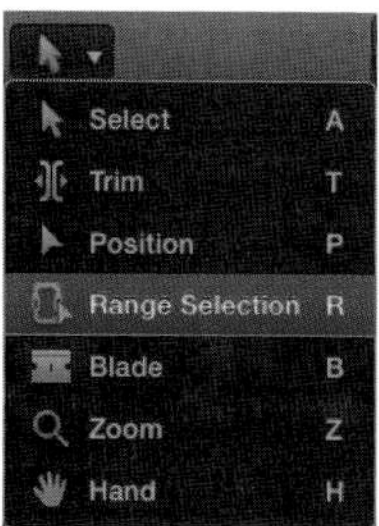

FIGURE 6.16 The Range tool allows you to select a portion of a clip.

FIGURE 6.17 In the Timeline, select the range within a clip, or between clips, that you want to replace with a new shot.

FIGURE 6.18 Here's the new shot inserted into the Timeline. Notice that no media was lost creating this Insert edit.

The Skimmer Can Confuse You

The results of an insert, connect, or overwrite edit vary, depending upon whether the skimmer is active and/or in the Timeline.

- If the skimmer is active and in the Timeline, the edit will place the new clip at the position of the skimmer.
- If the skimmer is active but not in the Timeline, the edit will place the new clip at the position of the playhead.
- If the skimmer is inactive, whether inside or outside the Timeline, the edit will place the new clip at the position of the playhead.

Overwrite Edit

● **NOTE** Can I Lock the Playhead in Place?

Yes. If you want to prevent the playhead from moving when you click the skimmer, just press the Option key when clicking the skimmer, and the playhead won't move. This is very useful when marking clips or when working with effects.

While it is helpful that you can insert into a range in the Timeline, you rarely want to preserve what's in the range. More often than not, you want to replace it.

The append edit is new with Final Cut Pro X; however, FCP 7 editors may be wondering whether their favorite edit, the overwrite edit, made the transition, because that would be perfect for this task. Fortunately, while the overwrite edit didn't get its own button, it did make the trip and has its own menu choice and keyboard shortcut.

Unlike an insert edit, which places a new clip into the Timeline by moving all the downstream clips to the right, an overwrite edit replaces whatever is on the Timeline with the new clip. This means that an overwrite edit, unlike an insert edit, will never change the duration of your Project, unless you edit the clip to the end of your Project.

Let me use some different footage to illustrate this. **Figure 6.19** shows a Project of two clips. The Project runs exactly 15:00.

FIGURE 6.19 Here's the Project you are about to do an overwrite edit into.

In the Event Browser, I have selected and marked a new clip. To overwrite edit this new clip into the Project, either select Edit > Overwrite or press D (Figure 6.19).

Ta-da! The new clip was edited into the Project at the position of the playhead, replacing what was in the Timeline for the duration of the new clip and without changing the duration of the Project (**Figure 6.20**). (The Project still runs exactly 15:00.)

FIGURE 6.20 The new clip replaced what it landed on and did not change the duration of the sequence.

Overwrite Editing into a Range: A Three-Point Edit

Just as you can insert edit into a range, you can also overwrite edit into a range. The procedure is similar.

1. Select the Range tool (press R).
2. Select a range in the Timeline. For the example in **Figure 6.21**, the range spans two clips and runs exactly 3:00. The entire Project runs 15:00.
3. Mark a clip in the Event Browser. In this example, the duration of the Event clip is exactly 7:00; clearly this is longer than the range in the Timeline.
4. Press D to perform an overwrite edit (or choose Edit > Overwrite). The duration of the Project does not change, and the new clip edits into the selected range (Figure 6.21) as the Timeline duration supersedes the Event duration.

FIGURE 6.21 After the edit, the Timeline duration remains unchanged, and the inserted clip is exactly 3:00 in duration.

NOTE What About Storylines?

Yup, you guessed it! By default, an overwrite edit is applied to the primary storyline. However, if you want to overwrite a clip to a connected storyline, click the dark-gray bar above the connected storyline to select it, and then position the skimmer (or the playhead) where you want the clip inserted before pressing D. This technique does not work with connected clips, but you probably guessed that by now.

After the edit, the Timeline duration remains 15:00. This process of overwrite editing into a range is often called a *three-point* edit, because you need three points—the Start and End in the Timeline and the Start in the Event Browser—in order to perform the edit.

Backtime Edit

Sometimes, and sports comes instantly to mind, you care more about where a clip ends in the edit than where it starts. (Think of a runner crossing the finish line in a highlights reel—the end is much more important than the start.)

This type of edit is called a *backtime* edit, and you can do it in Final Cut Pro X as well. Here's how.

FIGURE 6.22
Here's the next clip; you want to edit the clip based upon the End of the shot.

1. Select the clip in the Event Browser that you want to edit into the Timeline. Notice that in the last frame of the shot the tip of his hand is almost touching the wooden rail (**Figure 6.22**). (He's been throwing stones in the lake.)
2. Deactivate the skimmer—I find the skimmer doesn't give me the accuracy I prefer, though using the skimmer is faster than moving the playhead. Both work.
3. Place the playhead in the Timeline where you want the last frame of the selected clip to *end*.
4. Press Shift+D. (There is no button for this, nor is there a menu option.)

   The Event Browser clip is edited to the Timeline such that the *last* frame of the Browser clip matches the position of the playhead in the Timeline. You can see this in **Figure 6.23**. The small image on the left is the Browser clip; his hand is just touching the rail. The big image on the right is the Timeline clip, where his hand is just touching the rail. Perfect match!

FIGURE 6.23
Just double-checking that the ending of both clips match.

In addition to a backtime overwrite edit (which is what this is), you can also do a backtime insert edit (press Shift+W) and a backtime connected edit (press Shift+Q). I'll get into connected edits after this next section on replace edits.

Replace Edit

A replace edit replaces the contents of one clip, or a selected range, with another clip. A replace edit can be done to any clip in the Timeline. You can replace from the start of a clip or the end of a clip. This is a big change for Final Cut Pro 7 editors, where you could also replace from the position of the playhead, which you can't do in FCP X.

You can also use replace edits to add clips to Auditions, which I'll talk about later in this chapter.

FIGURE 6.24
Dragging a clip on top of another clip turns the bottom clip white—this is the indicator for a replace edit.

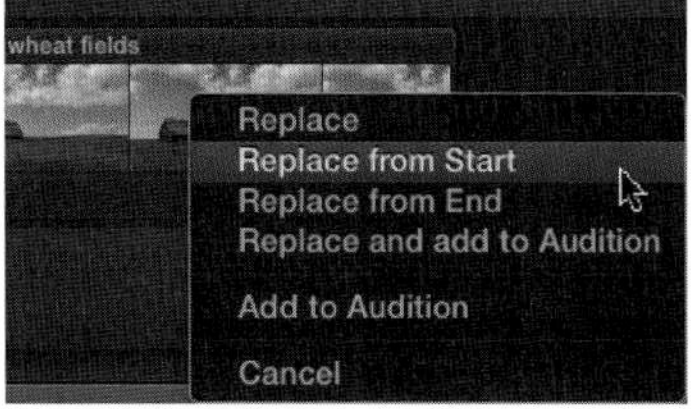

FIGURE 6.25
There are three options for a replace edit, plus the ability to create an Audition.

Replace edits don't exist on any menu. Here's how you do it:

1. Select and mark a clip in the Event Browser that you want to use to replace a clip in the Timeline.
2. Drag the clip from the Browser directly on top of the clip you want to replace in the Timeline. The Timeline clip turns white (**Figure 6.24**).
3. Let go of the mouse.
4. Make your selection from the pop-up menu that appears (**Figure 6.25**):
   - **Replace:** The Timeline clip is replaced by the Browser clip. If the durations of the two clips are different, the Timeline is altered to match the duration of the Browser clip. The start of the newly replaced Timeline clip matches the start of the Browser clip.
   - **Replace from Start:** The Timeline clip is replaced by the Browser clip, starting at the beginning of the Browser clip. The duration of the Timeline clip does not change.
   - **Replace from End:** The Timeline clip is replaced by the Browser clip, starting from the end of the Browser clip. The duration of the Timeline clip does not change. (Think of this as a backtime replace edit.)

   The two Audition selections (Replace and add to Audition and Add to Audition) will be discussed in Auditions, in just a few pages.

● **NOTE** **Can You Replace Edit Into a Selected Range?**

No, but there's a workaround.

The replace edit works only with whole clips. However, you can use the Razor Blade tool (press B) to slice the Timeline clip into the sections you need and then replace the section. Chapter 7 discusses the tools in the Tool menu in more detail.

Replace with a Gap

There's a special form of a replace edit, called replace with a gap. This replaces the selected clip with a gap, which is video and audio black. Unlike FCP 7, in order to create a gap in the primary storyline, you have to add a specific object, called a *gap*, if you want to separate two clips. I'll talk about this more in the next two chapters.

If you select a clip and press Shift+Delete or press the small Delete key, the selected clip will be replaced by a gap of exactly the same duration as the clip you deleted.

There are two keyboard shortcuts for these replace options:

- **Shift+R:** Replaces a clip based on the duration of the Browser clip
- **Option+R:** Replaces a clip from the Start, based on the duration of the Timeline clip

Connected Edit

▲ **TIP** Connecting to the Storyline

All clips outside the primary storyline must be connected to the primary storyline—either as a connected clip or as a connected storyline.

Connections are new with Final Cut Pro X. They are essential for B-roll, sound effects, music, and many effects. What connections allow is to stack clips vertically, which allows you to have more than one image or sound playing at the same time.

Connections also allow keeping connected clips in sync with clips in the primary storyline. Connections are always placed into the primary storyline. You can't connect a clip to another connected clip or connected storyline.

A *connected clip* is a single clip connected to the primary storyline. A *connected storyline* is one or more clips grouped into a single entity that is connected to the primary storyline. The principle reasons for using connected storylines are for trimming and transitions. (See Chapters 8 and 10.)

To edit a connected clip to the Timeline, place the skimmer or playhead where you want the clip to connect, and select and mark the clip in the Browser (you should be getting good at this by now). Then do one of the following:

- Click the connected edit button (**Figure 6.26**).
- Choose Edit > Connect to Primary Storyline.
- Press Q.

The selected clip is placed above the primary storyline if the clip contains video (**Figure 6.27**). If the clip is audio-only, it is placed below the primary storyline. Clips can be moved above or below the primary storyline by dragging them.

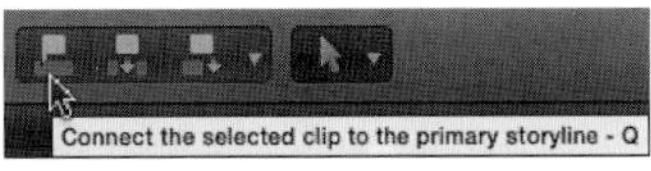

FIGURE 6.26
The first button on the left allows you to create a connected edit.

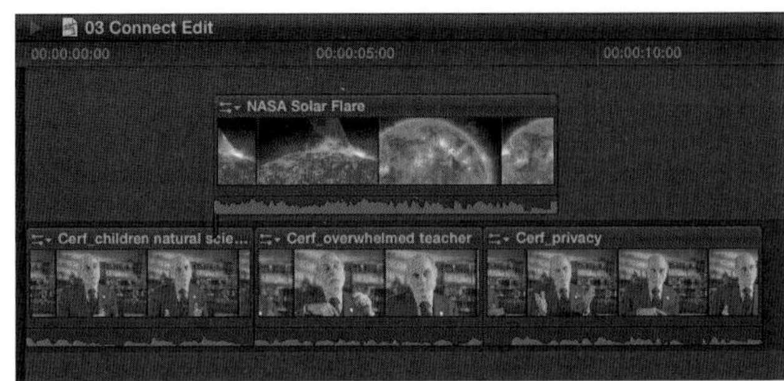

FIGURE 6.27
This is a connected B-roll clip, attached to the primary storyline.

Does It Matter Which Clip Is on Top?

Yes. By default, all video clips are 100 percent full-screen and 100 percent opaque. This means that a video clip on top of another video clip blocks the clip below it. This is why B-roll images are always placed above the video they illustrate. The way you adjust which video clip you can see is via opacity and other effects. I start talking about effects in Chapter 11.

Also, by default, audio clips are placed below the primary storyline. This is because regardless of where an audio clip is placed, you'll be able to hear it. The way you determine which audio clips you want to hear is through audio mixing, which I cover in Chapter 9.

Connections are indicated by small vertical lines connecting the primary storyline with the connected clip or storyline (**Figure 6.28**). If too many connections makes viewing the Timeline difficult, turn them off using the Switch in the lower-right corner of the Timeline. Click the Switch and uncheck Show Connections. The hooks disappear. You can turn them on by clicking the checkbox again.

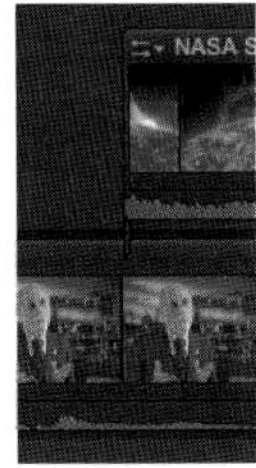

FIGURE 6.28
This is a close-up of the hook, or connection, connecting the top clip with the primary storyline.

The main reason for turning this display off is when you have so many connected clips that the lines between clips get to be distracting. You are not deleting the connections, just making them invisible.

Can You Move a Connection?

By default, the connection point is placed on the first frame of the connected clip. However, you can move the connection. Hold Option+Command and click the connected clip (or the dark-gray bar of a connected storyline) where you want the connection to move.

This is very useful if you want the transition to the connected clip to occur just before an edit but you want the connected clip to link to the clip after the edit.

Special Case: Editing a Connected Clip to or from the Primary Storyline

Sometimes, you may want to move a connected clip to the primary storyline or move a clip from the primary storyline to become a connected clip. If you just drag it, it will ripple changes throughout the entire Project.

Instead, there are two options:

- To move a selected clip, or clips, from the primary storyline, choose Edit > Lift From Primary Storyline, or press Option+Command+Up arrow. The clip moves up, and the space in the primary storyline is replaced with a gap.
- To move a selected connected clip down to the Primary Storyline, choose Edit > Overwrite to Primary Storyline, or press Option+Command+Down arrow.

Several notes about this: First, this works only with clips, not with storylines. Second, you can't move a connected audio-only clip to the primary storyline. And, third, if you don't want to use the keyboard shortcuts, you can achieve the same results using the Position tool, which I cover in Chapter 8.

Connected Storylines

As mentioned, there is a second kind of connected clip, called a *connected storyline*. This is one or more clips grouped together and connected to the primary storyline. Connected storylines have a variety of benefits compared to connected clips. Some include more trimming options (Chapter 8) and transitions (Chapter 10). For this reason, I won't spend a lot of time with them here.

To create a connected storyline, select a connected clip and do one of the following:

- Press Command+G.
- Choose Clip > Create Storyline.

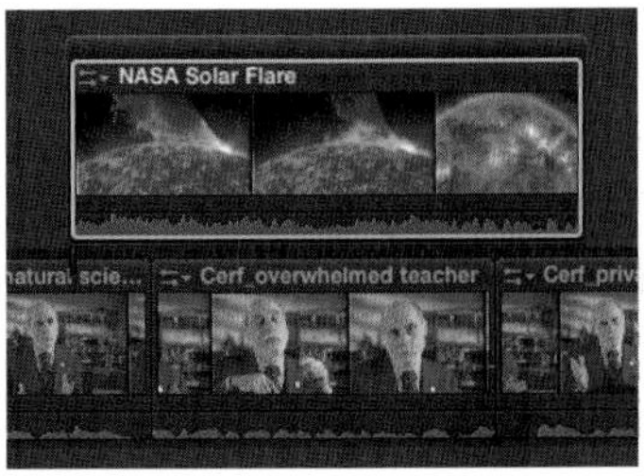

You can tell a connected storyline from a connected clip by looking for the dark-gray bar above the clip, which is the symbol of a connected storyline (**Figure 6.29**).

FIGURE 6.29
Connected storylines have a dark-gray bar across the top. Connected clips don't.

Just as you can edit clips into the primary storyline, you can edit clips into a connected storyline. The procedure is nearly the same. The key difference is that you need to select the connected storyline first and then edit into it.

Specifically, you can do the following:

- Append edit
- Insert edit
- Insert into a range
- Overwrite edit
- Overwrite into a range
- Backtime edit
- Replace edit

All the standard edits that you just learned in the primary storyline work the same in a connected storyline.

You can also drag a clip into a connected storyline or remove a clip from the storyline by dragging it out. A clip that is dragged out of a connected storyline becomes a connected clip, unless you drag it out and into the primary storyline.

You can disassemble a connected storyline into its component clips, by either selecting Clip > Break Apart Clip or pressing Shift+Command+G.

The Importance of Being a Storyline

The power of using storylines lies in far more than just editing. A connected storyline can be moved around like a single clip, supports a wider range of trimming, and allows you to add transitions. The main difference between the primary storyline and a connected storyline is that you connect media to the primary storyline, which you can't do for a connected storyline (or clip).

Connected clips are simple to add, but connected storylines are much more flexible. The one thing you can't do to a connected storyline is apply effects to it, but you can apply effects to the individual clips inside the connected storyline. To apply effects to a group of clips, you use compound clips, which I will discuss in Chapter 7.

Dragging Clips from the Finder

You can even drag clips into your Project directly from the Finder. When you do, a few special rules apply:

- You can drag clips from the Finder directly into the Timeline or on top of the name of the Event in the Event Library.
- Finder clips are analyzed according to current preference settings.
- Finder clips that you drag into the Timeline are linked to the source Event that you selected when the Project was first created.
- Finder clips that are dragged into an Event are linked to that Event.

Dragging Finder clips allows you to do one of four edits:

- **Append edit:** Drag clip to the end of the storyline you want the clip added to.
- **Insert edit:** Drag the clip between two other clips.
- **Replace edit:** Drag the clip on top of the clip you want it to replace.
- **Connected edit:** Drag the clip above the clip on the primary storyline where you want the clip to connect.

To drag a clip from the Finder into FCP X, you need to see both the clip in the Finder and FCP X.

Creating Auditions

Just as connections are new with FCP X, so are Auditions. An Audition is a group of clips that act as a single clip in the Timeline. Auditions are not like multiclips, as in Final Cut Pro 7, where you can see multiple images at the same time. Instead, think of an Audition as a very fast way to do a replace edit—switching from one clip to the next until you find the shot that works best.

For example, you could use Auditions to determine the best take in a performance, choose the best B-roll clip to use to illustrate a point, or compare different endings to find which works the best.

You can create Auditions in the Event Browser or the Timeline. Because an Audition keeps all the clips in it "live," it is a good idea to finalize an Audition in the Timeline when you've picked the version you want to use.

Caution: Auditions Use Whole Clips

Because you cannot set a Start and an End on more than one clip in the Event Browser, when you build an Audition, the entire clip is included. This means you will need to trim the final Audition clip in the Timeline after you decide which version to use.

However, there is a workaround. You can select the region you want to use in each clip and mark it as a Favorite. Then, in the All Clips menu, display only Favorites. You can build an Audition from just those Favorite selections.

Let's illustrate this with an example. I have an interview with Dr. Vint Cerf in which he discusses the interplanetary Internet (a conversation, by the way, that I found flat-out mind-bending). I want to use an Audition to pick the best NASA video clip to illustrate what Dr. Cerf is talking about.

In the Event Browser I selected three of the NASA video clips.

1. Once your clips are selected, create an Audition by doing one of the following (**Figure 6.30**):

FIGURE 6.30 Auditions are easiest to create in the Event Browser. Select the clips you want to combine into an Audition, and then create the Audition from the pop-up menu.

- Right-clicking one of the selected clips and selecting Create Audition
- Pressing Command+Y
- Choosing Clips > Audition > Create Audition

2. The Audition clip appears in the Browser with the Audition icon in the top-left corner. Each of the clips inside it can be easily accessed using either a keyboard shortcut (Control+[left/right arrow]) or a menu choice. Audition clips are indicated by a small "spotlight" icon near the top-left corner. Edit the Audition into the Timeline—generally, as a connected clip.

Caution: Spaces Interferes with Auditions

Spaces, the ability to extend your desktop using multiple workspaces, uses the same keyboard shortcut as Audition. You can change the Spaces keyboard shortcut in the Finder by choosing[Apple logo] > System Preferences > Keyboard > Keyboard Layouts.

3. To see the contents of an Audition, select it and press Y (or choose Clip > Audition > Open Audition (**Figure 6.31**).

   This opens a small window where you can see all the different clips in the Audition. The clip that is currently displayed in the Audition is called the *pick*.

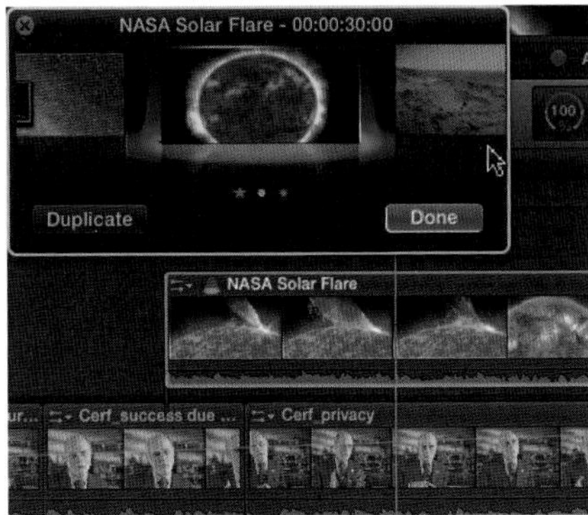

FIGURE 6.31
To view the contents of an Audition, press Y.

4. With the Audition window active, switch between clips by either clicking near the left or right edges of the Audition window or using the keyboard shortcut right arrow to go to the next clip in the Audition or left arrow to go to the previous clip.

   If the Audition clips were different durations, the duration of the Audition would change as different clips were selected as the pick. This duration change would shift all the downstream clips so that sync would be maintained.

5. When you have found the clip you want to use, click Done.

6. You can add a clip to an Audition, or replace an existing clip, by dragging a clip from the Event Browser directly on top of the Audition until the Audition turns white. Then, let go of the mouse (**Figure 6.32**).

   Replace and add to Audition: FCP will replace the currently displayed clip with the new one.

   Add to Audition: The new clip will be added to the Audition without affecting any of the other clips.

   If you select one of the top three replace options, the Audition will be replaced by the clip you dragged down from the Browser.

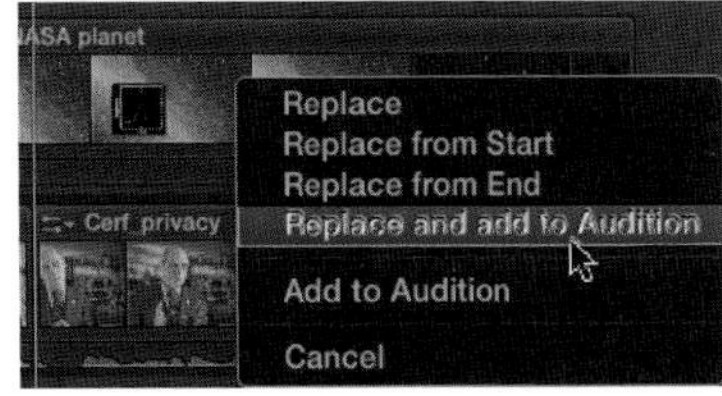

FIGURE 6.32
Not only can you replace individual clips, you can also add to, or replace, clips in an Audition.

7. To remove a clip from an Audition, open the Audition (press Y), display the clip you want to delete in the small window, and press the Delete key.
8. To finalize an Audition, which removes all the clips you don't want, display the clip you want to use in the final version, and then do one of the following:
   - Right-click the Audition and choose > Audition > Finalize Audition.
   - Press Shift+Option+Y.
   - Select Clip > Audition > Finalize Audition.

   All the clips you don't want disappear, leaving just the clip you do want.

NOTE Can You Apply Effects or Transitions to Auditions?

Yes. You treat an Audition as though it is a stand-alone clip. Apply transitions and effects with no problem. As you switch between clips, the transitions and effects switch with the clip. The only potential problem is that if the Audition clip does not have sufficient handles for the transition, the transition is either shortened or removed.

I think Auditions have a lot of potential, but they have two limitations you need to be careful of:

- Because the Event Browser does not remember the Start and End of more than one clip, creating Auditions requires using whole clips. A workaround to this is to view only favorites or clip ranges in a keyword collection before creating Auditions.
- You can't set a duration for an Audition. The duration of the Audition changes as the pick clip changes. While you can trim the duration for each individual clip, if you add a new clip to the Audition, the Audition duration changes to match the new clip. This means that changing between three different Audition clips creates wildly different durations in the Timeline.

If precise clip duration is important, it might be faster to simply use replace edits—which do respect the duration of the clip in the Timeline.

Auditions provide an alternative way of previewing clips in context, and the ability to switch quickly between them can help you find the right shot faster.

Summary

Editing is central to why you use Final Cut Pro X. Editing is also central to good storytelling. Editing video has two principle goals, one creative and the other business. Our creative goal is to craft a compelling visual story that other people want to watch. Our business goal is to create this story as efficiently as possible, while still maintaining the highest possible quality.

The tools covered in this chapter help you meet both these goals. The more software helps you achieve both these goals, the more likely you are to sleep better—and longer—at night.

Keyboard Shortcuts

Shortcut	What It Does
Command+N	Create new Project
I	Set the Start (In) of a clip
Shift+I	Jump playhead to Start of a clip
Option+I	Delete the Start of a clip
O	Set the End (Out) of a clip
Shift+O	Jump playhead to the End of a clip
Option+O	Delete the Out of a clip
X	Select the entire clip the playhead or the skimmer is in
N	Toggle snapping on or off
S	Toggle the skimmer on or off
Shift+S	Toggle audio skimming on or off
E	Perform an append edit
D	Perform an overwrite edit
Shift+D	Perform a backtime overwrite edit
W	Perform an insert edit
Shift+W	Perform a backtime insert edit
Q	Perform a connected edit
Shift+Q	Perform a backtime connected edit
Option+1	Enable audio and video edit
Option+2	Enable video-only edit
Option+3	Enable audio-only edit
Shift+?	Play around current playhead position
Y	Open Audition
Command+Y	Create Audition

continues on next page

Keyboard Shortcuts (*continued*)

Shortcut	What It Does
Control+Command+Y	Preview Audition
Shift+Option+Y	Finalize Audition
Control+[right arrow]	Move to next Audition pick
Control+[left arrow}	Move to previous Audition pick
Command+[comma]	Open Preferences window
R	Select the Range Selection tool
A	Select the Selection (Arrow) tool
Control+D	Change clip duration
/	Play selected clip, or range, from Start to End
Up/Down Arrows	Jump to earlier, or later, clip positioning the playhead on the Start of the clip
Shift+R	Replace edit based on Browser clip
Option+R	Replace edit based on Timeline clip
Shift+Command+G	Break apart the selected storyline or compound clip
Option+click	Lock the playhead in place so it doesn't jump to the skimmer position
Option+Command+click	Move a connection to the location of the click

ORGANIZING YOUR EDIT

In the previous chapter, you learned new ways to edit your clips into the Timeline. There, the goal was to get a rough cut built so you could see what you actually had to work with.

In this chapter and the next, you'll turn that rough cut into a polished gem. This chapter looks at all the different ways you can organize your clips, from tools to techniques to technology, with a special section on the new Roles feature in version 10.0.1. In the next chapter, you'll discover how to adjust the edit point—that place where two clips touch—in a process called *trimming*.

Making Selections

The number-one interface rule of Final Cut Pro X is "Select something and do something to it." Invariably, whenever you want to accomplish a task, you need to select something first. So, let's start at the beginning and make sure you know how to select things properly.

There are several ways you'll be selecting or deleting your clips. The tables on the right provide summaries based on the following categories:

- **Selecting Clips**

  The best place to start is to learn how to select clips. **Table 7.1** summarizes how to select clips according to the results you want to achieve.

- **Selecting a Range**

  Table 7.2 summarizes how to select a range within a clip.

- **Deselecting Clips**

  Table 7.3 summarizes how to deselect a clip.

- **Deleting Clips**

  Table 7.4 summarizes how to delete a clip.

Using Markers and To-Dos

Markers are a feature of every version of Final Cut Pro, but To-Dos are new with FCP X. Markers are reference points attached to clips. Think of them as frame-accurate yellow sticky notes, which you can position and write on however you want.

Markers can be added to clips in either the Event Browser or the Timeline. If you add markers to a clip in the Event Browser, they are visible in both Filmstrip and List views. Plus, Event Browser markers travel with the clip down to the Timeline.

A key difference with markers in FCP X is that markers are always applied to the clip; Timeline markers don't exist. Markers can be applied to any clip in the Event Browser or the Timeline. They are not visible in the Viewer. Markers can be added in real time, during playback, or by specifically positioning the skimmer (or playhead) on the exact frame you want to mark.

TABLE 7.1 Selecting Clips

What You Do	What It Does
Click a clip	Selects a single clip
Hover skimmer over a clip and press C	Selects the entire clip underneath the skimmer
Click the first clip and Shift-click the last clip	Selects every clip between the first and last clips, including the first and last clips
With the Arrow tool (A), drag a rectangle around a group of clips	Selects every clip touched by the border of the selection rectangle
Hold the Command key and click a variety of clips	Selects whatever clips you click, whether they are next to each other or not
Select a single clip and then press Command+A	Selects all clips in selected pane
Choose Edit > Select All	Selects all clips in selected pane

TABLE 7.3 Deselecting Clips

What You Do	What It Does
Click a different clip	Deselects the previously selected clip
Command-click selected clips	Deselects the clips clicked on
Press Shift+Command+A	Deselects all selected clips
Choose Edit > Select > None	Deselects all selected clips
Click in the background of a pane	Deselects all selected clips

TABLE 7.2 Selecting a Range Within a Clip

What You Do	What It Does
In the Event Browser, drag across any clip	Selects a range within a single clip
In the Timeline, use the Range Selection tool (R) and drag	Selects a range across a single, or multiple, clips
In the Browser or Timeline, position skimmer or playhead and press I, move skimmer or playhead, and press O	Selects Start and End of range
Move skimmer (or playhead) over a clip and press X	Selects range selection for entire clip (range selections can be adjusted for duration; clip selections can't)

TABLE 7.4 Deleting Selected Clips

What You Do	What It Does
Press the big Delete key for clips in the Timeline	Deletes selected clip(s) in the Timeline and any connected clips, pulling up all downstream clips so there is no gap.
Press the small Delete key (next to the End key)	Deletes the selected clip(s) and replaces them with a gap. This means the downstream clips don't move.
Press Shift+Delete	Same results as pressing the small Delete key.
Press Command+X	Cuts selected clip to the clipboard. Downstream clips move left to close any potential gap.
Select the dark-gray bar of a connected storyline and press Delete	Deletes the entire connected storyline.

FIGURE 7.1 Here's a marker—the blue dot at the top—added at the position of the skimmer.

Adding and Changing Markers

Whether you are working in the Event Browser or the Timeline, the process of adding and changing markers is the same. To add a marker to a clip in the primary storyline, position the skimmer or the playhead where you want the marker to appear and do one of the following:

- Press M (which also allows adding markers in real time).
- Choose Mark > Markers > Add Marker.

Markers appear as small blue shapes at the top of the clip. There is only one marker color: blue (**Figure 7.1**). (Well, there are also red and green markers, but these are a special case I will discuss later.)

▲ TIP Hey, Can You Add Markers in Real Time?

Yes. Press M as you are playing or skimming your Timeline or clip. By default, markers will be added to the primary storyline, unless you select another clip before you start skimming...or playing.

To add a marker to a connected clip or connected storyline, select the clip or storyline first, and then press M.

The Marker Information window (**Figure 7.2**) allows you to add text to the marker, convert it to a To-Do item, or delete the marker.

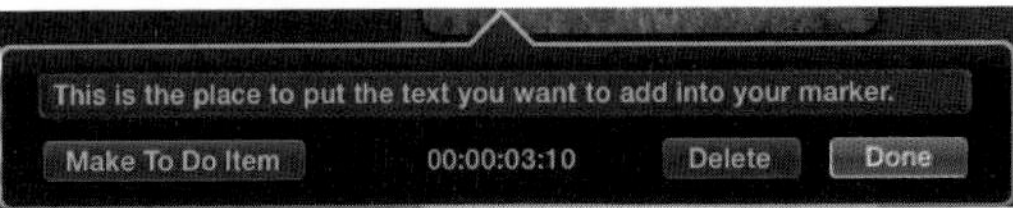

FIGURE 7.2 This is the new look of the Marker Information window.

To open the Marker Information window, do one of the following:

- Double-click the marker.
- Navigate to the marker, and then press M.
- Select the marker by clicking it and press Shift+M.
- Select the marker and then choose Mark > Markers > Modify Marker.
- Right-click the marker and select from the pop-up menu.

▲ TIP A Recommendation

Shift+M is a better choice for opening an existing marker than pressing M, because M always creates a new marker. If the skimmer or playhead is not precisely parked on the marker, you run the risk of creating a second marker very close to the original marker. Pressing Shift+M opens the Marker Information window, without first creating a marker.

Introducing To-Dos

Although markers are blue, there are two other marker colors: red and green. A red marker is an uncompleted To-Do item, while a green marker is a completed To-Do item (**Figure 7.3**).

FIGURE 7.3 A To-Do marker reminds you that you have...wait for it...something to do!

A To-Do is a special kind of marker that allows you track tasks. Figure 7.3 shows a To-Do; these are very simple; you can't assign dates, priorities, or resources. Think of it, instead, as a reminder. You'll see this again later in this chapter when I talk about the Timeline Index.

To convert a marker to a To-Do, do one of the following:

- Open the Marker Information box and click Make To Do Item.
- Right-click the marker and select Make To Do Item from the pop-up menu.

You'll never guess what you need to do to turn a To-Do into a Completed To-Do. Darn! You guessed.... Whether you add markers in the Event Browser or in the Timeline, the process and the look are exactly the same. However, markers are not visible in the Viewer.

Moving Markers

You can also move markers—either by nudging or in large increments (**Figure 7.4**). To nudge a marker, click the marker to select it, and then do one of the following:

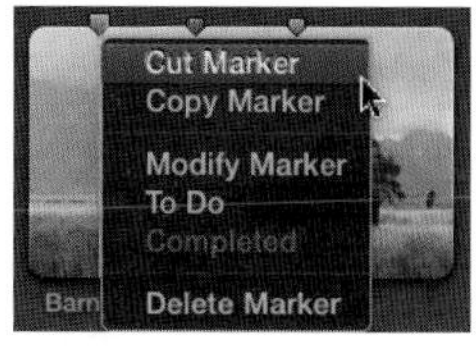

FIGURE 7.4 Markers can be nudged, moved, copied, and pasted.

- Press Control+[period] to move the marker one frame to the right.
- Press Control+[comma] to move the marker one frame to the left.
- Choose Mark > Markers > Nudge Markers Right (or Left).

To move a marker, right-click it and choose Cut or Copy from the pop-up menu. Then, move the skimmer to the new marker location and paste it via one of the following:

- Choose Edit > Paste.
- Press Command+V.
- Right-click and select Paste from the pop-up menu.

Unlike Final Cut Pro 7, you cannot move a marker by dragging it. Delete a marker by doing one of the following:

- Click the Delete button in the Marker Information box.
- Right-click a marker and select Delete Marker from the pop-up menu (**Figure 7.5**).
- Select a marker by hovering the skimmer over it and pressing Control+M.
- You can also delete a marker in the Event Browser when it is in List view by right-clicking a marker and selecting Delete Marker from the pop-up menu.

● **NOTE** What Happens If You Press the Delete Key?

In this case, you won't delete the selected marker. Instead, you'll flag the frame the marker is on as Rejected.

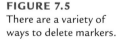

FIGURE 7.5 There are a variety of ways to delete markers.

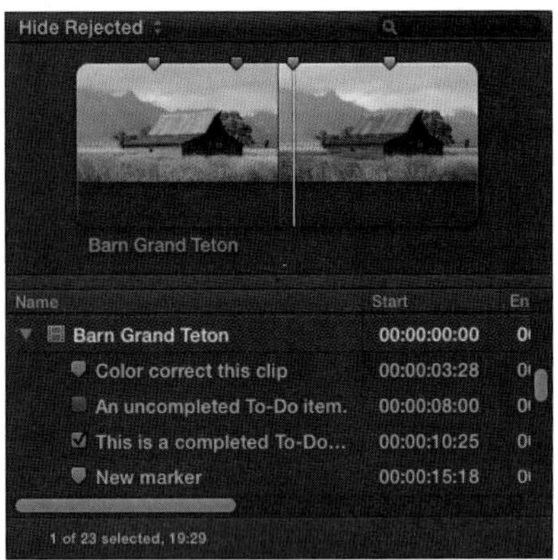

FIGURE 7.6
Markers, like keywords, are also displayed in List view in the Event Browser.

Accessing Marker Options

When clips are displayed in the Event Browser in List view, a small triangle to the left of the clip name indicates when keywords, ratings, or markers are applied to a clip (**Figure 7.6**).

In this example, there are two markers, plus an uncompleted To-Do and completed To-Do associated with this clip. (You can also complete a To-Do by checking it in this list.)

Right-clicking the marker icon or name provides an additional way to access marker options. You can quickly use this right-click technique to access the Marker Information window. While you cannot change the marker name in Filmstrip view, you *can* change the marker name in List view.

Markers are like yellow sticky notes—they provide reminders, locations, and general assistance during the process of editing a project.

Are FCP X Markers Like FCP 7 Markers?

FCP X markers don't do as much as markers in Final Cut Pro 7. FCP X markers don't

- Have as many colors (aside from red, green, and blue)
- Move by dragging
- Link to the Timeline (rather, they link to the clip)
- Include both a title and a label
- Display in the Viewer
- Allow individual colors to be displayed or hidden
- Export as a tab-delimited text file (markers are included, though, in an XML export)

Copy and Paste Options

Copy and Paste still exists, though you probably gathered that already during the markers section. Specifically, you can copy (Command+C) or cut (Command+X) a clip. Then position the skimmer or the playhead and paste (Command+V). A connected clip will always be pasted as a connected clip. A primary storyline clip is generally pasted back into the primary storyline; however, you have two options to paste it as **Table 7.5** illustrates.

TABLE 7.5 Clip Pasting Options

Name	What You Do	What It Does
Paste as Connected	Option+V	Pastes the clipboard as a connected clip and connects it to the primary storyline
Paste Insert	Command+V	Insert edits the clipboard at the location of the skimmer or playhead

I'm not sure where to talk about this, so I'll cover it now. Most of the time, you want connected clips to stay separate from the primary storyline. However, choosing Edit > Overwrite to Primary Storyline merges the connected clip with the primary storyline.

Select the connected clip you want to merge and press Option+Command+[down arrow]. The connected clip does an overwrite edit straight down into the primary storyline. This makes it very easy to merge a connected clip into the primary storyline.

The Magnetic Timeline

The Magnetic Timeline is a huge new feature—and one that I am enjoying more and more as I work with it. However, there isn't much to write about it. The beauty of the Magnetic Timeline is that as you move a clip or a group of clips, everything else gets out of the way. The first time I saw it, I was reminded of the Knight Bus in the *Harry Potter* books, where buildings scrambled to get out of the way of a wayward bus driven by a demented bus driver.

Anyway, the Magnetic Timeline is always on (though you can override its normal behavior using the Position tool, which I'll discuss soon). Grab something and drag it. Watch what happens. Giggle. Do it again (**Figure 7.7**). You'll like it!

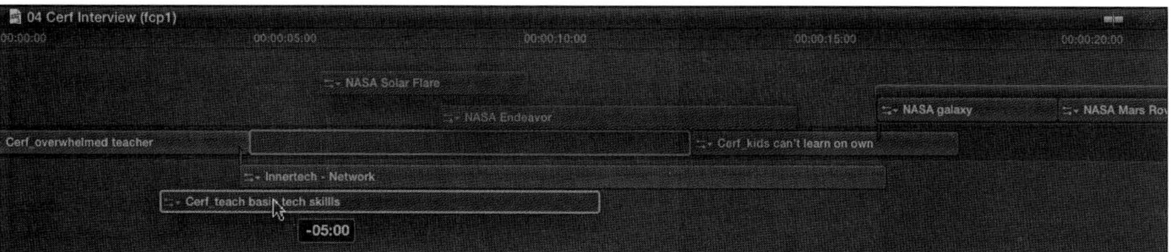

FIGURE 7.7 The Magnetic Timeline is hard to write about and terrific fun to play with.

NOTE Really? That's It?

The Magnetic Timeline always does an Insert edit between two clips. When dragging clips with the Arrow (Selection) tool, you can drop clips only between clips, never in the middle of two clips. This prevents you from accidentally splitting a clip (or splinching, if you want to continue the Harry Potter analogy...).

The Magic of Compound Clips

Compound clips are not new with Final Cut Pro X, but they are repackaged. In Final Cut Pro 7, we called them *nests*, and they allowed you to edit one sequence into another sequence. While sequences don't exist in FCP X, the ability to put one collection of clips into another remains possible. You do this using compound clips.

A compound clip is a collection of media—video, audio, and/or stills—that can be manipulated as though it were a single clip. They can be reedited, have effects applied, moved around, used more than once—all the things you would expect of a single clip. They also allow you to simplify a complex portion of the Timeline.

Compound clips can be created in the Event Browser or in the Timeline. The benefit to creating compound clips in the Event Browser is that you can use them in more than one Project. The benefit to creating compound clips in the Timeline is that you can use them to simplify a complex sequence or apply a single filter to a group of clips.

Create a Compound Clip in the Timeline

Here's a simple example of how to create a compound clip in the Timeline. In this Project, I have a connected storyline and two separate connected clips—one video and one audio (**Figure 7.8**).

FIGURE 7.8 Here are several connected elements, attached to several primary storyline clips.

1. Select the clips you want to combine into one compound clip—in this case, I'll coalesce everything into one compound clip.
2. Choose File > Create Compound Clip, or press Option+G; or, right-click and select New Compound Clip from the contextual menu.

   Notice how a compound clip reduces all the selected clips to a single clip that's easy to find and move. You could now apply an effect, color correction, or...well, now that all these clips are in one place, you could do just about anything with them (**Figure 7.9**).

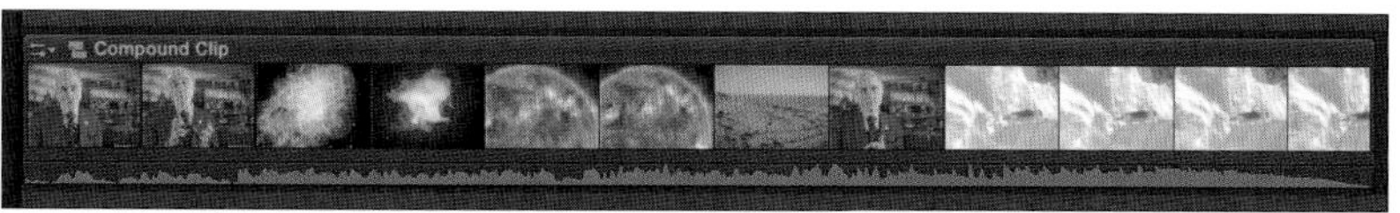

FIGURE 7.9
A compound clip reduces all the selected clips into a single, easy to find and move clip.

If you selected clips in the Timeline, the compound clip appears in the Timeline; If you selected clips in the Event Browser, the compound clip appears in the Event Browser. The process is the same: Select a group of clips, and then create the compound clip.

3. Open a compound clip in the Timeline by double-clicking. This allows you to see its contents and reedit them.
4. Compound clips can be renamed at any time—in the Inspector. Select the compound clip you want to rename, go to the Inspector, and click Info at the top (**Figure 7.10**).
5. Be sure you are in either Basic View or General View (Basic View is the default) and scroll up to the top. Change the name in the Name field.

FIGURE 7.10
Compound clips can be renamed in the Info tab of the Inspector.

Disassemble a compound clip by doing the following:

1. Select the compound clip.
2. Choose Clip > Break Apart Clips or press Shift+Command+G.

Essentially, a compound clip acts just like any project. All clips can be edited, replaced, modified...everything. In fact, the settings of a compound clip don't even have to match the settings of the Project they are placed in.

Create a Compound Clip in the Event Browser

The process of creating a compound clip in the Event Browser is the same as in the Timeline:

1. Select the clips you want to include in the compound clip in the Event Browser.
2. While you can create a new compound clip from the File menu, you can also do so from the contextual menu. Right-click a clip and select New Compound Clip
3. Just like a Project file, you need to give the compound clip a name and assign it the same technical characteristics you provide to a new Project (**Figure 7.11**). In this case, you are creating a new compound clip named Nature Scenes. These settings, including timecode, do not need to match the Project settings.

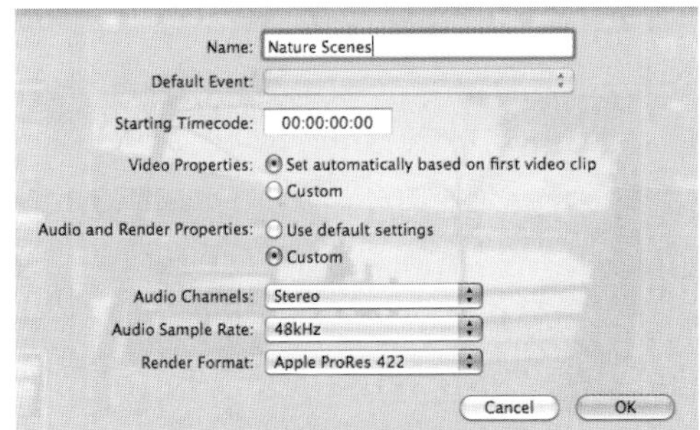

FIGURE 7.11
Just like a Project, you need to set, or confirm, the properties of a compound clip. These do not need to match the properties of the Project.

FIGURE 7.12
Note the small symbol in the top-left corner? This is the only indication this is a compound clip.

4. When you click OK, the new compound clip appears in the Event Browser. Notice the small "interlinked hands" symbol in the top-left corner? This is the indicator for a compound clip (**Figure 7.12**). In this case, it displays the name you gave it: Nature Scenes.

The real advantage—and it is a *huge* advantage—with creating a compound clip in the Event Browser is that you can add whatever clips you want to it, and they all remain in the Event Browser.

For example, double-click a compound clip in the Event Browser, which opens it into the Timeline. There, you can add, rearrange, or delete whatever clips you want. When I close this compound clip, by opening another Project, it goes back to the Event Browser, *not* the Project Library.

For instance, you could use a compound clip to create a standard program open that could be updated and reused for every show, create a reusable split-screen effect, collect all your SD clips to include in an HD Project, or desaturate an entire group of clips....

In other words, compound clips behave similarly to Projects, except compound clips can be stored in the Event Browser, and you can add filters and effects to them as if they were a single clip. Plus, and this is a huge benefit, the same compound clip can be reused over and over in multiple projects.

▲ TIP Create an Empty Compound Clip

You can also create an empty compound clip in the Event Browser, into which you can add clips as necessary. To do this, make sure no clips are selected in the Event Library and then choose File > New Compound Clip. The new, empty, compound clip appears in the Event Browser.

Pssst...Wanna Build a Selects Sequence—Fast?

A really handy use of a compound clip is to build a collection of all the clips you want to use for a particular scene—these are often called a *selects reel*, or just *selects*.

Command-click all the clips in the Event Browser that you want to add into a compound clip, and then choose File > Create New Compound Clip. All selected clips are added to the compound clip based on the sort order of the Event Browser. You can then rearrange them as much as you want inside the compound clip.

Deconstruct a Compound Clip

If you need to break apart the compound clip to restore all the individual clips, you can—and there are three ways to do it (**Figure 7.13**):

- Right-click the compound clip and select Break Apart Clip.
- Choose Clip > Break Apart Clip Items.
- Press Shift+Command+G.

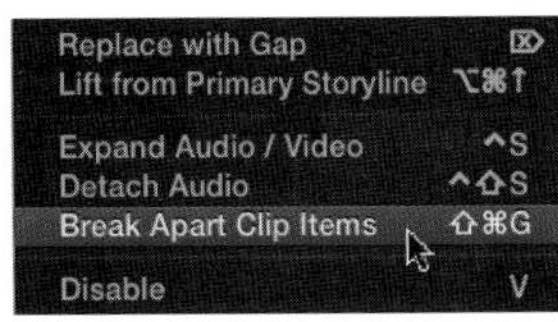

FIGURE 7.13 Compound clips can also be disassembled by keyboard shortcut or menu choice.

Moving clips into and out of compound clips is a fast way to move large groups of clips, organize the Timeline, or build "mini-projects" that you can use over and over in different projects. Compound clips are easy to create, versatile, and very, very handy to know.

Compound Clips Have Fixed Durations

If you add clips to a compound clip only to discover that the clips at the end are dim with cross-hatching, this means that the compound clip is not long enough to include all the clips you have added (**Figure 7.14**). (FCP 7 editors may recognize that left-pointing arrow at the top of the Timeline as an Out, which indicates the end of the compound clip.)

FIGURE 7.14 Compound clips, unlike Projects, have fixed durations.

To fix this problem, go back up a level to the Project (or compound clip) that contains this compound clip and increase its duration. When you step back into the compound clip, the cross-hatching will move to the right and the Out will be reset to the new duration.

Navigating the Timeline History

When you double-click a compound clip contained in the Timeline, there is something new: two arrows in the top-left corner of the Timeline. The text changes depending upon where you are (**Figure 7.15**). The arrows both indicate and navigate the Timeline History.

If you are just in the Timeline, the Project name is displayed at the top left. If you are in a compound clip inside the Timeline, the text shows the path from the master Project to where you are now.

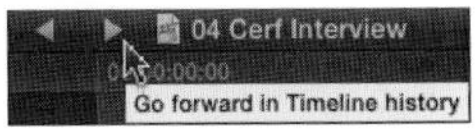

FIGURE 7.15 These two arrows constitute the Timeline History—allowing you to quickly switch between Timelines that have been opened this session, including compound clips.

The Timeline History is a list of every Project or compound clip that you opened since you started Final Cut Pro for this session. The Timeline History offers a fast way to move between Projects and compound clips and is there to help you navigate between Projects without having to return to the Project Library all the time.

Click the left arrow to move back up a level to the containing Project you were working on previous to the current Project; or you can press Command+[. Click the right arrow to move forward deeper into the Project you were working on; or you can press Command+].

A Grab Bag of Tools

There are a number of tools that you'll find are pretty handy in the editing process. This section covers a bunch of them.

Enable, Disable, and Solo Clips

By default, all clips are visible, 100 percent full-screen (except, potentially, for stills), and 100 percent opaque. Apple calls these clips *enabled*. However, there is a simple keystroke that can make a clip invisible, or *disabled*.

For instance, **Figure 7.16** shows two copies of the same clip: The left clip is visible, and the right clip is invisible. Notice the difference in clip color?

FIGURE 7.16 Enabled clips glow brightly in the Timeline; disabled clips are dim.

To toggle the visibility of a clip, press V, or choose Clip > Enable. When a clip is disabled, it won't display in the Timeline, it won't render, it won't make a sound, and it won't export. It acts as though it is not there—except that it is.

Also, there is a special audio feature I should mention: soloing. To *solo* a clip means that you can hear *only* that clip and no others (**Figure 7.17**).

FIGURE 7.17 When active, the Solo button glows gold. A soloed clip glows with color, while all other clips turn gray.

To solo a clip, select it and press Option+S. Or, choose Clip > Solo. Or, and my personal favorite, click the Solo button in the top-right corner of the Timeline. Notice that all the clips in the Timeline are black-and-white except the soloed clip? To unsolo a clip, click the Solo button again. You can solo more than one clip at a time.

While enable and disable apply to both audio and video, Solo applies only to audio clips.

The Tool Palette

Just as with earlier versions of Final Cut, there are a variety of tools to help in the editing and effects process. You find them by clicking the Select tool just to the left of the Dashboard (**Figure 7.18**).

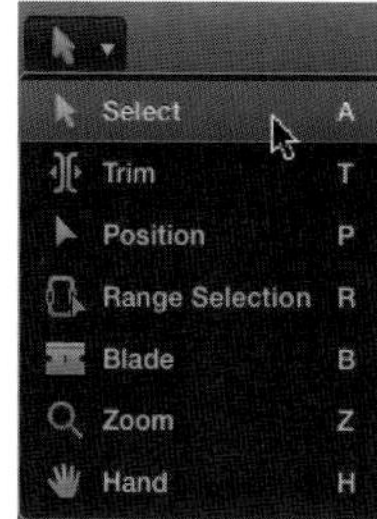

FIGURE 7.18
There are seven tools in FCP X—all stored in the Tool palette.

The **Select tool** (often referred to as the Arrow tool) is the default, general-purpose tool that you've been using all along. It selects stuff, moves stuff, and, in general, accomplishes virtually everything you need, except when you need something specific—which is where the rest of the tools come in. (Keyboard shortcut: A.)

The **Trim tool** is used exclusively for trimming where two clips touch—called the *edit point*. The process of trimming is really important, and this tool plays a vital role. It's so vital, in fact, that I'm devoting the next chapter to explaining how it works. (Keyboard shortcut: T.)

The **Position tool** is new with FCP X and really helpful. It allows you to move clips so they either leave gaps or override each other. I'll explain more about this in a few paragraphs. (Keyboard shortcut: P.)

You've already met the **Range selection tool**. It allows you to select a portion of a clip or a portion of a group of clips in the Timeline. This is just a Timeline tool, because you can easily select ranges in the Event Browser with the Select tool (though not a range between two clips). (Keyboard shortcut: R.)

The **Blade tool** cuts clips wherever you click it. However, it cuts only one clip at a time—by default, it cuts the clip in the primary storyline. More on this in a second. (Keyboard shortcut: B.)

The **Zoom tool** allows you to zoom into, or out of, the Timeline by clicking or dragging. I rarely use this because I tend to use Command+[equals] to zoom in, Command+[minus] to zoom out and Shift+Z to get everything to fit into the Timeline window. (Keyboard shortcut: Z.) The nice thing about the Zoom tool is that it will zoom into wherever you drag it. Using the keyboard shortcut zooms into either the skimmer or the playhead.

▲ TIP Switching Tools

To temporarily switch to a tool—any of those listed here—press and hold its keyboard shortcut. When you let go, the tool reverts to whatever was selected before you pressed the key. For instance, to quickly switch to the Trim tool from the Select tool, press and hold T. When you let go, the tool reverts to the Select tool. Cool!

When Is the Blade Not the Blade?

When you use something different. There are two blade tools in FCP X: one in the Tool palette and the other in the Edit menu. The Blade tool (B) cuts whatever clip you click it on. If you want to cut a connected clip, you need to select the clip first and then cut. The Blade tool needs to be over the clip it is supposed to cut. However, you can't cut multiple clips simultaneously with the Blade tool. Unlike the Blade tool, the Blade command (Command+B) cuts all clips wherever the skimmer or playhead is located. This command also allows you to cut in real time as you play back. (This is similar to Control+V in Final Cut Pro 7.)

The **Hand tool** allows you to scroll horizontally through a zoomed-in Timeline or Viewer. This works, but I tend to use Shift+scroll wheel on a mouse, the horizontal slide gesture on a track pad, or Multi-Touch mouse. (Keyboard shortcut: H.)

How to Get Rid of a Range of Clips

Let's look at the Blade tool in action. This trick for getting rid of a range of clips is really cool.

Select the clips you want to cut and position the skimmer over the place where you want the cut to occur. It is important that you select only one clip on the primary storyline (**Figure 7.19**).

Press Command+B, and all clips are cut at the position of the skimmer (**Figure 7.20**).

Select the clips containing the remaining portion of the range, and position the skimmer where you want the cut to take place (**Figure 7.21**).

Press Command+B (remember the Blade tool cuts only one clip at a time), and all clips are cut at the position of the skimmer (**Figure 7.22**).

Select the clips in the portion you want to get rid of and press the big Delete key.

FIGURE 7.19
Select the clips containing the range you want to delete. Limit the primary storyline selection to one clip.

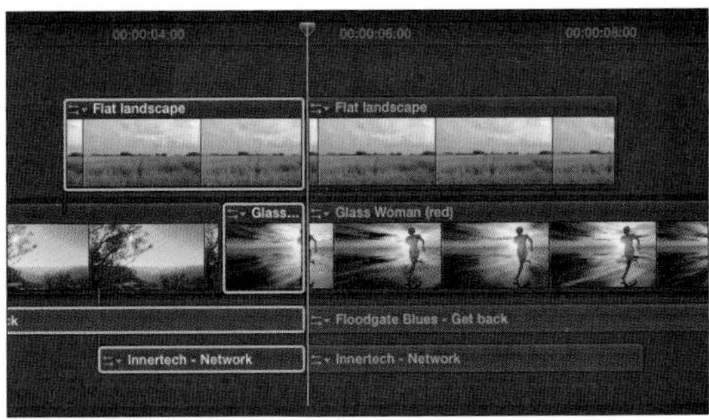

FIGURE 7.20
Pressing Command+B cuts all selected clips across all layers at the point of the skimmer.

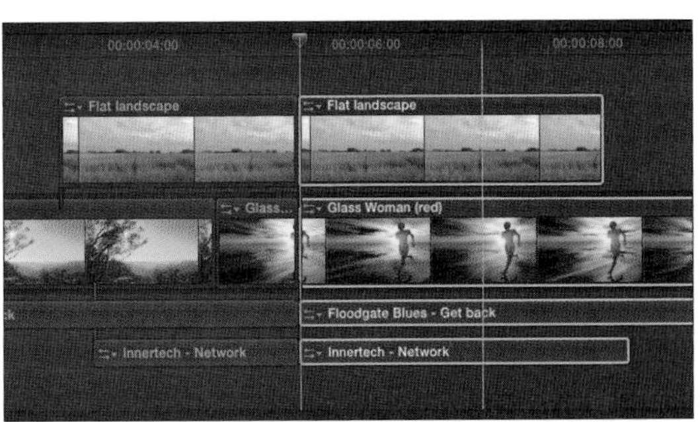

FIGURE 7.21
Select all remaining clips containing the range, and position the skimmer.

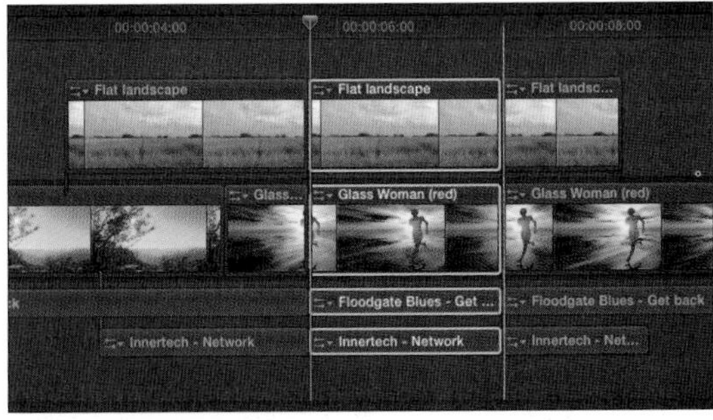

FIGURE 7.22
Press Command+B at the end of the range you want to remove.

Creating Gaps

The primary storyline does not allow you to edit a clip into it and leave a gap. That does not, however, mean you can't create gaps in the Timeline. You can, but you need to use a different tool—the Position tool. (You can also use a menu choice. I'll cover that in a page or two.)

The Position tool (P) allows you to move a clip or group of clips in two ways:

- Select a clip and drag it to the right with the Position tool. When you let go, FCP X inserts a gap between where the clip was and where it is now (**Figure 7.23**).
- Or, you can select a clip (or, as usual, clips) and drag to the left. When you let go, the clip you moved deletes whatever it landed on top of.

FIGURE 7.23
To create a gap, drag a clip, or clips, with the Position tool.

The benefit to using the Position tool is that you just need to grab something and drag it to insert a gap. However, if you want more precision, choose Edit > Insert Gap (press Option +W), and Final Cut will put a 3:00 gap at the position of the skimmer or playhead in the primary storyline.

Gaps are primarily used with the primary storyline. By definition, there are always gaps between connected clips. You can add gaps in a connected storyline using the Position tool, same as the primary storyline.

To adjust the duration of a gap, select it, and choose Modify > Change Duration (or press Control+D). Then, type the new duration into the Dashboard. You can also trim the gap; I'll talk about trimming in the next chapter. To remove a gap, select it and delete it.

A placeholder allows you to reserve a space in your Timeline for a clip that has not yet arrived. I'll cover placeholders in more detail in Chapter 13, because to use them fully, I need to cover both Generators and the Inspector—and I'm a couple of chapters away from tackling the Inspector.

However, here's something simple you can use to tide yourself over. Put the playhead at the place where you want to insert the placeholder. This can be between clips or in the middle of a clip. From the same menu you used for inserting a gap, choose Edit > Insert Placeholder (or press Option+Command+W). At the position of the playhead, a new clip is inserted, and all downstream clips slide right to make room for it. By default, it has a duration of 3:00—same as a gap (**Figure 7.24**).

FIGURE 7.24
Placeholders reserve space for yet-to-come shots. This placeholder uses the default image. Chapter 13 shows you how to configure both the actors and the location.

However, it uses the default generator for a placeholder, which is a single woman standing outside in a field in the daytime. (Yes, you can change this for location, time, number of people, and gender. That's part of what I cover in Chapter 13.)

As with gaps or other clips, you can adjust the duration, add transitions, and otherwise leave room for the clip to come. When that clip arrives, do a replace edit into the placeholder, and all your timing, transitions, and effects will remain as you set them for the placeholder.

Moving Clips Using Timecode

One of my favorite features in FCP 7 also made the transition to FCP X—moving things with timecode. For example, select a clip inside a connected storyline and then, using the keypad or keyboard, type, say, **+30** and press the Enter key. This moves the selected clip 30 frames to the right. Typing **-30** and pressing the Enter key moves a clip 30 frames to the left.

How Are Numeric Timecode Values Calculated?

When you enter values for timecode, you don't need to enter punctuation. Just type numbers; Final Cut even does the math for you.

- Positive numbers move right.
- Negative numbers move left.
- Enter one to two numbers, and FCP interprets them as frames.
- Enter three to four numbers, and FCP interprets them as seconds and frames.
- Enter five to six numbers, and FCP interprets them as minutes, seconds, and frames.

  For example:

  - Enter **20**, and FCP will interpret that as 20 frames.
  - Enter **60**, and FCP will interpret that as two seconds of 29.97 fps video.
  - Enter **1000**, and FCP will interpret that as ten seconds.

Roles

Roles are a new keyword category in version 10.0.1, which allow you to assign special keywords to clips. Roles are new, exciting, and something we haven't seen before in any version of Final Cut Pro. Personally, I am fascinated with what we can do with Roles.

FCP X is trackless. This means that the "age-old" method of putting the same clips in the same track—say to group all your Spanish titles in one track or to put all dialogue in specific tracks so that you can mix all your dialogue separately from your effects—won't work. Instead, you use Roles, which are special keywords that are either automatically or manually applied to a clip.

Roles can apply to video, titles, or audio. All default Roles have keyboard shortcuts, and you can add as many new Roles as you want. You can even add *Subroles*, which are Roles related to other Roles.

Here are three examples that showcase how Roles can be used:

- Organize a complex Timeline to keep track of all your different clips by function.
- Create an English and Spanish version of the same Project in one project, which could include both language-specific titles and narration.
- Create audio submixes, called *stems*, one for dialogue, another for effects, and a third for music, at the same time and in the same project as the master mix.

In this chapter, I'll show how you can use Roles for organization. In Chapter 17, you'll learn how to use Roles to export different versions of the same Project in a single pass.

Every clip contains one and only one Role; a synced audio and video clip would have one audio Role and one video Role. However, a clip in the Timeline can have a different Role than the same clip in the Event Browser.

When it comes to organization, you can do the following:

- Hide all clips assigned to the same Role
- Solo all clips assigned to the same Role
- Group clips by Role in the Event Browser
- Select all clips assigned to the same Role

In this next section, I'll show you how to assign, create, modify, and delete Roles. Then I'll show you how to use Roles with the Timeline Index.

Applying and Changing Roles

There are five default Roles for video, titles, dialogue, music, and effects. You cannot change or delete any of these default categories. You can create new categories, and, within a category, you can add Subroles.

Most of the time, you don't need to assign a Role; it's automatic. When you import a clip or add a clip from a Browser to the Timeline, FCP X looks at it and assigns one of the five default Roles. (If it makes a mistake, you can easily change it; I'll show you how in a minute.)

You can change or apply Roles in either the Timeline or the Event Browser. To do so, select the clip and choose Modify > Assign Roles. Select the Role you want to apply to the clip. (The five default Roles also have keyboard shortcuts assigned.)

You can have only one Role assigned to each video clip and one Role assigned to each audio clip. (Combined audio and video clips have one Role each for audio and video).

Apple suggests that the best workflow is to create and assign Roles in the Event Browser, but you can easily change a Role later. Since Events and Projects are separate databases, the Role is copied to the Project database when the clip is used in the Timeline.

Creating Custom Roles

You create new Roles and Subroles by selecting Modify > Edit Roles. Most often, you will be creating Subroles.

1. In the Edit Roles window (**Figure 7.25**), select the category you want to create the Subrole for.

FIGURE 7.25 Create new Roles and Subroles by choosing Modify > Edit Roles. Click the plus button to create a new category or Subrole.

2. Then, click the plus button and enter the name for the Subrole. In this case, I've created two Subroles: English and Spanish.
3. Once you are done creating custom Roles, close this window. You assign custom Roles the same way as one of the five default Roles, using Modify > Apply Roles.

Modifying or Deleting Roles

Currently, according to Apple's Help files, once you create a custom Role, you can't change or delete it. But that's not totally true. You cannot change any of the default five Roles. Nor can you change or modify a custom Role that you've applied to a clip. But you can change a custom Role that hasn't been applied to a clip.

If you have *not* applied a Role to a clip and are still in the Edit Role window, you can double-click the name of the Role in the Edit Role window and change the text. If you have closed the window but not applied it to a clip, then quit and relaunch Final Cut Pro. The Role will disappear, and you can re-create it.

If you *have* applied the custom Role to a clip, you need to remove the Role from all clips to which it is applied before you can delete it. You do this by highlighting all the clips with that Role (I'll show you how in the next section), selecting all the clips in the group, and changing them to another Role. Once no clips in active Events or Projects are using that Role, relaunch Final Cut Pro X. This will delete all unused Roles.

Using Roles in the Event Browser

The benefit of using Roles in the Event Browser is that you can group clips by Role. There are three ways to select this option:

- Choosing View > Event Browser > Group Clips
- Using the Gear pop-up menu under the Event Browser
- Right-clicking in the Event Browser and choosing Group Clips > Role

As you can see in **Figure 7.26**, all the video clips are grouped, and a count (24 items) is displayed for the number of clips in that group.

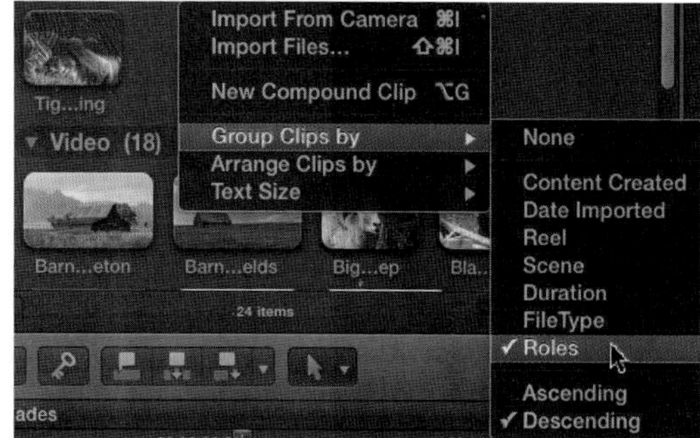

FIGURE 7.26
Use Roles in the Event Browser to group clips by Role. This is a fast way to gather all the same clips together.

● **NOTE** Using Roles as Bins

Because you can do a keyword search using Roles, you can create a Smart Collection of, say, all your music tracks. Then, with one click of the mouse, you can find all your music tracks in a project. This is what you used bins for in FCP 7—for example, storing all your graphics in one bin. Now, you can achieve the same thing using Roles and Smart Collections, without needing to hide files in a bin.

The Timeline Index

Roles are a big benefit in the Timeline because they allow you to solo, mute, hide, or highlight all the clips in a selected Role. This is such a powerful feature that Apple modified a major section of the interface to make this easier to use: the Timeline Index.

Like Roles, the Timeline Index is also new for Final Cut Pro X—and the only reason I saved it until last was because there was a lot of other stuff to cover first. However, this provides features you've never had access to before, and I've found myself using it more and more.

The Timeline Index allows you to view, navigate, and search a Project. Plus, the 10.0.1 release of FCP adds support for clip notes and Roles within the Timeline Index.

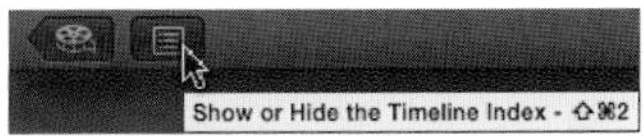

FIGURE 7.27
This button displays, or hides, the Timeline Index—a very useful new feature of FCP X. (Keyboard shortcut: Shift+Command+2.)

To display the Timeline Index (**Figure 7.27**), do one of the following:

- Click the button in the lower-left corner of the Timeline.
- Press Shift+Command+2.
- Choose Window > Show Timeline Index.

The Timeline Index appears on the left side of the Timeline. Unlike the Project Library, however, the Timeline itself does not go away. For example, this Project has a variety of clips, markers, keywords, analysis, To-Dos, and Roles (**Figure 7.28**).

FIGURE 7.28
The Timeline Index is on the left; the Timeline is on the right.

The whole purpose of the Timeline Index is to help you find stuff in a project, especially a very complex project. For instance, click Clips at the top and get a list of all Project media clips, sorted in Project timecode order. Video clips are indicated by rectangular icons, while audio-only clips are indicated by small speaker icons (**Figure 7.29**).

Another new feature is that the Timeline Index now displays the count of items displayed in the Index, along with the duration of all the selected items (assuming, of course, that they have a duration). This is a very fast way to get a quick count and timing for a portion of a project. In this example, the selected clip runs four seconds.

For a list of just the video clips, click Video at the bottom. Clicking Audio provides a list of all audio clips, and clicking Titles lists all titles used in the project.

Notice that the Notes field for each clip is displayed in the Timeline Index. This is often a faster way to add notes than using the List view in the Event Browser. Either way, this is the same information, displayed in two different places.

To see a list of all markers, keywords, analysis keywords, To-Dos, and completed To-Dos, click Tags at the top (**Figure 7.30**). To find a marker in the Timeline, click the marker name in the Timeline Index. To jump to the marker and open the Marker Information box, double-click the name. Also, click the To-Do icon to convert an uncompleted To-Do to completed, or a completed To-Do back to undone.

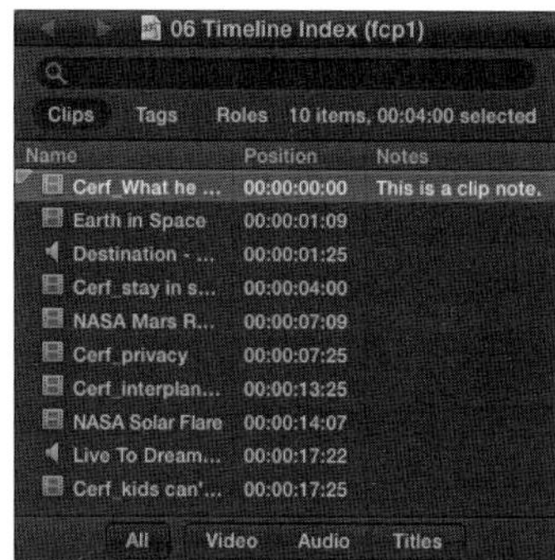

FIGURE 7.29
The Timeline Index allows you to quickly see selected elements within the Project.

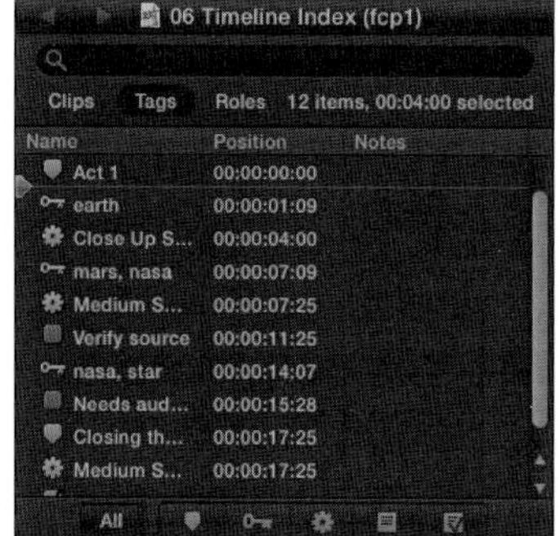

FIGURE 7.30
Click Tags to list all keywords, markers, To-Dos, and analysis keywords.

Use Roles to Organize the Timeline

One of the great new benefits to using Roles is that the Timeline Index allows you to use Roles to organize your Timeline (**Figure 7.31**).

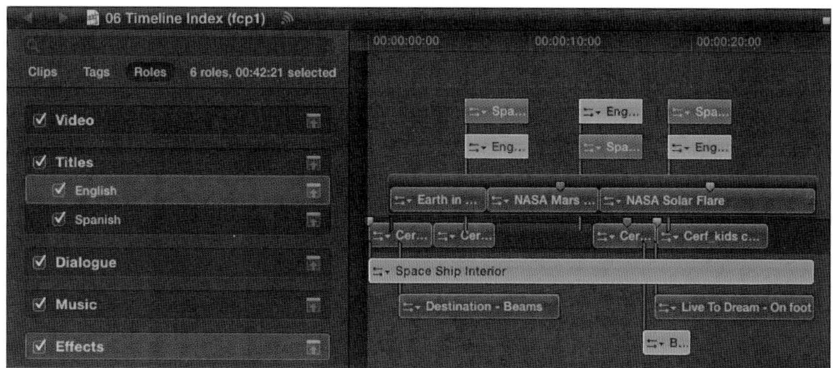

FIGURE 7.31
Roles allow you to organize Timeline clips, display or hide groups of clips, export groups of clips, and simplify working with multiple languages or complex audio mixes. Here, I created English and Spanish as Subroles of the Titles Role.

Click the name of a Role in the Timeline Index to highlight all clips that have that attribute. (Notice that clips assigned the same Role can be on multiple layers, as in Figure 7.31.) Uncheck a Role to make all clips linked to that Role invisible or inaudible. Click the box to the right of each Role to minimize the height of all clips with that Role in the Timeline. Select a Role to view the total duration of all clips assigned to that Role at the top of the Timeline Index. To deselect all Roles, click below the bottom Role in the Timeline Index.

Imagine you need to create a sequence with both English and Spanish titles. You assign English as the Subrole for all your English titles and Spanish as the Subrole for all your Spanish titles.

Take this one step further and add English and Spanish narration. Assign Dialogue > English to your English narration clips and Dialogue > Spanish to your Spanish narration clips. By simply toggling these Roles, you can switch the same project from one language to another without reediting a thing!

Speed Up Your Editing

Go back to the Clips section. Select a single clip in the Timeline by clicking the name. Select a range of clips by dragging across the names (**Figure 7.32**). Select a variety of clips by Command-clicking the clip names. Notice that the duration of all selected clips is displayed at the top. (I'm a big fan of durations!)

Here's another speed feature. You can even use the Timeline Index to delete a Timeline clip. Just select the clip in the Timeline Index and press the Delete key to delete the clip and close the gap.

You can use the Timeline Index to search for file names, keywords, marker text—or any of the other text elements displayed in the Timeline Index. For example, in **Figure 7.33** I am searching for all clips that contain the word *NASA* in the filename. This can really help manage large projects by allowing you to quickly find what you need without scrolling through the Timeline.

To make finding clips even faster, if the Timeline is active, pressing Command+F opens the Timeline Index. Not only that, it puts the cursor in the text entry box, ready for you to search for something.

The Timeline Index is designed to make large Projects manageable.

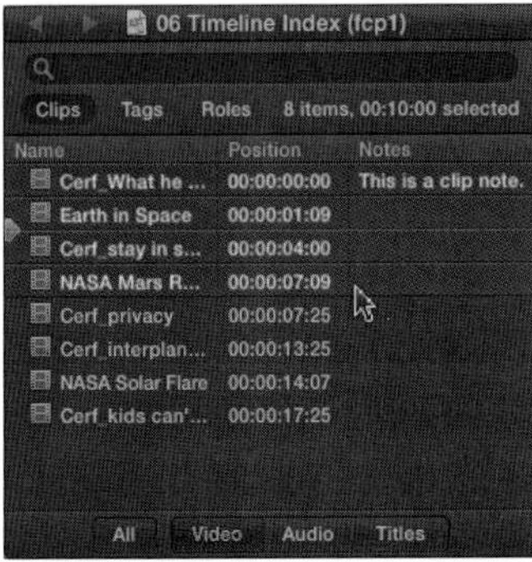

FIGURE 7.32
Use the Timeline Index to select a range of clips—by dragging, Shift-clicking, or Command-clicking.

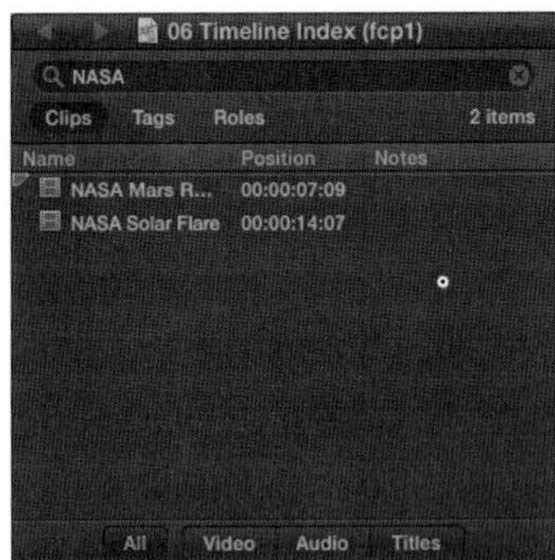

FIGURE 7.33
Another benefit of the Timeline Index for large projects is the ability to search for specific clips.

Summary

This chapter is a "catchall" for lots of different things that can make your editing easier. It's like building a bookcase. Once all the hammering, sawing, and nailing tasks are done, you still have a lot of work to do before the bookcase looks beautiful. That's where the tools in this chapter come in. They help you to get your Project into shape for trimming and effects.

Keyboard Shortcuts

Shortcut	What It Does
M	Add marker at position of skimmer or playhead
Shift+M	Open Marker Information window of selected marker
Option+M	Add marker and open Marker Information window
Control+;	Jump playhead to previous marker
Control+'	Jump playhead to next marker
Control+M	Delete marker under skimmer or playhead
Option+G	Create Compound Clip
Shift+Command+G	Break apart a Compound Clip
Command+[	Go back (up) one level in the Timeline History, i.e., between Compound Clips
Command+]	Go forward (down) one level in the Timeline History, i.e., between Compound Clips
V	Enable/disable the selected clip(s) in the Timeline
Option+S	Solo, or unsolo, the selected audio clips in the Timeline
Shift+Z	Fits existing Project into Timeline, complete image into Viewer, or displays one thumbnail per clip in the Event Browser, whichever is selected
Command+[equals]	Zoom into the Timeline
Command+[minus]	Zoom out of the Timeline
A	Choose the Select tool
T	Select the Trim tool

continues on next page

Keyboard Shortcuts (*continued*)

Shortcut	What It Does
P	Select the Position tool
R	Select the Range tool
B	Select the Blade tool
Z	Select the Zoom tool
H	Select the Hand tool
Option+W	Insert a gap at skimmer or playhead
Option+Command+W	Insert placeholder at skimmer or playhead
Shift+Command+2	Toggle display of the Timeline Index
Command+F	Open Find window in Timeline
Control+Option+V	Apply Video Role
Control+Option+T	Apply Title Role
Control+Option+D	Apply Dialogue Role
Control+Option+E	Apply Effects Role
Control+Option+M	Apply Music Role

8 TRIMMING YOUR EDIT

Trimming is the process of adjusting where two clips touch. (The point where they touch is called the *edit point*.) To me, trimming makes the difference between a home movie and a professional film. Trimming is the process of finding that one spot where two clips transition so smoothly that the viewer barely notices that an edit has occurred.

That's the good news. The bad news is that you can spend 30 minutes trimming to create the perfect edit; then, when you play it for your friends, it goes by so smoothly that they don't even notice it.

But the audience notices, because a well-trimmed video captures their attention and holds it in the story, while bad trims keep jarring them back to reality.

Getting Ready to Trim

There are four basic trims, and Final Cut Pro X does all four:

- **Ripple.** A *ripple* trims *one* side of the edit point (one edge of a clip) by moving it to occur at a different time. A Ripple trim always changes the length of a clip and the Timeline.
- **Roll.** A *roll* trims *both* sides of the edit point (the End of one clip and the Start of the next) but moves each edge in opposite directions. A roll trim changes the location of the edit point but doesn't change the duration of the Timeline.
- **Slip.** A *slip* edit changes the content of a shot, without changing its duration or its location in the Timeline.
- **Slide.** A *slide* edit changes the location of a clip in the Timeline, without changing its duration or its content.

Additionally, FCP X provides a new trimming interface, called the Precision Editor, and a new trimming tool, called the Position tool, that make the process of trimming both faster and more intuitive. I'll start with the Precision Editor, because it makes trimming easier to understand.

The last time I counted, Final Cut provides a dozen different ways to trim clips, with multiple ways to accomplish the same thing. Choose the technique that works best for you, because regardless of which technique you select, the end result is the same.

Three Types of Transitions

A *transition* is a change from one shot to another. There are three basic transitions: cuts, dissolves, and wipes.

- A *cut* is an instantaneous change from one shot to another. Aesthetically, a cut creates a change in perspective.
- A *dissolve* is where two clips are superimposed, or blended, on top of each other so that you see both images at once, though in varying degrees, throughout the transition from one shot to the next. Aesthetically, a dissolve implies a change in time or place.
- A *wipe*, these days, can be darn near anything. Wipes have clips and pieces of clips flipping, flopping, and skedaddling all over the screen. Aesthetically, wipes break the story and take you someplace different. Wipes work best when you don't use them too much.

This chapter on trimming assumes you are working with cuts. Chapter 10 explains how to work with dissolves and wipes.

NOTE When Does FCP Use the Skimmer and When the Playhead?

The skimmer always takes precedence over the playhead unless one of these two conditions is true: The skimmer is turned off or the skimmer is not in the same window as the selected clip.

Why Trim?

Imagine you have two shots. The first shows a wide shot of a person walking up to a door and putting his hand on the door handle, opening the door, and walking through the door. The second shot is a close-up of the door handle, where you see a hand reach in, turn the handle, open the door, and a person walks through the door as the door slowly closes after it.

Now, edit those two shots to the Timeline. In shot 1, you see the person walk up to the door and touch the door handle. In shot 2, you see the door handle but need to wait for several seconds before the hand reaches in to touch it. In this case, the *order* of the shots is correct, but the *timing* of the shots is not correct. You need to trim, or adjust, the Start of the second shot so that it starts just as the hand reaches in to turn the handle. In other words, you need to match the action between the first shot and the second shot.

This concept of matching the action is one that underlies much of trimming. You need the action in the first shot to easily flow into the action of the second shot. Sometimes, finding that match is easy. Other times, though, it is devilishly difficult.

Once you've matched the action—generally done with a ripple trim—now you have an aesthetic decision to make: *When* do you want the edit to occur? To go back to the example, do you want the edit to occur *before* the person reaches the door, which creates a sense of anticipation? Comedy uses this kind of a cut all the time—where you see what's going to happen before the people on-screen see what's going to happen.

Or, do you want the edit to occur on the action of turning the door handle? This is emotionally neutral and is used by documentaries to keep a story moving forward without making an editorial comment about it.

Or, do you want the edit to occur late, after you watch the person walk through the door, and then cut to the close-up of the door slowly swinging shut, which creates a feeling of dread or suspense, which the horror genre uses all the time.

In all three cases the two shots are identical. The action is identical. Yet the emotional impact is different. What creates this difference is the timing of the transition, the cut, between the two shots. Changing the timing of a cut is generally done with a roll trim.

Another example of when trimming is necessary is in sports. Let's say you are doing a sport highlights reel and you are cutting clips to the beat of the music. Each shot runs exactly four seconds and ten frames. So, you edit a shot that runs exactly 4:10—but *which* 4:10 do you need? The start of the play? The end of the play? The middle of the play?

The answer depends upon what you are trying to highlight—the *story* of your highlights reel, as it were. So, what you need to do is adjust what that B-roll looks like once you have it edited to the Timeline. That trim is generally done using a slip edit.

For me, the slide edit has been totally replaced by a connected clip. So, in the interest of fairness, I'll show you both—and after you compare them, you'll never use a slide edit again.

Explaining Handles

Handles are extra video before the Start (In) point and after the End (Out) point. Handles are needed for adjusting the location of the edit point between two clips.

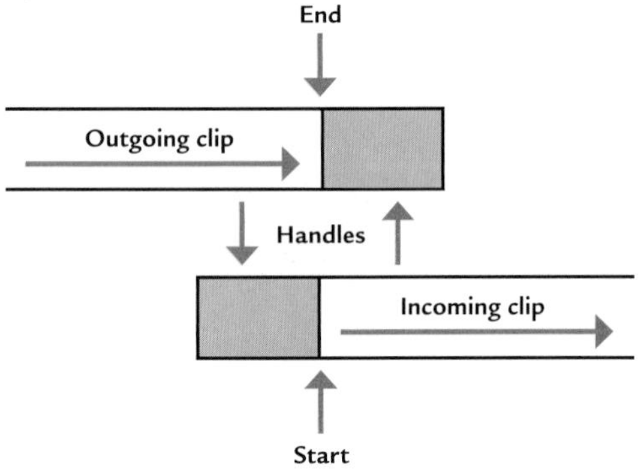

FIGURE 8.1
Handles, the gray areas, are extra video after the End point and before the Start point.

For example, in **Figure 8.1**, the gray section after the End in the top clip is the handle—extra video that is part of the clip but not displayed in the Timeline. In the bottom clip, the gray area before the Start is also the handle—part of the clip but also not displayed in the Timeline.

When you trim the End, for example, you are adjusting its location in the clip—moving it later, into the handle, or earlier, into the clip. If there were no handle, you couldn't move the End any farther to the right to extend the clip; you could move it only to the left, shortening the clip.

Setting Preferences for Trimming

One preference setting makes trimming a whole lot easier—so much so that it should be on by default. (The only reason you might want to turn it off is to improve trimming performance if you are editing HD video in a nonoptimized camera format like H.264 or AVCHD.)

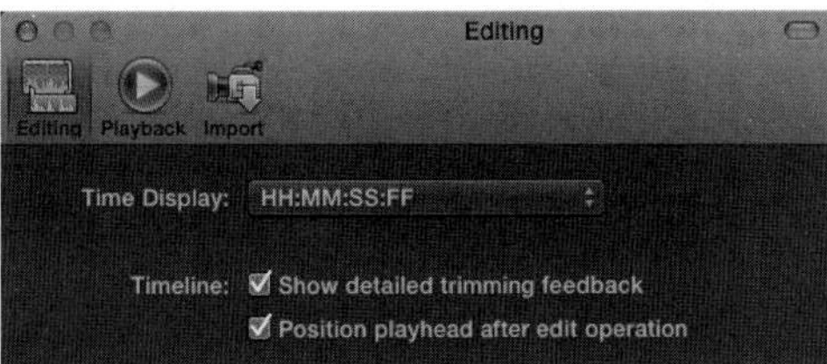

FIGURE 8.2
Trimming preferences are set in this screen.

Open Final Cut Pro's Preferences window (press Command+[comma]) and click the Editing tab (**Figure 8.2**). Then, select "Show detailed trimming feedback." This preference switches the Viewer to a special trimming view—called *two-up display*—when trimming clips. I find this option really helpful.

TIP Switching Your Preference

In case you forget to change this preference, you can quickly switch to two-up display by pressing and holding the Option key. If two-up view is off, this turns it on. If two-up view is on, this turns it off. As soon as you let go of the Option key, the Viewer resets to its default display setting.

Setting the Scene

Figure 8.3 shows the scene you will be using for most of this chapter. (Thanks, John Putch, for sharing this with us!) This is a six-shot dialogue scene, where one actor comes downstairs to comfort an upset actor. Two physical moves occur between shots—one where the blonde actor crosses from the bookcase to stand next to the couch. The second is where they hug. The order of the shots is correct, but the timing between them is messed up.

FIGURE 8.3 This is the six-shot scene, from the movie *Route 30, too!* that you will use in this chapter.

Here's the first problem: At the end of shot 3 (**Figure 8.4**), the two women are standing next to each other. Yet, at the beginning of shot 4, the blonde has not yet entered the frame. (I've added a yellow border to make it easier to see the two frames.) The outgoing shot is on the left (the End of shot 3), and the incoming shot is on the right (the Start of shot 4).

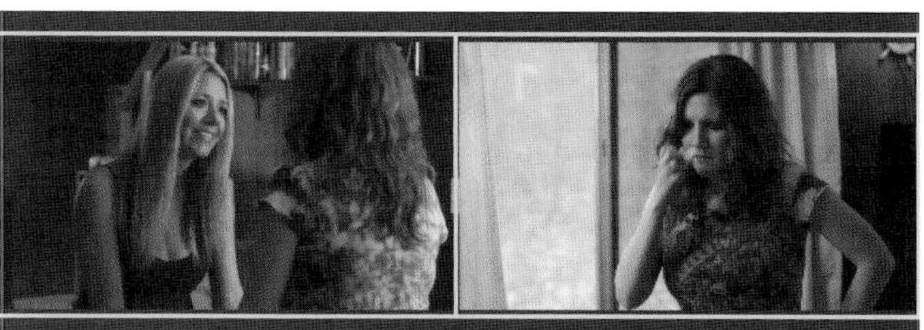

FIGURE 8.4 In the shot on the left, the two women are together. In the shot on the right, they are still apart. The shot order is correct, but the trimming is not.

Here's the second problem: At the end of shot 5 (**Figure 8.5**), they are in the middle of a hug. At the start of shot 6, the hug has not yet started. (Again, the outgoing shot is on the left, and the incoming shot is on the right.)

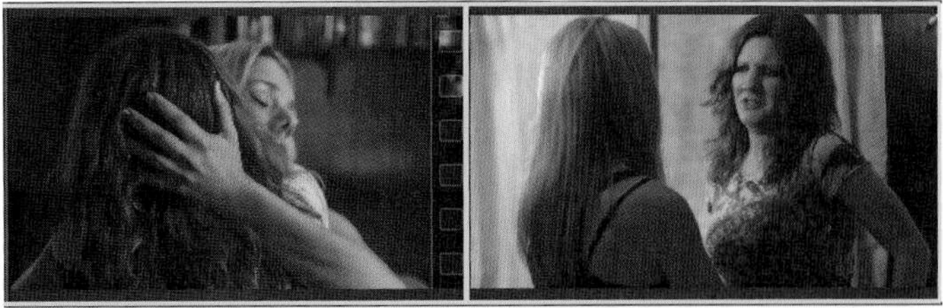

FIGURE 8.5 Another example of a trimming error. In the first shot, they are hugging. In the second shot, they are not yet touching.

As long as I am pointing out problems, the first shot has a problem, because I edited the shot to the Timeline before the director called "Action." I need to remove the excess video before the start of the first shot.

The Precision Editor

Apple added a new trimming tool to FCP X called the Precision Editor. To open the Precision Editor, double-click the place where two clips touch (the *edit point*) on the primary storyline. The Precision Editor only works with clips on the primary storyline; I'll talk about trimming connected storylines later in this chapter.

The Precision Editor presents an expanded view of the two clips (**Figure 8.6**); the outgoing clip is on the top, and the incoming clip is on the bottom. The brighter portions of each clip are what you see in the Timeline. The dimmer portions are the handles, the unused portion of each clip that you use for trimming.

FIGURE 8.6 The Precision Editor provides a highly accurate and intuitive way to trim your clips.

The yellow highlight allows you to move the edge of a single clip, which is a ripple trim. The gray "thumb" between them in the middle allows you to change the position of the edit point itself, which is a roll trim.

Perform a Ripple Trim

To fix the problem of the actors not being in the same physical position (see the earlier Figure 8.4), you need to adjust the Start of the incoming clip so that the position of the blonde actor matches the end of the outgoing clip. When you are adjusting one clip but not the other, you are doing a ripple trim.

FIGURE 8.7
The yellow highlight indicates which edges of an edit point are selected. In this case, the last frame of the End (or Out) is selected.

Let's take a closer look at the edit point (**Figure 8.7**). Notice that there is a yellow bar highlighting the end of the outgoing clip. This highlights the End (or the Out) of the clip—the last frame of that clip that appears in the Timeline when you play your project.

1. To select the Start (or In) of the incoming clip, click the leading frame of the bottom clip. The selection is indicated by a yellow bar.
2. Using either the Select tool or the Trim tool (which I haven't really talked about yet), grab the yellow bar and drag the edge left to move the Start of the clip earlier or drag it right to move it later (**Figure 8.8**). The small number box shows how much you are moving the edge of the clip in seconds and frames. Positive numbers mean you are moving to the right; negative numbers mean you are moving to the left. (In Figure 8.8, I moved the edit point 1:22 to the right.)

   When you trim, you are changing where a clip starts or ends.

   In this case, you are moving the Start of the bottom clip to occur later so that the ending action in the top shot matches the starting action in the bottom shot. Drag the yellow bar until the action of the two shots essentially matches. (I say "essentially" because it will rarely ever be perfect. Your goal is not perfection but believability.)

FIGURE 8.8
Drag the yellow bar in the bottom clip to change the Start of a clip to more precisely match the action from the top shot (outgoing) to the bottom shot (incoming).

But What If My Selection Glows Red?

Clip edges display one of two colors—yellow or red (**Figure 8.9**). If a selected edge glows yellow, it means it has handles. If a selected edge glows red, it means it has reached the end of a clip and there is no more unused video. A clip with no handles can be made shorter, but not longer, at that edit point.

FIGURE 8.9
A red highlight indicates a clip with no handles.

▲ TIP

Cool Skimmer Tip!

Here's a very cool trick you can use in the Precision Editor. Once you have the edit point selected (Start, End, or both), position the skimmer on the frame you want the edit point to move and click. The selected edit point jumps to the frame you click.

Thoughts on Setting an Edit Point

Oscar-winning editor Walter Murch offers his thoughts on what priorities to use when setting the edit point for a dramatic scene:

Priority 1: Set the edit point to reflect the emotion of the scene.

Priority 2: Set the edit point to advance the story.

Priority 3: Set the edit point to match the action in a smooth-flowing way.

Priority 4: Set the edit point to match where the audience is looking.

Priority 5: Set the edit point so that it respects the 180-degree rule.

Priority 6: Set the edit point so that it respects where the actors and set were positioned in the previous shot.

Murch writes: "Emotion, at the top of the list, is the thing that you should try to preserve at all costs. If you find you have to sacrifice certain of those six things to make a cut, sacrifice your way up, item by item, from the bottom." (Walter Murch, *In the Blink of an Eye*, 2001.)

As you move the edge, the display in the Viewer changes (**Figure 8.10**). The left clip remains the same, because you did not change the End of the outgoing clip. Instead, the right image changes as you move the Start of the incoming clip.

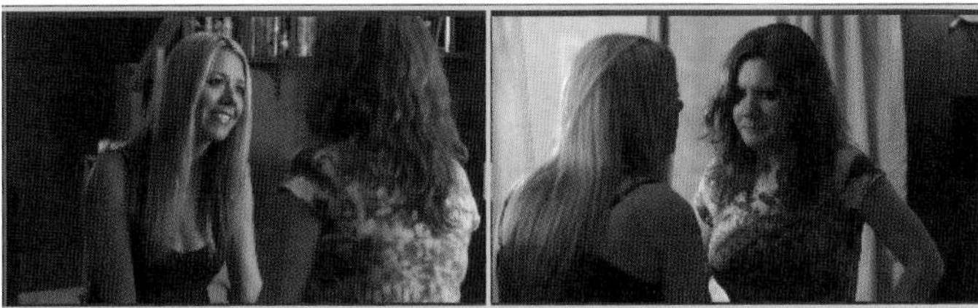

FIGURE 8.10 The two-image display in the Viewer continually shows you the results of dragging the edge. Notice that now the two women are standing together.

3. When you are done trimming these two clips, press the Return key to close the Precision Editor.
4. To preview the edit, press Shift+/. This backs up the playhead a few seconds, plays for several seconds through the original location of the playhead, and then resets the playhead to its original position. (This is one of my favorite keyboard shortcuts.)

That's it. You've done your first ripple trim! As you'll discover, there are lots of different ways to do a ripple trim, but they all do the same thing—move one side of the edit point, the Start or the End, to the left or the right to get the shots to match.

Perform a Roll Edit

Now that you have the two clips in sync—*sync* means that the action matches between the two shots—you get to decide when you want the edit to occur. Do you want to change shots before the blonde woman starts walking? During her walk? After she stops walking? Any of those options could be correct.

FIGURE 8.11 Moving the "thumb" between the two clips in the Precision Editor changes the position of the edit point earlier or later in the Timeline; this is a roll trim.

As you'll discover, there's no one aesthetic way to trim an edit. The technique is the same, but the aesthetics continually change. For example, maybe you decide that you need to cut while the blonde actor is walking toward the actor near the couch. (There is a major school of thought that says, when in doubt, cut in the middle of action, rather than when the action is complete.) If so, you should change the End of the outgoing clip, not the Start of the incoming clip. There's no right answer; it all depends upon your story.

A roll trim allows you to change the location of the edit point by moving both the Start and the End the same amount but in opposite directions (**Figure 8.11**).

1. Double-click the edit point to open the Precision Editor.
2. This time, grab the handle in the middle and drag it. Now, both images in the Viewer change because you are moving both—but in opposite directions. This keeps the action in sync while you figure out the best place to put the edit point.

   In this case, I decided the best place to put the edit was after the two women came together (**Figure 8.12**).

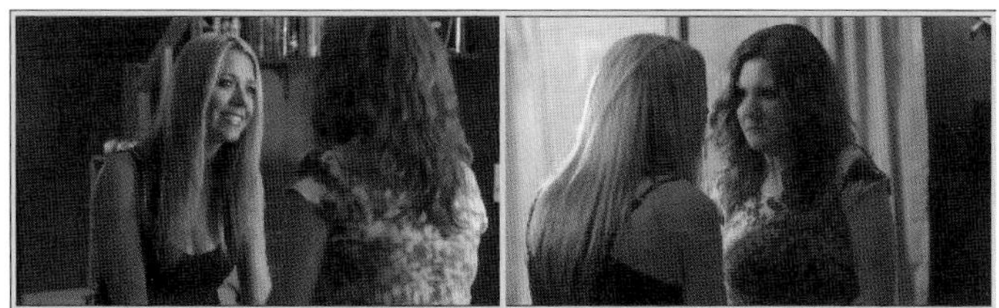

FIGURE 8.12 The edit point is now positioned so the two women are holding hands. Both the outgoing and incoming edges were moved using a roll trim.

To summarize, a ripple trim adjusts one side of the edit. A roll trim adjusts both sides of the edit.

● NOTE How Can You Move to Different Edit Points in the Precision Editor?

When you are done trimming an edit point in the Precision Editor, before you close it, press the Up or Down arrow key to jump to the next or previous edit point. This is a fast way to trim a number of edits by quickly loading each into the Precision Editor.

Trimming the Beginning or Ending of a Clip

Here are some fast ways to trim excess footage from the beginning and end of a clip (**Figure 8.13**):

- To trim from the beginning of a clip, put the skimmer where you want to trim and press Option+[.
- To trim from the end of a clip, put the skimmer where you want to trim and press Option+].
- To trim away footage outside a selected range, use the Range tool (press R) to select a range inside a clip and press Option+\.

FIGURE 8.13
FCP X also has the ability to quickly trim the start or end of a clip.

Twelve Trimming Techniques

In addition to the Precision Editor, there are a number of different ways to accomplish both these trims. For example, here is a list of all the different ways you can do a ripple trim. (The following techniques all assume you have sufficient handles on the selected edge of the clip.)

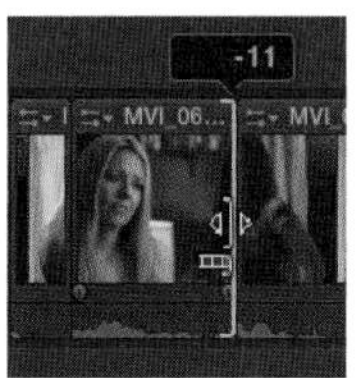

FIGURE 8.14
Here I'm using the Selection tool to drag an edge in the Timeline, without first opening the Precision Editor.

1. Using the Select tool, select the edge of the clip you want to move, that is, the Start or the End. In **Figure 8.14**, I have selected the End of the outgoing clip.
2. Then, do one of the following:
   - Drag the selected edge with the Select tool.
   - Position the skimmer or playhead where you want the selected edit point to be placed, and press Shift+X. This jumps the selected edit point to the position of the skimmer. (This shortcut can also be used in real time to trim an edit point.)
   - Press [comma] to move the selected edit point one frame left.
   - Press Shift+[comma] to move the selected edit point ten frames left.
   - Press [period] to move the selected edit point one frame right.
   - Press Shift+[period] to move the selected edit point ten frames right.
   - On the keypad, press [minus] followed by a number; then press Enter. This moves the selected edit point the number of frames you typed to the left.

- On the keypad, press [plus] followed by a number; then press Enter. This moves the selected edit point the number of frames you typed to the right. (Negative numbers move left; positive numbers move right.)
- Pressing Option+[trims from the beginning of a clip to the skimmer.
- Pressing Option+] trims from the end of a clip to the skimmer.
- Pressing Option+\ trims everything outside the selected range.

▲ **TIP** Keyboard Shortcuts in the Precision Editor

All the keyboard shortcuts in this bulleted list work exactly the same way in the Precision Editor, too.

Where You Drag Makes a Difference

When you drag the edge of a clip, be sure to drag nearer the top or the bottom of the edge of a clip. If you drag at the exact center of the edge, you'll create an audio fade-in or fade-out (**Figure 8.15**). If that happens, just drag the fade handle back to the edge of the clip. Then, grab a little higher, or lower, along the edge and try again. (I'll discuss fade handles in Chapter 9.)

FIGURE 8.15
Oops! Instead of dragging the edge of a clip, I am dragging an audio fade button. To avoid this, drag nearer the top or bottom of the edge, not the middle.

● **NOTE** On Editing and Trimming

In spite of what you may think, there is no one perfect place to edit and trim anything. It all comes down to your story. Every edit carries both emotion and information with it as it transitions from one shot to the next. Your job is to figure out how to trim your edit to enhance your story—partly this is experience, partly it is learning from others—and keep the story you are trying to tell firmly in mind as you trim your project.

Introducing the Trim Tool

The Select tool allows you to do ripple trims without needing to resort to the Precision Editor. But it won't allow you to do a roll trim. That's where the Trim tool comes in. The Trim tool allows you to do roll, slip, and slide trims.

As you've seen in the Precision Editor, a roll trim adjusts the edges of two touching clips at the same time, and it's used to adjust the position of the edit point in the Timeline.

1. To do a roll trim, without using the Precision Editor, select the Trim tool (press T) or select it from the Tool menu (**Figure 8.16**).

   With the Trim tool, do the following:

2. Click the edit point you want to adjust. The two edges will glow yellow (**Figure 8.17**). (If one edge glows red, it means that clip has no handles. You can make the red-edged clip shorter but not longer. If both edges glow red, you have no handles on either clip, which means you won't be able to alter the timing of this edit point.)

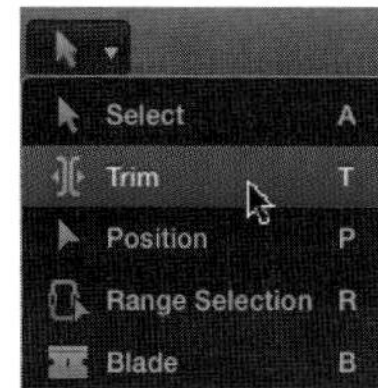

FIGURE 8.16
A portion of the Tool pop-up menu, showing the trimming tools.

FIGURE 8.17 In this specially constructed image, I am rolling the edit point in the Timeline at the bottom, while watching the effect of the roll in the two-up display in the Viewer, above.

3. Drag the Trim tool in the direction you want to move the edit point.

In this example, I'm dragging the roll tool to the left to move the edit point to where the blonde woman is reaching forward to take the hand of the red-haired woman. I am cutting during the action, rather than afterward.

Every keyboard shortcut that we discussed earlier with the Ripple tool works exactly the same in moving the Roll tool, with the keyboard, skimmer, mouse, and timecode. Specifically:

- Drag the selected edit point with the Trim tool; the Select tool does *ripple* trims, and the Trim tool does *roll* trims.
- Position the skimmer or playhead where you want the selected edit point to be placed, and press Shift+X. This jumps the selected edit point to the position of the skimmer.
- Press [comma] to move the selected edit point one frame left.
- Press Shift+[comma] to move the selected edit point ten frames left.
- Press [period] to move the selected edit point one frame right.
- Press Shift+[period] to move the selected edit point ten frames right.
- On the keypad, press [minus] followed by a number; then press Enter. This moves the selected edit point the number of frames you typed to the left.
- On the keypad, type [plus] followed by a number; then press Enter. This moves the selected edit point the number of frames you typed to the right. (Negative numbers move left; positive numbers move right.)

To be truthful, I use roll trims far more than ripple trims in my own editing.

Perform a Slip Edit

A slip edit changes the content of a shot without changing its duration or location in the Timeline. The most common way of using this is for cleaning up the content of B-roll; however, you can use this trimming technique everywhere: primary storyline, connected storyline, and connected clips.

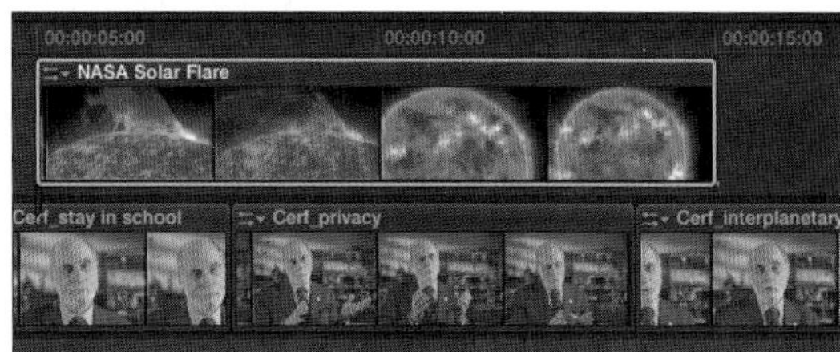

FIGURE 8.18
To illustrate a slip edit, I selected a connected clip with a clear color difference from the beginning to the end of the clip.

In **Figure 8.18**, I have a single connected clip as a B-roll over Dr. Cerf's interview. For the purposes of this example, I used a clip with a clear color difference from the start to the end of the clip. This is still a single clip, as you can see from the yellow outline. Notice, also that the clip starts exactly at 5:00 in and ends at 15:00 in the Timeline.

1. Select the Trim tool (press T) and click in the middle of the selected clip.
2. Drag the clip with the Trim tool. As I drag the contents of the clip, notice that the duration is not changing. Nor is its location in the Timeline (**Figure 8.19**). However, the *contents* of the clip shift, depending upon which way I drag the Trim tool.

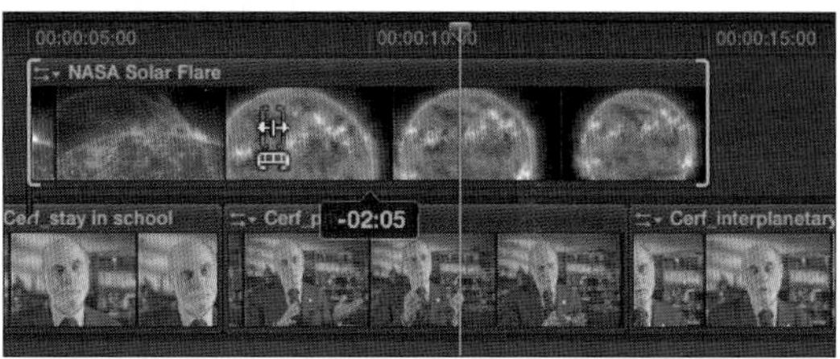

FIGURE 8.19
Dragging the middle of the clip with the Trim tool moves the *content* of the clip earlier, or later, without changing its position in the Timeline or its duration.

This is a very powerful edit that allows you to change the content of a clip without changing anything else. I use this tool constantly when editing B-roll, sports, and music—just about everywhere when I want to get the best possible content to fit within the clip.

Perform a Slide Edit

A slide edit is a holdover from the days of Neanderthals; though, perhaps, I'm being a bit biased. In 35 years of editing, I've never used this technique. However, as soon as I leave it out of the book, I'll be inundated with e-mails, so here goes....

A slide edit moves a clip in the primary or connected storyline earlier or later in that storyline relative to the clips before it and after it, provided the clips on both sides of this clip have sufficient handles. If either clip is missing handles, you won't be able to slide the clip.

For instance, here I have a clip sandwiched between two other clips (**Figure 8.20**). The slide edit allows me to move the clip earlier but *not* earlier than the previous clip. Or, it allows me to move this later but *not* later than the following clip.

FIGURE 8.20
Here are three different clips in the Timeline. I will slide the middle one.

FIGURE 8.21
Holding the Option key while dragging the Trim tool performs a slide edit. I cannot tell you how thrilled I am.

● NOTE When Is a Slide Edit Useful?

I've been reminded that a slide edit is still relevant if a series of B-roll clips are connected as a storyline and you want to slide a B-roll clip in the middle of the connected storyline to position it better with the underlying narration or sound bites.

To slide a clip, hold the Option key while dragging the middle of the clip with the Trim tool. As you see here, the clip has moved significantly to the left, while the duration of the three clips remains the same (**Figure 8.21**). The content remains the same, the duration remains the same, but the location changes.

The problem with this edit is that the middle clip cannot move earlier than the start of the clip before it or later than the end of the clip after it. The slide edit was invented when editing software supported only two tracks of video. With the unlimited layers that Final Cut Pro X offers, it is *much* easier to simply edit your B-roll clip as a connected clip, at which point you can move it wherever you want, without being limited to the boundaries of the clip before it or the clip after it.

Special Case: Split Edits Between Audio and Video

● NOTE Trimming Keyboard Shortcut

When in slip or slide mode, you can nudge a selected clip one frame left or right using [comma] or [period]. Nudge it ten frames left or right using Shift+[comma] or Shift+[period], always provided you have sufficient handles at the end of the clip.

I haven't talked much about audio yet. The reason for this is that it is easier to understand the techniques of editing if you take things in small steps. Once you add audio, your projects get much more interesting—and complex. However, since this is a chapter on trimming, I should explain how trimming works with audio.

A split edit is an edit where the video and the audio between two clips change at different times in the Timeline. It is used when you want to hear one thing and see something different. Split edits have a variety of names, including L-edit, L-cut, or video-precede-audio (forming the shape of an *L*) where the video edits before the audio; and J-edit, J-cut, or audio-precede-video (forming the shape of a *J*) where the audio edits before the video.

● NOTE When to Use Split Edits

This technique is used constantly in dramas, documentaries, reality TV, and just about everywhere two people are shown talking.

For example, John is yelling at Martha. Most of the time, you want to see the person doing the yelling. However, in this case, his anger is undeserved, so you want to *see* Martha react while you *hear* John yell. This requires a split edit, where the video (Martha) precedes her audio when she responds to John.

One of the new features in FCP X is that the audio is attached to the video so that when you edit a clip to the Timeline, the audio and video travel together. You can see the *waveforms*—that is, a visual representation of the volume of a sound associated with a clip—by turning them on using the Switch in the lower-right corner of the Event Browser or by selecting one of the four left icons in the Switch in the Timeline.

For instance, **Figure 8.22** shows what the waveforms look like attached to three clips in the Event Browser. And, "attached" is the right word. Until you disconnect them, the audio and video clips are permanently attached and show as a single clip.

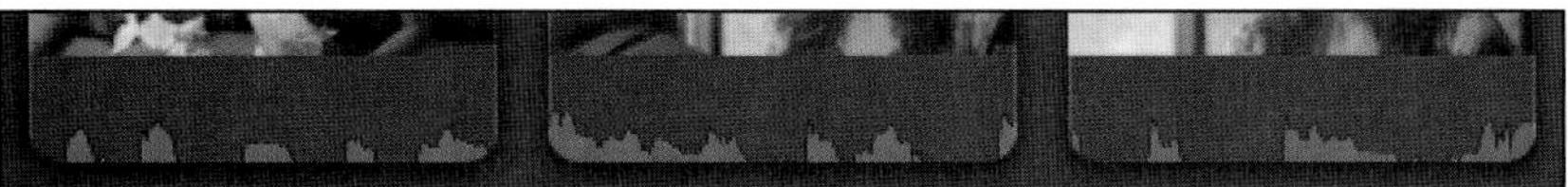

FIGURE 8.22 Waveforms are the visual representation of the volume of sound, displayed at the bottom of a video clip. Human speech is "bursty." This means that when we talk, every syllable is a single "puff" of waveform.

The small puffs of lighter blue represent the volume of the sound. Where the puffs are missing, the sound is silent. Where the puffs are tall, the sound is loud. The puffs vary in size as the sound varies in volume. When we speak, each syllable is a separate burst of sound. Generally, you edit audio where the waveforms are shortest.

● NOTE Can You Tell What People Are Saying?

By reading waveforms? No. All you can tell from looking at waveforms is how loud a sound is. (Well, that's not totally true. After ten years of editing the sound of my own voice, I was finally able to recognize the waveform for "Um." Clearly, a breakthrough in my editing.)

Let's go back to the scene where the two women are talking. Say you want to see the blonde woman listening while the red-headed woman is talking. Currently, you are changing shots to see each actor as they speak.

You create this effect using a split edit. Here's how:

● NOTE On Overlapping

Overlapping is good for sound effects but generally bad for dialogue. (As always, there are exceptions.)

1. As usual, select the two clips where you want to create a split edit.
2. Choose Clip > Expand Audio/Video, or press Control+S.

   The audio separates from, but does not detach from, the video. In this example, both clips are still selected (**Figure 8.23**).

   FIGURE 8.23 When you expand the audio and video, the clips remain attached, but you can see the two different components of each clip.

3. Using the Select tool, drag an edge of the audio. In this example, I am dragging the audio of the second clip to the left so that I hear the incoming clip's audio start sooner (**Figure 8.24**).

   In this example, I am hearing *both* the incoming and outgoing audio at the same time. To fix that problem, I would also drag the outgoing audio clip to the left so that the two don't overlap.

FIGURE 8.24 To create a split edit, drag the edge of one of the audio clips.

FIGURE 8.25
You can use the Trim tool to roll the video edit point to create the split edit. This is generally a better choice to avoid audio overlap, as you saw in the prior example.

▲ TIP Reactions Are Everything

Drama, in many cases, is not in the person speaking but in the face of the person reacting to the person speaking. Keep this in mind as you are trying to figure out what to show in a scene.

Or, select the Trim tool, click the edit point between two video clips, and drag (**Figure 8.25**). In this example, I'm dragging the outgoing video portion of the clip to the right so that you see the video of the outgoing clip while listening to the audio of the incoming clip.

While you can't use the Trim tool to roll the audio edit point, you can use the keyboard. Place the playhead at the expanded edit point, and press Shift+\ to select the audio edit point. Then, press [comma] or Shift+[comma] to roll the audio in one, or ten, frame increments to the left. Use [period] or Shift+[period], to roll the audio in one, or ten, frame increments to the right.

The result, when all the dragging is complete, is that you have created a J-edit where the audio of the incoming clip starts before the video of the incoming clip (**Figure 8.26**). This allows you to watch the face of the blonde woman reacting to what the red-haired woman is saying.

4. When you are done, you can collapse the clips back to a single level condition by choosing Clip > Collapse Audio/Video.

   However, the problem I have with collapsing clips with split edits is that the darker blue area of the Timeline where the audio overlap occurs is so very hard to see that you may forget it is there (**Figure 8.27**). My recommendation is that once you expand your audio, leave it expanded so you know it's there.

FIGURE 8.26
Notice, with this selected clip, that the audio starts earlier than the video. This is called a *split-edit* or a *J-edit*.

FIGURE 8.27
After creating a split edit, collapsing clips makes seeing the split edit very, very difficult, as this screenshot illustrates.

Special Case: Trimming Connected Clips

Trimming connected clips is simpler than trimming inside a storyline, because some trim tools no longer apply. For example, the Precision Editor cannot be used for connected clips. A roll trim can be done only inside a storyline where two clips touch. And a slide edit can be done only inside a storyline where three clips touch.

However, that doesn't mean you can't trim a connected clip. For example, you can change the length of the clip by dragging the Start or End of a clip. Since this isn't really a trimming tool, changing the duration of the connected clip has no effect on any clips before or after it—unless they bump into each other.

Also, the slip edit works the same way it does in the primary storyline: Select the Trim tool and drag inside the connected clip.

Special Case: Trimming Connected Storylines

Connected storylines have two significant benefits compared to connected clips: They support trimming and transitions.

For this reason, it often makes sense to convert even single connected clips to connected storylines. To do this, select the clip or clips you want to convert and choose Clip > Create Storyline or press Command+G. Once connected clips are converted into a connected storyline, all the trimming techniques you learned earlier in this chapter will work—with the exception of the Precision Editor.

Special Case: Trimming Stills

Working with stills is also a special case, for the same two reasons: trimming and transitions.

Although you can edit stills directly to the Timeline, more often than not, you are using the stills to illustrate what someone is talking about in the primary storyline. It is far smarter to convert and edit your stills into a connected storyline. (By the way, Chapter 12 shows you how to create moves on your stills.)

For instance, I started with three full-screen still images that are edited as three connected clips and selected. To convert them into a connected storyline, press Command+G or choose Clip > Create Storyline. This converts the selected clips into a connected storyline indicated by the dark gray bar at the top of the clips (**Figure 8.28**).

FIGURE 8.28
Three still images converted into a connected storyline (notice the dark gray bar over the top of the images).

At this point, a connected storyline acts just like the primary storyline for trimming—except that you still can't use the Precision Editor.

To do a ripple trim, drag the edge of a clip. Notice that as you do, the duration of the connected storyline changes. To do a roll trim, select the Trim tool (press T), click an edit point, and drag—just like you learned earlier (**Figure 8.29**). And, as you learned, a roll edit does not change the duration of the connected storyline.

FIGURE 8.29
Use the Trim tool to drag an edit point left or right to do a roll trim. In this example, the edit is rolling to the left 2:03.

How Do You Set the Default Duration for a Still?

There is no limit to the duration of a still image clip. You can adjust durations using any of the trimming techniques I discussed in this chapter. The default duration of a still image is four seconds and you can change this in the Editing preference pane (**Figure 8.30**).

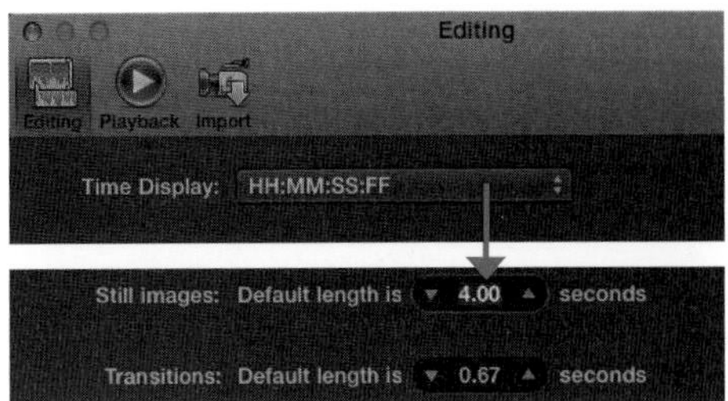

FIGURE 8.30 By default, all stills have a duration of 4:00. You can change this in Editing preferences.

To change the duration of multiple still images in the Timeline, select the images you want to change, press Control+D, and then enter the new duration into the Dashboard.

This last technique, changing duration using the Dashboard, is my favorite technique for changing the duration of anything—clip, still, transition, everything. I use it in both the Event Browser, to set the duration of a clip, and in the Timeline.

Summary

Editing and trimming are central to creating video that other people want to watch. Just as there are a wide variety of editing techniques you can use to edit your clips to the Timeline, there is an equally wide variety of trimming tools you can use to get it to flow smoothly.

This chapter on trimming wraps up the first half of the workflow I introduced in the first chapter—picking the content and telling the story. After you make a side trip into the world of audio in the next chapter, you'll pick up the workflow again and follow it into the second half—making your video look perfect using transitions and effects.

Keyboard Shortcuts

Shortcut	What It Does
Shift+/	Preview around an edit point
A	Select Arrow tool
T	Select Trim tool
Control+E	Display/Hide the Precision Editor
Control+S	Toggle expanding audio from video
[comma] / [period]	Move selected item one frame left/right
Shift+[comma]	Move selected item ten frames left
Shift+[period]	Move selected item ten frames right
Shift+X	Jump selected edit point to skimmer or playhead (also works in real time)
Command+G	Convert selected clips into a connected storyline
Option+[	Trim from Start to skimmer
Option+]	Trim from End to skimmer
Option+\	Trim to range selection
Control+D	Modify duration of selected clip(s)
Shift+\	Select audio edit point between two expanded clips

AUDIO

I've covered editing in significant detail. But I concentrated on the video. Special features and controls apply when you add audio to the mix. This chapter builds on what you've learned already and extends it to the world of sound.

There are two elements of audio that will be covered later in the book: Chapter 10 offers a unified discussion of transitions for both audio and video, and audio effects are discussed in a bonus chapter you can download according to the instructions in this book's Introduction.

However, before I cover audio in Final Cut Pro X, let's review some audio basics.

Audio Basics

Human hearing is defined as a range from 20 cycles per second at the low end to 20,000 cycles per second at the high end. (This also assumes you are 18 years old; as you get older, you slowly lose the ability to hear higher frequencies.)

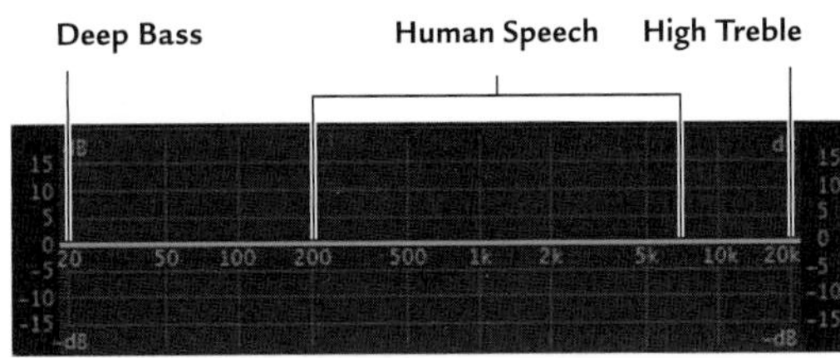

FIGURE 9.1
Normal human hearing goes from 20 cycles to 20,000 cycles, with bass on the left and treble on the right.

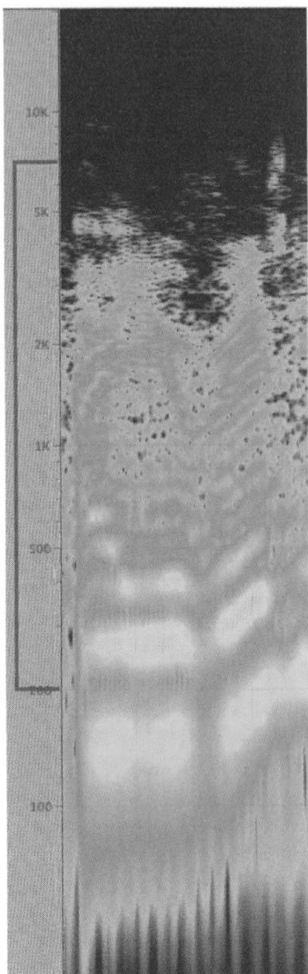

FIGURE 9.2
This is a graph of human speech based on frequency.

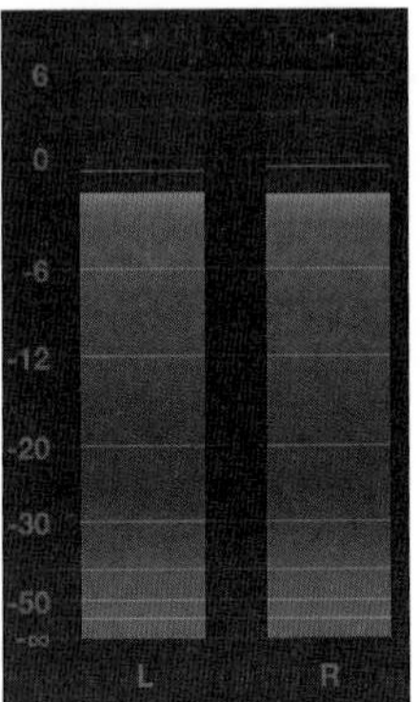

FIGURE 9.3
Audio volume is measured using meters. Louder sounds create taller green bars. Sound is displayed as peaks measured in dB (decibels) indicated by the numbers on the left.

Whenever we graph human hearing, we always draw a line, with bass on the left and treble on the right (**Figure 9.1**). Twenty cycles per second (most often, just called *cycles*) is such a low pitch that it feels more like a vibration than a specific tone; 20,000 cycles per second is such a high frequency that it sounds more like wind through the pine trees than an actual pitch.

All noise, music, speech—everything we hear—is carried within that range of frequencies. There isn't a separate musical frequency range that's just for music; instead, the frequency of everything we hear is located somewhere on that range from 20 to 20,000 cycles.

While human hearing goes from 20 to 20,000 cycles, human speech does not. Human speech ranges, roughly, from 200 cycles to 7,000 cycles; men are slightly lower, and women are slightly higher. Kids are definitely higher. (The frequency range of human speech is indicated by the bracket in Figure 9.1.)

Another interesting thing about audio is that it isn't linear; it's logarithmic. It isn't a straight line; it's a hockey stick. In **Figure 9.2**, the numbers on the left indicate the frequency of the sound. The colors on the right indicate the amount of sound at that frequency—ranging from yellow (a lot) to blue (very little).

Every time the frequency doubles (or cuts in half), the pitch of a sound moves up (or down) an octave. This means that human hearing covers a 10-octave range from 20 to 20,000 cycles.

Sound is displayed using peak levels in decibels (dB), as shown in **Figure 9.3**. (In fact, FCP X uses a system called dBFS—Decibels Full Scale.) The loudest a sound can be is 0 dB. All softer sounds are measured as negative numbers. It is also interesting to note that, like frequencies, audio volume is also logarithmic.

Each time the audio level drops by 6 dB, the perceived audio volume is cut in half. That means an audio level of -6 dB is 50 percent of the gain at 0 dB. I'll have more to say on this before this chapter ends, but this is so important that I want to start by mentioning it now.

● NOTE Vowels Are Not Consonants

Vowels—a, e, i, o, and u—are generally low-frequency sounds. Consonants—um, all the other letters—are high-frequency sounds. The warmth, character, and sexiness of a voice are carried by the low frequencies. Diction and clarity are carried by high frequencies. You'll see how this applies when I talk about audio effects later in the book.

What's the Relationship Between Sample Rates and Frequency?

Glad you asked! Audio is an analog wave. The computer stores digital bits. The process of converting an analog signal to digital bits is accomplished by *sampling*. The more samples per second, the more accurate the digitized audio. And, as I'm sure you remember from high school physics, the Nyquist Theorem states that the sample rate divided by 2 equals the frequency response of the digitalized audio.

All low-frequency sounds digitize well, regardless of the sample rate. However, faster sample rates are necessary to properly digitize high-frequency sounds.

When recording sound for video, audio is most often recorded at 48,000 samples per second, which is often abbreviated as 48 kHz, or just 48k. FCP X supports audio sample rates from 32 kHz to 192 kHz. Using the Nyquist Theorem, this means that a sample rate of 48k supports a frequency response of 24k—which exceeds normal human hearing. In fact, a sample rate of 22,050 yields a frequency response of 11k—which exceeds the requirements for high-quality reproduction of human speech.

Also, for the record, bit depth determines the amount of variation between the loudest and softest portions of an audio clip. Most audio recorded for video is recorded at a 16-bit depth. FCP X supports bit depths from 8- to 24-bit.

● NOTE The Funny Letters F and S

The letters F and S are called fricatives. A fricative is caused by forcing air across a small space, like the lower lip and upper teeth. The frequency needed to distinguish the letter F from the letter S is 6,100 cycles for a man's voice and 8,000 cycles for a woman's voice.

● NOTE A Joke

It always amuses me that the absolute maximum, in other words, the loudest, a sound can be equals 0. And all audio levels are measured in negative numbers where the bigger the number, the softer the sound. Well, it seems funny to me.

Audio in Final Cut Pro X

Working with audio in Final Cut Pro X provides a new set of controls and a new dimension of the interface for you to learn. In Chapter 8, you learned about waveforms. A *waveform* is a visual representation of the volume of the sound in a clip. When the waveforms are tall, the sound is loud. When the waveforms are small, or nonexistent, the audio is soft. Human speech tends to go in bursts, while music tends to move more like waves.

FIGURE 9.4
The meters on the right side of the Dashboard display audio volume. Clicking them toggles the display of the large audio meters.

The Audio Meters

You measure audio levels—which are also called *volume* and *gain*—using the audio meters. There are two sets of audio meters in Final Cut Pro. The small version is located to the right of the dashboard (**Figure 9.4**).

Or, if you click the small audio meters in the dashboard, it opens the large audio meters on the right of the Timeline (**Figure 9.5**). Drag the left edge to resize them. (You can also press Shift+Command+8 to display the audio meters, but it is *much* cooler to click the icon!)

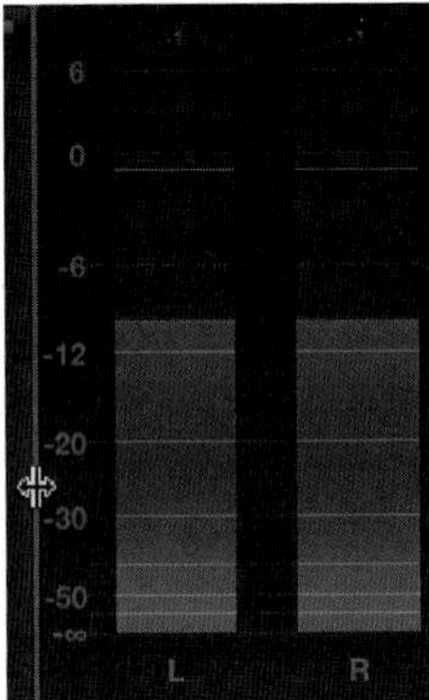

FIGURE 9.5
These larger audio meters are much more useful for accurately measuring the volume of a sound.

As you look just above the bouncing green bars, you'll see a thin white line. Because Final Cut's audio meters measure peak levels, the green bars are continually bouncing during playback. They're bouncing so much, in fact, that they become difficult to read.

So, Apple added that thin line just above them—called a Peak Hold indicator—that indicates the loudest the audio has been during the last second. That way, you always know how loud your audio is during playback.

How Do You Know If Your Audio Is Too Loud?

The absolute, number-one, *most important* rule about audio is that your audio levels in the final export must never exceed 0 dB. Not once, not ever.

While excessive levels frequently happen during editing, because you are not worrying about audio levels when editing a rough cut, levels over 0 dB must be fixed during the final audio mix, before export.

When your audio levels go over 0 dB—also called *too hot*—two things happen: First, a big red light at the top of the audio meters lights, and second, the peak hold indicator glows red (**Figure 9.6**). The red lights stay lit until you start playing your sequence again, just to make sure you saw them.

You can also turn off the red lights by clicking them.

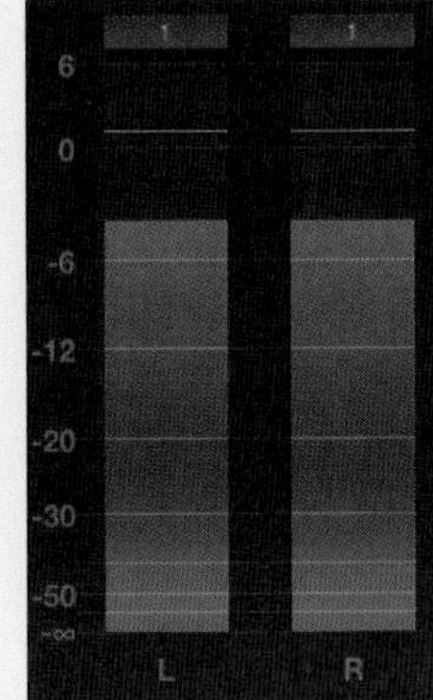

FIGURE 9.6
Red lights at the top of the meters indicate your audio is too loud. This *must* be fixed before you export your final program.

It is critical that you fix this audio problem by adjusting the levels on your clips before you export your finished program. I'll talk about setting levels and audio mixing later in this chapter.

Audio Skimming

Another nice feature in FCP X is audio skimming. Just as you can skim the video in a clip, you can also skim the audio. This gives you a high-speed way to review what a clip sounds like.

To turn audio skimming on, video skimming must be turned on first (**Figure 9.7**). (Keyboard shortcut S.) Then, turn on audio skimming by either clicking the button indicated in the screenshot or pressing Shift+S.

FIGURE 9.7
Clicking this icon, or pressing Shift+S, toggles audio skimming on or off.

What's cool about skimming is that it is pitch-corrected. Normally, if you dragged quickly across an audio clip, the pitch would rise sharply. Or, if you dragged slowly, the pitch would sound truly lugubrious (it's a word; you can look it up). However, Apple added pitch shifting so that no matter how fast or slow you drag the audio skimmer, the tempo will change but not the pitch. Neat.

Viewing Audio in a Clip

You can view the audio associated with a clip in several ways. Click the Switch in the lower-right corner of the Timeline, and then click any of the four icons to the left to display waveforms in the Timeline (**Figure 9.8**).

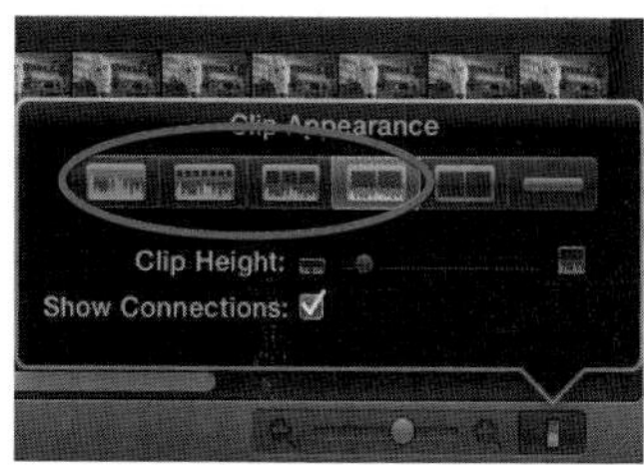

FIGURE 9.8
Click the Switch and then click one of the four left icons to display waveforms in the Timeline.

As you saw in Chapter 8, another way to see the audio attached to a video clip is to select the clips you want to expand and then choose Clip > Expand Audio/Video, or press Control+S.

This separates the audio from the video but keeps the clips attached. You use this technique to create a split edit. Also, as you'll discover in the next chapter, you expand clips to create an audio transition. The benefit of expanding the audio is that because the clips are still attached, there's no risk that the audio and video will go out of sync. To collapse the audio back into the video, choose Clip > Collapse Audio/Video or press Control+S.

▲ **TIP** Display Faster!

A fast way to expand the audio from the video is to double-click the audio waveforms.

You can also *detach* clips, which creates separate audio and video files. The danger with this method is that it becomes very easy for the audio and video to get bumped out of sync. When that happens, unlike Final Cut Pro 7, there is no indicator to show that clips are out of sync. By the way, to reconnect audio that is detached from the video, select both clips and create a compound clip. Aside from a simple Undo, there is no way to reattach audio once it has become detached.

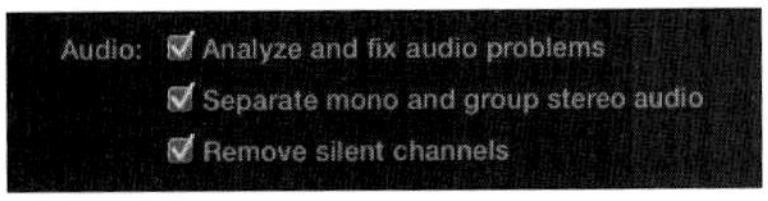

Audio: Analyze and fix audio problems
Separate mono and group stereo audio
Remove silent channels

FIGURE 9.9
These are the three analysis options for audio.

Audio Analysis on Import

When you import a clip that contains audio, or later when it is in the Event Browser, you have the option of analyzing the audio of a clip (**Figure 9.9**). This analysis provides three options:

- **Analyze and fix audio problems.** This looks at three common problem areas: loudness, background noise, and hum removal. Loudness tries to fix clips that were recorded too loud or too soft to make the levels more uniform. Background noise removal *reduces*, but does not *remove*, noises like air conditioners. Hum removal reduces common electrical hum at either 50 Hz or 60 Hz. Final Cut will automatically fix problems it thinks are severe and flag problems it thinks are moderate. You can decide later whether to accept these changes.
- **Separate mono and group stereo audio.** Interviews are almost always recorded as mono, either by putting the same signal on both audio channels or by putting one mono signal, such as the interviewer, on one channel and a second mono signal, such as the guest, on a second channel to create dual-mono audio. Stereo is where similar, but not the same, audio is placed on both channels. When this option is checked, Final Cut Pro converts channels improperly captured as stereo to dual-channel mono, and vice versa. When it comes to mixing, dual channel mono is *much* more flexible than stereo.

A Digression: Mono, Stereo, and the Sonic Field

By definition, a mono clip always appears centered between two speakers. This is because, also by definition, a mono clip plays the same volume out both speakers in a stereo system, giving the illusion of sounding in the center.

Pan allows you to adjust where this sound appears between the two speakers. For positioning sounds in space (left and right), mono audio provides the greatest flexibility. The space between two speakers is called the *sonic field*.

Also, by definition, a stereo clip plays the left channel (most often this is the odd-numbered channel) from the left speaker and the right channel (the even channel) out the right speaker. The placement of sounds within the sonic field for a stereo clip totally depends upon how the audio was mixed, or recorded, before it was imported into Final Cut.

When you want to determine the placement of the sound, work with mono audio. When you want to accept the placement based on how the sound was recorded, use stereo. For interviews, mono is best. (I think of this as "one mouth, one mic, one channel.")

- **Remove silent channels.** If, by accident, you fed audio to only two channels but your camera recorded six, when you import from the camera, you are bringing in four unnecessary audio channels that are just taking up hard drive space. This option mutes the channels you don't need so they don't get in your way.

By the way, when discussing audio, I use *channels* and *tracks* essentially interchangeably. Since FCP X uses a trackless timeline, don't confuse my use of the word *tracks* with the horizontal audio and video tracks in an FCP 7 Timeline. There's probably a deep, dark, difference between these two words...but in this book, I'm using both words to mean the same thing.

You can analyze clips in the Event Browser, after they were imported, by selecting the clips and choosing Modify > Analyze and Fix. Once a clip is edited into the Timeline, the options change. To analyze Timeline clips, select the clip, or clips, and then do one of the following:

- Select Auto Enhance from the Enhancements menu—the Magic Wand icon (**Figure 9.10**).
- Choose Modify > Auto Enhance Audio.
- Press Option+Command+A.
- Click the Auto Enhance button in the Audio tab of the Inspector.

FIGURE 9.10
Once clips are edited into the Timeline, you can analyze them using the Enhancement menu.

In addition to the three tests performed on a clip during analysis, auto-enhancing a clip adds one more: equalization. This lets you adjust ranges of frequencies in a clip to boost the bass, reduce the treble, or match the sounds between clips. This allows you to perform a variety of simple EQ modifications.

Introducing the Inspector

The Inspector is new to Final Cut Pro. The Inspector is "where you make changes." You've seen it in other applications, but this is the first time for FCP. You use the Inspector to make changes to clips, transitions, and effects. You won't use the Inspector much for editing, but you will use it constantly for effects.

To display the Inspector, click the Inspector icon (the small letter *i*) or press Command+4. When the Inspector is closed, the icon is gray. When the Inspector is open, the icon is blue (**Figure 9.11**).

FIGURES 9.11
Click the Inspector icon (indicated in blue) to toggle the Inspector open or closed. The keyboard shortcut is Command+4.

There is a great deal of depth and power in the Inspector. For now, I just want to point out the Audio Enhancements feature.

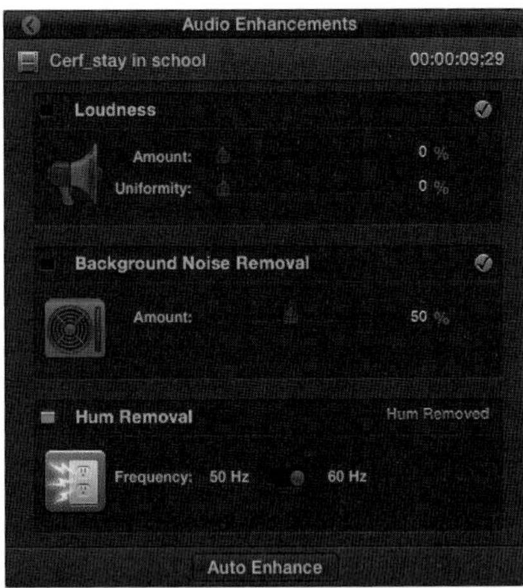

FIGURE 9.12
The Inspector is where you are able see, modify, or disable audio enhancements. Click a blue square to enable or disable a feature.

FIGURE 9.13
To edit just the audio of a clip in the Event Browser into the Timeline, check Audio Only in this pop-up menu.

Choose Window > Show Audio Enhancements or press Command+8. This opens the audio enhancements pane in the Inspector. Three settings are displayed: Loudness, Background Noise Removal, and Hum Removal (**Figure 9.12**).

A green check mark (on the right) indicates that the clip was checked for that potential audio problem and it wasn't found. A blue box (on the left) indicates a problem was found (in this case too much hum) and that the hum was removed. (Click the slider to set the hum removal to either 50 or 60 cycles. North America uses 60 cycles for power; just about everywhere else uses 50 cycles.) If you don't want to apply a particular enhancement, click the blue box to turn it off. When no blue box is displayed, that enhancement is disabled.

How do you decide whether to use a setting? Listen to it. Whichever sounds better—on or off—is the one you should use. If you are not quite happy, drag one of the sliders a little bit in each direction and listen to hear whether things improve or get worse. If they get worse, drag in the opposite direction. If they get better, keep dragging until the audio sounds as good as it can.

Audio Techniques

Because audio deals with sound, rather than picture, there are specific techniques you can use to make editing audio easier. This section presents several of them.

Editing Audio

The process of editing audio is the same as editing video—everything I've already covered still applies. For instance, to edit a clip audio-only from the Event Browser to the Timeline, you still need to set a Start and an End. However, before you edit the clip, either select Audio Only from the small pop-up menu next to the Edit buttons or press Option+3 (**Figure 9.13**). When you edit the clip, only the audio moves down to the Timeline.

Audio can be edited in one of two ways in FCP X—attached to a video clip or as a separate clip. Audio can also be edited into three locations: into the primary storyline, as a connected clip, and into a connected storyline.

What's a little disconcerting about editing audio in FCP X is that the audio clip can appear below or above the primary storyline. (Yes, I know, the idea of audio above a video clip does smack of heresy!) But imagine you have multiple audio clips playing simultaneously and a few sound effect clips that are intended to play in sync with connected B-roll. Rather than always keeping video above and audio below and constantly scrolling vertically to see where the B-roll and sound effects are, you can move the sound effects above the primary storyline so they are closer to the B-roll clip and, thus, easier to locate, sync, and work with together.

Here, for instance, are four different audio examples (**Figure 9.14**):

- Audio as part of a video clip in the primary storyline
- Audio as a connected clip below the primary storyline
- Audio as a connected clip with video above the primary storyline
- Audio as part of a connected storyline

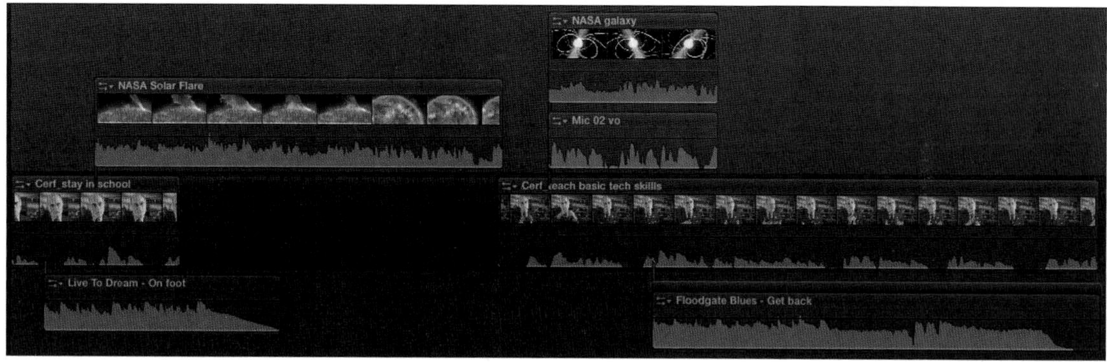

FIGURE 9.14 Four different audio configurations are illustrated here: audio in the Primary Storyline and as connected clips. Notice that connected audio clips can go *above* video!

In general, only audio synced to video edits into the primary storyline; all other audio is some form of a connected clip.

● **NOTE** How About Placing Video Below the Primary Storyline?

You can do that. However, unlike audio, vertical position makes a difference for video. Assuming you haven't made any changes to the video (such as applying an effect), video on higher layers always blocks video on lower layers. So, in general, place your audio wherever you want. But place B-roll video clips above the primary storyline.

Can You Match Frame Back to the Event Browser Clip?

Yes. *Match frame* means to find the source clip in the Event Browser that matches the selected clip in the Timeline. In fact, FCP X goes one step further. Not only does it display the matching clip, but it also matches the position of the Start, End, and playhead in the source clip to the selected clip in the Timeline.

To do this, first make sure the Event Browser is in Filmstrip view; then select the Timeline clip that you want to match to a source clip in the Event Browser. Press Shift+F (or choose Clip > Reveal in the Event Browser). FCP instantly displays the Event Browser version of that clip, creates a selection range that matches the Start and End of the Timeline clip, and puts the playhead in the same spot as the playhead in the Timeline.

Final Cut Pro 7 editors will recognize this as doing a match frame edit in FCP 7 but using a different keyboard shortcut.

Special Case: Music Video and Narration

When creating a music video, because you can't lock tracks in FCP X, it is generally a good idea to first edit the music clip into the primary storyline and then let all your video clips be connected clips, or, ideally, connected storylines, to that audio. This technique also works when you have audio-only narration that you want to illustrate using B-roll.

Placing audio in the primary storyline prevents any problems with the music slipping by mistake, while providing the greatest flexibility in editing and manipulating the video. Connected storylines also provide support for transitions between clips, which I will cover in Chapter 10.

The keyboard shortcuts to edit audio into the Timeline are the same as for video, which I illustrated in Chapter 6:

- E for an append edit
- D for an overwrite edit
- W for an insert edit
- Q for a connected edit

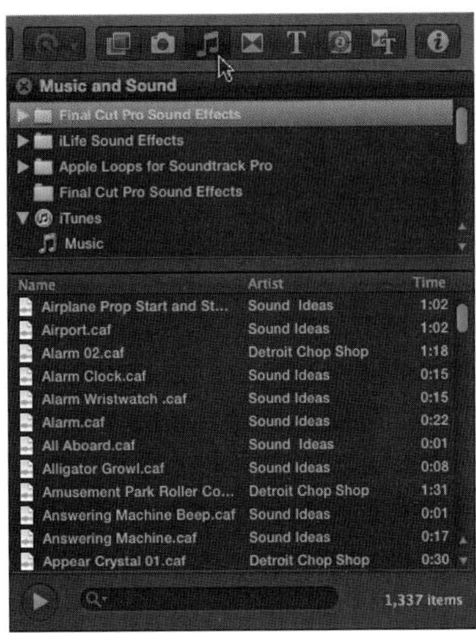

FIGURE 9.15
Each of the seven browser icons opens to display a wealth of resources.

The Music Browser

In addition to Events, there is one special place where you can find music and sound effects and, like the Inspector, it's a part of the interface I haven't talked much about: the Music and Sound Browser.

In fact, I haven't talked about the browsers at all. Allow me to introduce the browsers, located on the right side of the toolbar from left to right (**Figure 9.15**):

- Effects
- Photos
- Music and Sound Effects (the blue icon)
- Transitions
- Text and Titles
- Generators
- Themes
- Inspector (This isn't really a browser, which is why there is a space between its icon and the browser icons.)

1. Click the Music Browser icon to display the browser. The only browser that has a default keyboard shortcut is the Effects Browser. All other browsers need to be clicked to be opened. However, as you learned in Chapter 3, you can easily create custom keyboard shortcuts to open any browser.

   This browser contains audio that's part of the additional content you can download after you purchased Final Cut Pro X. (Since this content includes hundreds of royalty-free sound effects and other materials, it's worth the time to download. Use Software Update to get your copy.)

2. Each browser window has three sections: categories, individual files, and a search window. In this browser, the categories are at the top. Most of the time, the categories are on the left side.

   There are way too many elements to scroll through, so at the bottom of every browser is the search window. As an example, I entered the word *taxi*, and from those hundreds of clips, FCP found three taxi sound effects (**Figure 9.16**).

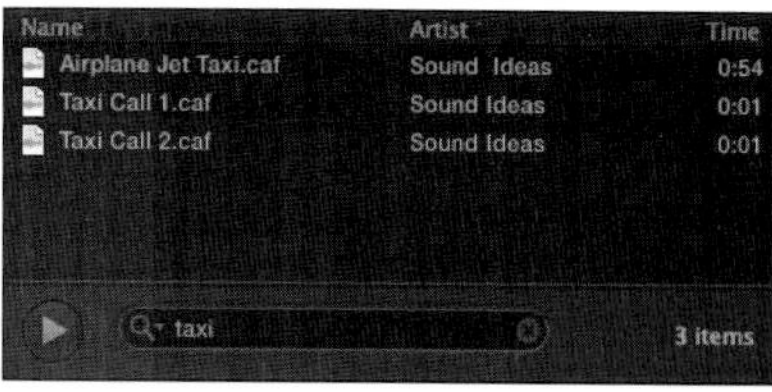

FIGURE 9.16
Use the Search text box at the bottom to locate elements by filename.

3. To preview an effect, click the Play arrow to the left of the Search box, or simply double-click the clip.

4. To reset the Search box to empty, which means you'll see all your clips again, click the cancel button—the *X* in a circle on the right side of the search text box.

   As an aside, if all your clips are suddenly missing, either your entire hard disk has gone missing, there's been a disruption in the Force, or, more likely, you have something entered in the Search text box. That's because when you close a browser, the Search text box doesn't empty. Click the Cancel button (the *X* in a circle) to clear it.

5. When you are done working with a browser, either click the Close button in the top-left corner (another *X* in a circle) or click the Browser icon in the toolbar.

Unlike editing from the Event Browser, there are no default keyboard shortcuts that quickly edit a selected element from an effects browser. In the case of audio, you need to drag the clip from the Music and Sound Browser to either the Event Browser or the Timeline. (Double-clicking is also an option when you get to placing effects, but this won't work for audio.)

As you saw in Figure 9.14, an audio clip can be placed above or below the primary storyline. This has *zero* impact on playing the audio. Audio clips play fine regardless of where they are placed.

The Timeline gives you a lot of flexibility in placing audio to help you keep your project organized, without worrying about whether it will play. (It will always play!)

Working with Clips

There are several things you can do specifically with audio clips, such as adding a fade-in or fade-out, adjusting pan, or selecting specific audio channels to play in the Timeline. (Because audio transitions are a special case, I will cover transitions between audio clips in Chapter 10.)

Fade-in and Fade-out

Whether skimming is turned on or off, when you move the cursor into an audio clip, two fade handles show up on either end of the clip, just above the black volume line (**Figure 9.17**).

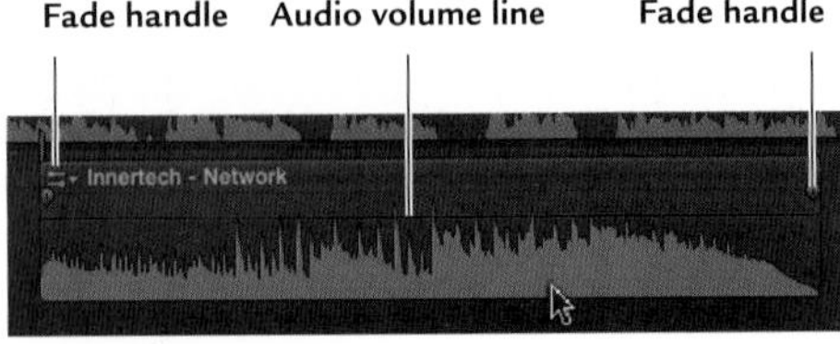

FIGURE 9.17
Each audio clip has fade handles at each end, allowing fades at the beginning and end of each clip, plus the horizontal volume line.

To add a fade-in or fade-out to a clip, drag a fade handle left or right. This is just like adding a video fade using the opacity slider. (The small black box measures the duration of the fade using timecode.) To remove a fade, drag the fade handle back to the edge of the clip.

Something that FCP X borrowed from Soundtrack Pro is the ability to change the shape of the fade—this is a feature I like a lot! To display the four fade shapes, right-click a fade handle (**Figure 9.18**).

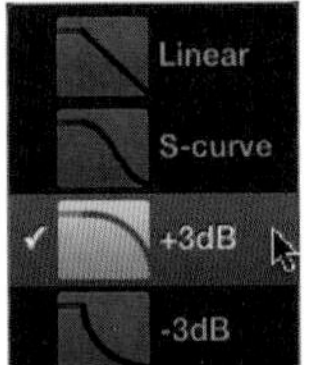

FIGURE 9.18
There are four different curves you can apply to an audio fade. Control-click a fade handle to select one.

- **Linear.** This performs a straight-line fade, also called *equal power.* This is best used when fading to and from black. If you use a linear transition when cross-fading between two audio clips, there will be a slight (-3 dB) drop in volume in the middle of the cross-fade.
- **S-curve.** This does an ease-in and ease-out of a fade, with the midpoint gain equaling 0 dB.
- **+3dB.** This adds a +3 dB boost in gain in the middle of the cross-fade; this shape is also called *equal gain*. This is best used when cross-fading between two audio clips. This fade is the default setting and is, generally, the best choice for most situations.
- **-3dB.** This adds a -3 dB drop in gain in the middle of the fade. This is best used when you need to avoid a noise at the very beginning (for a fade up) or end (for a fade out) of a fade.

To change the fade curve applied to a fade handle, simply select the curve you want. The shape of the current curve is displayed in the clip. Final Cut makes it easy to see at a glance what curves are applied to a clip.

Fade handles and fade curves also apply to audio which is attached to video. For example, as soon as the cursor enters the boundary of the audio waveforms attached to a video clip, the fade handles appear. As you add fades, the duration of the fade is indicated by the small black number box.

What Is This Thing?

In the top-left corner of every clip is this strange symbol (**Figure 9.19**). Click this icon to get shortcuts to effects I'll be covering starting in Chapter 12.

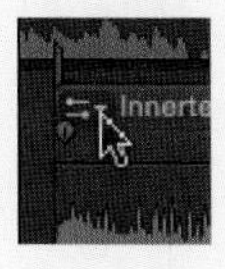

FIGURE 9.19
This icon provides access to animation and effects controls.

I will talk about mixing later in this chapter, for now I want to mention that adjusting the volume of an audio clip is easy—you just drag the "black rubber band" up (to make the clip louder) or down (to make the clip softer). Apple calls this line the *volume control* (**Figure 9.20**).

FIGURE 9.20
To adjust the audio volume of the clip, drag the volume line up to increase the volume or down to decrease it.

Dragging the black line this way changes the volume of the entire clip by the same amount.

Absolute vs. Relative Changes

Hey, you said audio levels can't go above zero! I did and they can't. However, while the audio meters display the *absolute* level of your audio, changing the gain of an individual clip is a *relative* change.

This means that when you change the audio of a clip, you are making the clip louder or softer relative to the level at which it was recorded. Most dialogue is recorded soft, which means you need to increase the levels. Most music is recorded loud, which means you need to decrease the levels so that you can hear dialogue over the music.

So, use the audio meters to determine the actual, absolute value of your audio. This must not go over zero. Use the volume settings on each clip to adjust the relative level so that each clip can be heard. I'll talk more about this in the "Mixing" section later in the chapter.

Adjust the Pan

Just as you can adjust the volume of a clip, you can also adjust the pan. Pan determines where, in the left-right space between two speakers, a sound appears. Although you can adjust volume in the Timeline, you need to use the Inspector to adjust pan. And, seeing as you'll be working with the Inspector for the rest of this book, this is as good a place as any to learn about it.

NOTE A Note on Panning

Generally, you want dialogue and narrator audio panned close to 0. This assures that principal dialogue can be heard, even if one of the speakers on the TV doesn't work. Sound effects can pan as far toward the edges of the sonic field as you want. Keep dialogue very close to the center.

1. Select the clip who's pan you want to adjust. Press Command+4 to open the Inspector.
2. Click Audio at the top of the Inspector. This displays the audio controls associated with a clip (**Figure 9.21**). For example, in the Inspector you can adjust the volume of a clip using the slider or type a value for the audio into the number to the right of the slider. (It turns blue when you can enter values into it.)

   Next to the words *Pan Mode* is the word *None*. This means that no special settings have been applied to the pan.
3. Click None, and the pan menu appears. Most of the time, the best choice is Stereo Left/Right. This allows you to change the pan settings for the selected clip. (Default means the default settings for the clip.) All the other settings in this pop-up menu relate to surround mixing.

   A pan setting of zero means a mono clip is panned to the center—evenly distributed between the two speakers. As you drag the pan slider left or right, the sound moves left or right between the two speakers. (A pan setting of 0 for a stereo clip means the left channel is coming out the left speaker and the right channel is coming out the right speaker. Generally, changing pan on a stereo clip is not a good idea.)
4. You can either drag the slider or type a value between -100 and +100. (Negative numbers move the sound left; positive numbers move the sound right.) In this example, I panned the dialog just slightly to the left, to -17 (**Figure 9.22**).

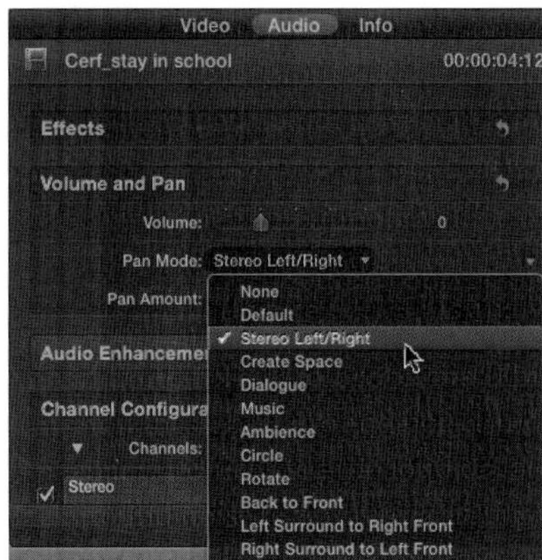

FIGURE 9.21
The Audio section of the Inspector. This allows adjusting volume, pan, channel configurations, and audio enhancements.

FIGURE 9.22
Drag the pan slider left to move the audio toward the left speaker or right to move the sound to the right.

Channel Configuration

Most audio clips are either mono or stereo. However, some camera formats record multiple channels of audio, and some audio-editing applications export six, or more, channels of audio. That's the good news. The bad news is that you may not want all those channels. Or, you may have an interviewer on one channel that you don't want to hear. In other words, you want to select which channels play in the Timeline. The Inspector solves this problem, too, by using the Channel Configuration option.

In this example, I imported a six-channel clip that was exported, by mistake, as a surround clip from Soundtrack Pro. The problem is that I want to use only two channels from this clip, as opposed to all six. Final Cut Pro correctly interprets this clip as a surround 5.1 clip—it has no way of knowing that I made a mistake.

Here's how to turn off the channels you don't need (and this trick also works if you bring in two channels and want to use only one).

1. Click the words *Surround 5.1* next to Channel Configuration (**Figure 9.23**), and change the setting to match how you want your clip to sound. In my case, I have six discrete channels, so I set this to 6 Mono. If you have a stereo pair that you want to convert to dual-channel mono, set this to Dual Mono.
2. The Inspector shows all channels associated with that clip. Uncheck the blue checkbox next to the channels you don't want to play, and you'll hear only the channels that are checked (**Figure 9.24**).
3. These excess channels are *not* deleted; they're merely muted so that you don't hear them. To hear them again, click the blue checkbox to turn it back on. Also, this has no effect on the source media stored on your hard disk.

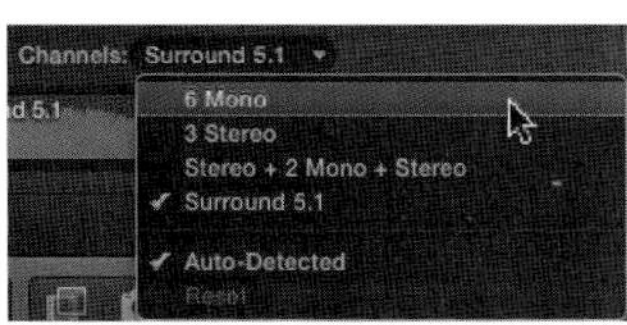

FIGURE 9.23
To change the number of channels audible in a clip or change a clip from stereo to mono, adjust the Channel Configuration setting.

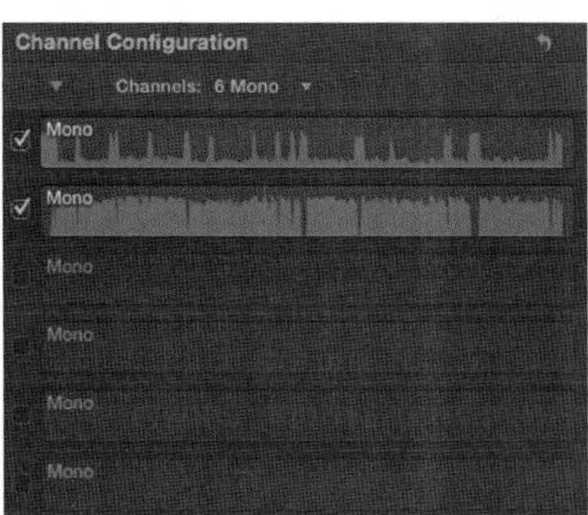

FIGURES 9.24
Set the Channel Configuration to mono, and then uncheck all the channels you don't want to hear. In this case, I turned off four channels.

Special Situations for Audio

Working with audio in FCP X is typically pretty straightforward, even when you encounter special situations. This section covers a few of those and gives you some techniques to use.

Working with Dual-Channel Mono

Many interviews are recorded using dual-channel mono audio, where the interviewer is on one channel and the guest is on another. When you edit the clip to the Timeline, you will automatically hear both channels. However, you have audio level control only on the stereo pair, not each individual channel.

If you want to hear only the guest, mute the interviewer's audio channel in the Inspector as just discussed. However, in the current release, if you want to hear both channels, with separate audio level control for each, the best way is to use the Razor Blade (B) to cut the clip when you want to switch between channels. Then, using the Inspector, mute the channel you don't want to hear for each portion of the clip.

Soloing and Muting Clips

It is often helpful to hear one clip, or a small set of clips, and have everything else silent. In Final Cut 7 you could do this using the green track visibility buttons on the left side of the Timeline, but tracks don't exist in FCP X. There's a very easy way to solve this—solo a clip.

1. First, as always, select the clip or clips you want to solo. (Soloing does not work on clip ranges.)
2. Click the Solo button—the letter *S* wearing headsets—in the top-right corner of the Timeline, or press Option+S. The button glows gold.

   All nonselected clips go gray and become inaudible. Soloing affects only the audio of a clip, not the video (**Figure 9.25**).

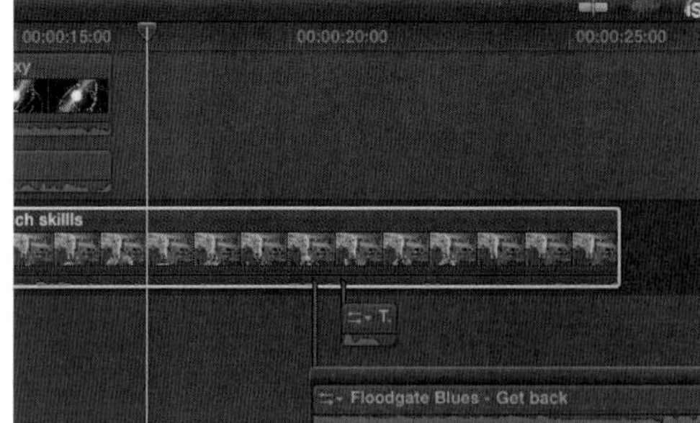

FIGURE 9.25 When the Solo button glows gold, all nonselected clips are grayed out—visible but inaudible.

3. To make everything audible again, click the Solo button, or press Option+S.
4. You can take this one step further and make a clip or selected group of clips inaudible *and* invisible.
5. Select the clips you want to hide and press V. This dims all the selected clips so they are visible as objects in the Timeline but not visible or audible during playback or export.
6. To bring them back, press V again.

Recording a Voice-Over

Voice-overs are a staple of video production. A *voice-over* is an audio-only recording of a narrator who is describing, in some way, what is happening on-screen. Most of the time, the narrator will be recorded outside the edit suite—either on-camera or in a recording studio. However, sometimes, you need to record a quick scratch track (*scratch* meaning temporary or for initial editing only) because you just don't have time to go to a studio. You need to record this audio *right now* and get the project done and gone.

Final Cut Pro makes it easy to record a voice-over, and here's how:

1. First, position your playhead where you want the voice-over to start. (Unlike FCP 7, recording a voice-over does not record in a range.)
2. Choose Window > Record Audio to display the controls to record your audio (**Figure 9.26**).
   - **Destination:** This is the Event that will store your voice-over recordings.
   - **Input Device:** This is the source you want to use for the audio recording. Generally, this will be a microphone attached to your computer.
   - **Gain:** Use this to adjust the level of your recording. In general, you want the audio meters (also called *VU meters*) to bounce around 75 percent of the distance from left to right. In other words, more green is good—up to a point.
   - **Monitor:** Check Monitor to allow you to listen to your audio as you are recording it. Generally, you would only monitor audio using headsets.
   - **Gain:** Use the lower gain slider to adjust the output volume.

   Configure the setup for your microphone and set the level (**Figure 9.27**).

FIGURE 9.26
This is the main interface to record voice-overs.

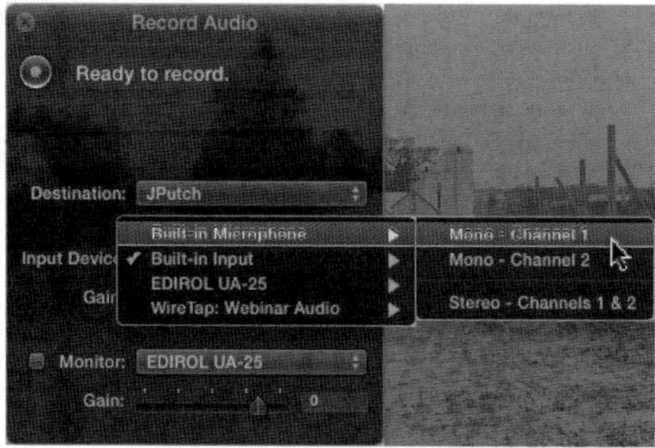

FIGURE 9.27
Use the input device to select the audio source. Generally, audio sounds better the closer the microphone is to your mouth.

3. Click the red button to start recording. Recording starts at the current position of the playhead in the Timeline and runs until you click the red button (or press the spacebar) to stop.
4. The voice-over appears as a stand-alone clip in both the Event Browser and the Timeline. Once it appears in the Timeline, you can move, edit, or trim this clip the same as any other clip.

The original recording file is stored in the Event folder that you set as a destination.

Syncing Double-System Audio

Final Cut Pro X has the ability to sync double-system clips. A *double-system clip* is one where the audio was recorded on one device and the video was recorded on another. A typical example of this is shooting with an (H)DSLR camera, which has very poor sound recording. So, the audio would be recorded on a digital audio recorder while the video is recorded on the camera.

Essential to getting the audio and video synced up is providing some common point—a clapper slate, a still camera flash, a production assistant clapping their hands—that provides a clear indication of where to sync the two files. This is called the *sync point.*

Final Cut Pro can sync multiple video and audio clips and, in doing so, creates a compound clip. The original clips in the Event Browser and the source media on the hard disk are not affected by this process.

Sync points can be markers (my personal favorite), matching timecode, file creation date, and audio content. If there are no matching elements, FCP syncs them based on the starting point of each clip.

For example, say two clips were shot double-system using a clapper slate. Put a marker where that slate "claps" by positioning the skimmer or playhead at the frame where you want the marker and pressing M. (As a note, if the clips are stored in two different Events, it is best to move one of the clips so they are both stored in the same Event.)

FIGURE 9.28
Use markers to create a sync point for both the audio and video clips, and then synchronize the two clips to create a single clip you can use for editing.

After you've created a sync point marker for each clip, select the clips you want to sync and press Option+Command+G, or choose Clip > Synchronize Clips (**Figure 9.28**).

A new compound clip is created and stored in the Event Browser. The name of the clip starts with *Synchronized Clip:* followed by the name of the video clip. When you open it, you'll discover the clips are aligned using their markers.

You can rename a compound clip in the Event Browser by double-clicking the name. To rename a compound clip in the Timeline, select it, and then go to the Info panel in the Inspector.

Double-click the compound clip to open it in the Timeline and notice that both clips are aligned based upon the position of the markers. You can add, modify, or delete clips in this compound clip the same as any other compound clip.

Precise Audio Editing

When you edit audio clips in the primary storyline, you are restricted by the frame boundaries between video frames to editing in single-frame increments. However, you can edit the audio in connected clips much more precisely. For instance, zoom into the Timeline using Command+[plus]. The light gray area extending to the right of the playhead represents a single video frame (**Figure 9.29**).

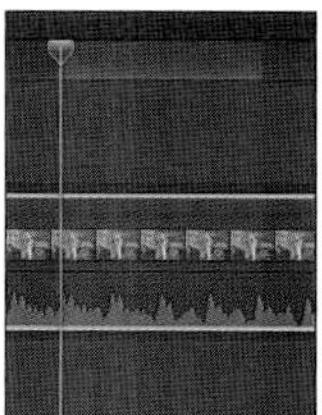

FIGURE 9.29
The light gray area represents the duration of a single video frame.

However, you can zoom in much further when you are editing a connected clip. Remember at the beginning of this chapter when I mentioned that sampling is how you convert analog audio into something the computer can store? Well, most audio recording for video uses 48,000 samples per second—which we call "48k" for short. All those thousands of samples provide lots of room for precise editing.

Go to the Final Cut Pro > System Preferences > Editing tab (or press Command+[comma]) and change the display from timecode to timecode plus subframes (**Figure 9.30**).

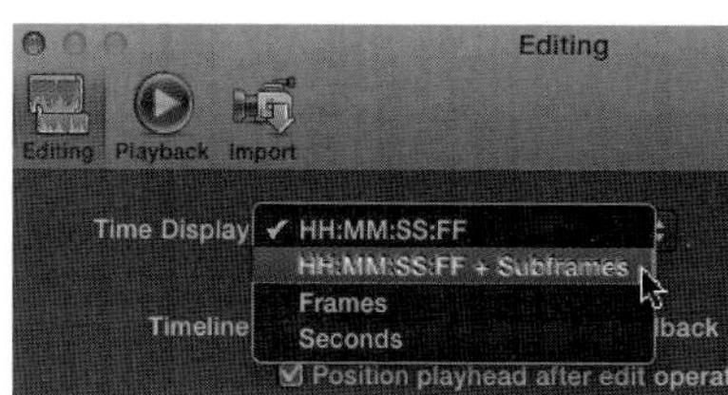

FIGURE 9.30
Changing this Editing preference to timecode plus subframes allows editing audio in connected clips to 1/80th of a frame.

A subframe divides the audio portion of a frame into 80 parts. Notice that now the Dashboard displays a timecode of hours:minutes:seconds:frames.subframes. Subframes mean you can make adjustments 80 times more precise than a video edit. (The smallest increment you can use for video editing is a single frame. So, if you are shooting at 60 frames per second, the shortest duration you can edit video is 1/60th of a second. For the same frame rate, you could edit audio down to 1/4800th of a second!)

FIGURE 9.31
Notice that now the Dashboard displays timecode plus subframes.

To see how this works, choose View > Zoom to Samples, or press Control+Z. Zoom all the way in. Notice, now, that as you move the skimmer around, the frames are not changing in the Dashboard (**Figure 9.31**). Instead, the subframe number changes. You are zoomed so far in that an entire frame more than fills the Timeline.

In the next section, on mixing, I'll show you how to add keyframes to adjust audio levels. By combining subframes with keyframes, you can cut out pops, clicks, and other audio weirdness without doing any damage to your video edit.

NOTE Caution

I was recently taken to task for suggesting specific levels for mixing. All audio and mixes are different, just like edits. If you are an experienced audio engineer, you already have your own system. If you are new to audio, use these numbers to get yourself in the ballpark. Ultimately, as long as levels don't exceed 0 dB, the only way to determine what's "right" is how it sounds.

Mixing

Mixing is the process of adjusting the levels, pan, and "sound" of each clip so that the audience hears what you want them to hear and doesn't hear what you don't want them to hear. Mixing primarily concerns itself with audio levels. However, Final Cut Pro X also contains world-class audio filters, borrowed from Logic, which can truly give your audio a unique sound. With more than 100 filters included in Final Cut Pro X, there are far more settings available than I can cover in this book.

In this chapter, I discuss mixing using pan and volume. The Audio Effects Cookbook (see this book's Introduction) is where I'll show you how to apply some of the more common—and powerful—filters in Final Cut Pro X.

Set Audio Levels

I've mentioned several times already that audio levels should not exceed 0 dB. But, what levels *should* we use for audio mixing? One thing I've learned over the years is that if you get five audio engineers in the same room at the same time, you'll have seven different opinions on what "proper" audio levels should be. (I guess this is analogous to asking five camera operators their opinions about what's the "best" camera.)

Nonetheless, given its current state of development, FCP X is optimized for mixing smaller projects with less demanding specs. It is not yet ready for mixing complex projects, or projects with exceedingly tight audio delivery specs, without relying on third-party plug-ins.

Still, FCP X can be ideal for anything going to the Web, DVD, or local cable, provided you set the right audio levels. So, let's answer that question.

There are three key rules for audio:

- Audio levels must not exceed 0 dB.
- Audio levels are additive; the more clips you have playing at the same time, the louder the total audio level.
- Total audio levels of the full mix should be as close to 0 dB as possible, without going over.

The only rule that will get you fired for breaking it is the first rule. So, be really sure your audio levels are safe.

That being said, **Table 9.1** shows my recommendations for audio levels. The only critical number is the level of the total mix. The other numbers are there to help you rough in your audio levels. How the whole mix sounds is the critical issue—the specific numbers for each clip are not important, as long as your total mix does not exceed 0 dB.

Missing Feature

One of the features I liked in FCP 7 was the ability to quickly scan a Timeline to see whether audio levels exceeded 0 dB (Mark > Audio Peaks). That feature doesn't exist in FCP X. Although you can see waveforms of individual clips, which glow yellow and red as the audio levels approach 0 dB, you can't see waveforms of the entire mix. You need to rely on the audio meters in Final Cut Pro to make sure your audio levels stay below 0 dB.

Also, for those of you in Europe, FCP X does not currently support PPM audio measurements.

● **NOTE** FCP X Displays Peaks

When looking at these levels, remember that FCP X measures peak audio levels, not average levels. There is no way to measure average audio levels, such as RMS, in FCP X.

TABLE 9.1 Audio Mix Levels

Type of Sound	Audio Level for Peaks
Total Mix	-3 to -6 dB
Principal dialogue and narration	-6 to -12 dB
Sound effects	-12 to -18 dB
Music underscore	-18 dB

The purpose of adjusting audio levels is twofold:

- So you can hear what you want the audience to hear
- So your levels stay below 0 dB

To that end, let's take a look at different ways you can adjust levels, starting with the mouse.

● **NOTE** Adjust Audio Levels in Real Time

All the techniques presented here also work in real time. To adjust and listen at the same time, start playback of your clip before adjusting the volume.

Adjust Audio with the Mouse

To adjust audio levels for the entire clip by the same amount, grab the black line, called the *volume line* or *black rubber band*, and drag up to make the sound louder or down to make it softer.

As you drag the line, notice that the waveforms displayed for that clip get taller or shorter (**Figure 9.32**). In fact, as the loudest portions of the waveforms approach 0 dB, the tips first glow yellow; then, when the volume of the clip exceeds 0 dB, they glow red. This is a *very* cool alert system!

FIGURE 9.32
As you drag the black volume level line, the height of the waveforms correspondingly changes.

● NOTE Displaying Audio Meters

Remember, you can't set audio levels by ear—your ears get tired quickly and are not accurate. You need to use, and trust, the audio meters. Press Shift+Command+8 to toggle the display of the audio meters.

While you can't adjust multiple selected clips at once with the mouse, though you can with the Inspector, you can copy effects settings from one clip to another. To do this, select the clip with the volume settings you like, and choose Edit > Copy, or press Command+C.

Then, select the clip or clips that you want to paste these settings into and select Edit > Paste Effects, or press Option+Command+V. The only disadvantage to this shortcut is that you must paste *all* effects from the first clip into the second. You can't choose—as you could in FCP 7—which effects would transfer and which would not.

Use Keyboard Shortcuts to Change Audio

There are keyboard shortcuts that also allow you to change audio for a single selected clip or multiple selected clips:

- To increase audio gain in 1 dB increments, press Control+= [equals].
- To decrease audio gain in 1 dB increments, press Control+- [minus].

Remember, you need to select the clips before adjusting levels.

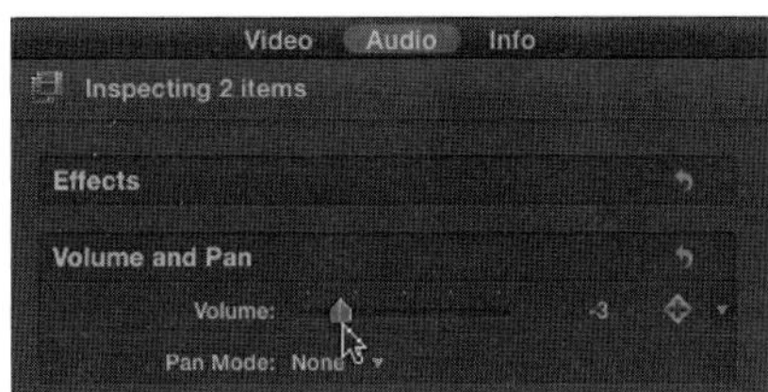

FIGURE 9.33
You can also use the Inspector to set both volume and pan settings.

Change Levels and Pan with the Inspector

You can also use the Inspector to change both audio levels and audio pan for a clip or a group of selected clips (**Figure 9.33**). Changing levels for a group of clips is a new option that you didn't have in Final Cut 7:

1. Select the clips.
2. Press Command+4 to open the Inspector (or click the Inspector icon in the toolbar).
3. Click the word *Audio* at the top.
4. Adjust the volume by either moving the volume slider left and right or entering a number in the text box to the right of the volume slider.

● NOTE Using the Inspector for Pan

As a side note, you can also do the same for pan—adjusting settings for multiple selected clips in the Inspector.

Adjust Volumes With a Menu

You can also adjust audio volumes using a menu:

- Modify > Volume > Up
- Modify > Volume > Down

Generally, I tend to use the mouse to set levels, just so you know. But, all these different techniques work, except...remember at the beginning of this section I said that this would "adjust audio levels for the entire clip by the same amount"? What if you want to adjust different portions of the same clip by different amounts? Can you do that? Yes, but it requires learning one more new thing before this chapter ends: keyframes.

Explaining Keyframes

Keyframes have a bad reputation. However, that's the wrong attitude, because keyframes can really make your life easier.

First, a definition. A *keyframe* is "a point of change during playback." If nothing changes during playback, then you never use keyframes. If you want something to change during playback, such as an audio level, keyframes make that possible.

This second rule is also useful when working with keyframes: You always use keyframes in pairs. There is always a "starting position" and an "ending position." It's like taking a trip; you can't complete the trip unless you know where you are starting and where your destination is. That's the same philosophy to use with keyframes. I like talking about keyframes when mixing audio, because mixing makes keyframes easier to understand.

However, keyframes are not just for audio. Actually, every clip effect, transition, and most built-in settings use keyframes. They may be hidden, but they are used everywhere inside FCP X.

There are two ways to set keyframes for audio levels:

- In the Timeline using the volume lines
- In the Inspector

Set and Adjust Keyframes in the Timeline

To set a keyframe, Option+click directly on the black volume line in a clip. (If you can't see the black line, go to the Switch and click one of the icons that displays waveforms.) Notice as you press the Option key that a small diamond attaches itself to the cursor. This indicates that you are in "keyframe setting mode."

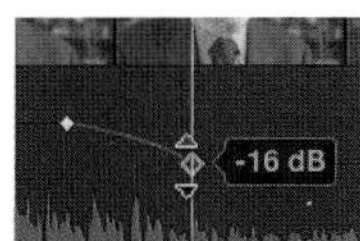

FIGURE 9.34 To set a keyframe, Option-click the black volume line. To adjust a keyframe, drag it.

Wherever you Option+click the line, you'll set a keyframe (**Figure 9.34**):

- To change the timing of a keyframe, drag it sideways along the volume line.
- To change the volume associated with a keyframe, drag it up or down. In this example, I am lowering the volume of the second keyframe so that the sound goes from -3 dB during playback to -16 dB.
- To delete a keyframe, click the keyframe once to select it, and then press the Delete key. Be careful that the keyframe is selected (has a golden border around it); otherwise, when you press the Delete key, you'll delete the clip, not the keyframe. You cannot select a range of keyframes and delete them as a group; keyframes need to be deleted one at a time.

You can adjust keyframes at any time by clicking and dragging. (If you can't select a keyframe, be sure you are using the Arrow [Select] tool.) To set keyframes for a range within a clip, select the Range tool (R) and select a range within the clip containing the volume you want to adjust (**Figure 9.35**).

FIGURE 9.35 You can use the Range selection tool to adjust the audio level within a portion of a clip.

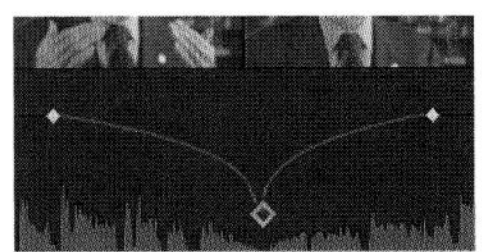

FIGURE 9.36 You can use keyframes to remove short noises like pops. This technique is especially useful in subframe audio editing.

Using either the Arrow or Range tool, drag the volume line inside the range up or down. FCP automatically sets keyframes for the start and end of the range and adjusts the level in the middle.

Keyframes are essential in removing clicks and pops in subframe editing (**Figure 9.36**).

For example, you could use three keyframes to fade the audio to minimize a loud pop:

1. Create a keyframe on either side of the pop.
2. Create a third keyframe directly on top of the pop.
3. Depending upon how long the pop lasts, move the two keyframes on the edges closer together or farther apart.
4. Lower the middle keyframe until the pop is no longer distracting; generally, though, this sounds better if you don't drag the middle keyframe all the way down so the audio becomes silent. This tends to leave an audible "hole" in the mix.

While using ranges within a clip to set keyframes is very helpful, you can't use ranges to set or adjust keyframes across the edit point between clips.

Set and Modify Keyframes in the Inspector

You can also set, modify, and delete keyframes in the Inspector. While not as convenient as setting keyframes directly in the Timeline, the benefit is that all other keyframes in Final Cut X are set using the Inspector. So, once you learn this technique, you will know how to set keyframes for everything else.

Remember, you always set keyframes in pairs, so you never set just one keyframe; you always set a starting and ending keyframe at two different times in the clip. (You can use more than two, but it really helps to think of them in pairs.)

To set a keyframe using the Inspector, follow these steps:

1. Put the playhead on the frame in the Timeline you want to set the keyframe and select the clip.
2. Click the gray plus icon on the right side of the volume slider.

   As soon as a keyframe is added, the plus sign color changes from gray to gold (**Figure 9.37**). This indicates a keyframe exists at that playhead position for that parameter. (Look over to the Timeline, and you'll see a keyframe is also set on the volume line for the clip.)

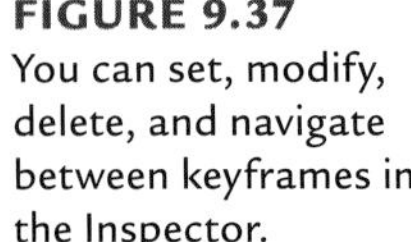

FIGURE 9.37 You can set, modify, delete, and navigate between keyframes in the Inspector.

3. Adjust the volume slider to set the audio level you want before moving the playhead off the keyframe. You can adjust a keyframe only when the playhead is parked on it.
4. Move the playhead to where you want to set the next keyframe and click the plus icon again. Notice that as you set keyframes, small left- and right-pointing arrows appear on either side of the Set Keyframe button. These allow you to jump from one keyframe to the next.

   Using these arrows is a *really* good idea—try to use these, instead of dragging the playhead or skimmer between keyframes. The reason is that these arrows take you *precisely* to a keyframe. If you drag the playhead or skimmer, you could be off by a frame or two and suddenly all your settings get screwed up.
5. Click the small downward-pointing arrow to the right of the keyframe button to display the keyframe pop-up menu (**Figure 9.38**). This allows you to jump between keyframes, add a keyframe (as long as you are not currently parked on a keyframe), or delete a keyframe (assuming you *are* parked on a keyframe).

FIGURE 9.38 Click the small downward-pointing arrow to the right of the glowing keyframe icon in the Inspector to reveal a pop-up menu.

A Quick Note on Surround Mixes

Final Cut Pro X has a built-in surround panner to create surround mixes. All the rules I just covered for stereo mixes are exactly the same for surround mixes—except for pan. The difference between stereo and surround is that stereo uses two speakers, whereas surround, as implemented in FCP X, uses six:

- Left and right front
- Center front
- Left and right rear
- Subwoofer

To take advantage of a surround system, you'll need a way to get audio out of your system as six discrete channels—the headset jack and the optical out are only stereo—and feed each channel to its own speaker. Since the main difference between stereo and surround is panning, I'll cover this briefly in the bonus chapter available for download (see the Introduction).

Summary

This chapter has primarily looked at audio editing and mixing. But audio is more than that—it's also about transitions and effects. Just as you have a wealth of visual effects—each creating exciting new looks for our projects—you also have a wide variety of audio filters that can make your audio sparkle.

However, simply to keep this chapter from turning into its own book, I'm going to cover audio transitions in Chapter 10 and audio effects in a chapter available for download (see the Introduction). There are two key filters that you *really* need to learn: EQ to shape your sound and the Limiter to work magic with audio levels. I use both of these constantly.

Up until now, I've talked about editing and building your story. Now you get to concentrate on making it look great. That is the realm of transitions and effects, which is where we are heading next.

Keyboard Shortcuts

Shortcut	What It Does
S	Toggle video skimming on/off
Shift+S	Toggle audio skimming on/off (video skimming must be on first)
Shift+Command+8	Toggle audio meter display on/off
Option+Command+A	Auto-enhance selected audio clips
Control+S	Expand/collapse audio/video clips
Control+Shift+S	Detach audio from video
Command+4	Toggle display of Inspector on/off
Command+8	Toggle display of audio enhancements
Option+3	Edit audio-only from the Event Browser to the Timeline
Shift+F	Find the matching Event Browser clip to a clip in the Timeline
Control+=	Raise selected clip volume 1 dB
Control+-	Lower selected clip volume 1 dB
Option+S	Solo selected clips
V	Toggle selected clip visibility, or audibility
Option+Command+G	Synchronize clips, generally audio and video, into a compound clip
Control+Z	Toggle subframe audio display on/off
[comma] / [period]	Nudge selected clip(s) left or right one frame
Option+Command+V	Paste all effects into selected clip(s)
Option+click	Set keyframe on volume line

TRANSITIONS

With this chapter, we make another transition—from editing to effects. The first half of the book covered techniques to help you tell your story. The second half examines ways to make your projects look and sound great!

So, it seems appropriate to me to make that transition by discussing transitions first.

Transitions Overview

At its simplest, a transition is a switch from one image or sound to another, to continue advancing the story. The reason we have so many different transitions to choose from is that each transition also contains an aesthetic meaning, or emotional impact.

Here are some examples:

- A **cut** is a change in perspective. You cut when you want the audience to see or hear something different. Cuts are generally, though not always, considered invisible.
- A **dissolve** is a change in time or place. You dissolve when you want to imply a shift from the previous scene and call attention to that shift in locale.
- A **wipe** is a break from the current scene into something totally different. You wipe when you want to forcefully interrupt the flow of the story.

Cuts and dissolves exist for both audio and video. Wipes, on the other hand, are visual only, although audio is increasingly using "whoosh" sound effects as the aural equivalent of a wipe.

A classic example of using wipes to break a story is in sports. A dramatic wipe—generally featuring a logo—flies out of the screen to make the transition from the real time of the game to the surreal world of replays: slo-mo, fast-mo, helmet-cam, grass-cam, blimp-cam, referee-cam, up/down/sideways-cam, then, whoops, *wipe* back to the action. The broadcaster uses the wipe to make the shift from reality to replay and back abundantly clear.

Handles Are Essential

Remember, in Chapter 8, when we talked about handles in trimming? Well, they are even more important when dealing with transitions. Handles are extra video before the Start and after the End. Handles are video contained in the clip, but not displayed in the Timeline (**Figure 10.1**).

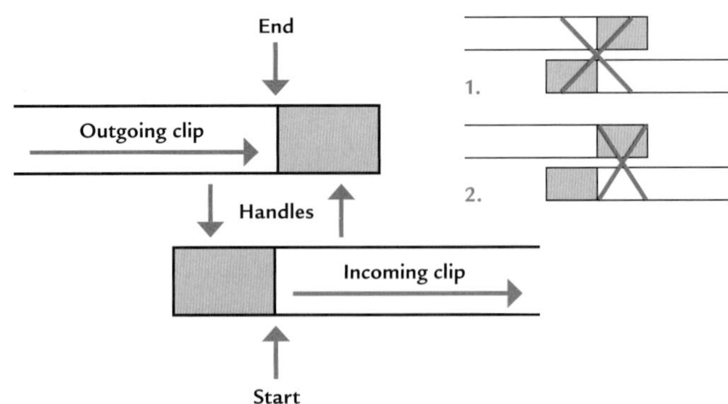

FIGURE 10.1 Handles are extra video before the Start and after the End point. A dissolve, like the two examples indicated by the *X*s in the upper-right corner, can only be created using handles.

In the past, as the box in the top right shows, if you wanted to put a dissolve (or a wipe) between two clips, you would need enough extra video at the end of each clip for the dissolve (indicated by the *X* in the top image). Essentially, each clip needed handles equal to at least half the length of the dissolve. If one of the clips didn't have sufficient handles, you could only dissolve if the other clip had enough handles for the entire transition (the *X* in the bottom image).

Final Cut Pro knows the importance of handles. In fact, when you select the Trim tool (*T*) and select a clip, the ends of the clip glow with one of two colors:

- **Yellow** means there is a handle at that end of the clip (**Figure 10.2**).
- **Red** means there is no handle at that end of the clip.

FIGURE 10.2
A yellow highlight indicates that the edge of the clip has handles. A red highlight indicates there are no handles.

In the past, a lack of handles meant you were out of luck trying to apply a transition, but Apple came up with a solution. In fact, FCP X gives you a number of new solutions. In this chapter, you'll discover a new way to apply transitions to clips that don't have enough handles, a new way of finding and applying transitions using the Transition Browser, new on-screen controls for manipulating transitions, the ability to apply keyframes to transitions, and a new Inspector for making changes to transitions.

Let's start by resolving the issue of how to handle handles, first by looking at FCP's Preferences.

Setting Preferences

You've heard the speech: "Final Cut Pro X was written from the ground up to support 64-bit memory addressing, multiple processors, and background processing!" But what does "background processing" mean?

Background processing means that while you are busy editing in the application, Final Cut Pro is working behind the scenes doing the heavy lifting of file and image processing. Most of the time, background processing is a good thing. However, every so often you may want to turn it off. (For example, when I do FCP X training live online, I turn off background rendering to make sure I don't interfere with the live Internet feed originating from my computer.)

Go to the Final Cut Pro > Preferences > Playback tab. To turn off background processing, uncheck the Background Render checkbox. Generally, you should leave this on. Only turn it off when background processing from Final Cut Pro is interfering with other background processing—like live Internet streaming—that you need to run on your system. The "Start After" setting determines how long the system will wait before starting background processing. Personally, I find the default to be fine.

NOTE Converting Frames to Seconds

I was going to present a table converting frames to seconds, but it got too tricky. Here's a fast formula that does the same thing: Transition duration in frames divided by video frame rate rounded up equals seconds. So, 20 frames at 30 fps (29.97 rounded up) equals 0.67 seconds. 20 frames at 24 fps equals 0.83. 20 frames at 50 fps equals 0.40.

At the bottom of the Editing tab (I reduced the size of this screen to save space) are two settings that affect transitions (**Figure 10.3**):

- **Default length** is the duration, in hundredths of a second, of the default transition. Final Cut Pro defaults to a one-second duration, which I find too long. My preference is a 20-frame dissolve, which translates to 0.67 seconds at 30 frames per second. So, I changed the default to get the duration I prefer. (As a note, some transitions, such as Static, have a built-in default duration, which ignores this preference setting. You can override this duration once the transition is applied to a clip.)
- **Apply Transitions using** includes two options:
  - **Available Media.** This is how Final Cut Pro has always worked. Transitions require handles. If you don't have at least four frames of handles on each clip, no transition is applied. If the available handles are shorter than the requested transition, the transition will be shortened to fit the available handles. This is the traditional way of applying transitions. It never changes the duration of the Timeline.
  - **Full Overlap.** This assumes handles are new to you, or you don't know if you have sufficient handles. When you apply a transition to an edit point, *regardless* of how long your handles are, the downstream clip slides left under the transition to provide handles. Because this requires the downstream clip to shift left, this always changes the duration of the Timeline. Full Overlap ignores any handles on both outgoing and incoming clips.

FIGURE 10.3 Transition preferences are determined by these two options in the Editing tab.

My personal preference is Available Media. If you are having trouble understanding handles, use Full Overlap. Choose the option you want from this pop-up menu.

Rendering and Background Tasks

You may have noticed an orange bar above the clips at the top of the Timeline. That bar indicates something that needs to be rendered. If you watch it closely, after a few seconds it disappears. I'm glad it's gone, but, um, what's going on here? That disappearing bar shows that FCP is busy in the background, rendering your transition so that you don't have to wait.

Rendering is one of those terms invented by geeks to intimidate the rest of us. To "render" simply means to "calculate." It's just that "calculating" doesn't sound as scary as "rendering." So when Final Cut Pro is rendering, it is simply calculating–in this case, calculating video. Thus, "I'm rendering this effect" means the same as "I'm calculating this effect." Final Cut Pro needs to render–calculate–all transitions, effects, retiming, color correction, and anything that changes the clip from the original format in which it was shot.

Rendering in itself is not a bad thing; at some point the computer needs to create finished video based on what you are creating in your Project. The problem with rendering is the time it takes. In the past, you needed to wait for rendering to complete before getting back to work. Now, rendering happens in the background, while you're able to continue working.

You can tell if a background task like rendering is running by looking at the clock in the Dashboard. Normally, when nothing is going on, the clock says 100% with a green circle. However, when background tasks start running, the clock changes color and displays the percentage of background tasks completed (**Figure 10.4**).

FIGURE 10.4 When the clock, on the left of the Dashboard, displays anything less than 100 percent that means background tasks are running.

To see the status of background tasks, click the clock face to display the Background Tasks window (**Figure 10.5**); or, if you must, press Command+9, but this is much less cool.

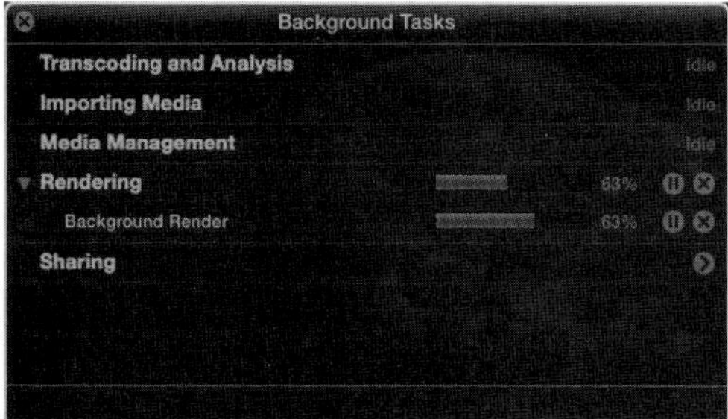

FIGURE 10.5 Click the clock or press Command+9 to open the Background Tasks window.

● **NOTE**

A Metaphysical Challenge

Your task, should you decide to accept it, is to figure out what the colors mean as the clock indicates background tasks are running.

The Background Tasks window displays everything FCP is working on in the background, along with current status. This is a monitoring window, so feel free to click and twirl anywhere you like. If necessary, you can also use this window to pause or cancel currently running background tasks by clicking the icons on the far right of this screen.

Project Properties

There's one other setting to consider as we talk about rendering: the video format of your render files. However, it's not a preference setting, because it doesn't apply universally. Instead, render settings can be different for each project.

This next option is *very* shy. To access Project Properties, choose File > Project Properties, or press Command+J. The Project Library appears, but nothing else.

FIGURE 10.6 Click the wrench icon to access project properties.

Move your gaze over to just above the blue icon for the Inspector and you'll see a wrench icon. Click it (**Figure 10.6**).

This opens the Project Properties window (**Figure 10.7**). We first saw this in Chapter 2, when we created our initial Project. This is where you can change the name of a Project, as well as adjust other settings. In our case, the setting we are concerned about for rendering is at the bottom: Render Format.

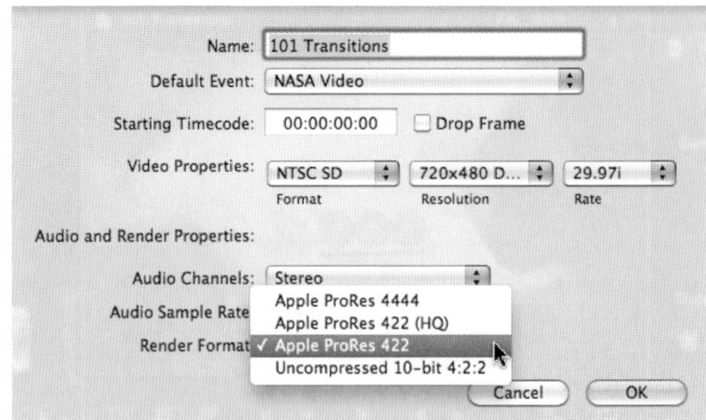

FIGURE 10.7 Project Properties determine the video format for render files, among several other settings.

We have four choices:

- **Apple ProRes 4444.** The absolute highest image quality. *Huge* file sizes. Only use when you need an alpha channel, which we will discuss later in effects.
- **Apple ProRes 422 (HQ).** Really high quality. I recommend using this when your lenses cost more than your camera and you're spending way too much time lighting a scene.
- **Apple ProRes 422.** The overall best choice, especially for less expensive cameras.
- **Uncompressed 10-bit 4:2:2.** For use when you need to render in a non-Apple format.

Render Tip

Most of the time, Final Cut Pro begins rendering almost immediately. However, just as with FCP 7, you can remind FCP X that it needs to render something "right now!"

There are two render options:

- Render All (Shift+Control+R) renders the entire project.
- Render Selection (Control+R) renders whatever is selected in the project.

Gone—thank goodness!!—are all the render bar colors of earlier versions of Final Cut Pro.

Apple's Help documentation states: "Transcoding files to the Apple ProRes 422 codec creates high-quality files that are optimized for fast and efficient editing. Apple ProRes 422 provides better performance during editing, faster render times, better color quality for compositing, and faster export times when compared to many standard video codecs. Apple ProRes codecs produce video that is indistinguishable from uncompressed high-definition (HD) video and needs less storage space than uncompressed standard-definition (SD) video."

Most of the time, I recommend using Apple ProRes 422. But you do have choices, and now you know where to find them.

Transition Basics

There are four ways you can apply a transition, in either the primary storyline or a connected storyline:

- Apply a matching audio and video transition.
- Apply a video transition with no matching audio transition.
- Apply an audio transition with no matching video transition.
- Apply an audio transition with a different duration than the video transition.

The first two are easy; the last two require additional work. Let's start with the easy stuff.

Apply a Matching Audio and Video Transition

Let's start with something simple—adding a matching audio and video transition between two clips in the primary storyline.

1. Using the Select (Arrow) tool, select the edge at an edit point, then press Command+T. Unlike FCP 7, you only need to select one edge, not the entire edit point.

   This applies the default transition—a cross-dissolve to the video and a cross-fade to the audio—to the selected edit point (**Figure 10.8**). Both the audio and video transitions have the same duration.

   The transition is centered on the edit point, and this centering can't be changed when using the keyboard shortcut. Nor can the default transition itself; it is always a cross-dissolve. However, as you'll learn in a few pages, you can easily replace one transition with another once a transition is placed on the Timeline.

FIGURE 10.8 This is a selected transition icon. Adjust its duration by dragging an edge left or right.

▲ TIP Adding Multiple Transitions at Once

If you select an edit point, the transition is added to the edit point. If you select an entire clip, transitions are applied to both ends of the selected clip. If you select multiple clips, transitions are applied to all edges of all selected clips. Unlike FCP 7, you cannot apply transitions within a selected range spanning multiple clips.

FIGURE 10.9
To change the duration of a transition, drag an edge. A red edge means you've reached the end of a handle.

2. To modify the transition using the mouse, drag an edge of the transition. The small number box shows the amount of change to the duration (**Figure 10.9**). If an edge turns red, you have run out of handles and can't make the duration of that transition any longer, though you can always make it shorter.
3. To delete a transition, select it and press Delete.

   If you delete a clip that has a transition attached to it, the transition remains after you delete the clip. If you want to delete both the clip and the transition, select both before pressing the Delete key.

▲ TIP Fading to Black

Unlike Final Cut Pro 7, you don't need to add a slug when fading to or from black. Simply add the default transition to the first clip in your Project. The transition will start fully in black and fade up to the clip. The same applies at the end of a Project. You don't need to add a slug to get the transition to fade fully to black. To fade to black in the middle of a scene, you can either use the Fade to Color transition, or add a gap between the two clips and apply the default transition to both sides of the gap.

Apply a Video-only Transition

Here's how to apply a video-only transition between two clips:

▲ TIP Expand that Audio

A fast way to expand the audio from the video is to double-click the audio waveforms.

● NOTE Can I Use Other Transitions?

Certainly, and we are coming to that. For now, though, I want to illustrate how to apply video-only and audio-only transitions because these techniques apply to all transitions, not just dissolves.

1. Make sure the Timeline is showing both video thumbnails and audio waveforms, then choose Clip > Expand Audio/Video, or press Control+S.

   The audio and video remain linked, but you can see them as two separate elements of the same clip (**Figure 10.10**).
2. If you can't see waveforms in the Timeline, go to the Switch for the Timeline and six icons appear at the top. Click one of the four icons on the left (**Figure 10.11**). If you select one of the two icons on the right, waveforms will not be displayed, even if you expand a clip.
3. Select just the video portion of the edit point and press Command+T.

   A video-only cross-dissolve is applied to the selected portion of the edit point (**Figure 10.12**).

FIGURE 10.10
Expanding the audio and video of two adjacent clips allows adding transitions to just the video. Notice the video Start is selected.

FIGURE 10.11
If you can't see waveforms, use the Switch to display them.

FIGURE 10.12
A transition is applied just to the video edit point between two clips.

4. As you learned, you change the duration by dragging an edge of the transition to make the duration longer or shorter. To delete the transition, select it and press the Delete key.
5. You can collapse the clip back into its solitary state by choosing Clip > Collapse Audio/Video, or pressing Control+S (**Figure 10.13**). However, if you do so, you can't tell whether the transition you applied to the clip is video and audio, or just video.

FIGURE 10.13 Here's a collapsed clip with just a video transition applied.

For this reason, although you *can* collapse clips, if you are doing video-only transitions, I recommend that you don't.

Apply an Audio-Only Transition

There are two ways to apply an audio-only cross-fade: manually, using fade handles; or automatically, using a transition. I prefer this manual method and here's how it works.

1. Select the two clips between which you want to apply the transition.
2. Choose Clip > Expand Audio/Video (or press Control+S).
3. Drag the edge of the outgoing clip to the right, to overlap it with the incoming clip.

4. Drag the edge of the incoming clip to the left, to overlap it with the outgoing clip.
5. Drag the fade handle for each clip to cross-fade from one clip to the next.

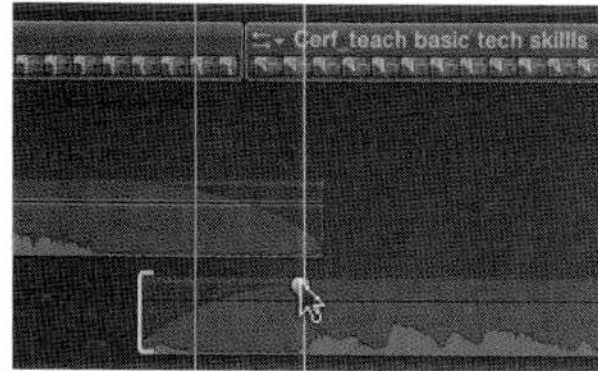

6. If necessary, right-click a fade handle to change the shape of each fade.

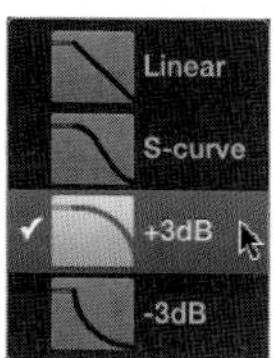

▲ TIP Use This Method Over Detached Clips Method

When I first learned FCP X, I didn't know about this technique. Now that I do, however, I find it far superior to the "detached clips" method we discuss in the next section.

This process of using fade handles to create transitions can be used for any audio clips, either on the primary storyline, connected clips, or connected storylines. The benefit of this approach is that you have complete control over the duration and shape of the fade. Plus, for clips in the primary storyline, you don't have to disconnect the audio from the video, which means you don't run the risk of losing sync between audio and video. The only disadvantage of this approach is that it takes more steps than simply selecting an edit point and applying a transition.

Advanced Transitions

Transitions require clips to be contained in storylines. So far you've spent most of your time with the primary storyline. Now you'll learn about connected storylines.

Connected Storylines

A connected storyline is a collection of clips connected to the primary storyline. A connected storyline can be one or more clips, audio only, video only, or both audio and video.

Stop the Presses! You Can Add Transitions to Connected Clips

With the release of FCP X 10.0.1, Apple added the ability to add transitions to connected clips. Select the edit point where you want to add a transition, and press Command+T (or drag a transition from the Transition Browser). FCP X automatically converts the connected clip into a connected storyline and applies the transition. This works for both connected video and connected audio clips.

FIGURE 10.14 The dark gray bar over a clip, or clips, indicates it's a connected storyline.

To add transitions to individual audio clips, you need to either use fade handles or convert them into connected storylines.

1. To manually convert a clip, or clips, into a connected storyline, select the clip(s) you want to convert and choose Clip > Create Storyline, or press Command+G. A dark gray bar appears over the top of the selected clip(s) indicating it is now a storyline (**Figure 10.14**).
2. Select the edge of the clip where you want the transition to appear—or select the entire storyline to apply transitions to all edit points at once—and press Command+T.

   The default transition appears at the selected edit point. You can modify the duration by dragging an edge.
3. As usual, delete a transition by selecting it and pressing Delete.

Detaching Audio for Transitions

In the last section, I showed how to create an audio cross-fade using fade handles. Now I want to show how to create an audio transition using transitions. (After you see this, you'll use the fade handles method, too.)

To apply a transition to audio, you need to convert the audio clips into connected storylines. (While the 10.0.1 release of FCP X will convert connected audio clips into connected storylines, it does not do so for clips on the primary storyline.)

1. Select the clips where you want to add an audio transition, and choose Clip > Detach Audio, or press Shift+Control+S. The audio separates from the video and becomes a connected clip (**Figure 10.15**). In this example, I have two connected audio clips attached to the video on the primary storyline.
2. With the latest 10.0.1 release, the process is simple: Make sure the Apply Transitions preference is set to "Available Media," then select the edit point between the two detached audio clips where you want the transition applied and press Command+T. This automatically converts the two connected audio clips into a connected storyline and applies the transition (**Figure 10.16**).
3. Change the duration of the transition by dragging an edge. An audio transition icon looks the same as a video transition icon.
4. As usual, delete the transition by selecting it and pressing Delete.

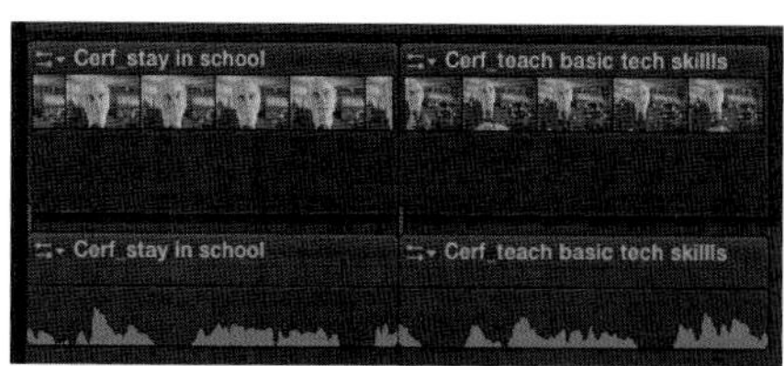

FIGURE 10.15
Detaching audio from video is another way to apply an audio transition.

FIGURE 10.16
These two audio clips, converted to a connected storyline, have an audio transition applied.

NOTE Another Way to Change the Duration

Yes, you can select the transition and press Control+D and type in the duration you want, or choose Modify > Change duration. You can also use the Inspector, which we are coming to shortly.

If you want to "reconnect" the audio and video elements, including the transition, select the detached clips and choose File > Create compound clip, or press Option+G. Once you've detached audio from video, you can't reattach it, except by using a compound clip.

FIGURE 10.17
Dragging the audio fade handles at either end of a clip allows you to add a fade up, or fade down, to each clip. And, if the clips overlap, you can use this to create audio cross-fades.

In addition to selecting an audio edge and pressing Command+T, you can add a fade-in or fade-out to an audio clip simply by dragging the fade handles. Change the duration of the fade by dragging one of the dots at the edges of the clip (**Figure 10.17**).

Warning! There Is No "Out of Sync" Indicator

One of the dangers of detaching clips is that there is no indicator if the detached audio and video elements go out of sync. (FCP 7 users will remember this indicator as a red flag at the start of a clip.)

This is why grouping the audio and video back into a compound clip is so important. If you don't, it is really easy to knock the audio out of sync and not realize it; and there is no easy or automatic way to get clips back in sync.

There is a workaround, however. Add a marker on the detached video and audio clips when you first detach them. If the markers drift out of alignment, sync has been broken. To fix sync, with snapping enabled, drag a range that snaps from one marker to the next, and see the range's duration in the information bar at the bottom. This duration helps you to manually move, slip, or slide the connected clips back into sync.

Because detaching audio can cause serious sync issues, I strongly recommend you create your audio fades for clips in the primary storyline using the fade handles method discussed earlier.

▲ **TIP** A Quick Way to Open the Precision Editor

A fast way to open the Precision Editor is to double-click the Roll trim icon of a transition. If no transition is applied, simply double-click the edit point.

Trimming Clips Under Transitions

One of the nice features in Final Cut Pro 7 and Final Cut Pro Express, that carried forward into FCP X, is the ability to trim clips even after a transition is applied. Here's how.

After you add a transition, look in the top left and right corners; each has a faint icon, as does the top center (**Figure 10.18**). The corners allow you to ripple edit the outgoing clip (left) or the incoming clip (right).

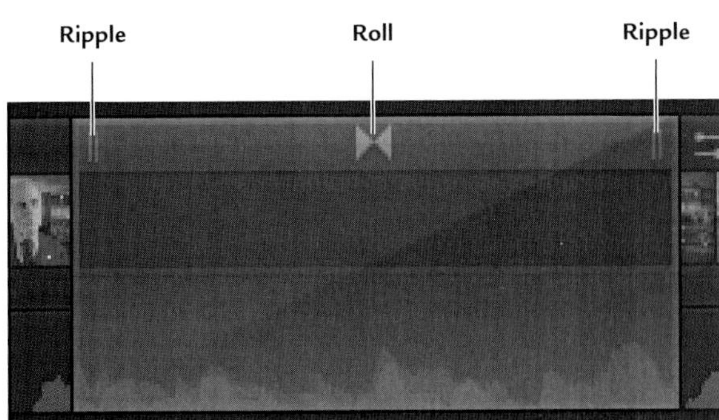

FIGURE 10.18 There are three icons that allow you to trim the clips under a transition.

The top center icon allows you to move the edit point itself—a Roll trim—simply by dragging, as seen here. You can also use the Trim tool to slip the content of a clip, without changing the location or duration of the transition. The nice thing is that trimming the clips does not affect the duration of the transition.

If the clips are in the primary storyline, you can also trim using the Precision Editor after a transition is applied to an edit point. Press Control+E to open the Precision Editor (**Figure 10.19**).

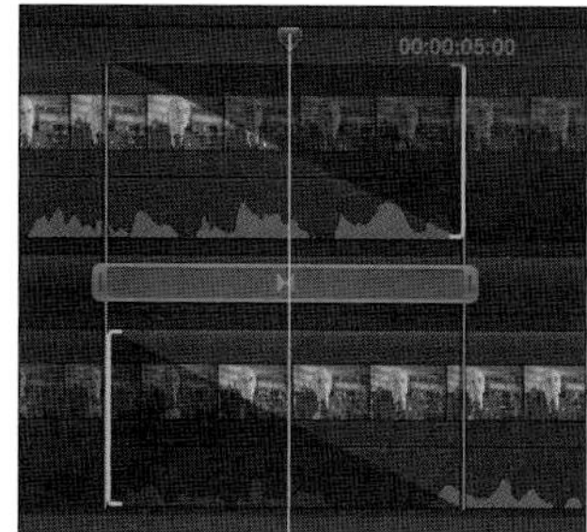

FIGURE 10.19
You can trim both edit points and transitions using the Precision Editor.

Using the Precision Editor, which we covered in Chapter 8, you can ripple trim the edge of either clip, roll the edit point to a different location, or adjust the duration of the transition. All you need to do is drag an edge. The key point here is that it is easy to make changes to any part of the edit quickly and easily.

NOTE Can I Duplicate a Transition?

Easily. You can use Copy/Paste, but an even faster way is to hold the Option key while dragging the transition to a new location. This makes a copy of the transition with all the settings of the original transition. Remember when using Copy/Paste that you need to select the new edit point before pasting the transition. If you drag or paste a transition to a location where a transition already exists, the existing transition is deleted and replaced by the new one.

Transition Inspector

As you learned in Chapter 9, the Inspector is where you make changes to all your effects. It is context-sensitive, so it changes depending on what you select in the Timeline. While you generally don't need this during editing, it is essential for all effects.

For example, select a transition in the Timeline and click the Inspector icon, or press Command+4. The Inspector window opens, displaying the settings you can change for this transition (**Figure 10.20**). As you'll see, other transitions—specifically wipes—provide many more settings you can play with. In this case, you have adjustable settings for both video and audio.

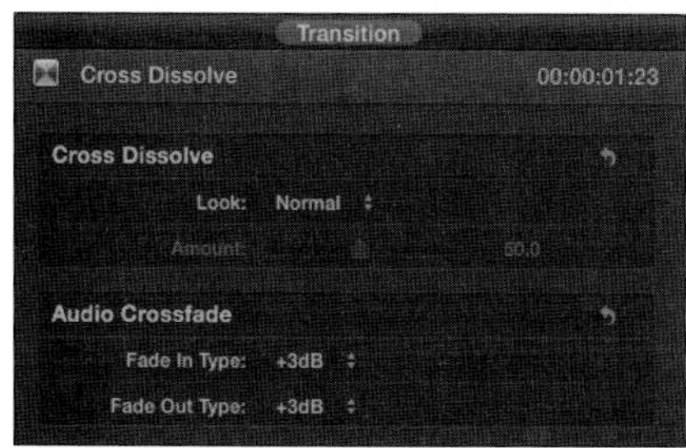

FIGURE 10.20
The Inspector is where you make changes to all transitions and effects.

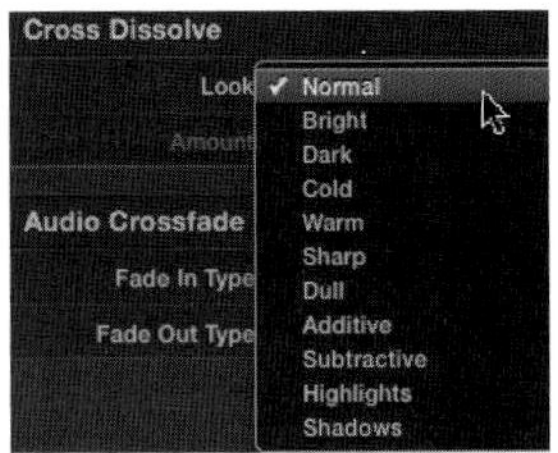

FIGURE 10.21
You can even change the look of a dissolve using this pop-up menu.

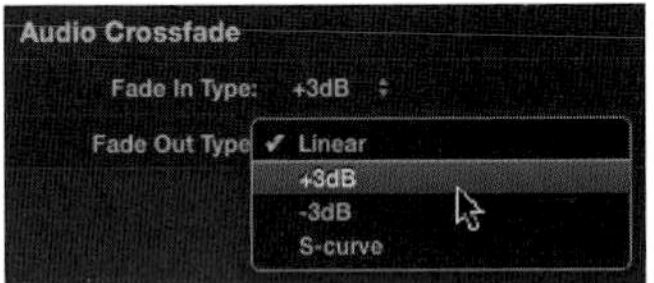

FIGURE 10.22
You also use the Inspector to change the shape of audio fades.

Click the word *Normal* and discover all the different ways you can change the look of a dissolve (**Figure 10.21**).

The nice thing about these different looks is there is nothing to adjust. If you like them, they are good; if not, change them to something that you like better. The default setting is Normal.

Just as you can set fade shapes on the audio fade handles, you can also set fade shapes on audio transitions using the Inspector (**Figure 10.22**). The settings do exactly what you learned in Chapter 9—only here you choose from a menu, not the icon you used when changing shapes in the Timeline.

My recommendation is to choose Linear when fading to or from black, and choose +3dB when fading between two different audio sources. However, each of these four settings has value, so feel free to experiment to find what sounds best to you.

It's interesting—I've spent all these pages talking about exactly one transition: a cross-dissolve, or cross-fade. Yet, Final Cut Pro has almost 100 different transitions you can use for your Projects. The cool part is that you already know how to apply and adjust them. But, um, you don't know where to find them.

That brings you back to the Browsers—which is where you will be spending a lot of time for the rest of this book. Let's take a look, now, at the Transition Browser.

Transition Browser

Like all Browsers, the Transition Browser allows you to find, review, and select elements you can use for your Projects—in this case, transitions. This is where the fun part of using transitions kicks in—there are dozens of transitions to choose from. Since all the browsers work the same, let me illustrate how they work using the Transition Browser as the example.

1. To open the Transition Browser, click its icon; there is no keyboard shortcut for this, though you can create your own in the Command Editor (**Figure 10.23**).

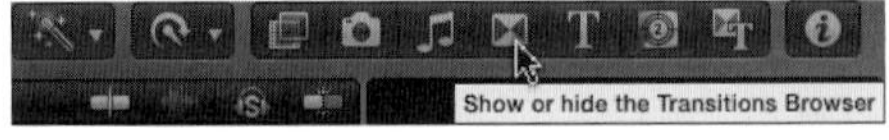

FIGURE 10.23
All Browsers are grouped in the Toolbar. Click the Transition Browser icon to open it.

2. On the left are different transition categories. Click a category and all the transitions in that category are displayed on the right. This screen shot has the Wipes category chosen (**Figure 10.24**).

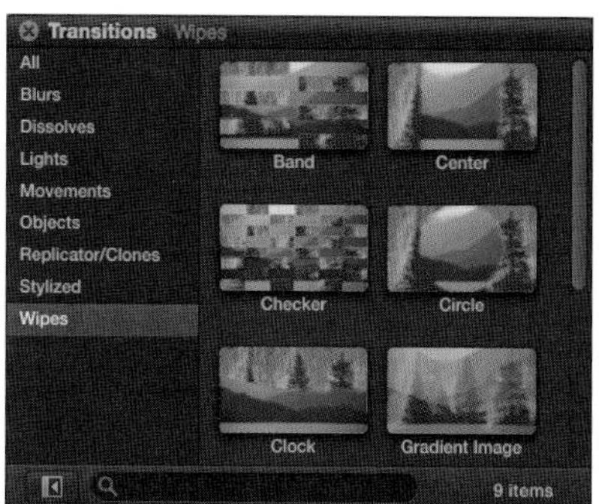

FIGURE 10.24
The Transition Browser. The Wipes category is chosen in the Categories column, showing nine different wipe transitions.

● **NOTE** How Are Transitions Created?

Transitions are created in Motion 5. Essentially, every effect and transition is a Motion template saved in such a way that Final Cut Pro has access to it. You can create your own transitions—even effects—in Motion 5 for your own Projects.

The Transition Browser displays individual transitions on the right. Skim across a few of these thumbnails and you'll see a preview of the effect—both in the thumbnail and in the Viewer above.

3. To search for a specific wipe, enter the text you want to search for in the Search box at the bottom, and the results will display in the Browser.
4. To reset the Search box to empty, which displays all transitions again, either delete the text you entered or click the reset icon—an *X* in a circle on the right side of the search box.

There are two ways to apply a transition from the Browser:

- Drag the transition from the Browser to the edit point.
- Select the edit point first, then double-click the transition inside the Browser.

Whichever you pick, the new transition is applied to the edit point. Then you can change its duration, copy it, move it, delete it; all the things I've talked about earlier in this chapter for dissolves also apply to any transition in the Transition Browser.

You can also replace one transition with another by dragging the new transition on top of the old one. This is just like a Replace edit. The new version inherits the same duration and location as the old transition.

As you'll quickly discover, many of these transitions are animated. As a general rule, be careful of using too many different animated transitions in one Project—it starts to look like a video ransom note. As much as possible, strive to give your Project an overall consistent visual style.

Animate Transitions

This transition animation is controlled from two places: the Inspector and on-screen controls in the Viewer. Let's take a look at both.

1. First, apply a transition to two clips. For example, from the Objects category, I applied a Star transition to two clips (**Figure 10.25**).
2. With the Star transition selected, look in the Inspector to see all the controls available—far more than the simple dissolve we looked at earlier (**Figure 10.26**). (Since this is a video transition, I did not capture the audio controls in this screen shot, but they are available in the Inspector as well.)
3. Play with a few of these settings so you can see what they do. Under Edge Treatment, for example, you can change the edge from feather to border, and set its width. One setting is the Center Point, which determines where the center of the transition starts. You could adjust the position by typing numbers in the Inspector, but it is much easier to use the on-screen controls in the Viewer. The on-screen controls let you change the position of an effect as well as other parameters, which vary by effect.

   The large, round white circle determines position (**Figure 10.27**). Drag the ring and the center of the effect moves; in this example, I'm moving it to the right, to reveal the runner.

   But there's a feature in FCP X that you haven't had before—the ability to add keyframes to a transition to animate it over time. For instance, let's say I want this star to spin as it transitions from one clip to the next. To do that, you use keyframes.
4. Using the arrow keys, move the playhead so it is over the first frame of the transition. The large *L* angle bracket in the lower-left corner of the Viewer indicates you are on the right spot; it marks the start of the incoming clip.

FIGURE 10.25
Here's a star transition applied between two clips.

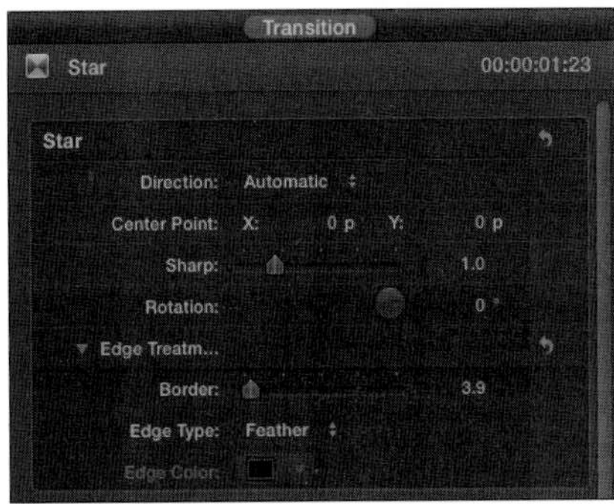

FIGURE 10.26
Use the Inspector to modify the settings for a transition. Animated transitions have more controls than a simple dissolve.

FIGURE 10.27
On-screen controls provide a faster and easier alternative to the Inspector. Drag the large white circle to change the position of the selected image.

5. With the playhead on the first frame of the transition, go to the Inspector and, as you roll your mouse over the word *Rotation,* a gray keyframe button—a diamond—appears on the right side. Click it to set a keyframe at the position of the playhead.

   When a keyframe is at the position of the playhead, the keyframe button turns gold (**Figure 10.28**). Note that keyframes are always set for specific parameters, not for the transition in general.

6. Again, using the arrow keys, position the playhead so it is over the last frame of the transition. The *J* angle bracket in the lower-right corner of the Viewer indicates you are in the right spot; it marks the last frame of the outgoing clip.

7. Set another keyframe for rotation—remember, you always work with keyframes in pairs—and in this example, I entered a Rotation value of 180. This means that during the transition, the star will rotate 180 degrees (**Figure 10.29**). As you play through the transition, you see the transition rotating, just as expected.

FIGURE 10.28
Click the diamond to add a rotation keyframe to the selected transition at the position of the playhead. Notice the rotation setting of 0.

FIGURE 10.29
You always add keyframes in pairs. Here, a second rotation keyframe is added at the end of the transition with the value set to 180.

This ability to add keyframes to transition parameters is very new and *very* cool!

Special Case: Multi-Image Transition

There is one special-case transition I want to cover before we wrap this chapter—a multi-image transition. Although these only work in the primary storyline, these create a very interesting effect, which I want to show you.

1. Search for the Pan Lower Right transition from the Stylized category. It contains multiple images on screen—specifically, six. Two are at the point of the transition, and the other four are randomly chosen from the clip before and after.

2. Select the transition, and the special yellow markers used by this transition appear. What you want to do is move these markers so you can select a better set of pictures to use in the transition (**Figure 10.30**).

3. To do that, drag a marker until it displays the image you want in the Viewer.

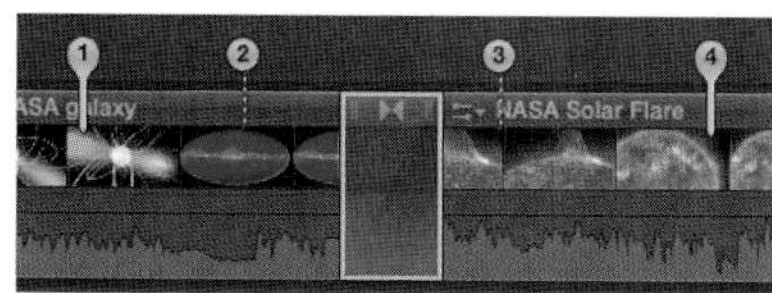

FIGURE 10.30
The yellow markers indicate where images will be taken for use in the transition. Each marker number corresponds to a specific image in the transition.

You can even position markers over different clips—in the primary storyline—to add even more variety to the transition.

Summary

With dozens of transitions to choose from, it's easy to indulge in "spot the stars" transition casting. However, try to avoid showing off every transition in the program in your Project! A consistent visual feel is always the best option. When in doubt, use a dissolve.

This chapter has introduced two new concepts that we will be working with for the remainder of the book: the Inspector and Browsers. In the next chapter, we'll take what we learned here and apply it to adding titles to our Project. For now, though, give yourself permission to play—you've worked hard to get to this point. Time to relax and enjoy yourself with some of these transitions!

Keyboard Shortcuts

Shortcut	What It Does
Command+[comma]	Open Preference settings
Command+9	Display the Background Tasks window
Command+J	Open Project Properties
Command+T	Apply the default audio/video transition
Control+S	Expand/collapse audio/video clips
Command+G	Create a connected storyline
Shift+Control+S	Detach audio from video
Option+G	Create compound clip from selected clips
Control+E	Open the Precision Editor for selected edit point
Shift+Control+R	Render entire Project
Control+R	Render selection

TITLES AND TEXT

Titles are what you use to add text to your Projects. And Final Cut Pro has more than 150 animated titles to choose from, in a number of categories.

This chapter shows you how to find, apply, modify, and delete titles. Along the way, I'll show you how to create commonly used titles for your own Projects.

Title Basics

If Browsers are new to you, read Chapter 10 to learn how to use a Browser.

The Titles Browser is part of the Browser buttons on the right side of the Toolbar. To open it, either click the letter *T* icon, which is the symbol for this Browser, or create a custom keyboard shortcut in the Commands Editor (**Figure 11.1**). Inside are more than 150 animated titles, grouped into six categories displayed on the left.

Let's start by adding a title to our Project that doesn't contain any animation—the Custom title.

1. To find this title, choose the All category on the left—otherwise the search just searches in the selected category—and type "Custom" in the search box at the bottom (**Figure 11.2**).
2. There are three options for applying a title:
   - Double-click it to connect it to the primary storyline at the position of the playhead.
   - Drag the title into the Timeline and drop it where you want it to connect.
   - Position the playhead in the Timeline where you want the title to appear and press the Q, E, D, or W key. Titles can be edited to the Timeline just like video clips.
3. Once the title has been placed in the Timeline, put the playhead in the middle of the title clip to see it in the Viewer (**Figure 11.3**). It is generally better practice to put the playhead, rather than the skimmer, in the middle of a title because that allows you to see the changes you are making in the Viewer.

NOTE Are Titles Always Connected Clips?

No. A title can be edited directly into the primary storyline, where it acts as a full-screen graphic. Most of the time, however, titles are connected clips.

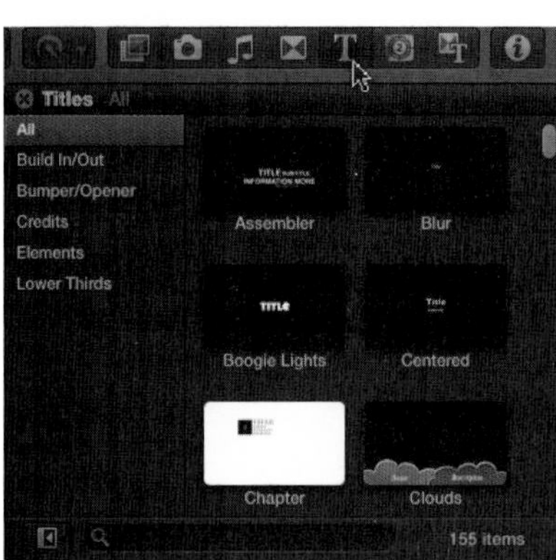

FIGURE 11.1
Open the Titles Browser by clicking its icon.

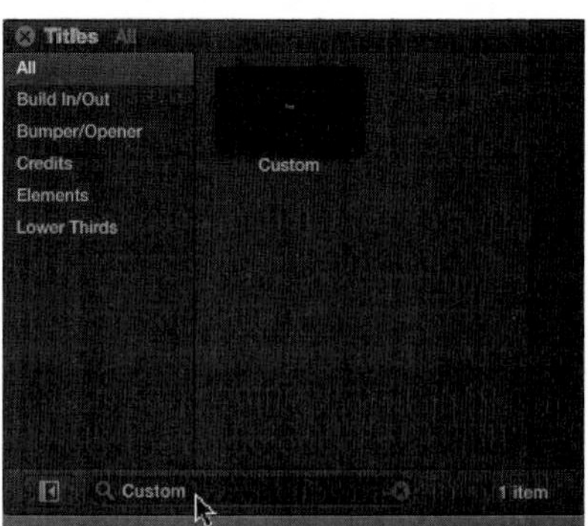

FIGURE 11.2
The Custom title is a good choice for a title that doesn't contain any animation.

FIGURE 11.3
Text in the Timeline is almost always a connected clip. Put the playhead in the middle of the title to see it in the Viewer.

When it comes to modifying a title, there are two things you can change:

- The text and styling in the title
- The location, duration, and animation of the title

You already know how to modify the duration of a title—drag an edge in the Timeline or use Control+D. So I won't spend any more time explaining what you already know. And it should come as no surprise that the way you delete a title is to select it in the Timeline and press the Delete key (just in case you needed reminding). I'll talk about Title animation in the next section. Here, I want to show you how to change the text and modify its style.

4. To move the text on-screen, double-click the text in the Viewer (**Figure 11.4**). The small position ring that you first saw moving the star animation in the last chapter shows up at the bottom of the text.
5. Drag the ring. In this example, I moved it to the upper-right corner of the Viewer.
6. Then, with the title text still selected, change the text. I changed the text—similar to changing text in Adobe Photoshop—by typing the new text directly into the Viewer (**Figure 11.5**).
7. Press the Escape (ESC) key to exit text-entry mode.
8. To add a fade-in to the text—assuming it doesn't have animation associated with it—select the edge where you want the transition to appear and apply the default transition. Adjust as necessary.

▲ **TIP** How Long Should a Title Be Displayed?

Ahhh... there's a raging controversy going on right now about that. Producers want titles up and out as quickly as possible. My feeling is the reason you put a title on screen is so that people will read it. Back in the day, you had titles hold for eight seconds. That would seem like an eternity now. I recommend that titles hold for at least five seconds, or long enough for you to read it out loud twice—whichever is longer.

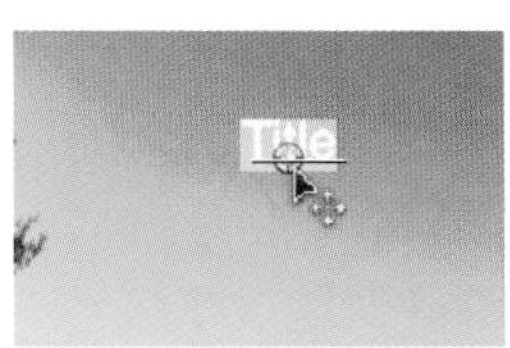

FIGURE 11.4
Double-click the text in the Viewer to display the on-screen controls, then drag the circle to move the position of a title. Select text in the title to make changes.

FIGURE 11.5
With the text selected, make changes by typing in the new text.

Modifying Titles

These basics are all well and good, but Apple did not give you 155 animated titles to only use the most boring one in the collection. So, in this section, I'll show you how to modify titles and animation using the Inspector. Then you'll learn a very cool way to find and replace text directly in the Timeline.

FIGURE 11.6
The Assembler animated title shows a collection of text all coalescing in the frame.

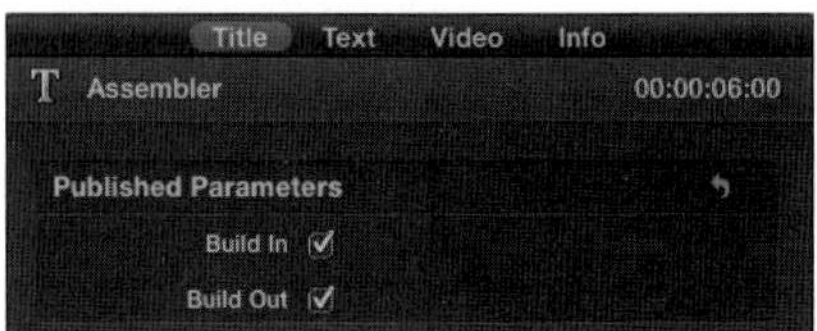

FIGURE 11.7
There are four tabs in the Inspector. The Title tab controls title effects, while the Text tab allows for adjusting the text.

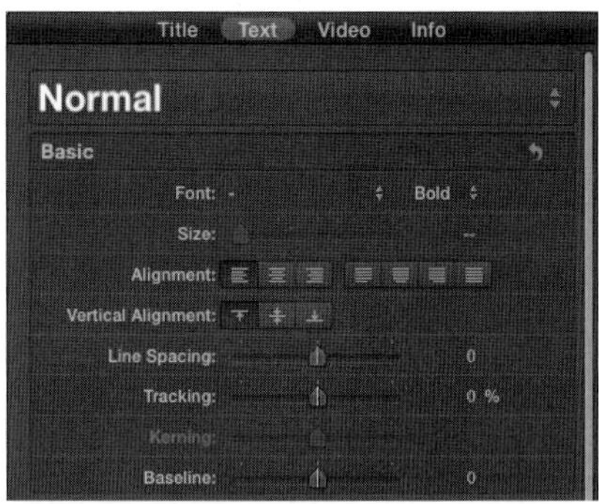

FIGURE 11.8
The Text tab offers extensive flexibility in how you format text.

In this case, I chose Assembler, from the Build In/Out category, and edited it to the Timeline by dragging. I selected the title and double-clicked each element in the Viewer—five in all—and changed the wording and position to match the screen shot here (**Figure 11.6**).

Let's take a look at this in the Inspector (**Figure 11.7**). As always, select the title in the Timeline before opening the Inspector. Ideally, put the playhead in the title so you can see it in the Viewer as well.

The **Title** tab controls the animation associated with the title and any related parameters. Build-in or Build-out determines whether to animate the start or the end of the title. Uncheck these to turn off animation.

The **Text** tab controls the look of the text on the screen.

The **Video** tab controls all the built-in effects associated with that clip. Chapter 12 goes over these settings in detail. I will ignore them in this chapter.

The **Info** tab provides access to the metadata that I talked about in Chapter 4.

For this example, I will leave the opening and closing animation for this title turned on.

Manipulate Text

Click the Text tab and you'll discover that, unlike with Final Cut Pro 7 or Final Cut Express, there's a ton of ways you can manipulate text—or at least a whole lot more than ever before (**Figure 11.8**).

These settings at the top control font, style, size, alignment—all the text controls that you'd expect in any program. Here are a few definitions for the new settings:

- **Alignment.** Determines the horizontal position of the text within the box that contains it. The right-hand buttons determine how a paragraph of text is formatted.
- **Vertical alignment.** Determines the vertical position of the text within the box that contains it—top, middle, or bottom.
- **Line spacing.** The vertical spacing between lines of text in the same paragraph.
- **Tracking.** The horizontal spacing between characters.
- **Kerning.** The horizontal spacing between two characters. To turn this on, put your cursor between two letters—such as *A* and *V*—in the text in the Viewer, and adjust the slider.
- **Baseline.** This is the position of the bottom of the text compared to the horizontal line drawn under the text.

Normally, you don't need to worry about changing kerning or baseline, as the default values for almost all Macintosh fonts are fine.

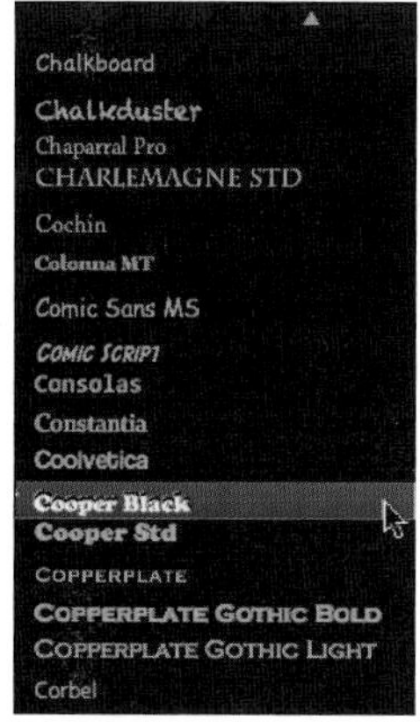

FIGURE 11.9
Fonts are displayed in their own typeface, which makes picking the right font a whole lot easier.

Font Settings

A very helpful new feature appears when you change fonts (**Figure 11.9**). When you select the font list, fonts are displayed in their native font. This lets you see what a typeface looks like without applying it to text in your title.

Scroll down to the bottom of the Text pane to see the settings, which allow you to change settings related to the text itself:

- **Face.** Controls type color, opacity, and blur.
- **Outline.** Allows you to add an outline around the text and control its color.
- **Glow.** Allows you to add a glow around the text and control the amount and color.
- **Drop shadow.** Allows you to add a drop shadow to text.

To turn a setting on, click the blue checkbox to its left.

I am a *huge* fan of drop shadows. Video, even HD, is very low-resolution compared with print. For this reason, whenever you add text to the screen that you want people to read, you must add drop shadows, especially when the text is placed over any color except black. Turn on drop shadows by clicking the blue box so it glows blue (**Figure 11.10**).

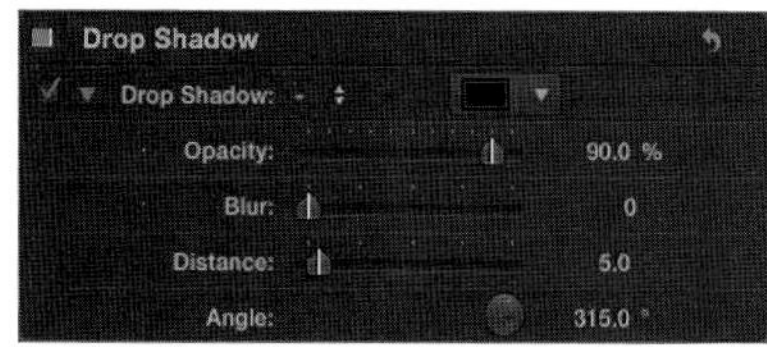

FIGURE 11.10
Turn on drop shadows by clicking the blue checkbox. These are my strongly recommended drop shadow settings.

The default drop shadow settings aren't bad—they get better with each version of Final Cut Pro—but I suggest making one change.

To adjust the settings, click the blue word *Show* to the right of the words "Drop Shadow," to reveal the settings underneath. Although you can change any of these, I recommend changing just the Opacity from 75 percent to 90 percent. This provides more sharpness to the shadow and makes the text easer to read. Figure 11.10 illustrates my recommended settings.

Can Drop Shadows Be Added to Other Visual Elements?

No. At this time, only text and the shape generator have a drop shadow setting. This is different from what you were used to in Final Cut 7. While we can use Motion 5 to design a drop shadow effect for Final Cut Pro, I hope more extensive drop shadows will be available directly in FCP X in the future.

Use Text Styles

FIGURE 11.11 An array of text styles is hidden at the top of the Text tab.

One of the hidden new features in the Text tab is the collection of text styles that you can use for your fonts. To display an otherwise hidden collection of text styles, click the word *Normal* at the top of the Text pane (**Figure 11.11**). This displays a wide range of text fonts and styles. Basic presets apply font settings. Style presets apply style settings to the current font. For example, if you were to save your favorite drop shadow setting as a custom preset, you would probably want to save it as a Style preset so you could apply it to any text regardless of its font.

To apply a preset to the text in your title, be sure the title text is selected in the Viewer, then click the style you like. If you decide that you don't like a particular style, you can remove the styling by choosing Basic Text and Shadow. *However*, this does not change the font back to the way you had it; instead it removes style attributes but leaves the font typeface and size changed.

To reset the font, click the triangle menu at the far right of the parameter, and choose "Reset Parameter." And if you've created a modified style you like, you can save it by choosing "Save All Basic + Style Attributes" at the top of this pop-up menu (**Figure 11.12**).

This is a very convenient way to create a text style, with a drop shadow, for all your lower-third titles. Presets allow you to quickly reuse a particular style without taking time to re-create it.

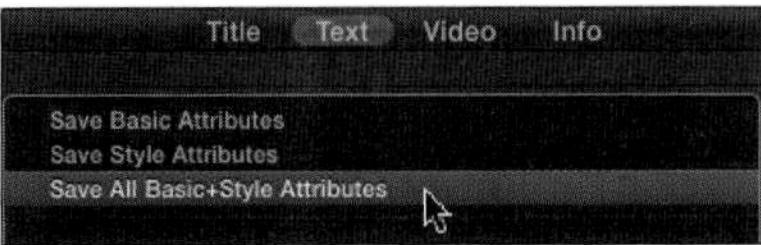

FIGURE 11.12 The ability to save a text style preset makes it easy to reuse styles in the future.

Displaying Action and Title Safe

One of the problems of adding text to video is that not all portions of the image are always displayed. Old CRT-based TVs are notorious for cropping the edges of a picture, as are more modern digital projection systems. On the other hand, video displayed on the Web shows the entire image from edge-to-edge.

This presents you with the worst of all worlds: needing to make sure the entire image is clean, with no light stands or stray production personnel standing along the edges (called "protecting the frame"), yet ensuring that all text and graphics can be seen regardless of how the image is displayed.

This problem has been around since the earliest days of television; to solve it, you create two boundaries within the frame:

- Action Safe, which is 5 percent in from all edges.
- Title Safe, which is 10 percent in from all edges.

To display these, click the Switch in the top right corner of the Viewer, then select "Show Title/Action Safe Zones" (**Figure 11.13**). Two boxes are displayed. Action Safe is the outside box, and Title Safe is the inside box (**Figure 11.14**).

All essential action, actors, sets, and movement need to be contained within the Action Safe boundary, which is 5 percent in from the outside edge. All essential graphics, logos, phone numbers, names, titles—all text elements—need to be contained inside the smaller Title Safe boundary, which is 10 percent in from the outside edge.

Keep in mind that the industry considers these essential boundaries and respect them in the work you create. When I am working with text, these boundaries are always on.

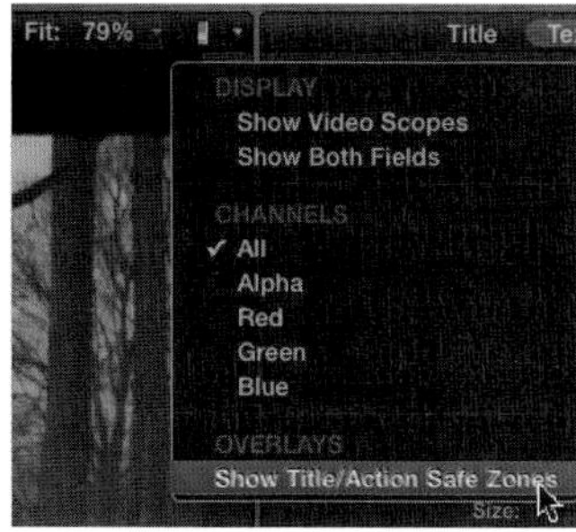

FIGURE 11.13
Click the Switch at the top right of the Viewer, then turn on "Show Title/Action Safe Zones."

FIGURE 11.14
Here's what the Action Safe and Title Safe boundaries look like. Title Safe is the inside box.

What About Video for the Web?

I make a slight exception for video that will be presented exclusively on the Web. In that case, I frame all my text so it is within Action Safe.

However, anything going to DVD, cable, broadcast, or digital projection gets framed considering both Action Safe (for actors) and Title Safe (for text). The worst thing you ever want to hear from a client is, "My mother couldn't read my phone number on her television! Fix it."

Finding and Replacing Text

One of the very cool features in FCP X is its ability to find and change title text. It can do this for an individual title or all titles in a Project. Here, for example, is a Project that has four titles (**Figure 11.15**). Three of them have the word *Jordan* somewhere in them; one doesn't. The placement of the text varies between titles, and each has a different text style.

FIGURE 11.15 This sample Project has four titles, three that contain the word *Jordan*.

Choose Edit > Find and Replace Title Text. In the Find and Replace Title Text dialog box, you can do a "Find" for an individual title, or all the titles in the Project (**Figure 11.16**). You have several options available to you depending on your needs:

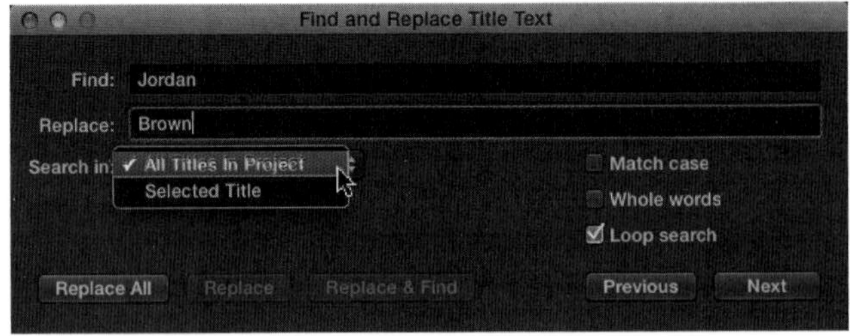

FIGURE 11.16 The Find and Replace Title Text dialog box makes it very easy to replace text in multiple titles.

- **Match case.** This means that FCP will only find text that matches the capitalization of the text in the Find box. In this example, if this option were turned on, it would find *Jordan* but not *JORDAN*.
- **Whole words.** FCP will only look for whole words containing the Find text. For instance, if this option were turned on, it would match *Jordan*, but not *Jordan's*.
- **Loop search.** FCP will continue the search from the beginning of the Project, if the search started in the middle. (The search starts at the current position of the playhead in the Timeline.)
- **Selected Title.** FCP will only replace the currently found and selected title, as opposed to all matching titles in the Project.

NOTE Why Won't It Find My Text?

If you added extra spaces between words, or a carriage return or tab, the Find Text box won't find your source text. Try to keep your source text—that is, the text inside your titles—as clean as possible, and use the formatting in the Inspector to get the looks and alignment you need.

Specific Title Examples

Let's take a look at some specific examples, adding a graphic with a picture.

This element starts with the underlying image full-screen, then zooms back, does a slow spin and zooms in, then brings the image back full-screen again. Creating this title takes just two steps:

1. I chose Push In from the Credits category, dragged it to the Timeline, and placed it so it starts one second after and ends one second before the underlying clip. This reduces the jar of having an animated title start or end too close to a shot change (**Figure 11.17**).
2. I double-clicked the on-screen text placeholders in the Viewer and added my own text, then styled them in the Inspector (**Figure 11.18**).

FIGURE 11.17
The Push In title starts one second after the start of the underlying clip and ends one second before the end of the clip.

FIGURE 11.18
Here's the Push In title with accompanying text.

Here's another example: adding a corner locator.

1. In this case, I chose Elements > Instant Replay. This is an animated upper locator used to establish where a shot was taken (**Figure 11.19**).

   The animation flies in from the right side and displays in the upper-right corner of the screen.

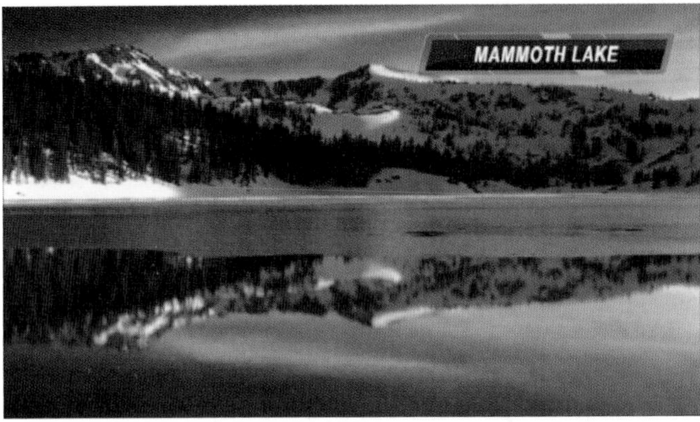

FIGURE 11.19 Another typical example is adding a corner locator to a title.

2. Rather than double-click the text in the Viewer, I changed the text in the text-entry box of the Inspector, then increased the Tracking to 6 percent at the bottom of the window, to increase the horizontal distance between the letters (**Figure 11.20**).

Here's another example, adding a lower-third name and title by choosing Gradient Edge in the Lower Thirds category (**Figure 11.21**).

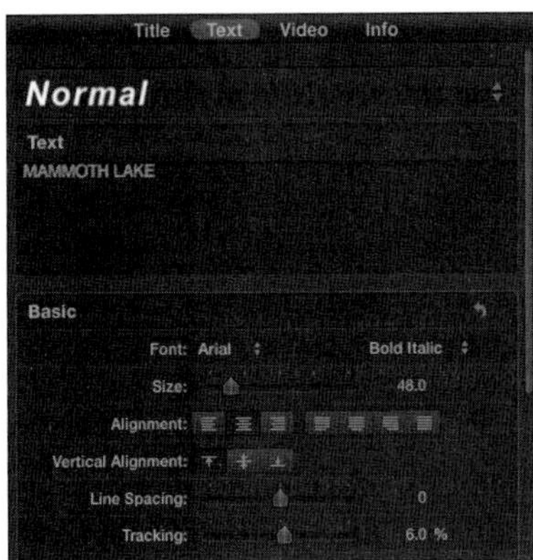

FIGURE 11.20 You can also add text to titles in the Text tab of the Inspector.

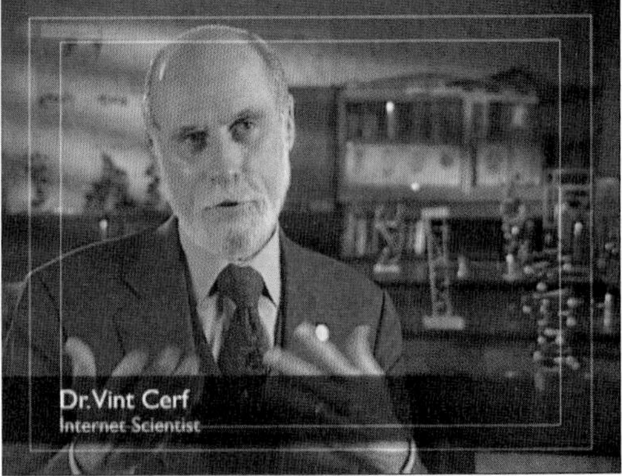

FIGURE 11.21 From the Lower Thirds category, choose Gradient Edge to get a standard lower-third title with a gray background.

Now, to be truthful, I find most of these Lower Thirds options almost useless. What I would like is a clean, simple, lower-third title with no animation and the ability to set it flush-left, center, or right. Two titles—Gradient Edge and Middle—tend to be my preference.

I changed the font from Futura—a font I like a lot—to GillSans, which is another font I like a lot. I changed the font colors and increased the font sizes (**Figure 11.22**). This title can be aligned left, right, or center, and the bar behind it can be any color.

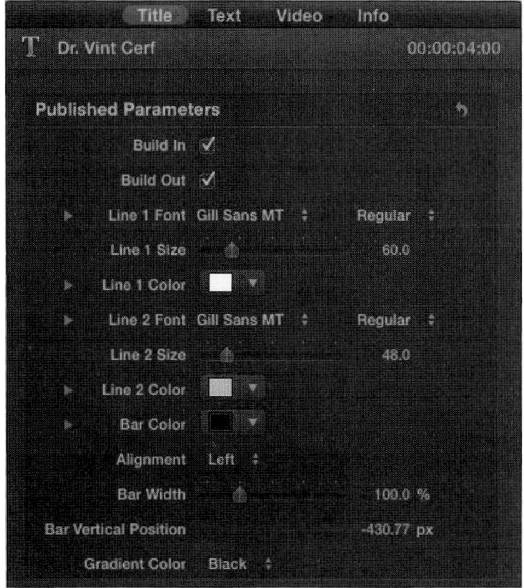

FIGURE 11.22
Here are the settings I changed. I also turned on drop shadows from the Text tab.

Since I enlarged the font size, the text no longer fits in Title Safe. You can either adjust the Baseline parameter, or as we'll see in Chapter 12, you can use the Transform parameters to reposition it. Keep in mind that drop-shadow settings are off by default and the title looks better with them on. (This is where creating a drop shadow style preset comes in handy.)

Summary

When used effectively, titles are the best way to communicate specific information to viewers. Keep in mind that the *look* of your title conveys more than just information; it also reinforces the feel of your Project. Final Cut Pro X gives you lots of new titles, bumpers, graphics, and animations to play with. Due to FCP's consistent interface, once you understand how one of these works, you are ready to work with any of them.

Finally, remember two things whenever you add text to your screen:

1. Add a drop shadow.
2. Pay attention to Action and Title Safe.

Keyboard Shortcut

Shortcut	What It Does
Command+4	Toggle the Inspector open/closed

BUILT-IN EFFECTS

The built-in effects for Final Cut Pro X are the foundation for almost all the other effects in the application. The set of built-in effects in FCP X is similar to, but more extensive than, the Motion tab in Final Cut Pro 7 or Final Cut Express. These consist of eight categories. One of them—Color Correction—has so many options that I've devoted Chapter 16 to discussing it in detail.

The purpose of this chapter is to provide an overview of all the built-in effects. However, because all these effects have a similar interface, I will start with some interface basics. Then, we'll take a look at each effect. The key thing about the built-in effects is that they are always available. They are called "built-in effects" because they are built into every clip. There is nothing you have to apply—they are ready whenever you need them, and out of the way when you don't.

FIGURE 12.1
Click the *i* icon to reveal the Inspector, or press Command+4.

Effects Basics

You access built-in effects through the Inspector. To reveal it, click the Inspector icon, at the far right of the Toolbar; or press Command+4 (**Figure 12.1**).

There are eight categories of built-in effects (**Figure 12.2**):

- Color correction (covered in Chapter 16)
- Transform
- Crop
- Distort
- Stabilization
- Rolling Shutter
- Spatial Conform
- Compositing

● **NOTE**
What Happened to Drop Shadow?

I don't know. At this point, the only elements that have a built-in drop shadow effect are Titles and the shape generator. And there isn't a filter effect that creates a drop shadow. However, you can use Motion 5 to design a drop shadow effect, plus there are some third-party shadow effects available as well.

You gain access to all built-in effects in the Inspector; however, some of these effects also have on-screen controls that you can change using the Viewer. I'll show you how these work as you go through this chapter.

With the Inspector open, click the Video tab to reveal the built-in effects. Each effect has several standard interface elements (**Figure 12.3**).

- The **checkbox**, on the left, turns an effect on (blue) or off (black). You can temporarily disable a setting without changing any of the values in it, by unchecking the checkbox. In this example, two effects are turned on (Transform and Crop) and two are turned off (Distort and Stabilization). This checkbox makes it easy to compare how a clip looks with, or without, an effect simply by clicking this on or off. Each of these is off by default.
- The blue words **Show** and **Hide** toggle the display of individual settings for this effect. The words appear only when the mouse rolls close to them. Click the word *Show* to reveal the specific settings available for each effect. Click the word *Hide* to hide them again.

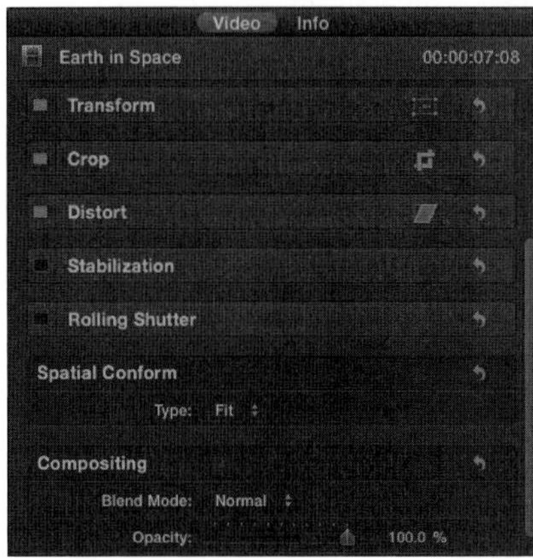

FIGURE 12.2
The built-in effects in FCP X are located in the Video tab of the Inspector.

FIGURE 12.3
The five standard interface elements: enable/disable an effect, show effect parameters, display on-screen controls, reset an effect, and the triangle on the far right displays a pop-up menu of additional options.

- The **icon** next to the word *Show* is a toggle to display the on-screen controls in the Viewer. As these icons vary by effect, they will be discussed individually below.
- The **curved arrow** on the right is the reset button for the entire effect. This resets all the settings for a specific effect back to its default state. There is no master reset for all built-in effects, just a reset for each effect.
- Just to the right of the reset button is a small, downward-pointing arrow. This reveals the parameter pop-up menu (**Figure 12.4**). This allows you to reset that specific setting, or work with keyframes. This arrow appears only when your mouse rolls close to it. I'll discuss keyframes in more detail after the Transform section in this chapter.

FIGURE 12.4
The built-in effects parameter pop-up menu lets you reset specific settings.

You can copy effects from one clip to another by first copying the clip that contains the effects you want to copy and pressing Command+C (or choose Edit > Copy). Then select one or more clips that you want to copy the effects to, and choose Edit > Paste Effects. If you have any filters or built-in effects settings applied to the selected clips, the pasted settings will override them.

As you add transitions or effects to clips, an orange bar appears at the top of the Timeline. This indicates that rendering is needed. Fortunately, rendering occurs in the background, so you don't need to wait for it to finish to keep working. For more on rendering, see Chapter 10.

● **NOTE** Can I Paste Just Some Effects from One Clip to Another?

No. Unlike in FCP 7, you can't specify which effects get pasted. All filters and effects settings associated with the first clip get pasted into the second clip.

Transform Effects

Transform effects control basic image sizing and positioning (**Figure 12.5**). Here's what these settings do specifically:

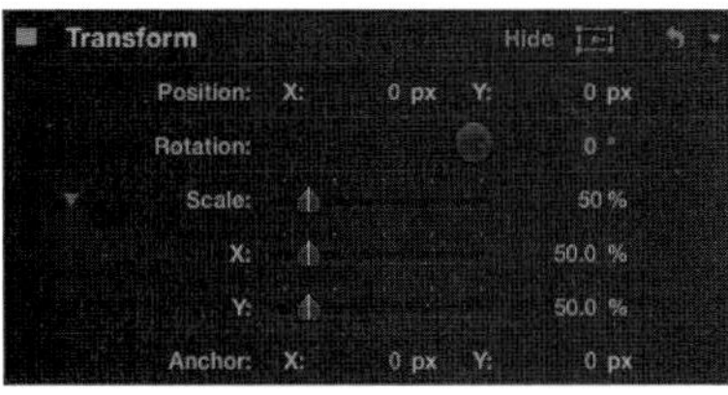

FIGURE 12.5
The Transform effects control size, position, rotation, and anchor point.

- **Position.** This determines the horizontal and vertical position of an element. Position moves the center of the image relative to the center of the frame. In the *X* box negative numbers move left, and positive numbers move right. In the Y box, negative numbers move down, and positive numbers move up. Negative numbers move left and down. Positive numbers move right and up.
- **Rotation.** This controls the rotation of the selected element.

● **NOTE** Positioning Changed in FCP X

Apple changed how the vertical position gets calculated from Final Cut Pro 7. In FCP 7, negative numbers moved up. In FCP X, negative numbers move down. Now, FCP X matches the same coordinate geometry system you learned in high school.

- **Scale.** This controls the size of the selected element. Keep in mind that all video elements are bitmapped. This means quality starts to be lost as you scale elements larger than 100 percent. Twirl down the small arrow next to the word *Scale* to adjust horizontal and vertical scaling separately.
- **Anchor Point.** This controls the point around which the selected element scales or rotates. By default, the anchor point is in the middle of the frame. The only place you can change the anchor point is in the Inspector; there are no on-screen controls for this. And you can't use the Distort tool to move it, as you could in FCP 7, because there is no specific Distort tool in FCP X.

Change Settings

To change a setting, either click the numeric value, so it turns blue, and enter a number; or, where available, slide a slider. Even cooler, click any number and drag up or down. This is the fastest way to change a setting.

While the Inspector is a perfectly fine place to change all these settings, it is not the most convenient. The Transform settings are much easier to see and control using the on-screen controls in the Viewer.

FIGURE 12.6
The easiest way to display the on-screen controls is using these three icons in the lower-left corner of the Viewer. This blue icon toggles Transform settings on and off.

There are three ways to display the on-screen controls:

- Click the icon (blue in this screen shot) in the lower-left corner of the Viewer (**Figure 12.6**). Blue means the icon is active, gray means it is not.
- Click the icon in the Inspector just to the left of the reset button for the Transform effect (see Figure 12.3).
- Press Shift+T.

That's It? Just Three Ways?

Well, no. There's a fourth.

Right-click anywhere in the Viewer window and select Transform—or one of the other options. "None," by the way, cancels any active on-screen controls (**Figure 12.7**).

FIGURE 12.7
Here's a hidden way to turn on a built-in effect: right-click in the Viewer.

To change the scale of the image display, but *not* the image itself, click the percentage number in the top-right corner of the Viewer and select the zoom ratio you want. You can also press Command+[plus] and Command+[minus], or Shift+Z, to rescale the image display to fit the entire image into the Viewer (**Figure 12.8**).

FIGURE 12.8
The Viewer contains three interface elements: A percentage number shows the scale of the image display, Done closes the on-screen effects, and the small box lets you move around an oversized image.

To accept your changes, do one of the following:

- Click the blue icon in the lower-left corner of the Viewer.
- Click the blue icon at the right of the Transform section of the Inspector.
- Press A to return to the Select tool.
- Click the Done button at the top-right corner of the Viewer. (I generally use this option.)

If you magnify the image display larger than will fit in the Viewer, a small white box with a red rectangle in it appears. Drag the mouse inside the white square to move around the image. This box disappears when the entire image is displayed in the Viewer. (You can also move around using the Hand tool from the Tool menu.)

Controls Specific to Tranform Effects

These on-screen controls appear for almost all the built-in effects, so now that I've mentioned them, I won't need to cover them again. However, there are also several controls specific to Transform effects that I want to show you next.

NOTE On-screen Controls

On-screen controls for built-in effects work only for clips in the Timeline, not for clips in the Event Browser.

Click the blue rectangular icon in the lower-left corner of the Viewer to turn on the on-screen controls for Transform, or press Shift+T (**Figure 12.9**).

FIGURE 12.9
The blue dots and center dots are the on-screen Transform controls.

Scaling the Image

▲ **TIP** A New Way to Constrain Image Movement

If you drag inside the image, you can move it anywhere. However, if you drag the circle in the center and press the Shift key at the same time, you constrain movement to either horizontal or vertical movement. Just discovered this. Very cool.

Around the edges of the image, eight blue dots appear. These allow you to scale the image. Drag a corner dot to scale while maintaining the aspect ratio of the image. Drag an edge dot to scale without maintaining the aspect ratio. If you press the Shift key while dragging a control point, you override the aspect ratio.

Press the Option key while dragging a control point to anchor the side, or corner, opposite where you are dragging. (Try it. This is easier to see than to explain.) Press both Shift and Option while dragging, and watch what happens.

The circle in the center allows you to position the image, but frankly, dragging anywhere inside the image will work. (Holding the Shift key while dragging this center circle constrains movement to 45-degree increments.)

Rotating the Image

The dot to the right of the center circle controls rotation (**Figure 12.10**). If you drag it to the right, the pivot bar expands, allowing you to be much more precise in rotating an image. The rotation dot glows gold when the Shift key is pressed, indicating rotation is constrained to 45-degree increments.

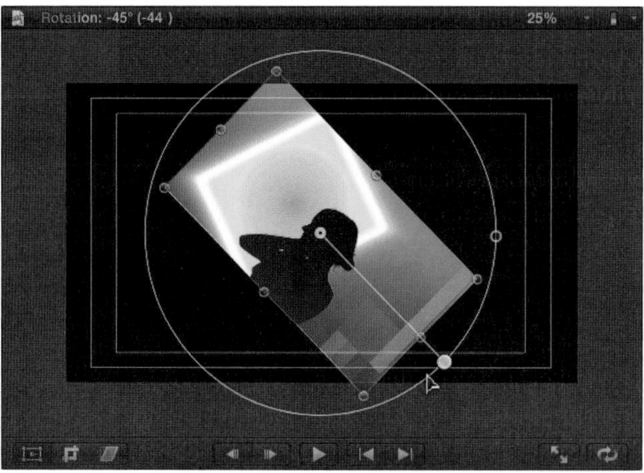

FIGURE 12.10 Drag the dot to the right of the center for rotation. Press the Shift key while dragging to constrain movement to 45-degree increments.

When you are done making changes, click the Done button.

Putting It All Together

Here's an example of a Transform effect, along with the settings that achieved it (**Figure 12.11**). The image is scaled to 50 percent and positioned to the top-right corner of Action Safe by adjusting the position *X* and *Y* coordinates. (*X* controls horizontal position, and *Y* controls vertical position.)

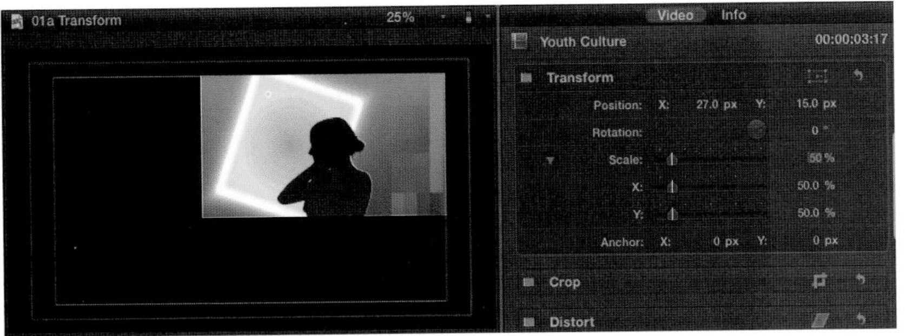

FIGURE 12.11 This is an example of the settings for a 50 percent scaled and repositioned image.

Just as a reminder, you turn the Action Safe rectangles on and off by using the Switch at the top-right corner of the Viewer.

Animate Using Keyframes

Another feature that runs through all effects (not just the built-in effects) in Final Cut Pro is that you can use keyframes for almost every parameter.

For example, let's say you want that last image, where it is scaled at 50 percent and positioned at the top and right corner of Action Safe, to fly into that position from full-screen. You do that using keyframes.

There are three ways to set keyframes: by way of the Viewer, the Inspector, and the Timeline. Let's take a look at each method.

> **NOTE** Definition of Keyframe
>
> A keyframe is a point of change during playback. Keyframes are used to provide animation with flexibility and precision. Corollary: You always apply keyframes in pairs—a starting position and an ending position. If you're using more than two keyframes, it is often easiest to think about them in pairs.

Set Keyframes in the Viewer

To set keyframes in the Viewer, follow these steps:

1. Select the clip you want to animate and position the playhead where you want the animation to start; this is not always at the beginning of a clip. (I often add markers to remind me where I want the animation to change; however, markers are not necessary to set keyframes.)
2. Turn on the Transform controls by clicking the Transform icon in the lower-left corner of the Viewer, or press Shift+T. Position the playhead on the frame in the Timeline where you want to create a keyframe.
3. Click the gray diamond in the cluster of three icons in the top-left corner; the diamond immediately turns gold (**Figure 12.12**). Gray indicates no keyframe at the position of the playhead; gold indicates the playhead is parked on a keyframe.

FIGURE 12.12 To add a keyframe in the Viewer, click the gray diamond. It turns gold when the playhead is parked on a keyframe.

When you create keyframes in the Viewer, you are setting keyframes for every parameter in Transform. (See all the gold diamonds in **Figure 12.13**? Each of those is a separate keyframe.) Setting keyframes in the Viewer is easy, but it often sets way more keyframes than you need. Read on for what I think is a better option.

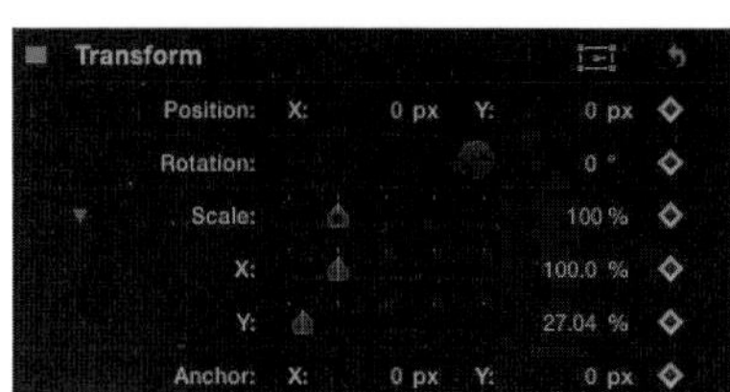

FIGURE 12.13 Setting keyframes in the Viewer is easy, but it creates keyframes for every Transform parameter.

▲ **TIP** Setting Keyframes

I often find it easier to create the ending position of an effect and set a keyframe. Then, move to the opening position and set a keyframe. Working from the finished effect backwards is often easier and faster.

4. Because you need to set keyframes in pairs—a starting value and an ending value—move the playhead where you want the animation to end. Then, adjust the image to its ending position and set another keyframe. Unlike FCP 7, FCP X does not set keyframes automatically.

   For effects that change position, the Viewer displays a red line trailing after the image. That's called a *motion path;* it shows how the center of the image moves from the first to the last keyframe.

5. When you have the final position set to your satisfaction, either click the Done button, press A to select the Arrow tool, or click the Transform icon at the bottom left of the Viewer. This locks all the settings so they don't change during playback.

6. To navigate to the previous keyframe, click the left arrow at the top left of the Viewer (**Figure 12.14**). To go to the next keyframe, click the right arrow. While I am not a fan of setting keyframes in the Viewer, I *am* a fan of using these arrows for navigation.

FIGURE 12.14 It is important to use these keyframe navigation controls in the Viewer to move between keyframes to avoid moving the playhead to the wrong position.

These navigation buttons are big, easy to see, easy to click, and guarantee that you are jumping exactly from one keyframe to the next. Never jump between keyframes by dragging the mouse—it is not only slow, but also highly inaccurate. All too often, you end up just missing the keyframe you want and creating a new keyframe where you *don't* want it, thereby totally messing up your animation. Always jump between keyframes using these arrows, or similar arrows in the Inspector.

The good news about setting keyframes in the Viewer is that it's easy. The bad news is that you often create more keyframes than you need, and this can cause confusion later as you try to figure out why your effect isn't working the way you expect.

To delete a keyframe, position the playhead on the frame containing the keyframe you want to delete (the diamond glows gold), and click the diamond. If the diamond icon is gray, clicking it sets a keyframe. If the diamond icon is gold, clicking it deletes a keyframe. It's a toggle.

▲ **TIP** Changing Parameter Settings

When you are in the Inspector, a quick way to change a parameter value, like Scale or Position, is to click the value itself and drag up/down or left/right. Watch what happens! Very cool. You could also just type in the value, but that's pretty boring.

Set Keyframes in the Inspector

Let's try this same effect another way in the Inspector.

In all cases when you want to add a keyframe, position the playhead on the frame where you want to add the keyframe and select the clip. (Press the Option key when clicking with the skimmer, to avoid changing the location of the playhead.)

In this case, I opened the Transform settings in the Inspector (by clicking the word *Show*, remember?) and added a keyframe for Position by clicking the gray diamond. Notice that the diamond turns gold; this means that a keyframe was added at the current position of the playhead (**Figure 12.15**).

▲ **TIP** A Warning First

If you create keyframes in the Inspector, you should make sure you haven't made any changes in the Viewer and the on-screen controls are turned off, or you will get strange and unexpected results.

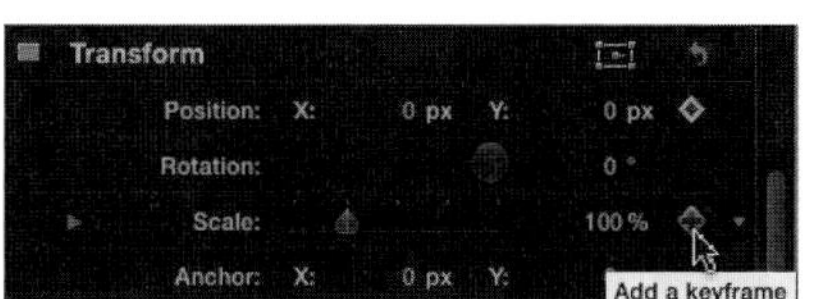

FIGURE 12.15 To add a keyframe in the Inspector, click the gray plus button next to the parameter you want to set. In this screen shot, I'm about to add a keyframe for Scale because the icon hasn't turned gold yet.

The benefit of adding keyframes in the Inspector is that you are only adding keyframes for the parameters you need, which makes figuring out problems a lot easier. However, it takes practice to figure out which keyframes you need to set.

Again—and this is important—move the playhead where you want the animation to stop, then add a new keyframe before adjusting the image. If you don't add a new keyframe where you want the animation to end, you'll unintentionally alter the previous keyframe . Notice that since you are setting keyframes in the Inspector, only the parameters that changed need keyframes; Rotation and Anchor have none.

Setting Keyframes in the Timeline

There's a third option for setting and adjusting keyframes: the Timeline. Simply follow these steps:

1. Select the clip you want to apply keyframes to and choose Clip > Show Video Animation, or press Control+V.

   Above the selected clip are options to add keyframes for most of the built-in effects. In this case, you want to add keyframes for Transform (**Figure 12.16**).

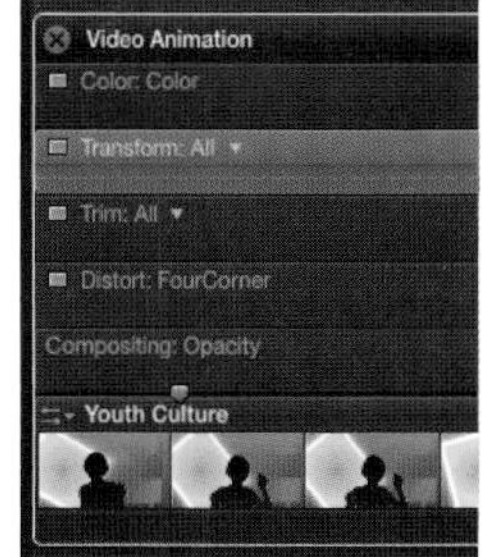

FIGURE 12.16 Pressing Control-V allows you to set, modify, or delete keyframes in the Timeline.

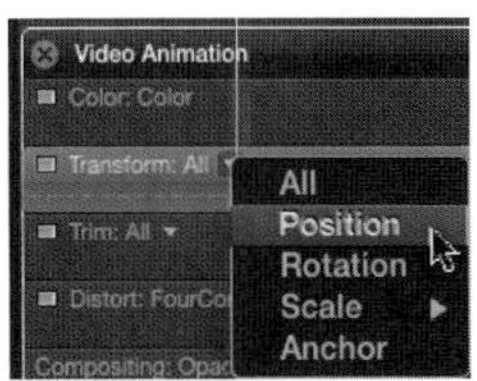

FIGURE 12.17 Click the small downward-pointing arrow next to Transform to display a pop-up menu.

2. Click the small downward-pointing arrow next to the word *Transform* to reveal a pop-up menu (**Figure 12.17**).
3. Choose All if you want to apply keyframes to every Transform parameter. Or choose just the parameter you want to apply a keyframe to. In this case, choose Position.
4. To add a keyframe, choose Modify > Add Keyframe to Selected Effect in Animation Editor, or press Option+K.

   A keyframe now appears in the Timeline at the position of the playhead or skimmer. (You can also Option-click the horizontal line to set or remove a keyframe.)
5. Switch between parameters using the pop-up menu to select the next parameter you want to add keyframes for, and press Option+K, which sets a keyframe at the position of the skimmer or playhead.
6. Move the playhead to where you want the animation to end, and add new keyframes for each parameter. Remember, keyframes are always added at the position of the skimmer, or playhead, if the skimmer is not active.
7. To delete a keyframe in the Timeline, click it to select it (turn it gold) and press the Delete key. Make *sure* the keyframe is gold; otherwise, you'll delete the clip.

FIGURE 12.18 To change the position of a keyframe, drag it sideways. To change its value, drag it up or down.

One of the advantages of creating keyframes in the Timeline is that if, by mistake, you set the keyframe in the wrong place, it is easy to drag it where you want it to go. Drag horizontally to change the timing. Drag vertically to change the value (**Figure 12.18**). (Not all keyframes can be dragged vertically.)

Summary of the Process for Setting Keyframes

Whether you add keyframes in the Viewer, the Inspector, or the Timeline, the process is always the same:

1. Set the playhead on the frame you want the animation to start.
2. Add keyframes to the settings you want to change.
3. Change the settings.
4. Move the playhead to the frame where you want the animation to stop changing.
5. Add new keyframes.
6. Adjust the image, which modifies the keyframe settings.
7. Repeat the steps until the entire animation is complete.

The animation I was creating here was a simple move between two positions. Many animations are just this simple, though they will often involve other parameters. Other animations can be much more complex, involving a number of intermediate steps.

▲ **TIP** Keyboard Shortcut

You can jump between keyframes using two keyboard shortcuts:

- Press Option+; [semicolon] to jump to the previous keyframe.
- Press Option+' [single quote] to jump to the next keyframe.

As long as you keep in mind that you are always working one parameter at a time, setting keyframes in pairs, you won't get lost, even in the most complex piece of animation.

Trim, Crop, and Ken Burns

A lot of what I covered in the Transform section is exactly the same for the rest of the built-in effects. So let me simply point out the differences as you move through the rest of this chapter.

The Crop parameter has three sections: Trim, Crop, and the Ken Burns effect.

- **Trim.** This acts like Crop in Final Cut Pro 7. It makes the edges of a clip transparent, without changing the size of the clip.
- **Crop.** This makes the edges of a clip transparent, then expands the remaining image to fill the frame. Keep in mind that image quality will degrade the more you expand an image.
- **Ken Burns.** This effect provides an elegant way to do moves (pans, tilts, and zooms) on an image. While this effect is generally used on still images, it works equally well on video, though with some degradation in image quality caused by zooming in on the image.

You have three ways to access these effects:

- On-screen controls in the Viewer
- The Inspector
- Video animation in the Timeline

Since the video animation controls work the same as for Transform, I'll illustrate the first two options for each of these three settings.

As always, first select the clip you want to modify in the Timeline.

Whether you want to trim, crop, or create a move on an image, either click the Crop icon in the lower left of the Viewer, or click the same icon to the right of the word *Crop* in the Inspector, or press Shift+C. This displays the on-screen controls in the Viewer (**Figure 12.19**).

In the top-left corner of the Viewer are six buttons, from left to right (**Figure 12.20**): Trim, Crop, Ken Burns, and the three keyframe buttons you learned about in the Transform section.

● **NOTE** What Are Pan, Tilt, and Zoom?

To *pan* is to move an image side to side, horizontally—for example, "Pan the camera right." To *tilt*. is to move an image up and down, vertically—for example, "Tilt up to show the sky." To *zoom* is to enlarge an image by adjusting the lens—for example, "Zoom in so I can see the detail."

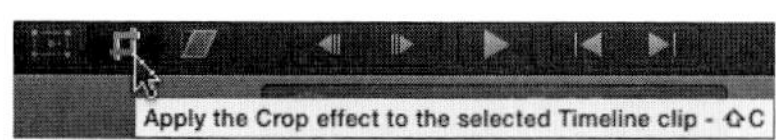

FIGURE 12.19
Click the crop icon in the lower-left corner of the Viewer to display the on-screen controls for Crop, Trim, and Ken Burns.

FIGURE 12.20
The three buttons on the left control effects. The three on the right set and navigate between keyframes.

Trim

▲ **TIP** Get Out of the Way!

If the Trim/Crop/Ken Burns buttons at the top of the Viewer get in your way, change the size of the Viewer by dragging the edge of the window. This should also change the aspect ratio enough so that the buttons are no longer in the way. This is what I did in Figure 12.21.

Click the Trim button to display the Trim controls. Trim removes the edges from a clip without changing the size or position of the clip. In Trim mode, the control points are blue rectangles and triangles (**Figure 12.21**). These blue controls are shaped differently from those you saw earlier for Transforms, or in the next section for Crops.

Drag one of the blue controls. Dragging an edge only affects that edge. Dragging a corner affects two edges. Watch what happens when you drag while pressing the following keys:

- **Shift.** This trims while constraining to aspect ratio.
- **Option.** This trims opposite edges.
- **Both.** This trims the opposite edges while constraining the aspect ratio.

The yellow guides show you where the center of the image is, vertically and horizontally. They appear as you start dragging stuff around.

When you are done dragging, everything outside the trimmed area is transparent (**Figure 12.22**). If there is a clip below this on the Timeline, you'll see it. If not, you'll see black. And this is really black; unless you export using Apple ProRes 4444, in which case the black area will be transparent.

You could get the same result by dragging sliders in the Inspector. Set the Type pop-up menu to Trim, then click Show to display the individual settings. But using the on-screen controls makes this both faster and easier.

FIGURE 12.21
This is a full-screen image with the blue Trim controls enabled and displayed. Note the blue crop icon in the lower-left corner.

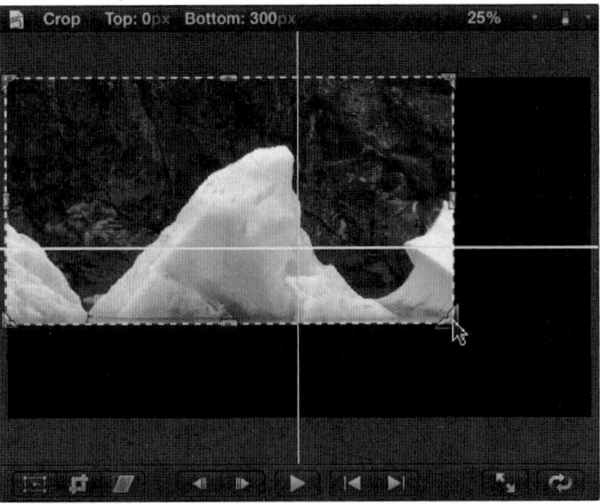

FIGURE 12.22
Here is the same image with a trim applied. Note that parts of the image are now missing. Trimming doesn't scale an image; it removes portions of it.

When you are happy with how the effect looks, click one of the following:

- Done in the top-right corner of the Viewer
- The blue crop icon in the top-right corner of the Inspector
- The blue crop icon in the lower-left corner of the Viewer
- Press A to return to the Arrow tool

The key benefit to using Trim is that you are not changing the size or position of the clip, just hiding parts of it. (No, this is not permanent. If you display the on-screen settings again, you can re-adjust the trim—as many times as you want.)

▲ TIP What If I Change My Mind?

You already know the answer: Click the Reset button (the arrow) in the Crop section of the Inspector. All the Crop settings reset to normal.

Crop

Cropping does the same thing trimming does, except it then takes the result and enlarges it so it fills the frame. Here, you need to be careful because if you scale an image larger than 100 percent, it will degrade quality. While this will rarely happen with high-resolution stills, it is very common when scaling video. Because Crop is designed to fill the frame, you can only trim the image in the same aspect ratio as your Project.

Here's how this works.

1. Click the same Crop icon in the Viewer or the Inspector, or press Shift+C (as you did in Trim) to display the on-screen controls.
2. Click the Crop button at the top left of the Viewer. Notice that the controls have changed: The blue rectangles in the middle of an edge are gone, and the shape of the four corner controls has changed.
3. Drag a corner and watch how the crop rectangle maintains the shape of your Project and highlights a portion of the image (**Figure 12.23**).
4. Drag the middle of the image to reposition the selected area. Areas of the image outside the crop are dimmed. When you are done, only the area inside the crop will be displayed in your Project.
5. To accept the Crop, click Done (or one of the crop icons). The cropped image is immediately enlarged to fill the entire frame (**Figure 12.24**).

You could get the same result in the Inspector, by setting the Type pop-up menu to Crop and adjusting the sliders. But for me, the on-screen controls are far faster and more intuitive.

FIGURE 12.23
This is the same iceberg image that you trimmed earlier. The crop rectangle is over a portion of the image, in the same aspect ratio as that of the Project.

FIGURE 12.24
The finished crop enlarges the selected area to fill the frame.

What's This "Image Degradation" Business?

All video images are bitmaps. This means they are composed of images made up of hundreds of thousands of individual picture elements, or pixels (**Figure 12.25**).

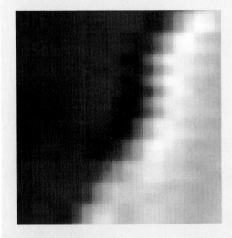

FIGURE 12.25
This is an image enlarged about 1000 percent to display the individual pixels in an image. Overenlarging a clip reduces image quality.

These pixels are fixed—both in number and in size. As you scale an image, you enlarge the individual pixels; you aren't adding any new image resolution. You are simply creating fat pixels. This image illustrates the problem: This is the edge of an iceberg against a dark cliff and enlarged about 1000 percent to clearly show the pixels, which display as square color shapes.

So to maintain the highest possible quality in your images, keep the Scale at 100 percent or less. You *can* scale larger, but remember that the larger you scale the image, the blockier and fuzzier it will look.

Ken Burns Effect

The Ken Burns Effect is named after legendary documentary filmmaker Ken Burns, who revolutionized documentaries with his innovative use of movement on stills. He has now been immortalized in software. This effect works best with still images. More important, it works best with still images that are larger than the frame size of your Project. Table 12.1 suggests some image sizes.

The whole reason to use this effect is to create the illusion of movement in a still image, or in a video clip that wasn't shot with movement.

Here's how this works:

1. Select the clip you want to apply the effect to, and display the on-screen controls (yup, click the crop icon or press Shift+C). (By the way, this effect can only be done on-screen; there are no Inspector controls for this.)
2. Click the Ken Burns button at the top left of the Viewer.

   Two frames are displayed: green and red (**Figure 12.26**). Both rectangles match the aspect ratio of your Project. (This is a still of the Yarra River in Melbourne, Australia.) The green rectangle indicates where the clip starts, and the red rectangle indicates where the move ends. The default move is a slight zoom into the center of the frame.
3. For instance, here I resized and positioned the green rectangle to start with a close-up of the right-side waterfront, then sized and positioned the red rectangle to do a move back to the bridge and skyline. The white arrow indicates the direction of the move (**Figure 12.27**).
4. Click the dual lightning symbol at the top to switch the position of the red and green rectangles.
5. Click the right-pointing triangle at the top to preview the effect.
6. When you are happy with the results, click Done.

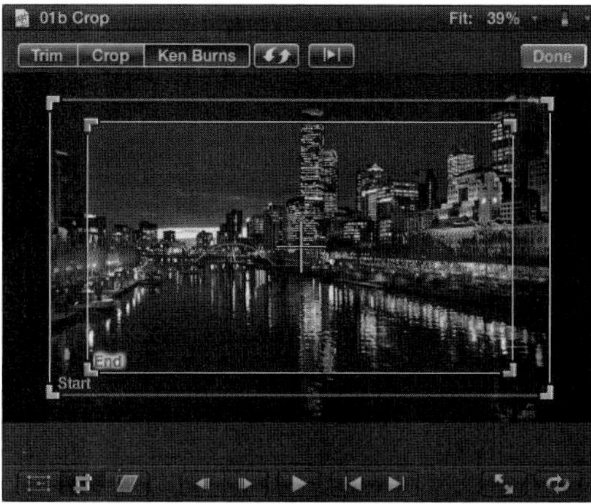

FIGURE 12.26
This is the default setting of the Ken Burns effect. The green rectangle signifies the starting position, while the red rectangle indicates the ending.

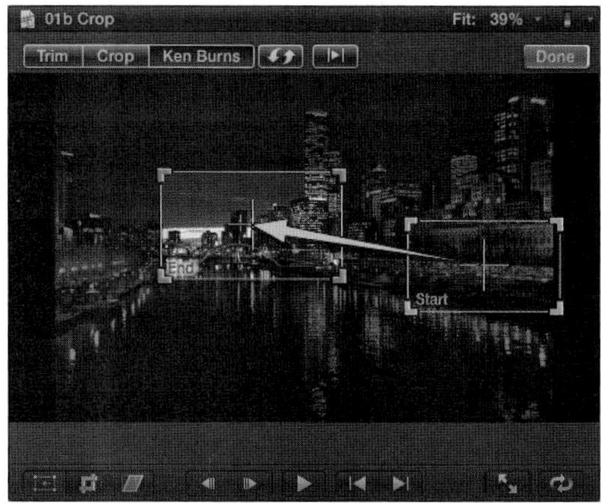

FIGURE 12.27
The images are resized and repositioned to pan slowly along the waterfront from the green to red rectangle.

▲ TIP Render the Ken Burns Effect

As with all effects in Final Cut Pro, you can preview the effect before rendering is complete. However, in the case of the Ken Burns effect, the playback will be jerky and the image quality severely reduced. Complete the rendering before making any final judgments on the effect.

Here's another example. This starts with a close-up of the bridge and zooms back to show a wide shot of the city (**Figure 12.28**). When you are happy with the effect, click Done.

FIGURE 12.28 This is another example of starting close and zooming out to the entire scene.

Sizing still images for moves gets *really* confusing. The basic idea is that if you are doing moves on a still image, that image needs to be bigger than the frame size of your Project.

Since all video is measured in pixels, **Table 12.1** will help you size images. The left column presents some popular video formats. The middle column shows size dimensions that let you create an image that perfectly fills the frame but doesn't allow moves. The right column contains dimensions that both fill the frame and allow moves, including zooms up to 250 percent.

TABLE 12.1 Sizing Still Images for Moves

Video Format	100 Percent Size (in Pixels) to Fill Frame	250 Percent Size (in Pixels) for Pan and Zoom
DV 4:3 NTSC	720 x 540	1800 x 1350
DV 16:9 NTSC	852 x 480	2130 x 1200
DV 16:9 PAL	1024 x 576	2560 x 1440
720 HD	1280 x 720	3200 x 1800
1080 HD	1920 x 1080	4800 x 2700

Note: All images should be designed at 72 dpi (dots per inch). DPI is a unit of measurement used for printers and is not relevant for video. Video exclusively uses total pixels across by total pixels down.

Why Would You Use Keyframes to Do Something This Simple?

You'd use keyframes because the Ken Burns effect runs from the start to the end of a clip. If you wanted to do this move in the middle of the clip, you would use either keyframes or the razor blade to cut the clip into the sections you need, then apply the Ken Burns effect to the section. Personally, I'd use keyframes; they are easier to work with than cutting clips. The only keyframes you need to set are for scale and position—in other words, you create a Ken Burns effect using just the Transform controls.

Distort, or Corner Pinning

Distort, also called "corner pinning," lets you take an image and manipulate it to give it a sense of perspective, or location in space. FCP X doesn't work in 3D space (though it can in combination with Motion 5). All you are doing here is providing the *illusion* of 3-D.

In Final Cut Pro 7 you used the Distort tool. In FCP X you can use either the on-screen controls in the Viewer or in the Inspector. In this case, the on-screen controls are *far* easier to use.

1. To distort a clip, select the clip, then do one of the following:
   - Click the Distort button in the lower-left corner of the Viewer (**Figure 12.29**).
   - Right-click in the Viewer and choose Distort.
   - Press Shift+Command+D.
   - Go to the Distort section in the Inspector.
2. When the on-screen Distort controls are turned on, a series of blue control dots appears around the edges of an image (**Figure 12.30**). Drag a corner to reposition it; drag an edge to reposition both corners at the same time. You can even drag corners outside the frame—although once they go out of the frame, that portion of the image disappears.
3. Drag the middle of the image to reposition the entire image. (When you reposition the entire image, you are actually adjusting the Transform settings.)

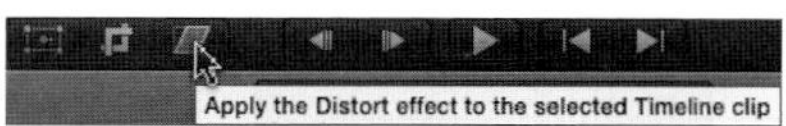

FIGURE 12.29
Click the Distort button to display the on-screen controls.

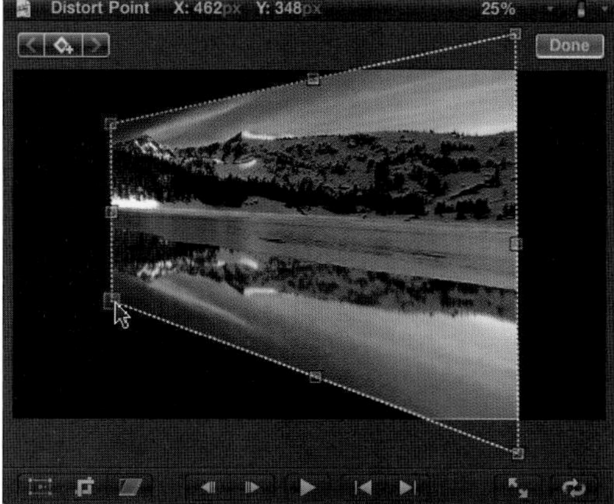

FIGURE 12.30
Using Distort, you can reposition each corner—even move it outside the frame!

In this example, the image has a sense of flying back in space, with the right side exploding out the front of the frame. This is a very popular technique to create the illusion of an image playing on a screen, or of the side of a building.

4. When you are happy with the Distort settings, either click the Done button, press A to select the Arrow tool, or click the blue Distort button in the lower-left corner of the Viewer.
5. To reset the settings back to their default, go to the Inspector and click the curved arrow to the right of the Distort settings. And, as with the Transform settings, you can use the Inspector to keyframe each of the four Distort corners to animate the distortion of the clip during playback.

Image Stabilization

High-definition images accentuate camera shake. This means the bigger your image will be viewed, the more stable your image needs to be. However, sometimes during production there just isn't time—or, more accurately, there doesn't *appear* to be the time—to put the camera on a tripod or dolly to stabilize the shot.

FCP provides an option to solve this problem by analyzing your image to reduce the apparent movement. FCP looks at how the image moves in the frame, then moves the image in the opposite direction. For example, if the image moved down during filming, FCP moves the image up by the same amount, giving the illusion of a stable image.

▲ TIP Can I Analyze a Range Within a Clip?

No. If you need to analyze a range, edit it into a compound clip, then analyze the compound clip.

Image stabilization requires analysis, and FCP allows you to analyze your clips during import, after import in the Event Browser, or once they are edited into the Timeline. However, analyzing during import takes a *long* time because FCP always analyzes entire clips. This means if you are bringing in lots of long clips, it can seem as if your clips are in background processing forever.

A better way to deal with this is to analyze your clips for image stabilization only when you know you are going to use them in your Project.

While you can analyze a clip in the Event Browser using Modify > Analyze and Fix, the most efficient way to analyze a clip is to do the following:

1. Edit the clip to the Timeline; analysis does not need to be complete before you can stabilize the clip.
2. Go to the Inspector (there are no on-screen controls for this), and turn on Stabilization by clicking the blue checkbox (**Figure 12.31**). This forces the clip to be analyzed.

FIGURE 12.31 Turn on the blue checkbox to enable the Stabilization controls in the Inspector.

3. FCP gets to work analyzing your clips in the background. As always, you can monitor the status of analysis using the Background Tasks window (press Command+9.)

   The image instantly zooms in slightly. As you play the clip, you'll notice it moves far less than before. Due to differences in clips and how they are shot, sometimes this stabilization is just magical. Other times, it needs adjustment. And in a few instances, it doesn't work at all.

There are three controls you can adjust to smooth out the stabilization:

- **Translation Smooth.** This adjusts compensation for horizontal and vertical movement. In almost all cases this should be used. Slide this to 0 to remove the compensation. Slide it to 5.0 for maximum compensation. The default setting of 2.5 is generally a good place to start.
- **Rotation Smooth.** This adjusts compensation for rotational movement. Slide this to 0 to remove the compensation. Slide it to 5.0 for maximum compensation. I generally set this closer to 1.0.
- **Scale Smooth.** This adjusts compensation for shaky zooms. Slide this to 0 to remove the compensation. Slide it to 5.0 for maximum compensation. I generally turn this off by setting it to 0.

This is an effect that is just not possible to demonstrate in a book. However, once you try it, you'll see how it works.

Rolling Shutter

Rolling Shutter is an artifact of rapid panning while shooting using the large, and somewhat slow, sensor in an (H)DSLR camera.

> **NOTE** What's This Term, (H)DSLR?
>
> To try to avoid confusion, the industry is trying to differentiate between digital cameras that just shoot stills (DSLR, or digital single-lens reflex) and those that shoot stills and high-definition video: (H)DSLR (high-definition single-lens reflex).

Here's what the problem looks like: See how all the vertical edges of the garbage cans and the light pole are leaning to the right (**Figure 12.32**)?

FIGURE 12.32 During this pan, both the garbage cans and the gray light pole are leaning heavily to the right.

This is caused by the pan moving the image so quickly over the image sensor that the camera can't capture the image all at one time. Instead, it captures the image moving from the top of the sensor to the bottom. (Lenses, as you know, invert the image on the sensor so the bottom is on the top.) This means that the bottom of the image is recorded slightly before the middle and top of the image are recorded. If the camera is holding still, this is not a problem, but if the camera is panning too quickly, you can get undesirable results.

To fix this, you analyze the clips using the same process used in image stabilization:

1. Edit the clip to the Timeline.
2. In the Inspector, turn on Rolling Shutter.
3. After analysis is complete, go to the Inspector and, if necessary, adjust the Rolling Shutter settings.

What FCP does is slightly zoom into the picture and shift the pixels proportionately to remove the lean (**Figure 12.33**). The image illustrates a medium setting, which is the default. You can minimize or exaggerate the correction by changing the settings from Low to Extra High. None turns off all image compensation. (More often than not, the default setting of Medium will be the best choice.) If you need to apply this correction to only a portion of a clip, cut the clip into sections using the razor blade (or press B).

FIGURE 12.33 All the edges appear properly vertical after applying a medium setting of the Rolling Shutter effect.

Keep in mind that this artifact only shows up when rapidly panning using (H)DSLR cameras. For other cameras, you can ignore it.

Spatial Conform

Spatial conform is a scary term. But it is a very useful tool because it solves a common problem: images that don't fit the frame. While spatial conform is most often used for still images that are not in the right aspect ratio, you can just as easily use this tool for video. I find myself using it in almost every Project.

Unlike other built-in effects, Spatial Conform is always on, with three settings to select from (**Figure 12.34**).

FIGURE 12.34 There are three spatial conform settings: Fit, Fill, and None. Fit is the default.

FIGURE 12.35
This image of Earth is using the default setting: Fit. This *fits* the entire image into the frame, even if that means seeing around the edges.

FIGURE 12.36
This is the same image using Fill. This zooms into the image until it entirely fills the frame. Some pixels around the sides are lost.

Fit. This is the default setting. It fits (by scaling) the entire image into the frame so that you see all of it (**Figure 12.35**). Unless the image is specifically designed to match the aspect ratio of your video, you will see around the edges—either black or, if one exists, the image below it.

Here's the problem. This is a 16:9 image that is superimposed in a 4:3 Project. The underlying image, which is on the primary storyline, is showing around the edges of the planet Earth image.

Fill. This scales the image so that the entire frame is filled. Notice in this example there is no black at the top and bottom, but you've lost some of the image on the left and right edges. This option is the best choice when you want a still image to fill the frame when it doesn't match the aspect ratio of the video (**Figure 12.36**).

None. This displays the image at 100 percent size, whether it fits in the frame or not. This option is the best when you want to use an image for a Ken Burns effect (**Figure 12.37**), or import a very small image to use within the frame.

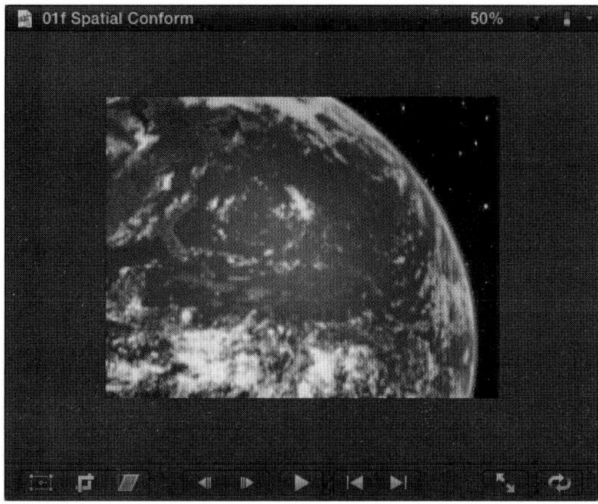

FIGURE 12.37
This is the same image set to None; it displays the image at a size of 100 percent.

Caution!

For anamorphic clips captured by older software, FCP will display this 16:9 clip as 4:3. Spatial Conform won't stretch it to fit the frame. Instead, it will zoom into the clip until the image fits the frame; this results in lost pixels along the left and right edge.

FCP X does not have the ability to change the aspect ratio of a clip from 4:3 to 16:9, or vice versa. That will need to be done outside of Final Cut Pro X prior to importing the clip. At the time of writing this book, QuickTime 7 Pro was the software of choice for this; Compressor 3 or 4 will also work.

Compositing

● NOTE Alpha? Luma? What?

The alpha channel determines how transparent a pixel is.Each pixel in a clip has four values associated with it: how red it is, how green it is, how blue it is, and how transparent it is—RGB plus alpha. Luma refers to the "shade of gray" values in the image. If you were to convert the color picture into a black-and-white version, what you would be looking at is the luma—short for luminance—values of the image.

Compositing can be defined simply as combining two or more images to form a new image. Thus almost all of the built-in effects in FCP are doing compositing in some way or another. Since a composite combines two or more images at the same time, the only way you can composite is to stack images vertically. Since FCP X allows for an unlimited number of layers in a stack, theoretically you can create some pretty dazzling effects.

However, stacking clips creates a problem. By default, every image is 100 percent full screen and 100 percent opaque. This means that the top image *always* blocks any images below it. Over the course of this book, you'll discover a range of ways to solve that problem. For now, though, you want to look at two specific built-in effects for compositing: Blend Mode and Opacity.

Both are amazingly flexible. Blend modes alone deserve an entire chapter. In fact, the best way to learn how to use blend modes is to read a Photoshop book. While blend modes are little understood in video, they are a staple of Photoshop image enhancement.

Opacity determines how opaque, or transparent, a clip is. Opacity lets you change the default clip setting of 100 percent using either the Inspector or the Timeline. (By the way, a clip that is neither opaque nor transparent is called "translucent." Gosh! The things we learn in video editing...)

Blend modes let you combine images from two or more clips based on five criteria:

- **Highlights.** These are the brighter portions of the image.
- **Mid-grays.** These are the middle gray portions of the image.
- **Shadows.** These are the darker portions of the image.
- **Color,** also called **chroma.** This is the color in an image.
- **Transparency.** This refers to either alpha channel or luma channel.

Opacity

At the bottom of the Inspector are settings for Blend Mode and Opacity (**Figure 12.38**). This setting moves to the top of the Inspector when you are working with a Title clip.

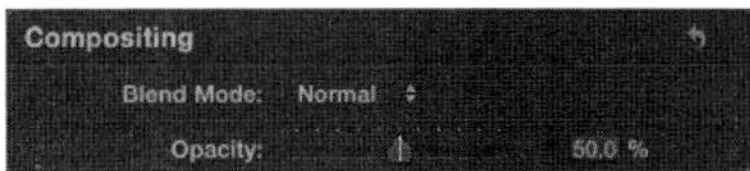

FIGURE 12.38
The Opacity and Blend Mode settings are at the bottom of the Inspector.

You only need to change the opacity on the top clip. The bottom clip can be left alone. This is true for all effects—always change the top clip.

Select the clip and, in the Inspector, drag the Opacity slider left to blend the two clips; type in a value in the numeric text entry, or drag the text value up or down. In this image, Opacity was adjusted to 50 percent, thus creating a blend between a sunset and a winter scene in a forest (**Figure 12.39**). The top image is called "translucent." When Opacity is set to 0 percent, the image is invisible.

FIGURE 12.39
Two clips were blended at 50 percent opacity for the top clip.

You can adjust Opacity in the Inspector, and you can also adjust it in the Timeline. When you adjust Opacity in the Timeline, two additional options present themselves: opacity fade handles at the beginning and end of each clip, and the ability see where you are placing keyframes (**Figure 12.40)**.

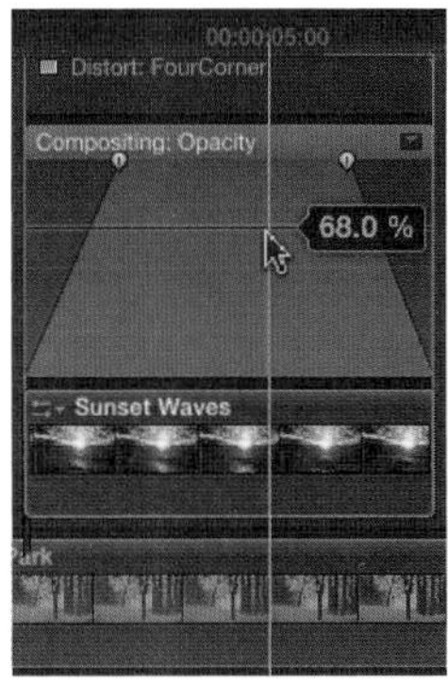

FIGURE 12.40
Adjust Opacity in the Timeline by enabling video animation and dragging the Opacity keyframe line.

To reveal the Opacity controls, select the clip and either choose Clip > Show Video Animation, or press Control+V. Double-click in the Opacity box above the clip to reveal the Opacity controls. Double-click this box again to close the animation window.

Drag the horizontal black line up and down to increase or decrease opacity (the maximum value is 100 percent).

To add keyframes to the black line, which would allow you to change the opacity settings during playback, Option-click directly on the black opacity line.

To add fades to the beginning or end of the clip, which I did for this clip, drag the gray dots at either end of the clip to adjust the opacity fade handles. These work exactly the same way as the audio fade handles you discovered in Chapter 9, except these control opacity. This is a fast way to do a fade-up or fade-out on any clip without using transitions.

Blend Modes

▲ TIP Normal Is Good

"Normal" turns all blend modes off.

Blend modes are used to combine textures between two images (clips or stills) that are stacked on top of each other. Blend modes combine the images based on the grayscale values of their pixels. There's a basic rule to using these: If you like it, it's a good effect; if you don't like it, it's a bad effect. There's nothing to adjust. Take it or leave it.

Blend modes are used far more than you might expect; in fact, they are central to creating believable effects. However, one place you see them a lot is in blending text with the background.

Let me just give you a few examples. Then you can experiment on your own.

The Blend menu is divided into several main categories (**Figure 12.41**):

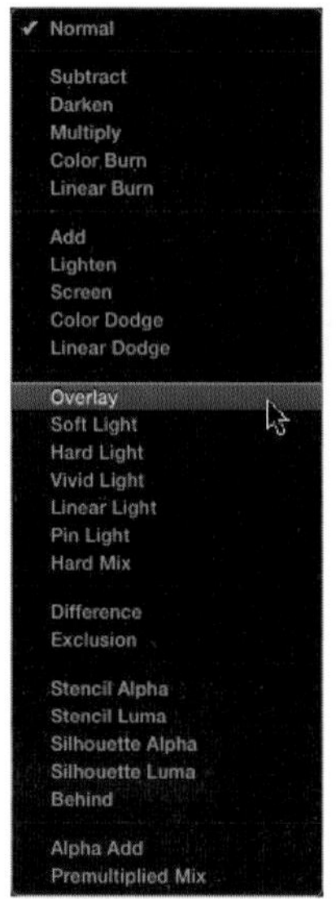

FIGURE 12.41 There are multiple categories of blend modes, with options in each category.

- **Subtract.** This category combines images based on darker pixel values. My favorite here is Multiply.
- **Add.** This category combines images based on lighter pixel values. (Avoid using Add, by the way, which creates white levels that are too bright. Use Screen instead.)
- **Overlay.** This category combines images based on midtone gray values. This is my favorite blend mode, and I always try using it first.
- **Difference.** This category combines images based on color values.
- **Stencil Alpha.** This category combines images based on transparency, either alpha or luma.

Not all of these settings work for all clips. Some will be dramatic, others much more subtle. In all cases, try it and see what you like. The three that I always try first are Overlay, Screen, and Multiply—in that order. After that, I start playing with the others.

Here are some examples.

This is a text clip that I created in Final Cut Pro (**Figure 12.42**). It is light gray in color and grayscale. Let's superimpose it over a background and change the blend modes.

FIGURE 12.42 This is our starting clip, with light gray text.

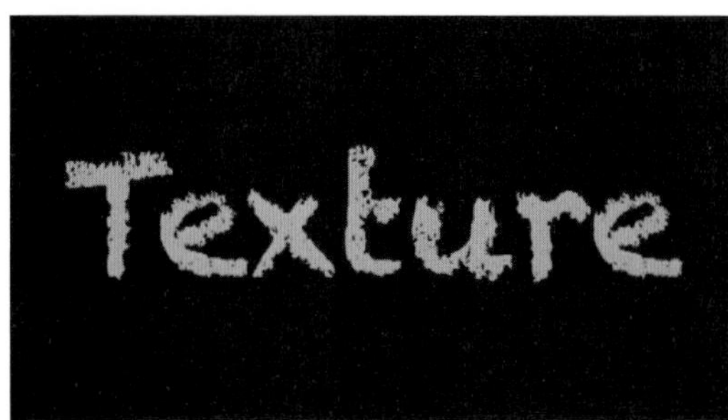

FIGURE 12.43
This is the text applied to a background using the Overlay blend mode.

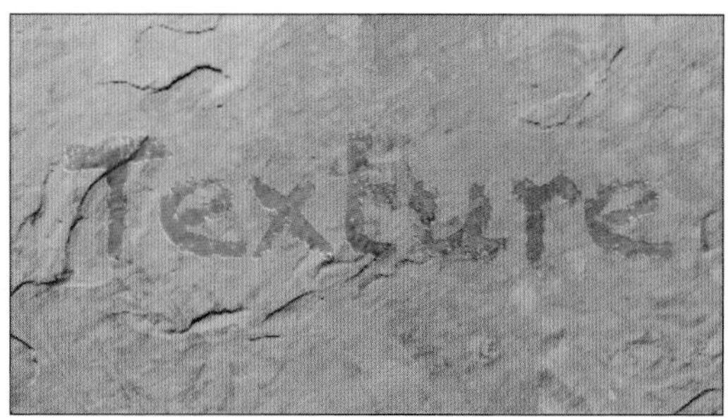

FIGURE 12.44
This is the text applied using the Linear Light blend mode.

The image in **Figure 12.43** uses an Overlay blend mode. Notice how the colors from the background blend into the text, and the shadow from the background runs through the *T*. This creates the effect of weathered text blended into the rock's surface.

The image in **Figure 12.44** uses the Linear Light blend mode. In this example I changed the color of the text to blue, because Linear Light works better with color text than white text. This gives more of a feeling of chalk scrawled on the rock.

FIGURE 12.45
This is the text applied using the Multiply blend mode.

The image in **Figure 12.45** uses the Multiply blend mode. In this example I made the text dark gray. Again, the two textures combine in ways that make the text look as if it is actually spray-painted on the rock. (By the way, this rock texture is actually a generator that ships with Final Cut Pro X. I'll talk about generators in the next chapter.)

Blend modes are a great way to share textures between images and a never-ending opportunity to make your effects look more "organic" and integrated than simply adjusting opacity, or doing a key.

Special Case: Use Compound Clips for Effects

Compound clips also play a large role in creating effects. A compound clip lets you treat a group of clips as though they were a single clip. (In Final Cut Pro 7, this was called a "nest.")

Let me illustrate with an example. I've stacked four clips on top of each other in the Timeline (**Figure 12.46**). What I want to do is rotate all of them, make them a bit darker, then add a title on top. The easiest way to do this is with a compound clip. Here are the steps:

FIGURE 12.46 Because I want to see four images at once, I start by stacking four clips in the Timeline. Note they all start and stop at the same time.

1. Using the Transform settings in the Inspector, scale the top clip to 50 percent size. (Use the top clip so you can see what you are doing in the Viewer.)
2. Copy this clip to the clipboard (choose Edit > Copy, or press Command+C).
3. Select the three remaining clips and choose Edit > Paste Effects. This pastes the Transform effect from the first clip to the three selected clips.
4. Using the on-screen controls for Transform, position all four clips until there is a clip in each corner of the screen (**Figure 12.47**).

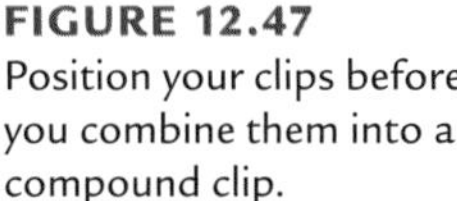

FIGURE 12.47 Position your clips before you combine them into a compound clip.

5. Select all the clips you want to combine into a compound clip, and press Option+G, or choose File > New Compound Clip. This condenses all four clips into a single compound clip stored in the Timeline (**Figure 12.48**). (If I had planned to use this effect with these clips more than once, I would have first created the compound clip in the Event Browser. Chapter 7 explains how.)

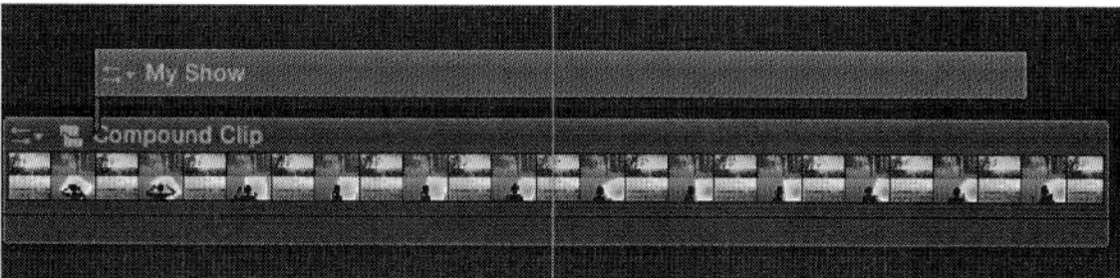

FIGURE 12.48 After combining the clips into a compound clip and adding a title, the Timeline looks like this.

6. I added the Drifting title effect from the Titles Browser on top of my clips. Then I changed the text font, changed the size of the text, and colored the bottom title. Oh, and I added a drop shadow.
7. I then selected the compound clip and, in the Transform section of the Inspector, I scaled it, rotated it, and decreased the opacity until I got to the final effect (**Figure 12.49**). After all these changes, when I play this effect, the video from each clip plays under the title.

FIGURE 12.49 This is the finished effect.

The compound clip made it easy to rotate all these separate clips and decrease their opacity. In real life, I would also blur this background and remove some of the color so the text is easier to read, but I haven't covered those effects yet, so I'll stop here.

Summary

The built-in effects are central to almost all the effects you create inside Final Cut Pro X. You are always looking to change the size of something, or reposition it, animate it, or blend it so that it works better for this Project.

More than any others, these are the effects you'll use to make all that happen.

Keyboard Shortcuts

Shortcut	What It Does
Command+4	Toggle the Inspector open/closed
Option+Command+V	Paste effects to selected clips
Shift+Control+R	Render entire Timeline
Control+R	Render selection
Command+9	Display Background Task window
Command+[plus]	Zoom into Viewer (if active)
Command+[minus}	Zoom out of Viewer (if active)
Shift+Z	Scale image to fit in Viewer (if active)
Command+[plus]	Zoom into Viewer
Command+[minus}	Zoom out of Viewer
Shift+T	Display on-screen Transform controls
Shift-drag the anchor point	Constrain movement
Option+;	Jump to previous keyframe in the Animation Editor
Option+'	Jump to next keyframe in the Animation Editor
Control+V	Display Timeline video animation
Control+A	Display Timeline audio animation
Option+K	Add keyframe to selected video/audio animation
Shift+C	Display on-screen Trim/Crop/Move controls
Shift+Command+D	Display on-screen Distort controls

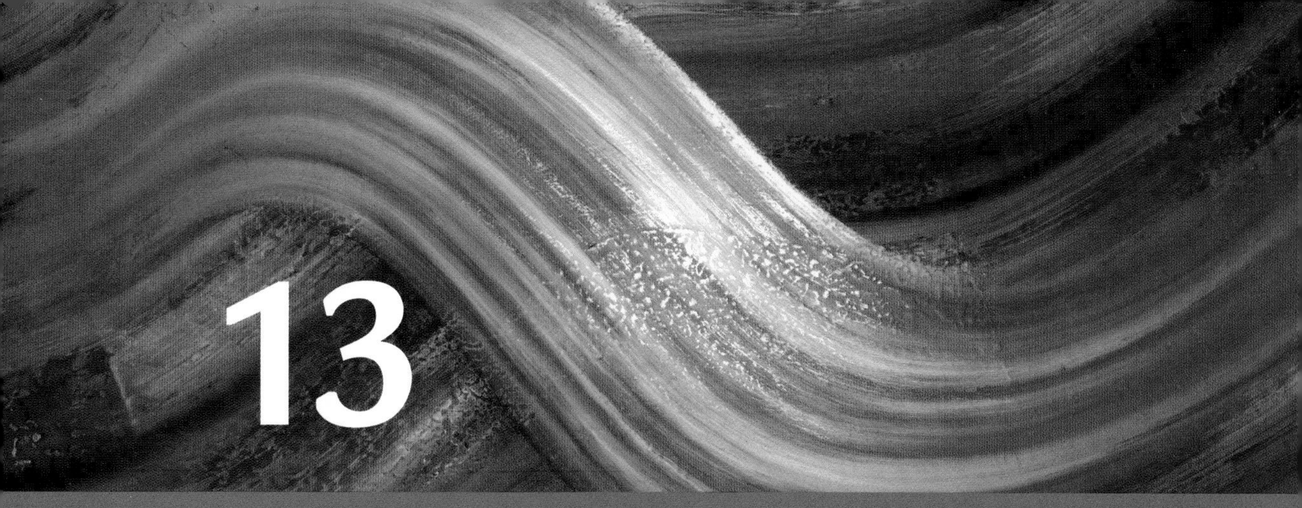

THEMES AND GENERATORS

After all the heavy lifting involved in learning how to use built-in effects, it's time for something a lot easier to understand: *themes* and *generators*.

Believe it or not, you already know how to use themes and generators—these are just plain fun. Themes, simply, are collections of transitions and titles that work well together. Generators create brand-new pieces of video on the basis of parameters that you set in Final Cut Pro.

Let's continue our exploration of effects by tackling these two short subjects.

Themes

FIGURE 13.1
Click the Theme icon to open the Themes Browser.

In Final Cut Pro X, themes are collections of video transitions and titles grouped into categories so that all the elements inside a single theme have a common visual look. You access themes in the Themes Browser (**Figure 13.1**). While there's no keyboard shortcut to open this, you can create one in the Command Editor.

Inside, you'll find more than 120 effects in 15 different categories (**Figure 13.2**). Within a category, elements are organized first by transitions, then by titles, with transitions on top. As you learned earlier, you can find specific themes by entering text into the search box at the bottom, or clicking a specific Themes category on the left.

To preview a title or a transition in the Browser, roll the skimmer slowly across it. The effect will be previewed in the Viewer. If you have clips selected in the Timeline, after a second or so FCP will use the images contained in the selected clips to illustrate the transition.

New with FCP X version 10.0.1 is the Tribute theme. This consists of one transition and four new titles (**Figure 13.3**).

Using a theme is as easy as using any other title or transition. As mentioned, all themes do is group existing effects into visual categories, and I've already discussed how to use transitions (Chapter 10) and titles (Chapter 11). So, the process of using theme elements is one you already know.

The cool part about themes is the categories. If, however, categories are not your thing, then you can safely ignore themes. There's nothing there you can't find somewhere else in FCP X.

● **NOTE** Can I Create New Themes?

Yes. You can also create new effects to put into themes. In all cases, titles, transitions, and effects are created in Motion 5. Then, when you save the new effect, you have the option of saving it as a template that FCP X can use. When you save this template, you can also either store it in an existing theme, or create a new theme category for your effects. It's easy way to organize the look for all the graphical elements of your Project.

● **NOTE** Changing Speed

While you can't apply speed changes, also called "retiming," directly to theme elements, you can if they are contained in a compound clip. (I'll explain speed changes in Chapter 15.)

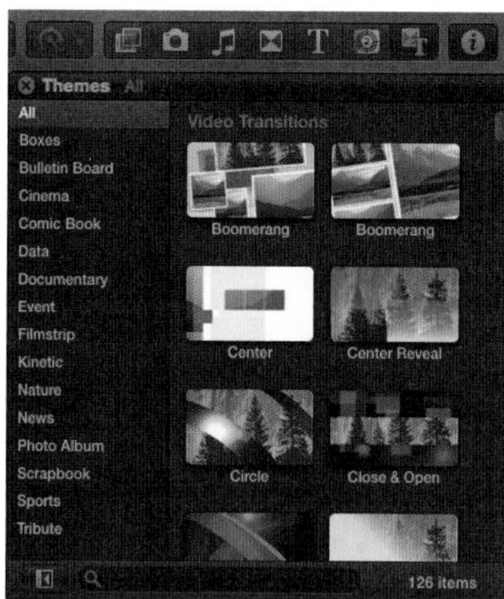

FIGURE 13.2
Like all Browsers, the Themes Browser shows categories on the left, while individual effects are grouped by transition and title on the right.

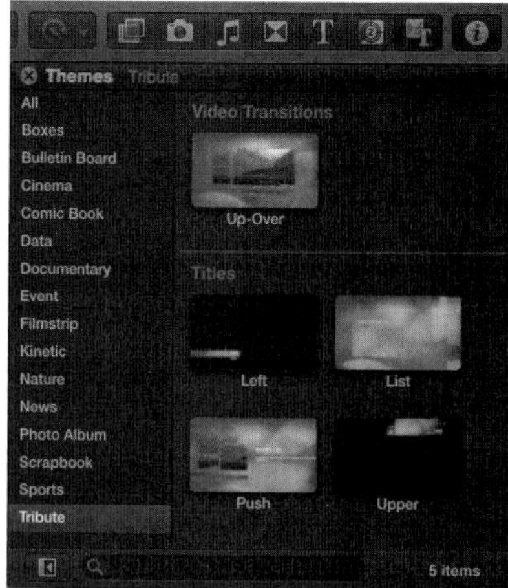

FIGURE 13.3
The Tribute theme is new with version 10.0.1 of Final Cut Pro X.

Generators

In FCP X a generator is a synthesized video clip that is created inside the application. Generators can be any image size, any frame rate, and any duration. Generators, like titles, transitions, and themes, are stored in a Browser. To see which generators are available, click the Generators Browser button, which is next to the Theme icon (**Figure 13.4**).

FIGURE 13.4
Click the Generator icon, next to the Themes icon, to open the Generators Browser.

One of the benefits of using generators is that, since these are synthesized video, they can be any image size or frame rate. This means you can use them in any of your Projects without worrying about a loss in image quality as the image size increases.

Like themes, generators are grouped into four categories (**Figure 13.5**): Backgrounds, Elements, Solids, and Textures.

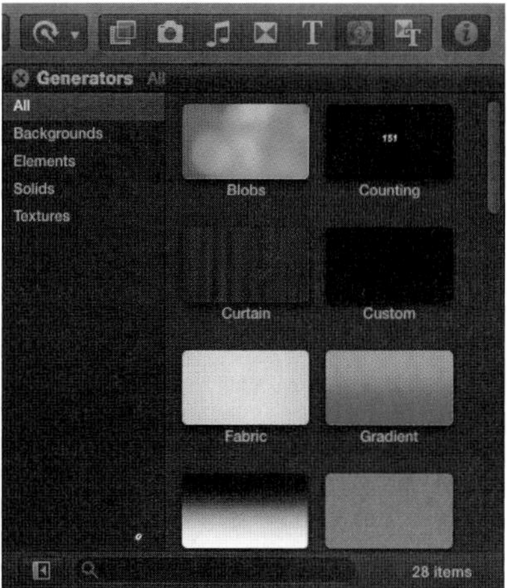

FIGURE 13.5
The Generators Browser has four categories and 28 effects.

All generators are video clips, so you can use the same built-in effects for generators as you do with any other clip. You can scale them, reposition them, add blend modes, and so on. In other words, anything you can do with a clip, you can do with a generator. The exception is you can't change the speed of a generator unless it is contained in a compound clip.

Generator Backgrounds

There are four background generators (**Figure 13.6**): Blobs, Curtain, Organic, and Underwater.

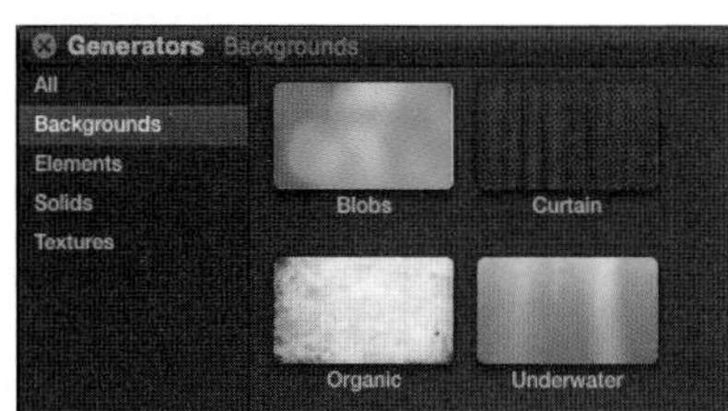

FIGURE 13.6
Generator backgrounds are good to use behind text or composited images.

The easiest way to edit a generator to your Project is to double-click it. This does an *insert* edit of the generator into the primary storyline at the position of the playhead. You can drag it from the Browser to the Timeline, which allows you to place it anywhere in the Timeline. And, using the E,D,W, and Q editing shortcut keys will also work.

Once a generator is edited to the Timeline, select it and go to the Inspector. Many generators can be modified in their look. For instance, you can change the color of both Curtain and Underwater.

Another feature of generators is that they can be connected below the primary storyline when you need to use them for a compositing background.

Generator Elements

Background Elements provide four useful utility clips (**Figure 13.7**):

- **Counting.** This creates a clip that counts up, down, or randomly, with or without decimals, at any speed you want. This clip can also be superimposed on any other clip or group of clips.

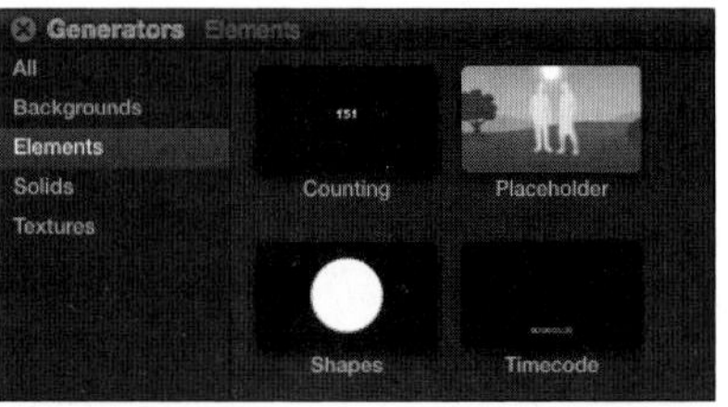

FIGURE 13.7
The Elements category is the most useful of the generators.

- **Placeholder.** This lets you place a clip of any length in your Project to hold the place for a clip that is not yet available—most often, a clip that has yet to be shot, or an effects clip still in development. You can also adjust this clip for the number of people and type of shot.
- **Shapes.** This lets you create up to 12 shapes, with or without borders, in any color you desire, with or without a drop shadow.
- **Timecode.** This lets you create a timecode display to key, or insert, into the clips in your Project that displays the timecode of your Project.

What Does "Key" Mean?

Key means to insert one image, like text, into another image so that both images are bright and clear. Chroma key, or green screen, is probably the most obvious use of this technique. (Chapter 14 covers chroma keys in detail.)

But the most common use of a key is inserting text into a background. Whether this is a title or timecode, keys let you have both the text and the background equally visible. A very old-fashioned way to blend text with backgrounds was by adjusting opacity. The problem this caused was that both images were dimmed. Keys solve that problem.

Counting

Once you edit Counting into your Project, select the clip and go to the Inspector. Here are some things you'll find there (**Figure 13.8**):

- You can change the color and font of the numbers.
- The speed the numbers change is determined by the duration of the clip.
- **Start** is the number displayed at the start of the clip.
- **End** is the number displayed at the end of the clip.

- If you want the numbers to count down, make the starting number greater than the ending number.
- **Decimals** allow you to display decimals.
- **Minimum Digits** pads the start of the number with zeros, so that "1" with a minimum display of 3 would show as "001."
- If you want the numbers to display randomly, click the **Random** checkbox.
- If you want to change the order of the random numbers, click the **Generate** button.
- To slow down the speed of the numbers, slowly increase the Hold Frame using the slider. (I like values between 5 and 10.)

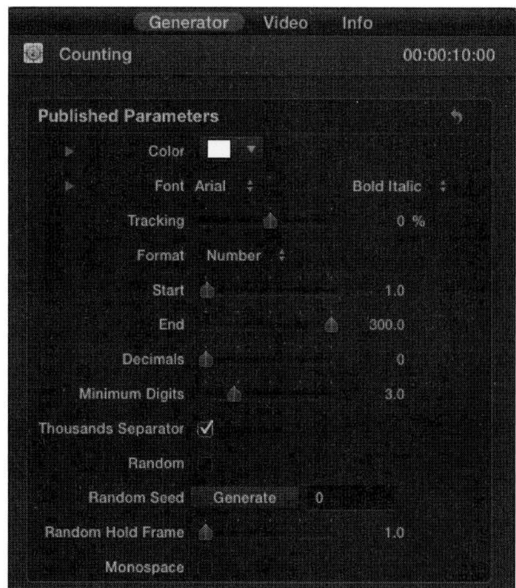

FIGURE 13.8
These are the settings for creating a clip that counts.

▲ TIP Random Numbers Aren't Random

When you turn on random numbers, the numbers are random, but they always display in the same order. To shuffle the order, either click the Generate button, or enter any number you want in the text box next to it. (For best results, enter numbers with four to six digits.) The order of your random numbers will always be the same, until you change the Seed with the Generate button. Otherwise, you'd never get the same sequence of numbers twice in a row.

Placeholder

While the simplest way to use placeholders is to choose Edit > Insert Placeholder, this generator offers more options. The real purpose of it is to hold a place in the Timeline for a clip that is yet to come (**Figure 13.9**).

FIGURE 13.9
Placeholders let you add temporary clips to your Project. The fun part is styling the placeholder.

However, Apple decided to spruce this up a bit and provide some additional options (**Figure 13.10**):

- **Framing.** You can specify what kind of shot you want, from a long shot to a close-up.
- **People.** You can display from zero to five people in the frame.
- **Gender.** You can display men, women, or both in the shot.
- **Background.** You can change the background graphic from pastoral to urban; there are 14 options.
- **Sky.** You can pick a sky condition, from starry night to high noon.
- **Interior.** Checking this puts a wall with a window behind the talent.
- The **View Notes** checkbox let you enter notes. Then, turning this checkbox on or off lets you display or hide your notes in the Viewer.

FIGURE 13.10
With placeholders, you can change framing, backgrounds, people, gender and, in general, totally mess with the clip.

FIGURE 13.11
Generators give you a range of geometric shapes to add to your Projects.

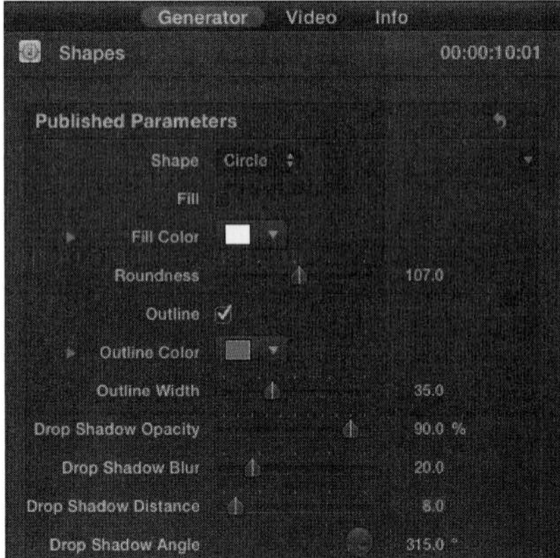

FIGURE 13.12
These are the settings for the circle in Figure 13.11. Shapes and titles are the only two effects that include drop shadows.

FIGURE 13.13
The Timecode generator lets you add a timecode display to your Projects.

Placeholders don't really need all these options. In fact, they don't need any of them. But they are still fun to play with and you can use them as storyboarding elements when determining if you need to shoot pickups.

Shapes

You can choose from 12 different geometric shapes to superimpose on other clips (**Figure 13.11**). Shapes, by the way, are the only clip in FCP X, other than text, that includes a drop-shadow setting.

However, unlike shapes in Final Cut Pro 7, to adjust these you must use both the Generator controls and the Transform controls, which are part of the built-in effects.

For instance, in Figure 13.11, I selected a circle shape, turned off Fill, changed the color of the outline to blue, and adjusted the outline width (**Figure 13.12**). Then, I clicked the Video tab at the top of the Inspector to switch to the built-in effects settings and, using Transform, adjusted the position of the circle so that it highlighted the actor's upper body.

▲ TIP **Switch Between Settings**

You switch between settings in the Inspector by clicking the words at the top, Generator and Video.

Timecode

Another very useful element is the Timecode generator (**Figure 13.13**). This is really helpful when you want to send a review copy of your sequence to a producer for comments. Add the Timecode generator as a connected clip that runs the entire length of your Project. It will exactly mimic the timecode of your Project.

Use the settings in the Generator tab to adjust font size and font color. Then, use the Transform settings to position the image where you want it in the frame.

This is a very popular technique for marking digital dailies, select reels, and rough cuts so that producers can reference their comments to a specific timecode in the Project.

▲ TIP Start at the End

Here's a very cool tip for making changes to your Project. When the producer sends you his or her notes, start at the end of the Project and make changes from back to front. If you start at the beginning, as soon as you change one clip, all the timecode references to later clips will be thrown off. By working from back to front, any changes you make will affect only the clips you've already changed.

Generator Solids

There are six solid colors shipped with Final Cut Pro, and each of these is useful in providing a variety of colors in a variety of shades. The Custom solid lets you select any color from the standard Mac color picker (**Figure 13.14**).

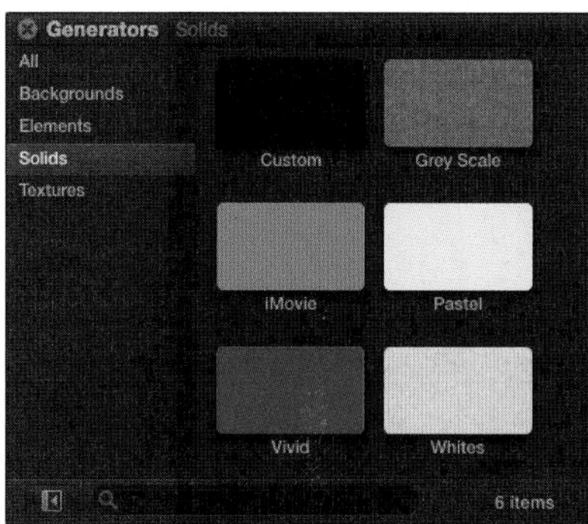

FIGURE 13.14
These solid colors are nice for generic backgrounds; the most flexible choice is Custom.

Once you've edited these to the Timeline, select the Generator tab and adjust the color in the Inspector. For the greatest color flexibility, use Custom. For shades of gray in 10 percent increments, use Grey Scale. For simplicity in picking colors, select any of the others.

Generator Textures

Textures include 12 different images, each with a variety of adjustable settings. These are most often used as backgrounds for text (**Figure 13.15**).

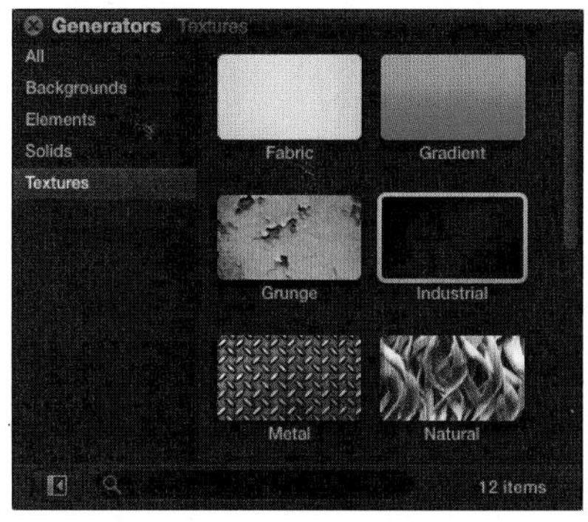

FIGURE 13.15
Textures provide more interesting elements to use as text fills and backgrounds. Each has a wide variety of settings to modify the look.

Edit a texture to the Timeline as you would any other clip. Then select it, and go to the Inspector to make changes.

Each texture provides a variety of settings and colors to play with. These are especially useful as text fills, or as backgrounds when combined with clip effects like Blurs or Stylize.

Adjusting a Generator in Motion

Any generator, effect, or title can be further adjusted in Motion 5. While explaining how Motion works is well outside the focus of this book, here are a couple of notes.

To send a generator to Motion, right-click it and click the "Open a copy in Motion" menu item. In Motion, make whatever changes you want, then save your changes.

The saved clip automatically appears back in the same Browser from which you sent it. To make additional changes, you can right-click it to "Open in Motion," but now the generator won't update until you relaunch FCP X. Unlike in FCP 7, you do not have continuous round-tripping between the two applications.

Also, if you need to delete a customized generator effect, it is stored in [Home Directory] > Movies > Motion Templates > Generators.

Where Can I Find Any Customized Effect?

Any effect, in any Browser, can be customized in Motion 5. The revised effect is saved back into [Home Directory] > Movies > Motion Templates. From there, they are stored in folders named by the Browser of the original effect and the category within that Browser.

In the Finder, a fast keyboard shortcut to the Home Directory is Shift+Command+H.

Summary

Themes are a fast way to find transitions and titles grouped by visual "look." Think of this as a shortcut to the Titles and Transitions Browsers.

Generators are special clips that provide a variety of backgrounds and other special effects that you can access at any time in any Project.

Any effect in any Browser can be further customized in Motion 5.

14 KEYING

Keying is the process of making one element in an image—a shade of gray or a particular color—transparent, so that you can put one image on top of another image.

You began exploring this, though not using this name, when you were looking at titles in Chapter 11. The process of inserting text on top of another clip is one form of a key. However, this chapter focuses on the most popular types of keying: luma key and chroma key.

Keying is used every day in productions big and small. This chapter shows you how to use this technique successfully.

Planning a Key

The reason keying became necessary is that many times, due to cost or physical impossibility, a script calls for putting an actor someplace where they can't go—for instance, standing on the soil of a distant planet, or inside the human body, or in front of an animated weather map.

Keying also saves time and money. Rather than fly an actor to a distant locale, you can use a local film crew to take pictures of that location, shoot the actor locally in front of a green screen, then composite (combine) the two images together in postproduction.

Sounds simple, doesn't it? The problem is that when green-screen work is not thought through properly, a visual train wreck ensues. Planning—especially *before* you start shooting—is essential to good keys. You should have a really good idea of what your background images look like before shooting. That way, you can answer aesthetic questions like these:

- Where should the actor stand in the frame?
- Where should the actor be looking?
- Where should the green-screen camera be positioned so it matches the position of the imaginary camera that is shooting the background?
- Where are light sources coming from and do they need to match?
- How much room does the actor have to move?
- Are there physical objects the actor needs to move around or be hidden behind?

You get the idea. Unless you know what the background looks like, it is really hard to make the foreground (the part of the image that contains the actor) look right.

Then there are technical issues you need to consider:

- Make the background as smooth as possible. Painting the background is always better than using a crumpled cloth.
- Light the background evenly.
- Foreground lighting does not need to match the background lighting. Light the foreground for drama. Light the background for evenness. Ultimately, you will make the entire background and its lighting disappear.
- Keep your actors at least 10 feet in front of the background. This avoids having the light wrap around their bodies, which makes creating a clean key really difficult. (The phrases "pulling a key" and "creating a key" are synonymous.)
- When in doubt, shoot your actors toward the middle of the frame, so you keep their entire body in the shot. You can always reposition later. (This way you avoid the problem of repositioning someone shot at the edge of the frame, only to discover that when you move the image, half of his or her body is missing.)

- Avoid thin, fly-away hair. Caps, shawls, braids, bonnets, hats, hoods, and hairspray all help to keep hair under control. The hardest thing to key is loose, wildly moving hair.

None of these questions can be solved in postproduction. Once the images are recorded, all you can do is work with them. The goal is to prevent problems by thinking about these issues *before* you start shooting.

Help on Set

If you are planning on doing a green-screen shoot, it is *really* helpful to bring an editor with editing gear on set. They can pull some quick keys on set so you can see whether you are getting the results you need before you send the crew home and strike the set.

It is *far* easier, and cheaper, to reshoot a scene to correct a problem when the cast, crew, and set are all together, than it is to fix it later in postproduction.

Creating a Luma Key

Luma keys are special effects that remove a black or white background to superimpose the rest of the image on a second clip. Luma keys were invented before chroma keys because black-and-white images predated color.

Luma keys can make the black background of an image transparent, while retaining the white portion as opaque. Or, conversely, you can remove the white portion while retaining the black—a luma key works both ways. In the "really old days" this technique was used for live talent. Today, you'll only need it when you are trying to key a JPEG graphic downloaded from the web.

NOTE
Stacking Order

When it comes to stacking clips, the foreground clip is always on a higher layer than the background. The stacking order determines what is foreground (top), midground (middle), and background (bottom).

Here's how a luma key works:

1. First, you need a JPEG file. This is Bob (**Figure 14.1**). He's an incredibly complex JPEG file that I could have downloaded from the Internet, except that I created this in Photoshop. (Bob is the reason people don't hire me as a graphics designer. Also, Bob could have been a variety of colors, instead of solid white. As long as the background is black, this effect would still work.)

FIGURE 14.1
This is Bob. He's a blob. But he really wants to go places.

2. In the Timeline, I edited a background clip into the primary storyline, then stacked Bob above it as a connected clip. (Remember, if you want to see two images at the same time, they need to be stacked above each other.) You could also put Bob in the primary storyline and connect the background clip below it.

FIGURE 14.2
Click the Effects Browser button, or press Command+5, to open the Browser.

3. In Chapter 12 you met the built-in effects. These are effects settings that are inherent in every clip. The Effects Browser has the rest of the effects you'll be using: clip effects—more than 100 effects that can be added to each clip. To display the Effects Browser, either click the Effects Browser button or press Command+5 (**Figure 14.2**).

   As usual, effects in this Browser are sorted by categories, and you can search for effects using the Search text at the bottom (**Figure 14.3**). For this chapter, I want to concentrate on the effects in just one category: Keying. There are four options for keying: Luma Keyer, Keyer, Mask, and Image Mask (**Figure 14.4**). I'm going to use the Luma Keyer filter.

FIGURE 14.3
This is the Effects Browser—the home for hundreds of effects.

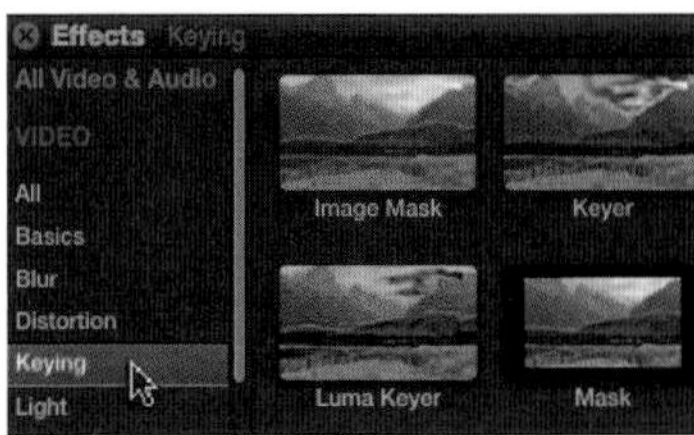

FIGURE 14.4
The Keying category has four effects.

● **NOTE** "Clip Effect" or "Filter"

This is a holdover from Final Cut Pro 7, where effects that could be applied to each clip were called "filters." I will try to call these "effects," but if I slip and call it a "filter," just substitute "clip effect." They mean the same thing.

4. To apply the Luma Keyer filter, either select the foreground clip (Bob) and double-click the Luma Keyer, or just drag the filter on top of Bob. Since clips on higher layers always block clips on lower layers, you always apply clip effects, and effects in general, to the clip on the highest layer.

   Poof! Bob is instantly placed over the background (**Figure 14.5**).

FIGURE 14.5
Bob is instantly transported to a new background!

With the foreground clip (Bob) selected, look at the effects settings in the Inspector (**Figure 14.6**). Though I will examine most of these in detail in the next section, I want to point out a few things:

- Effects are always placed at the top of the Inspector, above the built-in effects.
- The Invert checkbox lets you toggle between removing the black or removing the white. Click it and you'll see what I mean.
- If the edges of the key are fuzzy and not sharp, *slowly* drag the black or white Luma settings to adjust the key settings. Most of the time, these will be fine; when you need to adjust them, make small adjustments.

FIGURE 14.6
The Inspector shows the settings that got Bob where he is today.

The benefit of knowing how to create a Luma key is that it allows you to work with graphics that are downloaded from the web. However, most of the time you'll spend your time working with green-screen keys, or chroma keys. I cover that next.

Creating a Chroma Key

Chroma keys, green-screen keys, blue-screen keys—they all mean the same thing: making a background color transparent so you can put the rest of the shot on top of a different background. The reason you need to use this technique is that no video format shot by a camera contains an alpha channel.

Alpha Channel Defined

Every pixel ("picture element"—the smallest part of an image) contains four values when an image is displayed in Final Cut Pro X: red, green, blue, and alpha. The red, green, and blue values are pretty obvious—they are what give each pixel its specific color. The alpha value determines how transparent, or opaque, each pixel is.

However, when you shoot video with a camera, the camera doesn't record any alpha channel data. Every pixel is fully opaque. Green-screen techniques were invented to solve this problem—how to remove the background from an image. So when you bring the clip into FCP and apply the right effect, you convert all those opaque green background pixels into transparent pixels and store that information in the alpha channel—the part of a clip that remembers how transparent each pixel is.

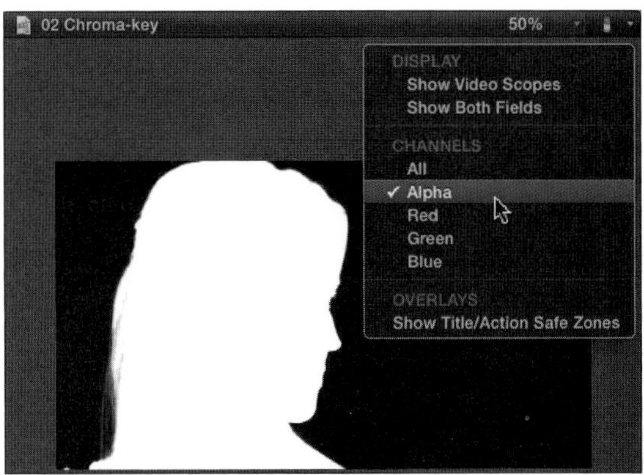

FIGURE 14.7
The alpha channel can be displayed using the Switch pop-up menu. White is opaque, black is transparent, and gray is translucent.

You can view the alpha channel by clicking the switch at the top right corner of the Viewer and choosing Alpha (**Figure 14.7**). White is opaque, black is transparent, and gray is translucent. In this case, the actor's head is white (opaque), and the background is black (transparent). This is what you would see when adjusting a chroma key. With "normal" video, the entire screen is white, meaning every pixel is opaque.

To be truthful, there are two video formats that do support alpha channels: Animation and ProRes 4444. (Avid's DNX format also supports alpha channels, but it isn't natively available in Final Cut Pro X.) The problem is that these formats are used only in postproduction to move files between applications while retaining all the transparency information. No camera uses either of these formats, and if one in the future did, the camera would still not record any transparency data, because it would have the challenging task of figuring out what is foreground and what is background. So, green screens will be with us for a long time to come.

Create a Simple Chroma Key

One of the really nice things about Final Cut X is that Apple has totally rewritten the Chroma-key effect. It is much simpler than in earlier versions and delivers much better results.

The steps to create a key are easy:

1. Place the green-screen shot above the background.
2. Apply the Keyer effect.
3. Adjust the effect for best results.
4. Repeat steps 1–3 for each green-screen clip.

FIGURE 14.8
This is the source clip for our first key.

In the source clip, notice how smooth and flat the background lighting is (**Figure 14.8**). Flat (smooth) lighting with no wrinkles in the green is *so* essential to creating great-looking keys.

You can either place the green screen clip in the primary storyline with the background clip connected below it or you can place the background clip in the primary storyline and the green screen clip connected above it. Which option you choose depends upon how you are transitioning into the effect.

In this example, I placed the background clip in the primary storyline. Then, immediately above it, I placed the green-screen clip. The markers are there to mark where I want to take screen shots for this book; they are not necessary to create the key (**Figure 14.9**).

FIGURE 14.9
This is one way to position clips in the Timeline: with the background on the bottom and green-screen on top as a connected clip.

Select the top (green-screen) clip and apply the Keyer filter by either double-clicking it or dragging it on top of the green-screen clip. This key uses the default settings for the Keyer effect. The hair keys without a bit of green spill—and even the loose hair is retained (**Figure 14.10**). Apple has done a *great* job with this effect. As long as the background is properly lit, pulling a clean key could not be easier!

FIGURE 14.10
Poof! One great-looking key.

When you open the Inspector, as you saw with the Luma key, the chroma-key effect is at the top, with the built-in effects below it (**Figure 14.11**). As you'll discover, you can move clip effects around and delete them. However, for now you only need one effect—the Keyer—and it is in exactly the right spot, at the top of the Inspector.

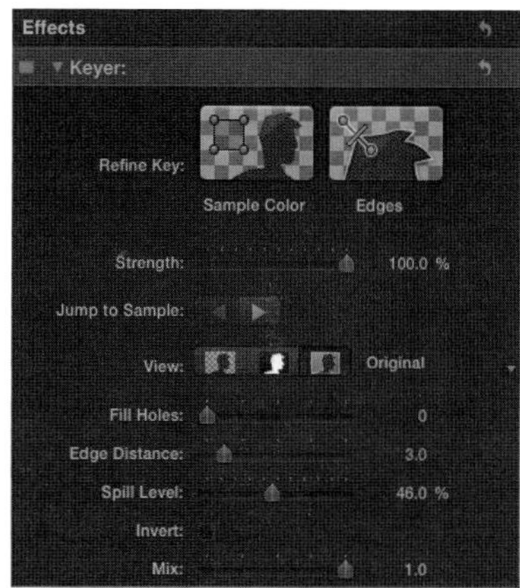

FIGURE 14.11
These are the Inspector settings for this key.

Sometimes you'll get lucky and the key will look perfect as soon as you apply the filter. But the worse your lighting, or uneven the background, the more likely you'll need to tweak the shot.

● **NOTE** Stacking Order Matters

In Final Cut Pro 7, the order in which filters were stacked in the Filters tab made a difference in the final effect. This is also true in FCP X. You can change the order of effects (filters) in FCP X by dragging the name of the effect up or down. However, you cannot drag an effect into the built-in effects. Clip effects always process before built-in effects. Most of the time this is fine, but every so often it causes problems. For keying, this won't be an issue.

News Flash! It Doesn't Have to Be Green!

Strange as it may seem, FCP really doesn't care what color the background is. For example, if you are creating effects for "The Lizard King from Outer Space," obviously you wouldn't use green for the background because it would conflict with the King's lovely green lizard suit.

So you'd use a blue background color. Final Cut doesn't care what color you use, although green and blue color data are easiest to isolate, and thus pull better keys than other colors

Go ahead, all you lizard aficionados, strut your stuff.

Refining the Sample Color

The best way to start cleaning up a shot is refining the sample color. The sample color is the color of the background that you want to remove.

1. Click the Sample Color drawing in the Inspector; you'll find it near the top of the effect.
2. Draw a rectangle near, but not next to, the actor's face (**Figure 14.12**). When it comes to keys, the most important element is getting the transition right between the face and the background. That's why hair is an important consideration. If our actors were wearing shag boots, it wouldn't really matter, because the audience is looking at their face. But because hair is right next to the eyes, any errors in keying hair are blindingly obvious.

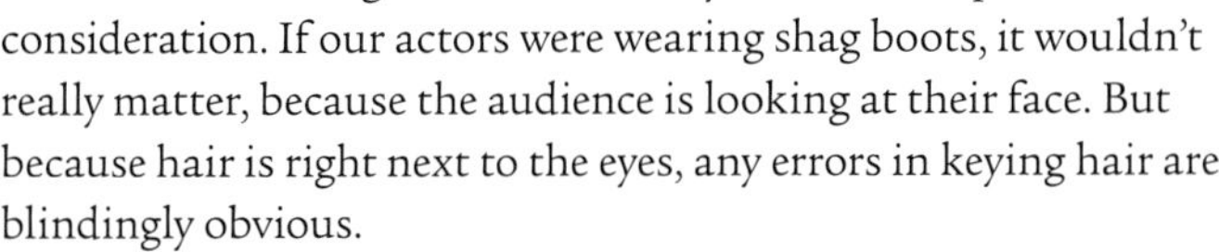

FIGURE 14.12
Draw a rectangle for a sample color near the face, but away from any loose hair or clothing.

For this reason, I make it a habit to always sample the background color nearest the eyes without getting any skin, hair, or costume in the sample. This is *critically* important; if any other color gets sampled, it will totally hose the key.

Generally, the only adjustment you need to make to improve a key is to refine the sample color.

Quick Clip Effects Tips

To reset all clip effects, but not the built-in effects, click the curved Reset arrow to the right of the word *Effects*, at the top far right of the Inspector.

To reset a specific clip effect, click the curved Reset arrow on the right side from the name of the effect (**Figure 14.13**).

FIGURE 14.13
Clip effects can be reset globally or for each effect.

To temporarily disable an effect, click the blue box on the left side of the effect; you use the same technique to disable a built-in effect.

To delete a specific clip effect, click its name to select it and press the Delete key. (You cannot delete built-in effects.)

Create a More Complex Key

Let's try creating a more complex key that illustrates what can be done with lighting and repositioning an image.

1. Place the green screen clip in the primary storyline (**Figure 14.14**).

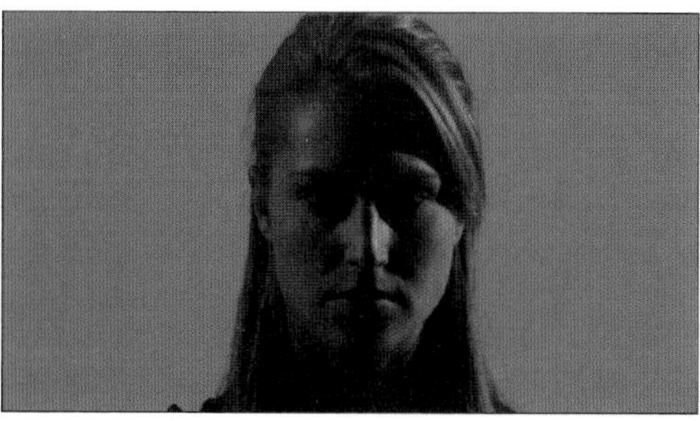

FIGURE 14.14 This is Lisa. It's also a dramatic moment in my script for a very suspenseful movie about the dark, seamy, underbelly of river life. So far, I have exactly this one shot for my movie, but, um, when I shoot the rest, "It's gonna be great!"

   In my example, notice how evenly lit the background is, but how dark and "contrasty" the foreground is. This is perfectly OK. As long as the background is evenly lit, you can light the foreground anyway you want that's in keeping with the story you are telling.

2. Select the foreground (top) clip and apply the Keyer effect.
3. Refer to Figure 14.11 for the full settings of this filter. Just below the Jump to Sample button is this three-way switch. This provides three views of the key (**Figure 14.15**):
   - **Composite** (or finished results) on the left
   - **Matte** in the center
   - **Source Image** on the right

FIGURE 14.15 In the middle of the filter is the View button, which displays (from left to right) the final composite, matte, and source image.

4. Click the blue Source Image button on the right. This allows you to sample the color of the foreground without seeing any of the background.

   You have a pretty nice key, but it still needs some adjustment.

5. Sample the background color near the face, being careful not to get any skin, hair, or costume in the sample. This becomes especially important when dealing with wrinkled or badly lit backgrounds (**Figure 14.16**).

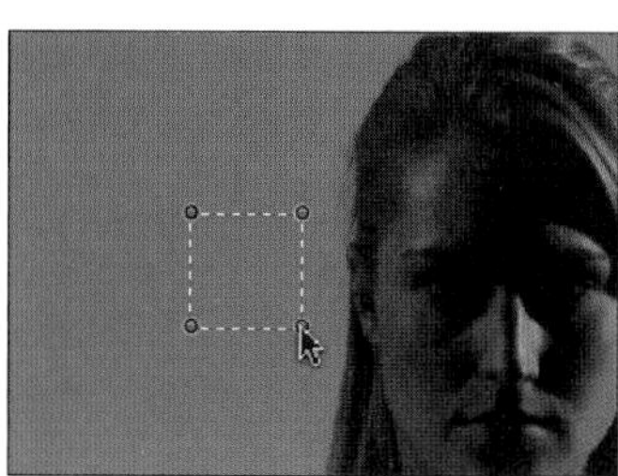

FIGURE 14.16 Again, to be sure of getting the best key, sample the background color close to the face. Press the Shift key and drag new rectangles, to create more than one sample of the background.

6. Click the middle Matte button (**Figure 14.17**).

FIGURE 14.17 When you click the Matte button, the foreground goes white (opaque), and the background goes black (transparent). The goal is to eliminate all shades of gray.

Removing Gray Shades

Your goal is to have the background be solid black and the foreground solid white. You want as few shades of gray as possible—none, in fact, especially in the middle of your actors. Shades of gray cause a weird twinkling effect, the hallmark of a bad key.

The problem is more pronounced with a wrinkled background that has many shades of green. To solve this problem, follow these next steps.

1. Switch back to the Source button and use the Sample Color tool to draw rectangles around the different wrinkles until the background matte is clean—solid black. Hold down the Shift key to create more than one sample on the same clip.
2. Switch back to the Matte button to evaluate the background.
3. Repeat steps 1 and 2 until the all shades of gray in the background are gone. If the interior of the foreground still has gray shades, adjust the Fill Holes slider to make the foreground solid white.

Click the left button to see the final composite (**Figure 14.18**). Very dramatic! I added some blur to the background to improve the perception of depth.

FIGURE 14.18 Here's the final composite.

Refining the Key

This key would look better if I moved Lisa to the left to make a more dynamic shot against the lights of the shore. (And thinking of lights, look at how the colors in her hair and cheek reflect the color of lights in the background. We, ah, planned that.)

1. Turn on the Transform on-screen controls and, while holding the Shift key, drag the center circle to the left (**Figure 14.19**). This constrains movement to just horizontal or vertical movement.

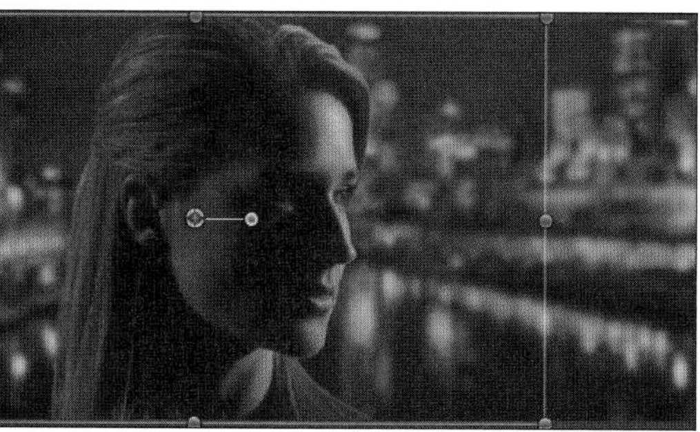

FIGURE 14.19
Use the Transform settings to move the actress horizontally so she looks more into the frame at the lights on shore.

2. Keep dragging the circle until her image positions in the frame better. When you are happy with the position, click the Done button; or press A to return to the Select Tool. This is important because you can't change effects settings if any of the on-screen controls are active.

Now you have a little "tearing," or edge softness, around her mouth. You can fix this by following these steps:

1. Return to the Inspector and click the Edges button.
2. Drag from just inside the foreground that's tearing across the boundary between foreground and background and slightly into the background (**Figure 14.20**). The goal is to help FCP figure out where the edges are.

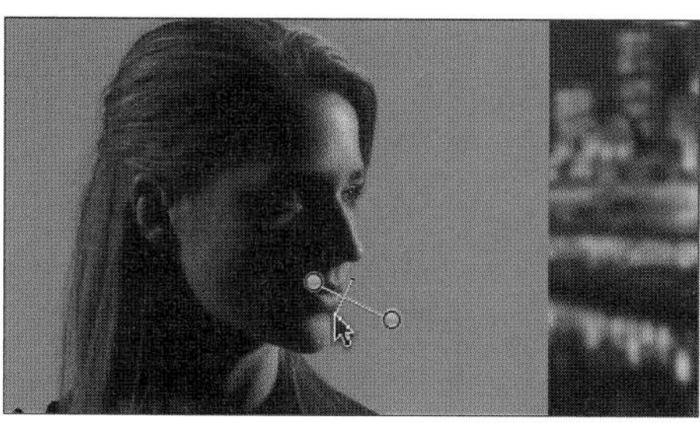

FIGURE 14.20
The Edges button lets you fine-tune the edges between the foreground and the green screen.

3. Drag the vertical slider in the middle of the line you just drew and slide it right to the edge between foreground and background—in this case, her lips.
4. To get rid of some green spill on her shoulder, adjust the Spill Level slider until you get the look you want.

Here's the final effect and the settings it took to get there (**Figure 14.21**).

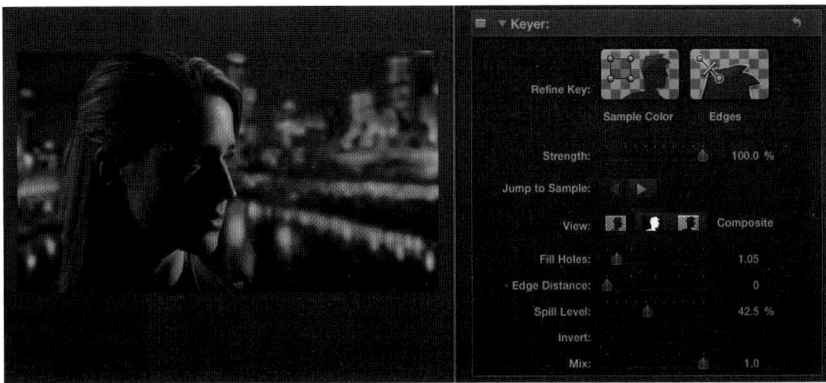

FIGURE 14.21 This is the final effect and the settings for it.

Important Note: Interlaced Footage

If your key uses interlaced footage for either the foreground or background, it is important that you match the interlacing between the two clips. If you don't, the foreground clip will go out of focus. You have two options to prevent this problem: Don't ever reposition the clips, or make sure the interlacing matches. Since you'll do repositioning all the time, here's how to match interlacing:

In the Transform setting, be sure the Y value (vertical position) ends in an even whole number. It can be positive or negative, but no decimals. It needs to end with 0, 2, 4, 6, or 8.

Note this rule does not apply to progressive footage.

Adding a Mask

● **NOTE** **Is There a Difference Between a Matte and a Mask?**

Yes. But no one except a few curmudgeons can remember the difference. For all intents and purposes, when using software, the two terms mean the same thing.

Quite often you'll be given chroma-key footage that has problems—the green-screen background doesn't properly fill the frame, or there are light stands in the shot, or some other garbage has crept in that you need to get rid of. While you can use trimming for this (I talked about this in Chapter 12), many times it is easier to use a mask.

The benefit of using a mask is that you can draw irregular shapes within the frame and feather the edges to soften the effect. That image inside the mask is from the green-screen clip. That image outside the mask is from the background clip. The mask in FCP X is a four-corner affair, which means it creates shapes with four sides. Always apply the mask after you've pulled your key. I've found this to be more reliable.

Follow these steps to create a mask:

1. Select your green-screen clip and, from within the Keying category of the Effects Browser, double-click the Mask effect.
2. This is the default setting of the mask (**Figure 14.22**). I turned off the key so the results of using the mask are easier to see. To change the settings, grab one of the white circles and drag.

FIGURE 14.22 The mask filter applied with its default settings.

3. If you want to feather the edges, drag the Feather slider—the feather can be either inside or outside the mask, depending on which way you drag the slider.
4. If you want to round the edges, drag the Roundness slider.

   You can keyframe Feathering and Roundness, but not the placement of the four mask points. I hope Apple will add that feature in the future. Fortunately, there are already a few third-party solutions for moving masks available for free online.

Here's a final result, with an asymmetric, feathered shape (**Figure 14.23**). Remember, when setting the mask, give your actors room to move. Masks are designed to hide garbage around the edges of the frame, not precise rotoscoping around the actor.

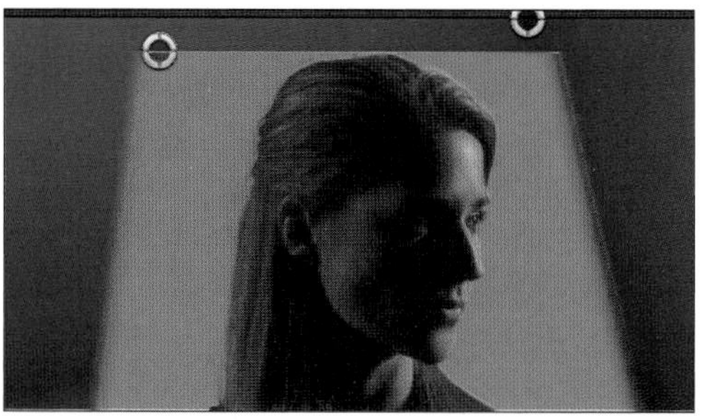

FIGURE 14.23 This is the result of moving the mask points and adding feathering.

▲ **TIP** Help! My Mask Won't Move!

Yeah, I had that problem, too. Masks don't work correctly for some types of clips, especially those in the primary storyline. If you run into this problem, try using trim instead.

Summary

Keys are an essential part of today's postproduction effects. The new Keyer in Final Cut Pro X makes keying a whole lot easier than ever before.

Remember, the key to a great key is to spend time in production creating a smooth background, then lighting it evenly. Oh! And it would also help if your actors didn't wear green in their costumes.

Keyboard Shortcuts

Shortcut	What It Does
Command+4	Toggle the Inspector open/closed
Command+5	Toggle the display of the Effects Browser

RETIMING

Retiming is the process of changing the speed of a clip. (I could have called this chapter "Speed Changes," but that wouldn't have sounded as exotic and sexy.)

There are three basic ways you can change speed: freeze a single frame, change the speed of an entire clip by the same amount, or change the speed of an entire clip by an amount that varies over time.

There are variations on these methods, but those are the basics. I cover all of them in this chapter.

The Basics of Retiming

▲ **TIP** Are Some Speeds Better than Others?

Actually, yes. When it comes to fast motion, any speed is fine. But for slow motion, there are certain magic numbers that tend to yield better results than others. Here's the secret: If you have a choice—and sometimes you don't—any speed percentage that divides evenly into 200 will look better than a speed percentage that doesn't. So, percentages such as 10, 20, 40, and 50 percent are all slow-motion speeds that play back especially smoothly. For extremely slow motion—less than 15 percent—you'll need to read on for some special techniques you can use to make your playback look smoother.

Every video clip runs at a fixed rate—for example, 24 frames per second (fps), 25 fps, or 30 fps. In fact, in the world of high definition (HD), there are about eight different frame rates. (It's so depressing.) What retiming does is change the number of original frames that play every second. For instance, if you have a clip that plays at 30 fps and you change the frame rate to play at 15 frames per second, you create the illusion of slow motion.

This is the heart of retiming: You take a clip that was recorded at one speed and play it at another speed. Speed changes only apply to true video and audio clips. Unless you put them in a compound clip, you can't apply speed changes to still images (duh!), generators, titles, or themes.

Rather than force people to figure out how many frames need to play per second, Apple expresses all speed changes as percentages. One hundred percent plays a clip at the same speed it was recorded (normal speed), 50 percent is slower than normal, and 200 percent is faster than normal.

You can set the speed of a clip to any percentage you want; however, FCP gives you some shortcuts you can use to set popular playback speeds.

By default, Final Cut Pro preserves the audio pitch of a clip, though you can turn this off if you wish. For freeze frames this doesn't make a difference, but for both constant and variable speed changes, it does. Preserving the pitch means that while the speed of the audio changes, the pitch, or frequency, of the clip remains constant. This makes it easier to listen to and understand the audio when the speed of the clip is changed.

Finally, simply for reassurance, nothing you do with retiming has any effect on the media stored on your hard disk.

Hold Frames

Final Cut Pro X calls them *hold frames*. I grew up calling them still frames. In Final Cut Pro 7 or Final Cut Express they were called freeze frames. They all mean the same thing: an image in your clip that doesn't change.

You can create hold frames anywhere in a clip: at the beginning, middle, or end. Hold frames default to a two-second duration, but can be adjusted to any length. However, you can only create hold frames in the Timeline, and, unlike FCP 7, you can't store them in the Event Browser. (But you could export the hold frame and reimport it into the Browser for reuse later. I'll show you how in the next section.)

Let's start with a simple case of adding one hold frame to the end of a clip with a fade-to-black at the end.

1. Position the playhead on the last frame of a clip and select the clip. (You can also use the skimmer, provided you remember the keyboard shortcut I'm about to give you.)
2. Click the Retime icon in the toolbar (to me, it looks like a Smurf wearing a headset; Apple says it is a speedometer with a circular arrow) to reveal the Retime pop-up menu (**Figure 15.1**). If the menu doesn't appear, make sure the clip is selected and the playhead is in the clip.
3. Choose Hold, or press Shift+H.

   The Retime Editor appears above the clip, and the top of the clip displays two colors: green, where the clip speed remains untouched, and red, which represents the hold frame (**Figure 15.2**).
4. By default, a hold frame has a two-second duration. However, you can change this by clicking the handle at the right edge of the red Hold bar and dragging to make the hold frame run longer or shorter. (You can only set hold-frame durations by clicking and dragging.)
5. To add a fade-to-black at the end of the hold frame, select the end of the hold frame and press Command+T or add any other transition from the Transitions Browser (**Figure 15.3**).
6. To delete the hold frame and reset the clip to normal speed, delete the transition, then choose Reset Speed from the Retime menu, or press Option+Command+R.

For you menu mavens, all retiming options are also available from Modify > Retime.

You can also create hold frames in the middle of a clip—or at the start, for that matter—by placing the playhead on the selected clip you want to freeze and pressing Shift+H, or using the Retime pop-up menu (**Figure 15.4**). There is no limit to the number of hold frames you can put in one clip. Just follow the same procedure.

The Retime Editor is the bar that appears at the top of every clip. This gives you the controls you need to change the speed of a clip. To toggle the display of the Retime Editor, press Command+R, or choose Show Retime Editor from the Retime pop-up menu.

You can also create a hold frame from a range within a clip (but not spanning across clips). Simply select the Range tool (*R*) and select a range within a clip (**Figure 15.5**). Press Shift+H, or choose Hold Frame from the Retime pop-up menu (**Figure 15.6**). The first frame in the selected range will hold, and the duration of the hold will match the duration of the range.

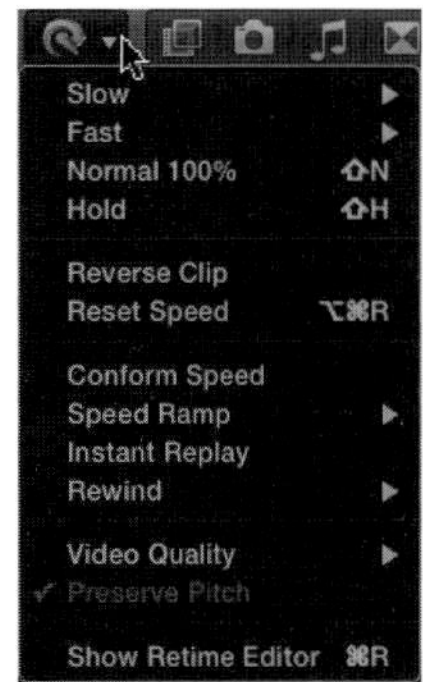

FIGURE 15.1
Click the Retime icon in the toolbar to display the Retime pop-up menu.

FIGURE 15.2
The Retime Editor appears above the clip, with a hold frame created at the position of the playhead.

FIGURE 15.3
Select the right edge of the hold frame and apply a transition to fade to black.

FIGURE 15.4
Hold frames can be created anywhere in the Timeline you can put the playhead.

FIGURE 15.5
To create a hold frame for a range, first select the range in a clip.

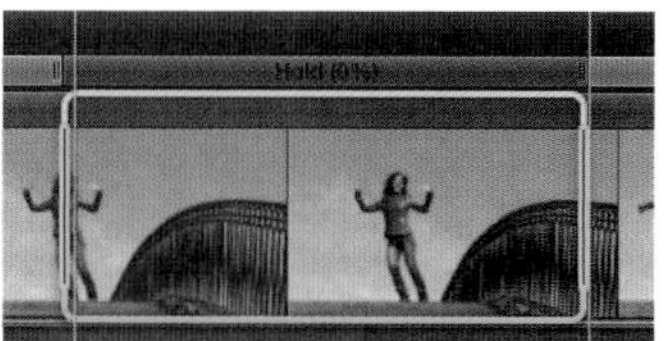

FIGURE 15.6
Choose Modify > Retime > Hold to replace the selected range with a hold frame, or press Shift+H.

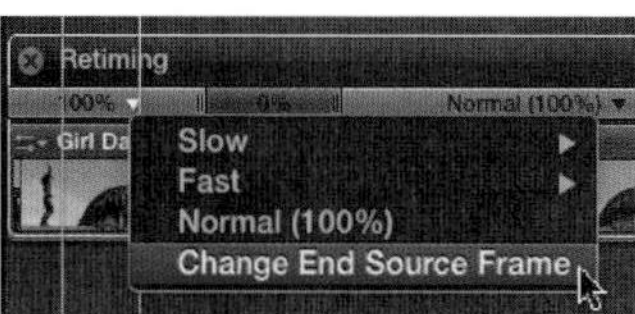

FIGURE 15.7
To change the frame for the hold, choose Change End Source Frame.

FIGURE 15.8
In the Retime menu, drag the little white frame to change the hold frame.

Sometimes you don't get the freeze frame quite right. In the past, changing the frame involved doing everything all over from the top. In this case, changing the frame is easy. Click the small, downward-pointing triangle in the green bar just before the hold frame, and choose Change End Source Frame (**Figure 15.7**). A small white frame appears in the Retime menu. Drag it to select a different frame to freeze (**Figure 15.8**). Simple, easy, sweet, and neat!

Exporting a Hold Frame

Many times, you need to export a frame from your Projects for marketing, for approvals, or just to pin up on your wall. Piece of cake—the export, that is. Getting approvals is an entirely different story.

In the old days, when video was being designed, no one ever expected to play movies on a Macintosh. So, video frames were designed without considering the computer. (Since this was the 1930s, perhaps that is understandable.)

The result of this was two evils that continue to bedevil us: *interlacing* and *pixel aspect ratios.*

FIGURE 15.9
Those thin, horizontal lines radiating from moving objects signify interlacing. Drives us all nuts!

Interlacing are those thin, horizontal lines radiating out from anything that moves in the frame (**Figure 15.9**). On a normal TV set, you won't see them. On a computer screen, they stick out like sore thumbs.

To get rid of them after exporting hold frames, you can open the frames in Photoshop and de-interlace the video. This will make those lines disappear and it will also make your video look a bit softer. When possible, always shoot progressive video.

Pixel aspect ratios are more insidious. In short, for all standard-definition video, and some high-def video as well, images use rectangular pixels rather than square pixels in their images. Then again, just to keep us humble, some video formats use square pixels. This means that video clips look great, but exported hold frames sometimes look squished. Fortunately, Apple added a menu choice that totally solves this.

Here's how to export a still frame of a video clip:

1. Select a clip on the Timeline. (You can't export stills from the Event Browser.)
2. Choose Share > Save Current Frame. There are a number of export options, but PNG and TIFF provide the highest quality (**Figure 15.10**).

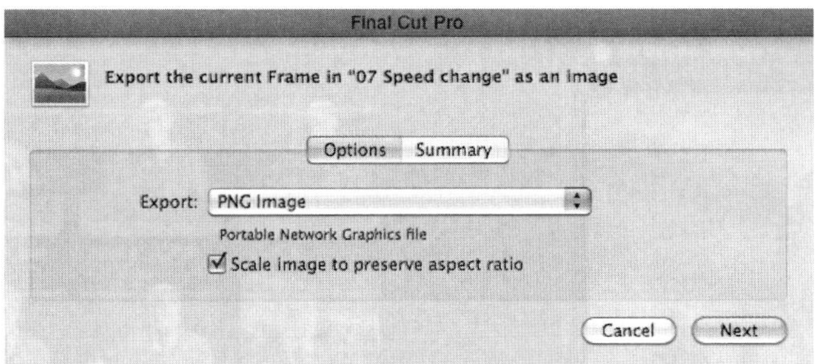

FIGURE 15.10
When exporting, use PNG or TIFF for the highest quality, PNG is the default setting.

3. Do one of the following:
   - Select the checkbox "Scale image to preserve aspect ratio" if you want the hold frame converted to square pixels. This is a very good idea for anything you want to work with in Photoshop or display on a computer. (You'll still need to deinterlace any interlaced images, however.)
   - Deselect the checkbox "Scale image to preserve aspect ratio" if you want to use this image in another video editing package—say you want to move it to Motion or After Effects. Maintaining the correct aspect ratio is important, so you would leave this unchecked.
4. Click Next, give the file a name and location, and click Save. After a few seconds, the export is complete. Apple has accelerated this export in version 10.0.1 using the GPU (graphics processing unit).

The "Scale image to preserve aspect ratio" checkbox option is worth its weight in pixels, because converting images to the right size used to be really, really complicated!

Constant Speed Changes

A constant speed retiming changes the speed of the entire clip by the same amount. Constant speed changes always alter the duration of the clip. You can apply constant speed changes to a single clip, a group of clips, a range within a single clip, or a range across multiple clips.

You have essentially two options:

- Use a speed preset, which is quick.
- Create your own custom speed, which is more flexible.

Let me show you how this works.

1. To apply a constant speed change, select where you want the speed change to apply, then do one of the following:
   - From the Retime pop-up menu, choose the speed you want.
   - Press Command+R to display the Retime Editor, and choose the speed you want.
   - Choose Modify > Retime and choose the speed you want.
2. Press Command+R to display the Retime Editor.
3. Then click the small, downward-pointing arrow next to the label to display the Speed pop-up menu. In this case, I'll select a slo-mo speed of 50 percent (**Figure 15.11**).

   The duration of the clip doubles as the speed is cut in half. The bar at the top of clip will display one of four different colors (**Figure 15.12**):
   - **Red** indicates a hold frame.
   - **Orange** indicates slow motion.
   - **Green** indicates normal speed.
   - **Blue** indicates fast motion.
4. To adjust the speed to make the clip run faster or slower than the preset, drag the far-right speed handle in the orange bar to change the speed. This is the same handle you drag to adjust hold frames. Even if you select a speed preset, say 50 percent or 200 percent, you can easily change the speed by dragging the speed handle at the right of the speed bar.

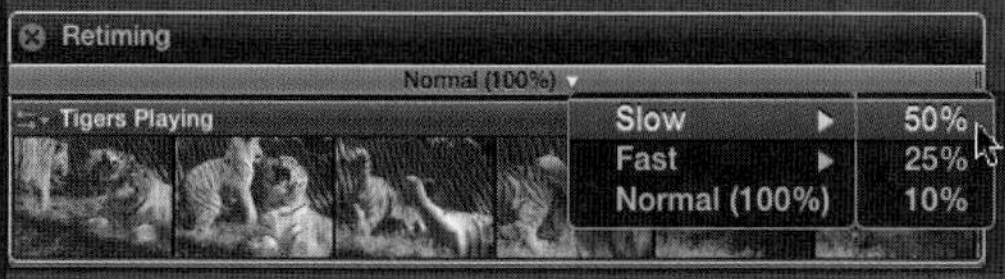

FIGURE 15.11
Choose the speed change from the Retime pop-up menu.

FIGURE 15.12
The bar color indicates speed; orange is slow.

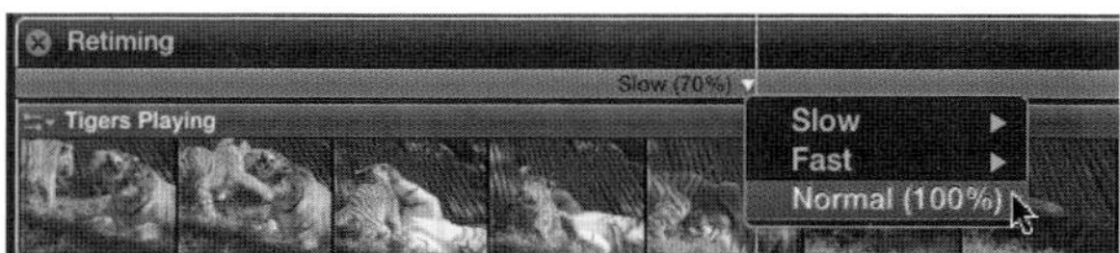

FIGURE 15.13
To reset the speed of a clip, choose Normal (100 percent) from the center pop-up menu.

FIGURE 15.14
You can also apply speed changes to a range in a clip.

5. To reset the speed of the clip back to normal, do one of the following:
   - In the Retime Editor, click the arrow and choose Normal (**Figure 15.13**).
   - Press Option+Command+R.
   - From the Retime menu, choose Normal.
   - Choose Modify > Retiming > Normal Speed.

▲ **TIP** Speed Tip

If you want to slow down a clip without adjusting (rippling) the clips downstream, make it a compound clip, then slow the clip inside the compound clip.

You can even apply a speed change to a range within a clip. For example, let's say you want the clip to run normally for a bit, then slow to 10 percent, then speed back up to 100 percent.

1. First select the range where you want to apply the speed change; this range can even extend across clips (**Figure 15.14**).
2. Then, using one of the techniques I just mentioned, change the speed of the clip. All speed changes within a range use ease-in/ease-out acceleration.

   The first frame of the range marks the start of the speed change, and the last frame of the range marks the last frame of the speed change.

When speeds get slower than about 25 percent, you'll start to see jerkiness in the playback. This is caused when too few frames are played too slowly.

Here's the problem. Video recorded at 30 fps—I'll pretend 29.97 NTSC video is running at 30 fps—and playing at 10 percent speed is only playing 3 original frames per second. (Ten percent of 30 is 3.) This makes the video look like a fast slide show.

To fix this, Apple provides three levels of video quality (**Figure 15.15**). These settings are only relevant for very slow clips. Here are my recommendations:

- **Normal:** Use for speeds greater than 30 percent.
- **Frame Blending:** Use for speeds between 15 and 30 percent.
- **Optical Flow:** Use for speeds slower than 15 percent.

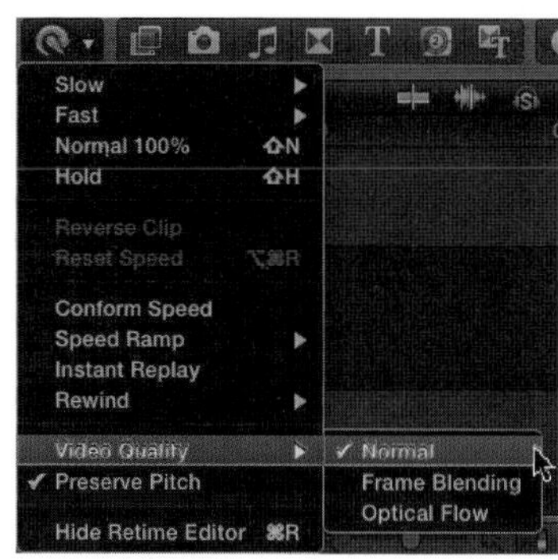

FIGURE 15.15
Video quality becomes important as speeds slow below 25 percent.

As you change settings, render times will significantly increase. There's nothing to adjust with these, so if you don't like how one of these settings looks, try something different. Allow these to render before making decisions on playback quality.

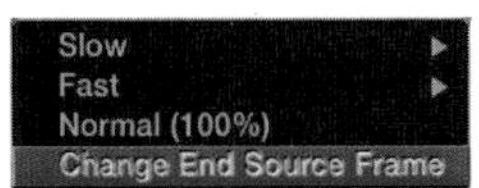

FIGURE 15.16
As with hold frames, you can adjust the frame where a speed change ends.

To reset the clip back to normal speed, select the *entire* clip and press Option+Command+R or select Modify > Retime > Reset Speed. If you want to change the frame where the speed change ends, without changing the speed of the selected range, click the downward arrow for the orange section and choose Change End Source Frame (**Figure 15.16**).

Variable Speed Changes

Variable speed changes are similar to a constant speed change, except that the speed changes during the length of a clip. Apple calls these "speed ramps."

Speed Ramp to Slow Down Clip

Here's a simple example. I want the speed of a clip to gradually slow down for the duration of the clip.

Select the clip, then, from the Retime pop-up menu, choose Speed Ramp > 0 percent (**Figure 15.17**).

The selected clip immediately divides into four sections (**Figure 15.18**). The first section runs at 88 percent of normal speed, the second at 63 percent, the third at 38 percent, and the fourth section at 12 percent. In other words, the clip slows down from beginning to end.

Variable speed ramps always divide the selected clip or range into four sections. You can change speeds and durations by dragging the speed handle on the right side of the color bar.

FIGURE 15.17
You choose variable speed changes from the Retime pop-up menu.

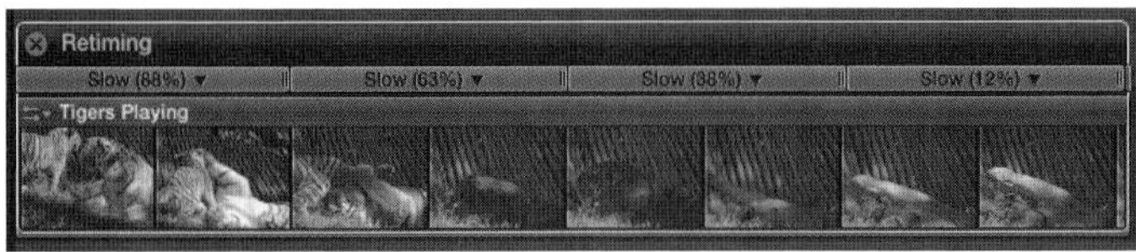

FIGURE 15.18
These four sections are the default speeds for a variable speed clip.

Speed Ramp to a Still Frame

Let's say you want the clip to play at 100 percent speed, then slow to a still frame. Here's how to make this happen.

1. Using the Range tool, select a range in a clip (or across clips).
2. Choose Speed Ramp > 0% in the Retime menu.

   The speed ramp is applied just to the range. You can adjust the speed of any section by dragging the speed handle at the right edge of any color bar. This allows you to make the ramp gentler or more abrupt.
3. Position the playhead on the last frame of the clip and select the *entire* clip, not just the range. (To avoid moving the playhead when selecting a clip, hold the Option key when clicking or press C.)
4. Press Shift+H, or choose Hold Frame from the Retime pop-up menu.
5. Drag the end of the still frame until you have the still frame duration you want (**Figure 15.19**).

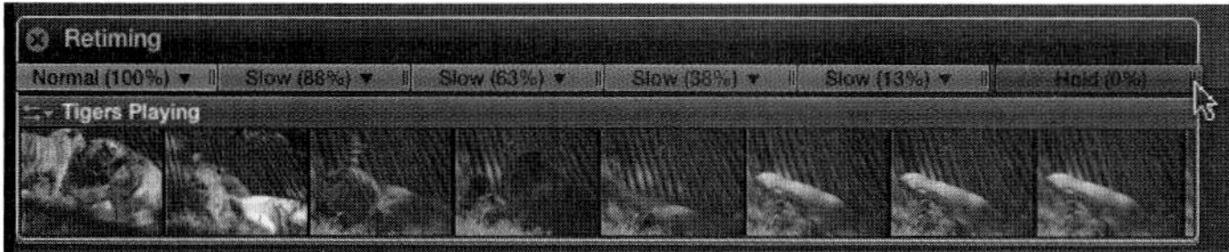

FIGURE 15.19
Add a hold frame to the end of the speed ramp and drag the duration as you see fit.

Speed Ramp to Slo-mo and Back Again

Here's one more version. Start playback at 100 percent, slow to zero, then speed back up to 100 percent.

Using the razor blade, divide the clip into four sections: the initial section that runs at 100 percent, the section that slows down, the section that speeds up, and the final section that runs at 100 percent speed.

Select the second section and, from the Retime pop-up menu, choose Speed Ramp to 0%.

Select the third section and, from the Retime pop-up menu, choose Speed Ramp to 100%.

Play all four sections. The clip starts at full speed, slows to zero, then speeds back up to full speed again.

Each orange bar section can be changed in speed and duration by dragging the speed handle at the right side of each bar.

● **NOTE** Extra Credit

Click the downward-pointing arrow for each section and watch what happens as you select different settings and different durations, and change the end points.

Other Speed Effects

The Retime pop-up menu hides a variety of other speed options.

Conform Speed. If the frame rate of your source media doesn't match the frame rate of the project, this enables the clip to play at the project's frame rate. For example, if you edit a 30 fps clip into a 60 fps Timeline, enabling Conform Speed will make it run at 60 fps or 200% speed. So, if you've intentionally applied speed effects with your camera using overcranking or undercranking, this allows your in-camera speed effects to play correctly.

Instant Replay. This option creates the effect of an instant replay like those used in sports. Select the range you want to replay, then choose Instant Replay from the Retime pop-up menu. The selected range is instantly duplicated starting at the end of the range (**Figure 15.20**).

FIGURE 15.20 The Instant Replay feature lets you replay a selected range of a clip.

To make Instant Replay more effective, choose Slow > 50 percent from the menu that appears when you click the small arrow at the top of the replay section (**Figure 15.21**).

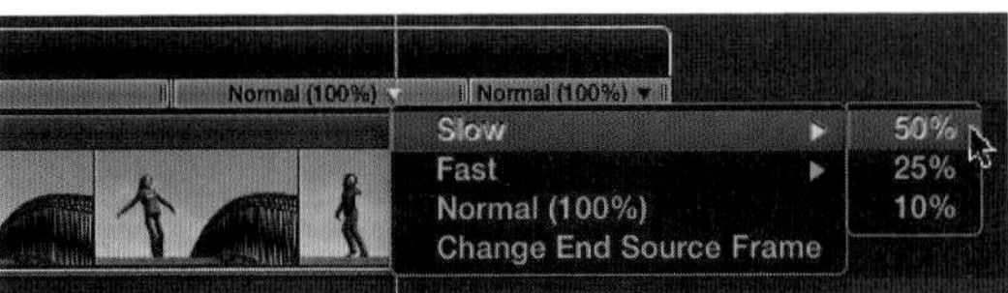

FIGURE 15.21 Adding a slo-mo effect makes Instant Replay more believable.

Rewind. This option lets you duplicate the selected range of a clip and play it in reverse at whatever speed you specify. To make this more effective, set the speed of the rewind section to 4X or faster.

Reverse Clip. To play a clip backward, select the clip, or range within a clip, that you want to reverse, and choose Reverse Clip from the Retime pop-up menu. Negative numbers in the Retiming Editor indicate a clip going backward.

Summary

Speed changes are a fun way to call attention to specific sections of a clip. Slow motion lets you see things that happen too quickly to appreciate properly in real time. It lends grace and delicacy to movement, even if it wasn't there in the first place. Fast motion lets you see patterns in movements that are too slow to perceive in real time.

Whether you are creating still frames, slo-mo, or high-speed extravaganzas, speed changes can add life and energy to your Projects.

Keyboard Shortcuts

Shortcut	What It Does
Shift+H	Create a hold frame at the skimmer or playhead position
Shift+N	Set clip speed to normal (100 percent)
Command+R	Toggle display of Retime Editor
Option+Command+R	Reset clip speed to normal (100 percent) and remove all clip speed settings
Option-click	Select clip without moving playhead
C	Select clip skimmer is positioned in

16 COLOR CORRECTION

Unlike all earlier versions of Final Cut Pro, color correction is now built into every clip. Apple has simplified automatic color correction, beefed up manual color correction, and shifted into a new color space—RGB.

Along the way, video scopes have undergone a transformation, the color-correction tools have a new interface, and everything is much, *much* faster.

In other words, there's a lot of new stuff to talk about!

Color Correction Basics

Color conveys emotion. Before you hear one word of dialogue or listen to one measure of music, your eyes are already getting emotional information from the colors in a shot. As filmmakers learned long ago, lighting is much more than illumination; lighting and color are as essential to the craft of storytelling as the script and the score.

The problem is that mastering this craft takes time and practice. Final Cut Pro X provides a variety of techniques you can use whether you are new to the craft or a longtime master at it.

There are two terms you hear a lot with color: *color correction* and *color grading*. In my view, color *correction* fixes problems and color *grading* creates looks. Let me start with some simple things you can do to improve the look of your Projects, then move on to the subtler and more complex ways you can fix and improve your color.

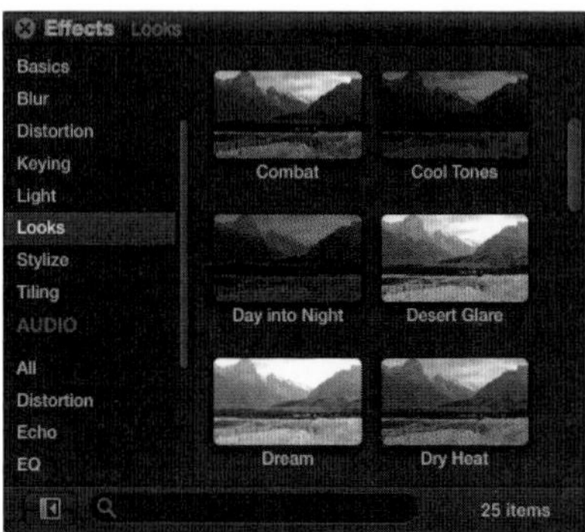

FIGURE 16.1
The fastest way to change the look of a clip, or group of clips, is to use a Look from the Effects Browser.

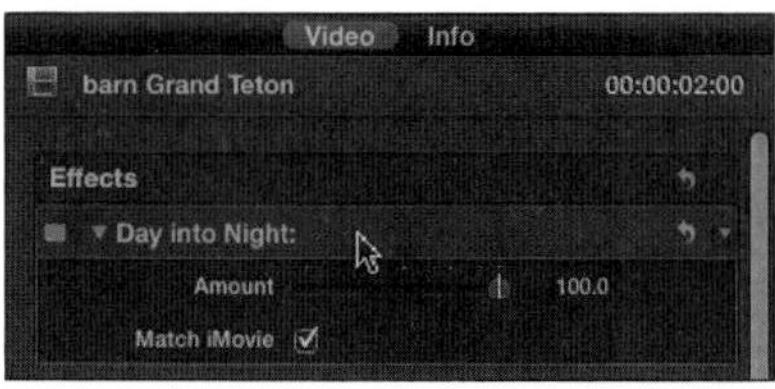

FIGURE 16.2
Each Look can be adjusted in the Video tab of the Inspector. To delete a Look, select its name in the Inspector, and press the Delete key.

Color Looks

When time is pressing and you just need to make your images look "different," the Effects Browser is the place to turn. (The beginning of Chapter 12 covers how to use built-in effects, in case you need a refresher.)

1. Press Command+5 to open the Effects Browser, and choose the Looks category (**Figure 16.1**). Here you can choose from 25 Looks that you can apply to visually change a clip.
2. To apply a Look, select the clip or group of clips to which you want to apply that effect. (You can't apply an Effects filter to a range within a clip.)
3. Then, either double-click the Look from the list on the right, or drag it onto the clips. (Double-clicking only works if something is selected.) Poof! Instant new look.
4. Looks allow a small level of adjustment, which you can modify by selecting the clip, opening the Inspector, and clicking the Video tab. All effects, also called filters, are listed at the top of the window (**Figure 16.2**).
5. To remove a Look, select the name of the effect in the Inspector and press Delete. (You can't delete built-in effects.)

This process of applying, adjusting, and removing an effect is the same for every effect in the Effects Browser.

The good news about Looks is that they are very easy to apply. The bad news is that you can't adjust them very much. Also, they don't fix color problems, such as when images are too blue because a camera wasn't color-balanced properly.

Color Correction with the Enhancement Menu

One place to turn, when you have color balance problems, is the Enhancement Menu in Final Cut Pro X. Let's look at what it does in more detail.

Analyze for Balance Color

One of the options when you import a video clip is to "Analyze for balance color." While the grammar in this sentence is a bit suspect, the power it represents is not.

There are two ways to analyze a clip for color problems: as you import it, or after it's imported and displayed in the Events Browser. (You can also analyze a single representative frame of a clip after it's edited in the Timeline.)

My recommendation, since color analysis takes time, is to either analyze clips for color after you've imported them and decided that you want to use them in your Project, or analyze a single, representative frame once the clip is edited into the Timeline. This way you analyze only the clips you need. However, all these options work fine, and analyzing during import means you never have to worry about it again.

To analyze clips for color problems during import, be sure to check the "Analyze for balance color" option in the Import window (see Chapter 4). To analyze clips in the Event Browser, select the clips, and choose Modify > Analyze and Fix.

You can also decide to skip color analysis entirely. However, if the clip has been analyzed, when making automatic color adjustments, Final Cut Pro makes its changes based on the entire clip. If the clip has not been analyzed, Final Cut Pro decides what to do by looking at the frame of the clip under the playhead or the skimmer when you select the Balance Color option.

Fixing Color Cast

There are two dominant colors of white light: the blue cast of daylight, and the yellow cast of indoor light. A common problem is that a camera has been set for the wrong color of light, resulting in shots that look either too blue or too orange.

In this shot, the overall image is too blue/green (**Figure 16.3**). This problem is called a *color cast*. A clip has a color cast when it contains an undesirable color affecting the entire image, such as the blue/green in this shot.

FIGURE 16.3
In this shot, the image is too blue/green.

FIGURE 16.5
The same train shot, with the color corrected and exposure adjusted.

FIGURE 16.4
The Enhancement Menu in the Toolbar is the perfect first stop when you want to improve a video clip or an audio clip.

Whether your shot is too blue or too orange, here's a fast way to fix it.

1. In the Toolbar, click the magic wand icon to open the Enhancement Menu (**Figure 16.4**).
2. For a quick and easy color correction, choose Balance Color, or press Option+Command+B. (Even when you're manually correcting a clip, this is often a good place to start.)

Instantly, the image color is corrected (**Figure 16.5**). FCP actually did several things here: adjusted the black level to make the shadow detail richer, adjusted the white level to maximize the exposure, and adjusted the color to fix the color cast with the clip.

Matching Color Between Shots

There's one more automatic feature, called Match Color, that also does a nice job of solving color problems.

It's a typical problem (**Figure 16.6**). The first shot, on the left, looks great, but the second shot looks too blue. The Balance Color option gets close, but the color of these two shots needs to match:

1. Select the clip to fix and apply Balance Color from the Enhancement menu.
2. Go back to the Enhancement Menu and choose Match Color, or press Option+Command+M.
3. In either the Timeline or Event Browser, use the skimmer to find a clip with the color you like and click the skimmer on a frame with the color you want. The clip with the bad color is immediately changed to match the clip with the desirable color.
4. Click the Apply Match button in the lower-right corner of the Viewer to apply the change.

FIGURE 16.6
Clearly, the two shots don't match. The Match Color feature helps fix this.

FIGURE 16.7
The color of the right-hand clip now more closely matches the color of the left.

I've found that choosing the right clip takes experimentation. If you don't like the result, try a different part of the same clip or a different clip entirely. Changes aren't "locked in" until you click Apply Match. In this case I had to try several clips before I found the right look to match the color of the clips (**Figure 16.7**).

One thing I really like about this feature is that you can select from *any* clip in the Timeline or the Event Browser. This makes it much easier to find a clip with the look you want.

Another benefit of using Balance Color and Match Color is that you don't need to understand anything about video scopes or color correction to improve the look of your shots. Both of these techniques will make your video look better.

But a wealth of additional color tools is hidden in Final Cut Pro that can really make your images sing. These tools take some training and practice to master, but the results are well worth the effort. However, in order to use them, first you need to learn how to read video scopes.

▲ TIP
Borrowing Looks

If you see a look that you like while watching a streaming movie or television show, take a screen shot or search the web for a still frame, import it into the Event, and use that as the source image for Match Color.

How to Read the Video Scopes

Final Cut has, essentially, four video scopes, each of which has a variety of settings: Histogram, Waveform, Vectorscope, and RGB Parade (**Figure 16.8**).

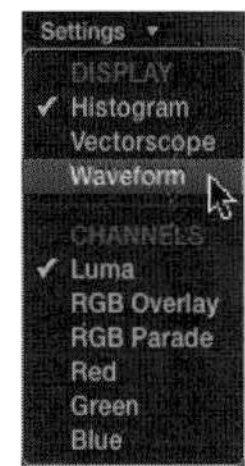

FIGURE 16.8
Video scopes can be accessed from Window > Show Video Scopes, or keyboard shortcuts. Once scopes are displayed, go to this Settings menu in the top-right corner of the Viewer to select which scope to display.

When you examine a clip using a scope, you are looking at two different things:

- Grayscale—also called contrast, luma, or exposure—which is the black-and-white portion of the image
- Color—also called chroma—which is the color portion of the image

It is generally best to look first at the grayscale, then examine the color.

To access the video scopes, choose Window > Show Video Scopes. Click the word *Settings* in the top right corner of the Viewer to choose one of the scopes.

Waveform Monitor

Even though Final Cut Pro defaults to displaying the Histogram video scope, the best place to start when examining images with scopes is the Waveform monitor; press Shift+Command+7 (**Figure 16.9**).

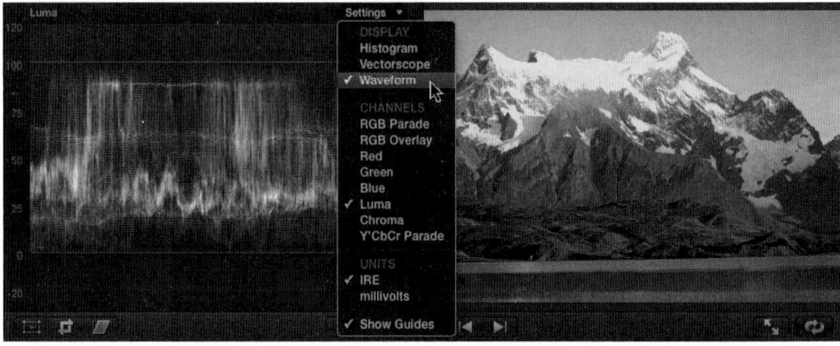

FIGURE 16.9 The Waveform monitor is the most helpful scope for analyzing video. It tells you almost everything you need to know about the grayscale of an image, but nothing about color.

The Waveform monitor displays the grayscale values in an image. The left edge of the Waveform corresponds to the left edge of the image, and the right edge of the Waveform matches the right edge of the image. So you *can* say things like, "The left side of the picture is a little darker than the right side." But vertically, the Waveform displays the brightness value of the pixels in the image. This means you *can't* look at the scope and say things like, "The dark part of the image is at the bottom."

Grayscale values are grouped into categories and measured by the scale on the left side of the scope:

- More than 100 percent: superwhites
- 100 percent: white
- 70 percent to 100 percent: highlights
- 30 percent to 70 percent: midtones, midgrays, or mids
- 0 percent to 30 percent: shadows
- 0 percent: black
- Less than 0 percent: superblacks

Superblack is a new category for Final Cut Pro 7 editors, because in FCP 7, Apple clamped black levels at 0 percent. This is no longer the case in FCP X. However, when you are adjusting black levels manually, it is very strongly suggested that black levels not extend below 0 percent.

In this example, the image has a wide range of grayscale, with the dark shadows near the shore, the medium grays in the water and mountains, and the highlights in the snow.

Histogram

The Histogram displays the range of pixels from black, on the left, to white and superwhite, on the right (press Command+7). (This is just like the histogram in Photoshop.) To see just the grayscale values, select the Luma option in the Settings pop-up menu (**Figure 16.10**).

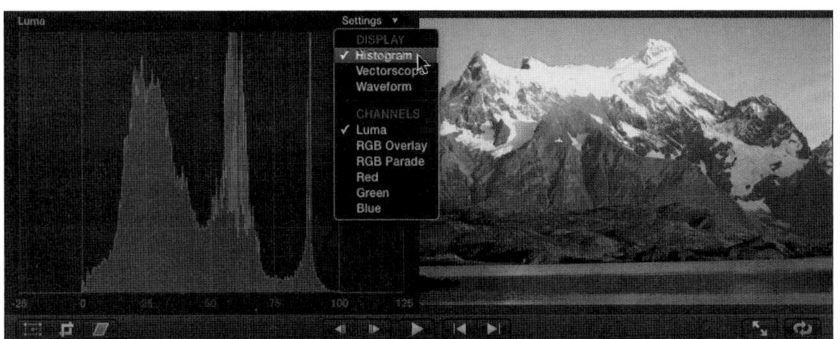

FIGURE 16.10 The Histogram in FCP works just like the one in Photoshop; it displays the range of pixels from black, on the left, to white, on the right.

For me, the Waveform monitor is much more useful, and while it isn't the default keyboard shortcut, I can quickly display it. Though I use the Histogram for setting black levels, most of my scope time is spent elsewhere.

Select the RGB Overlay option to see color values of the selected clip displayed along with the grayscale values. These RGB values are useful, but the RGB Parade scope in the Waveform monitor is a better choice because it makes comparisons between colors easier.

Vectorscope

The Vectorscope is the complement to the Waveform monitor (**Figure 16.11**). While the Waveform tells you everything about grayscale, the Vectorscope tells you everything about color (press Option+Command+7).

FIGURE 16.11 The Vectorscope is the other essential scope in Final Cut Pro. It tells you everything you need to know about color, but nothing about grayscale.

All shades of gray coalesce into a single dot in the center of the scope. The farther out from the center a pixel moves, the more saturation, or color, that represents. As you look around the circle, you see small squares—these are called "targets." Starting in the top left, and rotating clockwise, are Red, Magenta, Blue, Cyan, Green, Yellow, and back to Red. In this image, for example, there is a small thrust toward yellow, but the big "arm" of color is heading toward blue.

So, as the Waveform monitor describes a pixel (which is what all these white dots represent) in terms of how light or dark it is (as a percentage of white), the Vectorscope describes that same pixel using two numbers: what color, or hue, it is and how much color, or saturation, it contains.

These three numbers—for grayscale, hue, and saturation—define the image value of every pixel in the frame. (Another way of representing this is HSB—hue, saturation, and brightness.)

RGB Parade in the Waveform Monitor

The RGB Parade is a special-case scope: FCP X contains an RGB Parade scope as part of both the Waveform monitor (**Figure 16.12**) and the Histogram. The Parade scope shows the amount of red, green, and blue in an image.

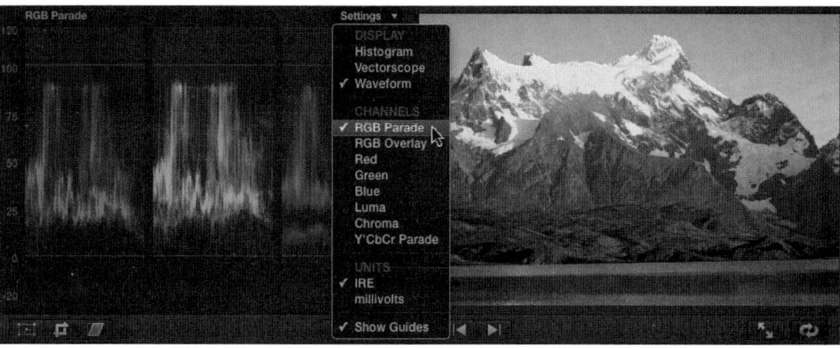

FIGURE 16.12 The RGB Parade is a special scope for both the Histogram and the Waveform monitor. The Waveform version, shown here, displays the amount of red, green, and blue in the image.

The Parade scope is essential to manual color correction, but still takes a second seat to the Waveform and Vectorscope.

Adjusting Grayscale and Color

Apple changed the underlying color model it used when it moved from Final Cut Pro 7 to FCP X. FCP 7 used YC_bC_r—though Apple called it YUV—and FCP X uses RGB. YUV was easier to calculate, but RGB provides greater accuracy, and it parallels the color space used in Color, DaVinci Resolve, and other high-end color grading systems.

The key points of difference between the old system and the new include the following:

- In FCP X, adjusting grayscale affects color values, *and* adjusting color values affects contrast.
- In FCP X, black levels can descend below 0 percent, but you need to prevent that.
- In both systems, white levels can exceed 100 percent, which you also need to prevent.

The steps to adjusting color remain the same between the two programs:

1. Set the black level first.
2. Set the white level second.
3. Adjust the midtones to get the exposure the way you want it.
4. Adjust color values.

Useful Settings

Before all the e-mails start, let me say at the outset that color correction is as much an art as a science. There is no one value that works for everyone. The story and your level of experience make every color grading session different.

On the other hand, if you don't know where you are going, a basic map can be a real help. So, here's a basic map, and then I'll show you how to apply it.

1. Set black levels to 0 percent.
2. Set white levels so that they do not exceed 100 percent (personally, I use 97 percent).
3. Adjust midtones to get the "vibe," feeling, or time-of-day look that you want.
4. Adjust colors so skin tones look normal.
5. Apply the Broadcast Safe filter to trap black levels below 0 percent or white levels greater than 100 percent.

Your goal here is not to make the colors in your clip look like reality, but to make them look believable. If directors wanted actors to look "real," no one would wear makeup.

There are two key rules in color correction:

- To remove a color, add the opposite color; FCP X makes this easy by also allowing you to subtract a color using the Color Board
- Equal amounts of red, green, and blue equal gray. Or, stated in a way that helps you color correct—if something is *supposed* to be gray, it *must* contain equal amounts of red, green, and blue.

Why Can't White Levels Exceed 100 Percent?

Well, if you are going exclusively to the web, they can. The web is very forgiving about both black and white levels. However, DVDs, broadcast, and cable have very specific technical specs. White levels in excess of 100 percent cause audio buzz, trembling pictures, and, in severe cases, can get a broadcaster fined by the FCC. To prevent this problem, incoming programs are often tested for excessive white levels. If your program exceeds specs, it will be rejected until you fix it. It is better to have your white levels correct in the first place, than to have to do the work twice.

However, sometimes you don't have something gray in the shot, in which case you need to do your color correction based on the skin tones of the actors. Remember, your goal is to make actors look believable. (One thing I've learned–if the actor's skin color looks believable, everything else in the scene looks good. If the skin tones are off, nothing else in the scene matters.)

Alexis Van Hurkman has written extensively about color correction, and **Table 16.1**, modified from his book *Encyclopedia of Color Correction*, is designed to help you get skin tones to look right. This assumes natural, studio lighting.

TABLE 16.1 Color Values for Skin Tones*

Ethnicity	Grayscale	Hue	Saturation
Caucasian–Female	50 to 70 percent	2 degrees above (to the right) of the skin tone line	40 percent
Caucasian–Male	40 to 65 percent	2 degrees above the skin tone line	35 to 40 percent
Hispanic	35 to 55 percent	0 - 2 degrees above the skin tone line	30 percent
Asian	35 to 55 percent	0 - 2 degrees below the skin tone line	30 percent
Indian	20 to 40 percent	4 degrees above the skin tone line	20 percent
Black	15 to 35 percent	2 degrees above the skin tone line	20 percent

*Note: Grayscale is measured on the Waveform monitor. Color is measured on the Vectorscope. The skin tone line is the diagonal line going left from the center to between the yellow and red targets.

Adjusting Grayscale

Let's apply these settings to a few clips to see how this works. Most digital cameras raise the black level a bit, giving the image a washed-out look. So, the first step in manually color correcting an image is to set the black level to 0 percent. (This assumes you have something very dark, like a shadow, in your shot. If you don't have something dark, don't set the black level to 0; it will create a "crushed" look to your image.)

Figure 16.13 is a good example of an image with washed-out shadows. The color is OK, but the exposure needs help. The black levels are very high—close to 20 percent—giving the image a washed-out look. Also, the white levels are down around 80 percent, and could come up a bit. You can fix both of these using the Color Board in the Inspector.

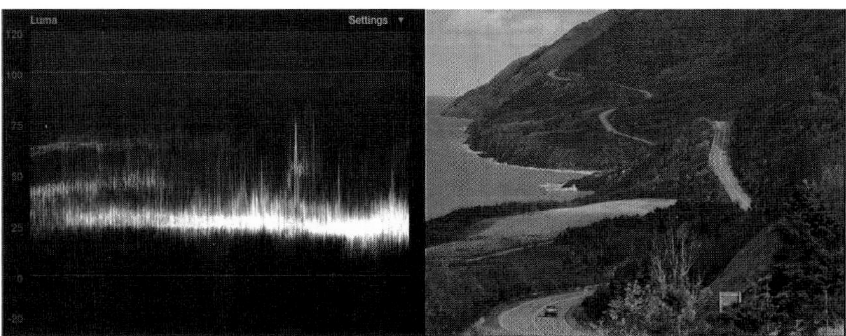

FIGURE 16.13 Here's a typical example of an image that looks washed-out. On the Waveform monitor the black levels are raised to almost 20 percent—way too high!

All color corrections are done in the Inspector. Press Command+4 to open it. The color settings are at the top of the built-in effects. To apply a correction, click the gray, right-pointing arrow (my cursor is parked on it in **Figure 16.14**). When a custom correction is created, this correction button displays a rainbow of colors.

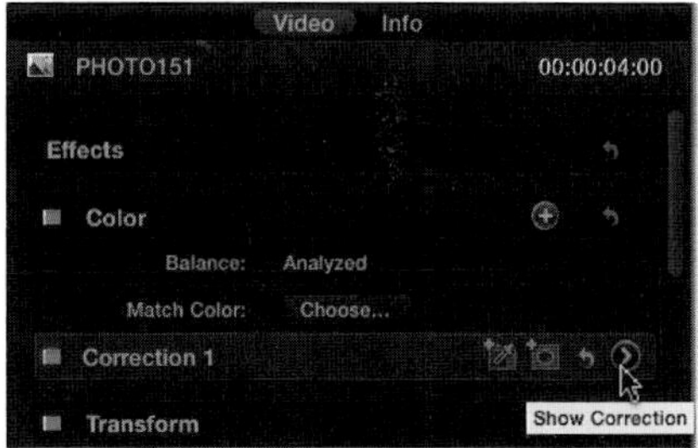

FIGURE 16.14 Open the Inspector by pressing Command+4. All the color settings are at the top. To apply a correction, click the right-pointing gray arrow next to "Correction 1."

Clicking the arrow opens the Color Board (or press Command+6). There are three sections in the Color Board:

- **Exposure** adjusts the grayscale in an image (press Control+Command+E).
- **Color** adjusts the hue (press Control+Command+C).
- **Saturation** adjusts the saturation (press Control+Command+S).

Any adjustment you make in any of these three panels affects the entire clip, not just the frame you are looking at in the Viewer. There is no limit to the number of color corrections you can apply to a clip.

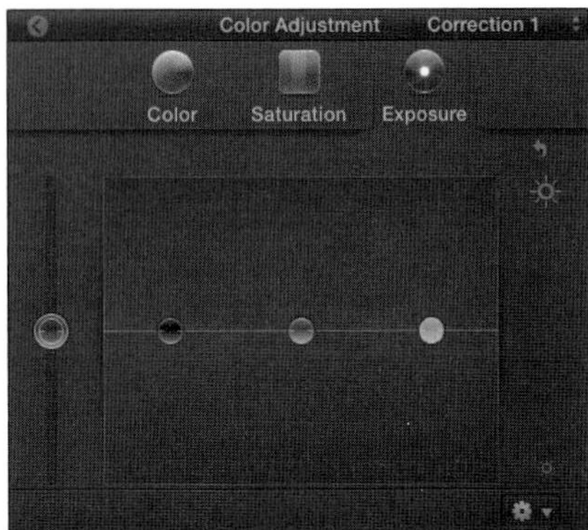

FIGURE 16.15
The default panel is the Exposure panel; to reveal it, click the Exposure icon. From left to right, the four sliders control global exposure, shadow levels, midtone levels, and highlight levels. (Apple calls this type of control a "puck.")

FIGURE 16.16
The Go Back button in the top-left corner returns you to the Inspector.

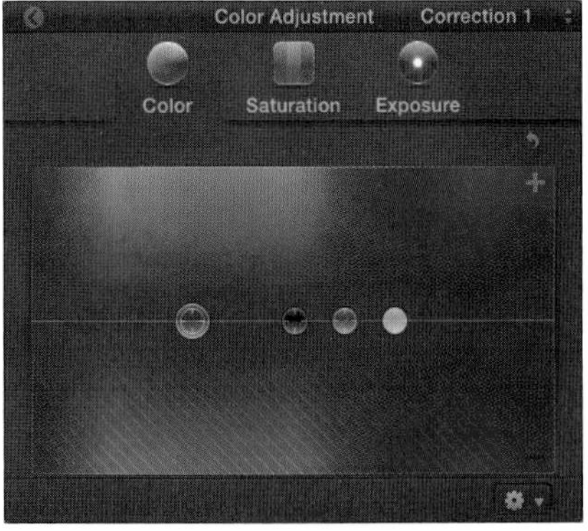

FIGURE 16.17
Click the Color icon to display the Color panel. From left to right, the four pucks control global hue, shadows hue, midtones hue, and highlights hue.

The Exposure panel has four sliders, called "pucks" because they can move in two dimensions (**Figure 16.15**). These are, from left to right:

- Global exposure
- Black, or shadow, levels
- Midtone levels
- White, or highlight, levels

Dragging a puck up increases the level. Dragging a puck down decreases it. Generally, you adjust the black level using only the black puck. Most of the time, leave the Global exposure puck alone.

To reset just this panel, click the hooked Reset arrow in the top-right corner. To reset the entire color correction, click the Color Reset arrow in the Inspector. To return to the main Inspector, click the Go Back button in the top-left corner (**Figure 16.16**).

The *hues* (or colors) in an image are controlled in the Color panel (**Figure 16.17**). The same four pucks control the hue globally, in the shadows, in the midtones, and in the highlights of the image. Drag up to add a color, drag down to remove a color, and drag sideways to change a color. This is the only panel whose pucks move both up and down as well as side-to-side.

In FCP 7, a color was removed by adding the opposite (complementary) color. With this new Color Board, you can still do that, but it is much easier to drag down to remove a color. For FCP 7 editors, replacing the color wheel with a color rectangle takes a *lot* of getting used to. (No, I still haven't fully gotten used to it myself.)

● **NOTE** Thinking Like the Color Board

The new rectangular shape of the Color Board makes it more closely resemble the Spectrum view in the Apple Color Picker. Also, you can assign keyboard shortcuts to Nudge Puck Up/Down/Left/Right using the Command Editor.

The *amount* of color in the image is controlled by the Saturation panel (**Figure 16.18**). The same four pucks control the saturation in the same four ways: globally, shadows, midtones, and highlights. Drag each puck up to increase saturation, or drag down to decrease it.

Returning to the original image to correct the washed-out effect, I clicked the Exposure panel, then lowered the black level until the darkest part of the waveform (at the bottom) was just touching the 0 percent line. This set the darkest shadows to grayscale black. Then I raised the white levels slightly to give the image some "pop," making sure the white levels did not exceed 100 percent.

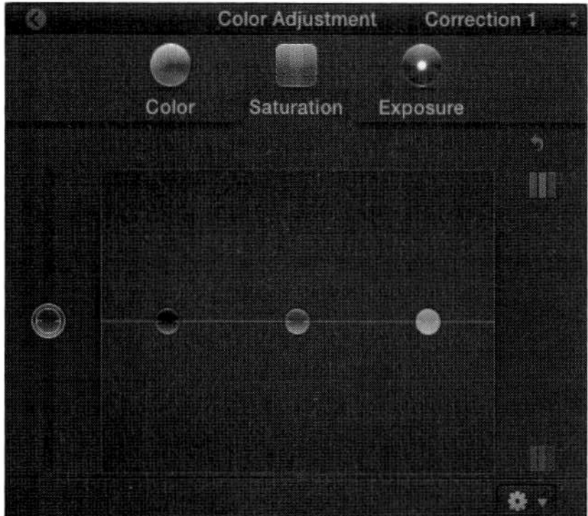

FIGURE 16.18
Click the Saturation icon to display the Saturation panel. From left to right, the four pucks control the *amount* of color globally, in the shadows, midtones, and highlights of the image.

Figure 16.19 illustrates the final settings I used for this image. Shadows add vitality, highlights add energy, and midtones set the emotion.

FIGURE 16.19
These are the Exposure settings that corrected the initial image.

How Do I Decide Which Puck to Use?

This secret took me *way* too long to learn.

You use the puck that represents the pixels you want to adjust. If the image is so dark that the brightest part of the image is around 50 percent, you adjust the image using the midtones puck. If you have a very bright image that you want to darken a bit, you use the highlights puck. If you want to adjust the darkest pixels, you use the shadows puck.

You don't adjust the puck where you want the pixels to *be*, you adjust the puck where the pixels *are*.

Adjusting Color

Here's another example: The skin tone of the girl in this image looks green, which is not a normal skin color (**Figure 16.20**).

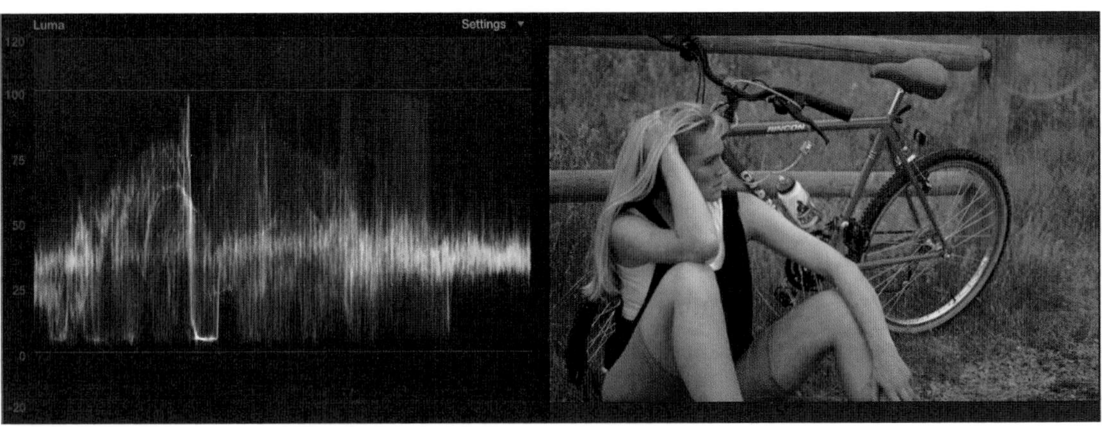

FIGURE 16.20
The girl's skin color in this image is green, which is not normal. I'll fix it.

Also, the black level is a little high. Since she's wearing a black vest, I would expect the shadows to sit right at the 0 percent line. Just by way of illustration, her black vest is the dark shadow about 1/3 of the way in from the left edge. The highlights on the top right side of the scope are from the reflection in the bike wheel at the bottom of the image. The waveform matches the Viewer from left to right, but not from top to bottom.

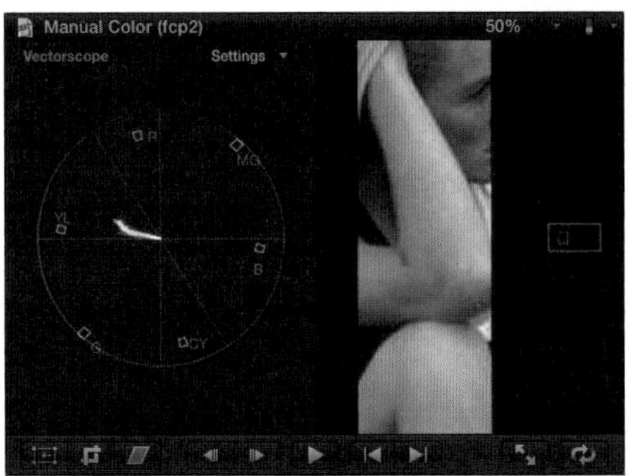

FIGURE 16.21
To correct the skin tone, I trimmed the clip to isolate the skin, then opened the Vectorscope to figure out exactly what colors I needed to fix.

Even though she is wearing white and black, which are easy to isolate and color correct, I'm pretending she's wearing other colors, as that makes the problem more challenging and the solution more applicable to other clips. Here is how I adjusted the color:

1. Using Exposure, I set the black level to 0 percent by lowering the shadows puck.
2. I went to the on-screen Crop tools and trimmed the image to isolate her skin (**Figure 16.21**).
3. To make the image bigger, I then scaled the image—pressing Command+[plus], or using the Scale menu in the top-right corner of the Viewer.
4. I displayed the Vectorscope and discovered just how green the image was—*very* green! Look at that huge spike heading right toward yellow.

Except, well, where *should* it be going? This, to me, is the most magical thing about color correction. Look closely at the Vectorscope in Figure 16.21. See that thin white line going up and left at about the 10:30 position? That's the skin tone line. All of us, whether we are black or white or any other shade of humanity, have the same color red blood under our skin. That line represents the color of red blood under skin. (In fact, skin without blood is gray—another weird fact you get to learn in this book!)

When adjusting color for skin tone, you *first* need to make the grayscale values correct (using the table I supplied earlier) and measure them on the Waveform monitor. *Then*, adjust the color using the Vectorscope so skin tones are placed on the skin tone line.

5. Because the entire image was green, I decided to apply a global color-correction setting and adjusted the global color puck. By dragging it down, I removed the green in the image. Dragging above the line increases the color; dragging below the line decreases it.
6. To add or remove a specific color, drag the puck over that specific hue in the panel.

Figure 16.22 illustrates the final skin tone image and the results as measured in the Vectorscope. (Though in my corrections, I often move individual pucks.)

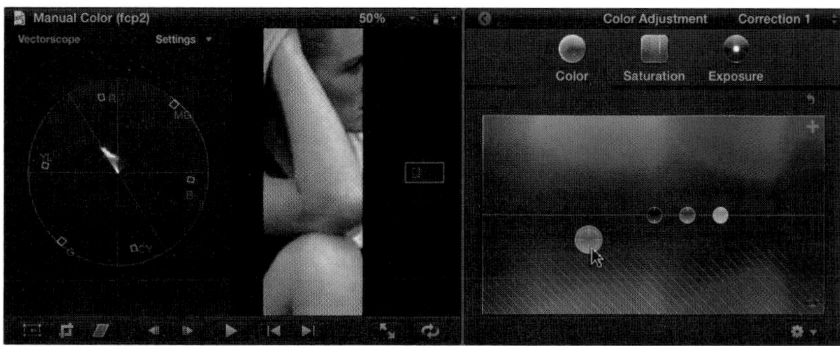

FIGURE 16.22
In the final result, you see corrected black levels and corrected color. Notice the skin tone sitting directly on the skin tone line, around 40 percent, out toward the targets.

Applying the Broadcast Safe Effect

Sometimes, especially with inexpensive digital cameras, white levels are recorded at levels greater than 100 percent. There's a simple effect, or filter, you can add that solves problems with superblacks and superwhites, as these excess levels are called. The Broadcast Safe filter clamps both excessive white and black levels to make your videos technically "safe."

Open the Effects Browser (press Command+5), choose the Basics category, and apply the Broadcast Safe filter to the clip or clips you want to protect (**Figure 16.23**). If the clips are already selected, double-click the filter. If not, drag the filter on top of the clips where you want to apply it.

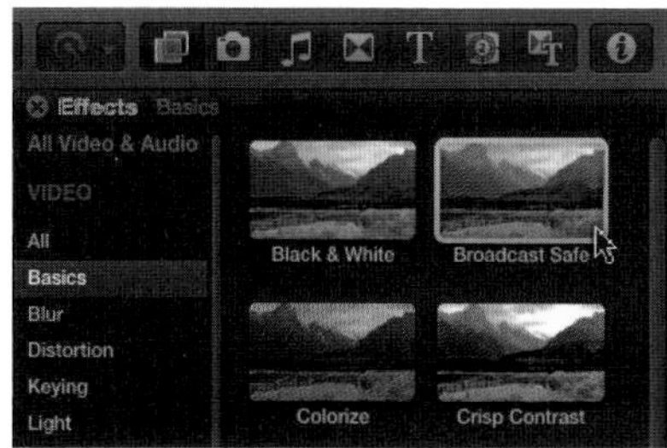

FIGURE 16.23
The Broadcast Safe filter (top right) protects your clips against excessive white or black levels. For web video, you don't need this. For DVD or broadcast, you do.

For web-only videos, this filter is not necessary. For everything else, it can keep you out of serious trouble. One of the advantages of a compound clip is that you can apply an effect, such as the Broadcast Safe filter, to the entire compound clip, which then applies that filter to all the clips inside.

To turn your entire Project into a single compound clip, select the Timeline, press Command+A to select everything in the project, then press Option+G to create a single compound clip from all the selected clips.

You can use this technique to apply a single effect to a group of clips. To adjust the effect in the Inspector, select the compound clip first.

A Really Important Point

Clip effects, like the Broadcast Safe filter, process *before* any built-in effects, like color correction. When you apply the Broadcast Safe filter to a clip, then make color adjustments to that same clip, those color adjustments are made *after* FCP processes the Broadcast Safe filter. This means you lose the protection afforded by the Broadcast Safe filter.

Ideally, the Broadcast Safe filter should apply after color correction, but since that is not how FCP X currently works, the best option is to always make color corrections directly to clips, then apply the Broadcast Safe filter to a compound clip containing those clips.

Using Masks for Color Correction

A new feature in FCP X is an improved ability to add masks for color correction. As you discovered in Chapter 14, a mask lets you restrict an effect, such as color correction, to only a portion of the frame.

There are two types of masks that are part of the color-correction filter:

- A **color mask** isolates a portion of the image based on a color range.
- A **shape mask** isolates a portion of the image based on a shape.

Here's an example, using three balloons. I want to keep the yellow balloon, but change everything else to black and white. (This is also called the Pleasantville Effect, named after the movie.)

1. Select the clip, open the Inspector, and click the Add Shape Mask button (**Figure 16.24**). This displays the on-screen mask controls:

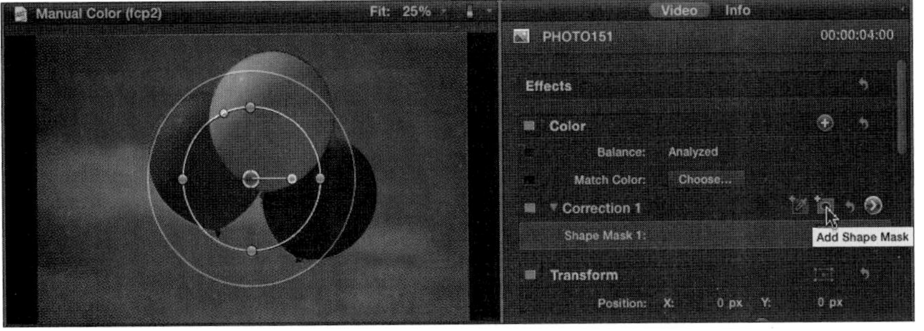

FIGURE 16.24 Clicking the Add Shape Mask button displays an image of three balloons with the default shape mask applied. The on-screen controls let you adjust the size and shape of the circles.

- The inner circle controls the shape of the shape mask.
- The circle in the center controls position.
- The dot at the end of the line to the right controls rotation.
- The white dot at the top, to the left of the top dot, morphs the shape from circle to rectangle.
- The outer circle controls feathering.
- Drag the four green control dots to adjust the shape of the circle.

2. Adjust the shape. In this example, the mask shape is adjusted to isolate just the yellow balloon with no feathering.
3. Once the mask is in position, open the Inspector and switch to the Color Board (press Command+6). There are two text buttons at the bottom:
   - **Inside Mask** makes all color adjustments inside the selected mask area.
   - **Outside Mask** makes all color adjustments outside the selected mask area.

   You can have separate settings inside and outside the mask.
4. In this case, you want to adjust the area outside the mask, so click the Outside Mask button (**Figure 16.25**).
5. Then, drag the global saturation puck all the way down, to remove all color from outside the mask area.

   All masks and color-correction settings can be keyframed using the techniques discussed in Chapter 12.

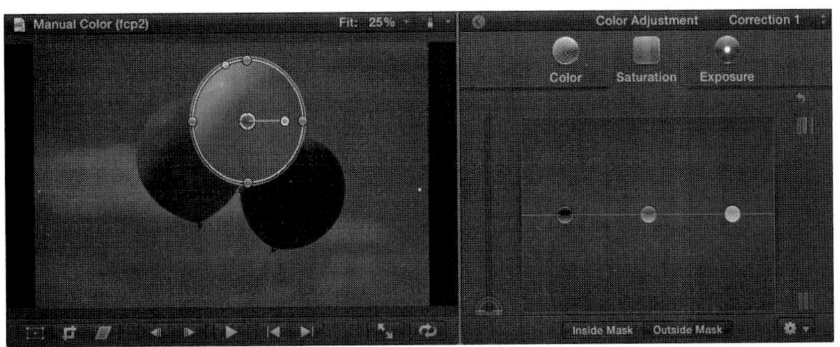

FIGURE 16.25 The mask is complete. In the Saturation panel, I clicked the Outside Mask button, then dragged global saturation way down.

There is no limit to the number of color corrections you can apply to a clip. There is no limit to the number of masks you can apply to a clip. And each mask can have different settings for inside and outside the mask.

Summary

The color-correction settings in Final Cut Pro X are flexible, extensive, and powerful. They also provide a never-ending opportunity to make your images look great.

Working with color is a skill that gets better with practice and studying the works and writings of others. The good news is that you will have to work very hard to outgrow the possibilities that Final Cut Pro X provides.

Keyboard Shortcuts

Shortcut	What It Does
Command+5	Toggle display of the Effects Browser
Option+Command+B	Toggle color balance on or off
Option+Command+M	Match colors between clips
Command+7	Toggle display of Histogram
Shift+Command+7	Toggle display of Waveform monitor
Option+Command+7	Toggle display of Vectorscope
Command+6	Toggle display of Color Board
Control+Command+C	In the Color Board, display the Color pane
Control+Command+S	In the Color Board, display the Saturation pane
Control+Command+E	In the Color Board, display the Exposure pane
Command+A	Select everything in the Timeline or Browser
Option+G	Create a compound clip from the selected clips
Command+4	Toggle the display of the Inspector

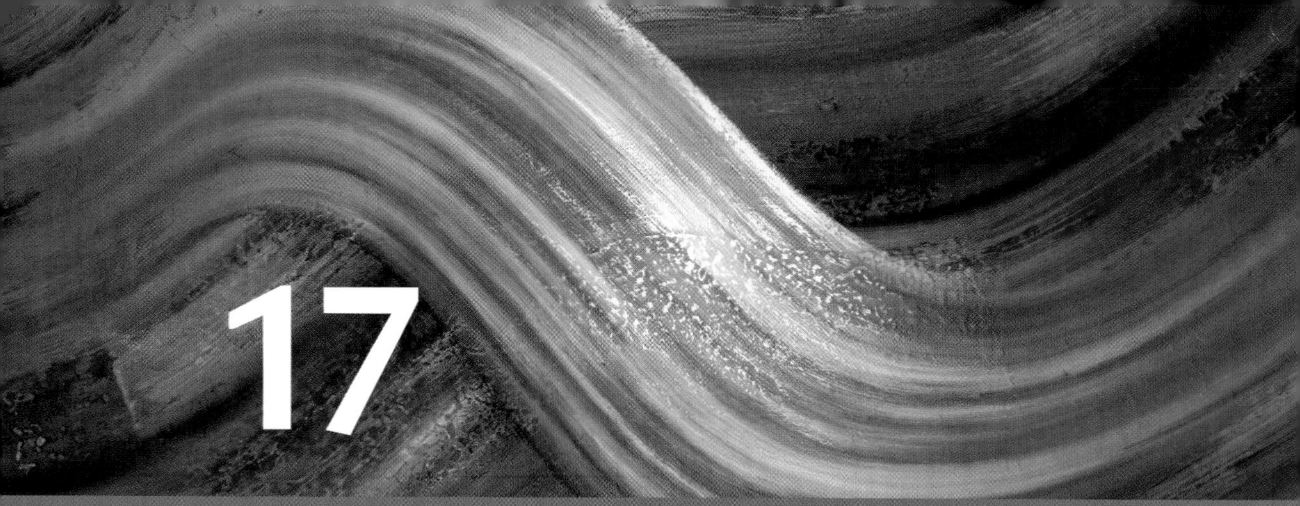

SHARING AND EXPORTING

Once your work is complete, it's time to share your Project with others. So it's fitting that sharing, or exporting, is the last chapter in this book.

The Share menu in Final Cut Pro X is the last step in the editing process, where you create finished versions of your Projects. You'll look at how to export a high-quality master file, plus the benefits of using Roles, then I'll provide an overview of how to share your files with popular websites.

Overview of the Output Process

Apple adopted a new philosophy on exporting with FCP X: It assumes that the person doing the exporting is not necessarily the one doing the editing. Since you export directly from the Project Library, the person exporting (who may or may not be the editor—in larger facilities and in broadcast, it would probably be someone else) can just select and change the output settings without opening the Project. This means that how the editor configured the Timeline no longer affects what gets exported.

Unlike FCP 7, in which the export process was directly affected by whether the editor had turned on or off all the appropriate audio and video tracks, FCP X allows the output process to be completely separate from the Timeline display, and therefore *what you set up in the Export menu is exactly what you get.* What makes this possible are Roles, which you first met in Chapter 7.

All output happens from the Share menu. Apple defines sharing as a two-step process: First you create a compressed version of your files, then you publish it. In the past, this consisted of a number of steps:

1. Configure the Timeline for export
2. Render the Project
3. Export the Project
4. Compress the Project
5. FTP the compressed file to a website
6. Update the website with data about your Project

● **NOTE** Exporting a Still Frame

See Chapter 15 for details on exporting a still frame.

Now, all of those steps can be condensed into a single menu choice. However, to be truthful, I rarely want FCP to do all these things at one time. The main reason is that my clients can't decide what they want to do. One day they want a YouTube video. A week later, they need something for their website. A few weeks after that, they need to burn a DVD.

I learned long ago that the best thing to do with any Project is to create a high-quality master file and archive it. Having a master file means that whenever a client needs a new version, I don't have to reopen the Project; I only have to recompress a new version of the master file.

A very cool feature of FCP X is that you don't have to open a Project to export it. You can select the Project you want to export from the Project Library and export from there. This also prevents accidentally making changes to a Project file that's been approved by the client.

So first I'll show you how to create a high-quality master file. Next, I'll talk about the new Roles feature in FCP X version 10.0.1, which provides some great flexibility in exporting both audio and video. Finally, I'll wrap up with a quick look at other export options, including sending your files to a variety of websites.

Exporting a High-Quality Master File

Once a Project is complete and approved by everyone who needs to approve it, it's time to create a master file of the Project. In Final Cut Pro 7 terms, you are creating a self-contained QuickTime movie. This option assumes you don't need to export any specific Roles from your Project (the next section covers what you need to know if you do).

In the latest update to Final Cut, the process of exporting a QuickTime movie is now faster—if you are working with optimized media, FCP just does a simple file copy of the ProRes in the Project to the ProRes of the export. Also, you can export a master QuickTime file and have it automatically loaded into Compressor while retaining the master file.

Apple also harnessed the power of the graphics card to speed exporting. This provides significant speed improvements in outputting a file. However, when you use the GPU (graphics processing unit), you can't export in the background.

1. To export your Project, simply select the Project in the Project Library; no need to open it in the Timeline and risk making changes to it.
2. Creating a master file of your Project in Final Cut Pro X is similar to how you did it in FCP 7; in fact, they both share the same keyboard shortcut: Command+E. You can also use Share > Export Media (**Figure 17.1**).
3. Set the export options on the first screen:
    - **Export.** This is self-evident. The default setting is Video and Audio.
    - **Video Codec.** Although you can use Final Cut to transcode into a variety of other formats, my recommendation is to use Current Settings. This matches the settings of your Project and, in almost all cases, yields the highest quality.
    - **After Export.** The Do Nothing option does exactly that. Open with QuickTime Player, the default, lets you quickly review your exported file. Open with Compressor exports the Project, then opens it in Compressor for compression. This tends to be my personal choice.

    By the way, you can skim your Project in this window by dragging the cursor across the image at the top; this is an easy way to be sure you have the right Project.

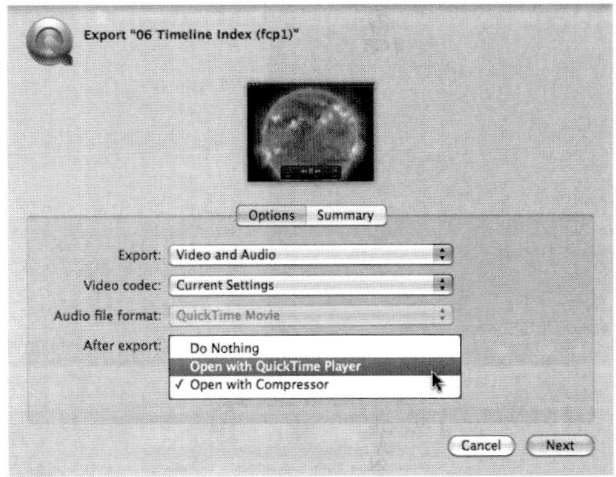

FIGURE 17.1
The settings to create a high-quality master file of your Project in Final Cut Pro X are similar to those in FCP 7.

The key point is that you access everything you need to export the Project from the Export Media screen. You no longer need to worry about which tracks are turned on or off, as you did in Final Cut Pro 7. So, to be specific, here's how I generally set my export options:

- Export: Video and Audio
- Video Codec: Current Settings
- After Export: Open with Compressor

4. Click Next to give the exported file a name and location, then click Save.

Most sharing can happen in the background, *except* for three menu choices:

- Exporting a high-quality QuickTime movie
- Exporting a single frame
- Sending to Compressor

These three run in the foreground so that the GPU can speed up the process of exporting. In my brief testing, exporting was two to four times faster than real time, assuming all rendering is complete.

NOTE What If I Need to Output to Tape?

Currently, Final Cut Pro X does not support output to videotape. Instead, you'll need to export a high-quality master file, then use a combination of software and hardware from companies like AJA (www.aja.com), Blackmagic Design (www.blackmagic-design.com), or Matrox (www.matrox.com/video/) to output your master file to tape.

Exporting Roles

Roles provide exciting new ways to get work done in less time. Because every clip is tagged with a Role, FCP X lets you group Roles for export. Roles are not the same as batch exporting. Roles let you export different versions of the *same* Project at the same time; batch exporting lets you export multiple *different* Projects at the same time.

Here are three scenarios that illustrate what you can do with Roles:

- **Scenario 1.** You have a single Project with both English and Spanish titles tagged with Subroles for each language during the edit. Roles let you quickly configure the export for a specific language, to create a master file of the Project.
- **Scenario 2.** You want to create a single multitrack QuickTime movie containing all the video, with three separate stereo pairs for the audio "stems." Stems are submixes of your Project: dialogue-only, effects-only, and music-only.
- **Scenario 3.** You want to create three separate audio files, one for each stem, in a single export. Using Roles, you can create a single export that creates all of these files in one pass.

Here's a sample Project: titles in two languages, with dialogue, effects, and music clips (**Figure 17.2**).

To illustrate that this contains titles in two languages, I highlighted the English titles. The clips are not all on the same layer, and, while the English titles are highlighted, both languages are active; neither Role is invisible. This Project also has multiple effects clips, with the clips on different layers. Remember, that you don't need to open a Project to export it.

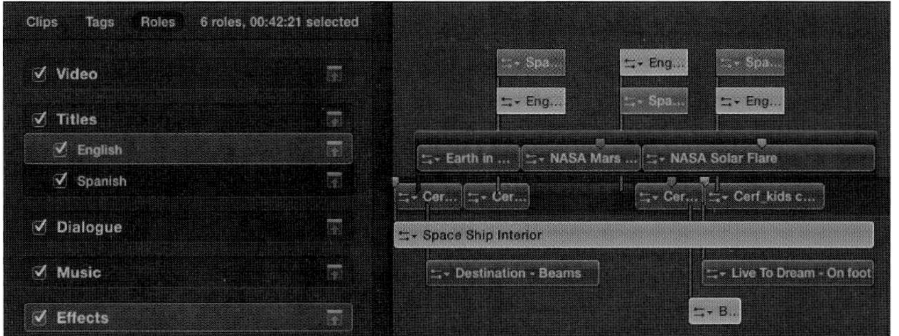

FIGURE 17.2
The Timeline Index, with the English titles and the Effects Role highlighted, has titles and effects on different layers.

Scenario 1: Exporting Selected Roles As a Single File

To export a specific language from a multilanguage Project, you need to do an export for each language:

1. Select the Project you want to export in the Project Timeline.
2. In the Export Media panel, set Export to "Roles As Multitrack QuickTime Movie" (**Figure 17.3**).
3. Click the Roles tab. This is where you configure what exports. From the Video menu, select just the Roles you want to export (**Figure 17.4**). In this example, all the video files plus the English titles are checked and will export.
4. In the first audio Roles pop-up menu, select all three options. This means that all three audio Roles will export into a single stereo pair audio file (**Figure 17.5**).
5. Click the minus button to the right of a Role to remove the other two audio Roles (**Figure 17.6**). This means the entire mix will export as a stereo pair.
6. Click Next, give the file a name and location, and click Save. The selected Roles will all export into a single QuickTime master movie.

● **NOTE** When You Use Roles, You Must Configure the Export

If you don't configure a Project that uses Roles, all layers and clips in the Project will export into one file where all layers and clips are visible and audible.

FIGURE 17.3
The Export setup window lets you configure the exact export you need, without reopening the Project.

FIGURE 17.4
Configure the Video Roles so that only the video you want to export is checked. In this case, both the video clips and English titles will export; the Spanish titles will not.

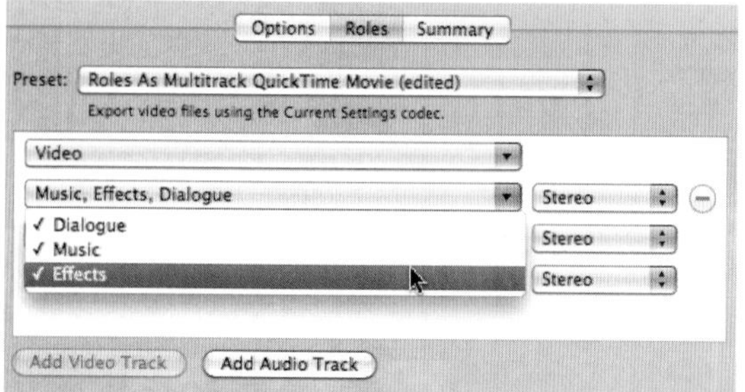

FIGURE 17.5
Condense the three separate audio Roles into a single export option. This means all your audio will export as a stereo pair.

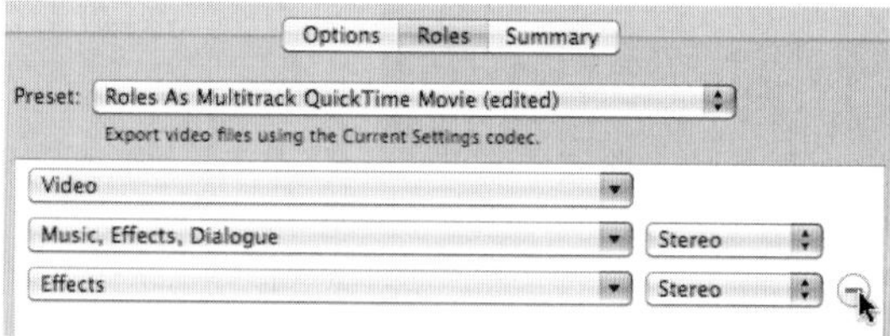

FIGURE 17.6
Remove the audio Roles that you no longer need to export as separate files.

Scenario 2: Exporting Multiple Roles to Separate Files in One Export

This next technique is very cool. Let's say you have multiple language titles in the same Project. You can export all the languages as separate files, all at the same time, plus a master audio file. Here's how:

1. Select the Project in the Project Library.
2. Choose Share > Export Media, or press Command+E.
3. In the Export pop-up menu, select Roles As Separate Files (**Figure 17.7**). This exports each selected Role, which you'll select in the next step, as a separate file. You can output as many different Roles as you have assigned to your Project. The other export settings remain, as I discussed in the first section.
4. Click the Roles tab at the top center.
5. In the Roles tab, specify which Roles you want grouped in each export. Here, the first export includes all video files, plus just those clips tagged with the English Subrole; in this example, that's the English titles (**Figure 17.8**).

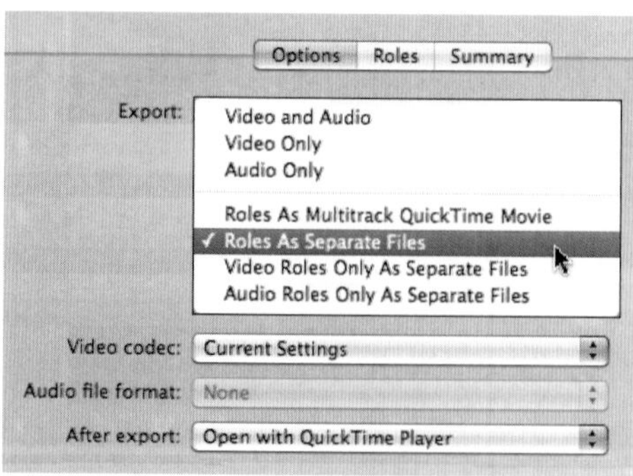

FIGURE 17.7
Select the Roles As Separate Files option to export each selected Role as a separate file—all at the same time.

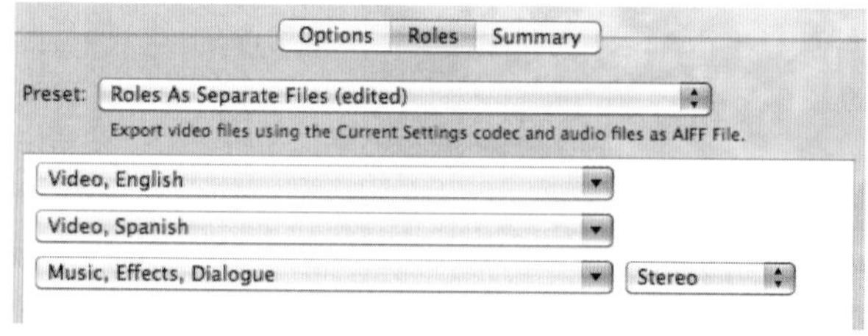

FIGURE 17.8
In the Roles tab, select the Roles you want to group in each exported file by combining them in one of the pop-up menus.

6. The second export combines all the video files with the Spanish titles.
7. The third export combines all the audio files into a single, stereo-pair mix.
8. To remove a Role you don't want to export, click the minus button on the right side. (You must export a minimum of one Role.)
9. To add a Role to export, click either the Add Video File or Add Audio File button at the bottom (**Figure 17.9**).
10. When the Roles are set, review what you are doing by clicking the Summary tab, then click Next. This allows you to give the files a name and location.
11. Click Export, and Final Cut Pro creates a separate file for each Role in the second screen—in this case a total of three—and includes the stem name as part of the filename.

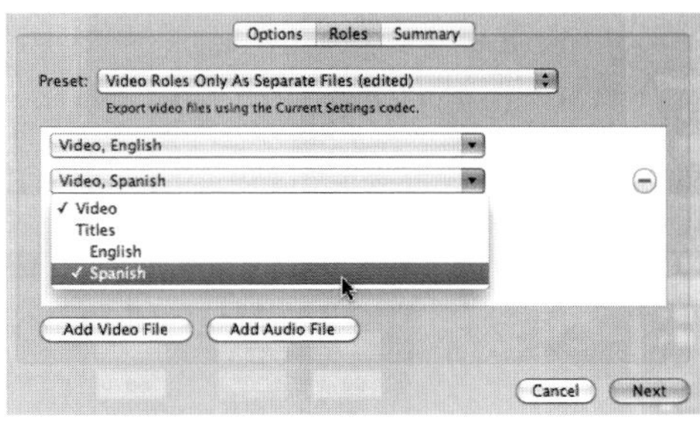

FIGURE 17.9
Combine multiple Roles in one pop-up menu to combine those elements in the exported file.

NOTE A Word of Caution

This technique separates the audio from the video, creating two separate files; but they can easily be imported and reassembled in another video application (such as QuickTime 7, or FCP X). However, for Projects destined for DVD authoring, such as DVD Studio Pro, this system for creating separate audio and video files is usually OK.

Scenario 3: Exporting a Single Multitrack File

In this scenario, I want to create a single master QuickTime movie containing the final form of my video, and separate tracks for the audio stems. This could be used for output to tape later, or simply for archiving all the final elements of my Project in one file.

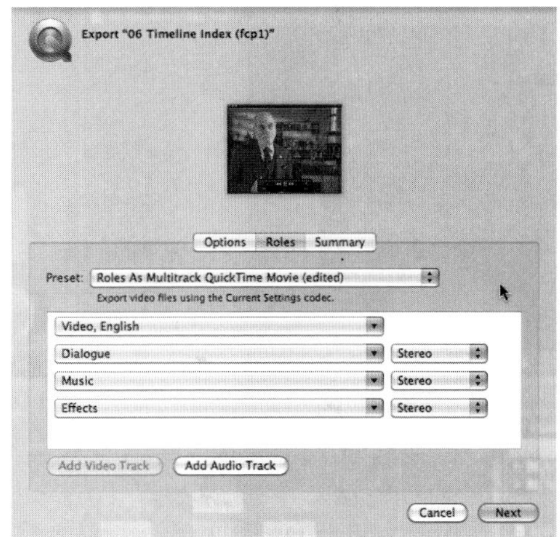

FIGURE 17.10
This scenario exports a single master QuickTime movie containing separate tracks for the audio stems.

Here's how to do it:

1. Select the Project in the Project Library.
2. Choose Share > Export Media (press Command+E).
3. In the Options tab, set Export to Roles As Multitrack QuickTime Movie.
4. Click the Roles tab.
5. Set the Video pop-up to match the settings of the Video Roles (**Figure 17.10**).
6. Click Next and give your export a name and location.
7. Click Save.

A single high-quality master QuickTime movie containing one video track and three audio tracks (in this example) will be exported.

Scenario 4: Exporting Separate Audio Roles (Stems) of the Same Project

The other major use of Roles is creating audio stems—separate mixes of dialogue, effects, and music, each of which is exported as a stand-alone file (**Figure 17.11**).

In this example, I want to create a separate audio file for each stem. Here's how:

1. Select the Project in the Project Library.
2. Choose Share > Export Media (or press Command+E).
3. In the Option tab, next to Export, select Audio Roles Only As Separate Files.
4. Click the Roles tab (**Figure 17.12**). Make sure each of the audio Roles that you want to export are displayed as separate lines in this dialog. The default setting is three.
5. Click Next, and give your export a name and location.
6. Click Save.

Final Cut Pro will export a separate audio-only file for each line item in the Roles panel and include the stem name as part of the filename.

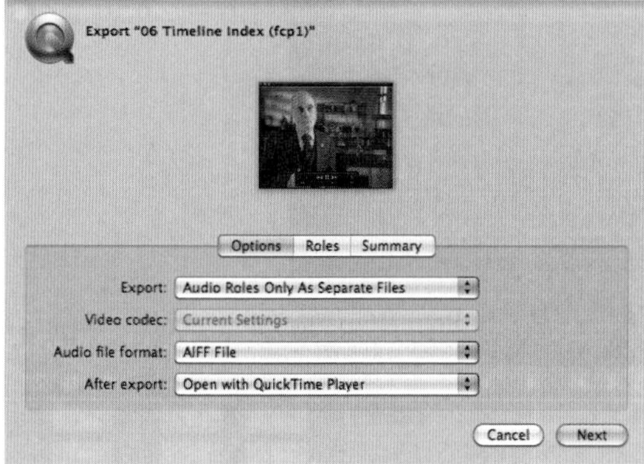

FIGURE 17.11
The other significant use of Roles is creating audio stems—separate files containing individual mixes for dialogue, effects, and music.

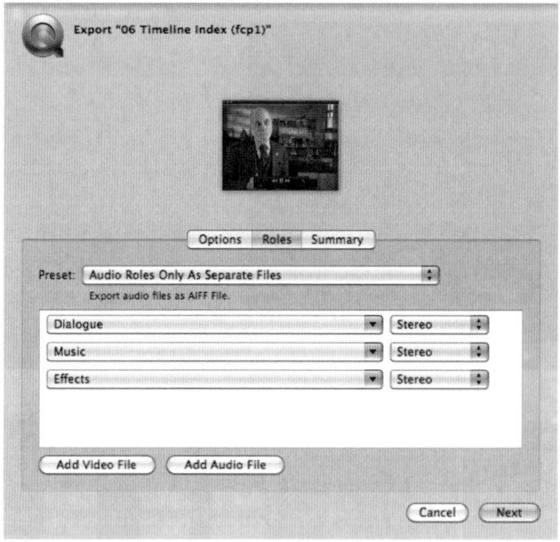

FIGURE 17.12
The three pop-up menus in the lower half of this window indicate that three separate audio files will be created.

Exporting XML Files

Also new with the FCP X 10.0.1 release is the ability to import and export XML files. XML exports can be made only from the Event Library or the Project Library.

For now, this feature is principally of interest to developers because they can now get information into and out of Final Cut Pro X. Over the long term, this will be an essential feature for every editor.

Fortunately, the process of exporting is simple:

1. Do one of the following:
   - Select the Project you want to export in the Project Library.
   - Select the Event you want to export in the Event Library. (You can only select one at a time for export.)
2. Choose File > Export XML.
3. Enter the filename and select a location.

At this point, you can import that XML file into any other application that supports it to quickly move your data into it from Final Cut Pro. (If you are interested in importing XML, I covered that at the end of Chapter 4.)

Other Options in the Share Menu

There are several other output options in the Share menu. Most are self-explanatory, but there are a couple I want to explain in a bit more detail.

In all cases, select the Project you want to export in the Project Library (the Share menu does not support exporting from the Event Library), then go to the Share menu and pick one of the following:

- **Media Browser.** This requires OS 10.6.8 or later, and exports files into the Media (also called Movies) Browser so that you can access your movie later from any Mac application that supports the Media Browser, such as Keynote, without needing to access the source Project. This export can run in the background.
- **Apple Devices.** This option lets you output movies optimized for the screen size and file-storage capacity of various Apple devices (**Figure 17.13**). You can output multiple versions at the same time and store them in iTunes. All Apple devices compress the video using MPEG-4 (H.264). This export can run in the background.

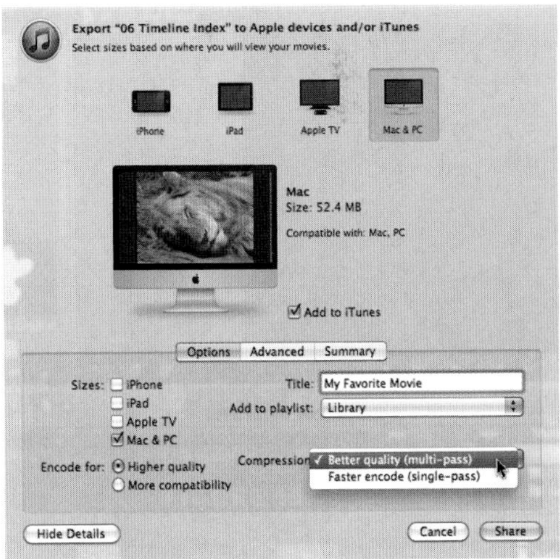

FIGURE 17.13
Using the checkboxes you can configure and output your Project for multiple Apple devices at the same time.

- **DVD.** This option lets you burn a Project to a DVD using a simple menu template. You can import your own background graphic for the menu, but this does not provide the same level of authoring as DVD Studio Pro. This export can run in the background.
- **Blu-ray Disc.** Similar to the DVD menu choice, this option lets you burn a Project to a Blu-ray Disc using a simple menu template. You can import your own background graphic for the menu, along with a logo and title. However, this does not provide the same level of authoring for Blu-ray Disc as do Adobe Encore or even Roxio Toast. This export can run in the background.
- **YouTube, Facebook, Vimeo, and CNN iReport.** These four options let you export and send Projects directly to these social media sites.

NOTE Do I Have to Own a Blu-ray Disc Burner?

No. Final Cut Pro supports a high-def format called AVCHD. This lets you burn your HD material using the standard SuperDrive in your computer. The only limitations are that the image quality is not quite as high as that of a standard Blu-ray Disc burned with a Blu-ray Disc burner, and the AVCHD disk will only hold about 20 minutes of material before it is full.

YouTube Example

For example, if you have a Project you want to quickly export to YouTube (**Figure 17.14**), simply follow these steps:

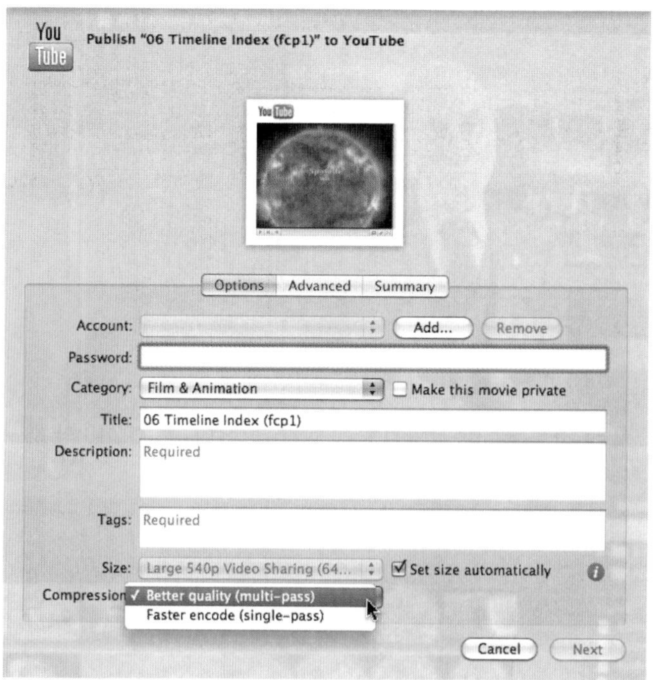

FIGURE 17.14 All the social media sites share a similar screen layout, like this one for YouTube.

1. Start by clicking the Add button and entering your account and password (no, sorry, I decided not to publish mine in this book).
2. Fill in the required fields, like Category, Title, and such. When all the fields are complete, pick the size you want to export. For YouTube, I select the size that matches my Project files. YouTube scales them as necessary.
3. Click Next. Accept the YouTube Terms of Service, and click Publish.

   Final Cut Pro exports and compresses your Project, then automatically sends it to your account at YouTube, in this example.

Best of all, since this process can run in the background, as soon as you click Publish you can get back to work in Final Cut Pro.

Monitoring Sharing

When you select any Sharing menu choice, except Export Media or Save Current Frame, the export can occur in the background. You can monitor the status of the export using the Share Monitor. Unlike the Batch Monitor with Final Cut Studio (3), the Share Monitor can only be accessed from within Final Cut Pro X, Compressor 4, or Motion 5.

As soon as you click Export, a new dialog appears displaying the status of the export (**Figure 17.15**). Click the Share Monitor button.

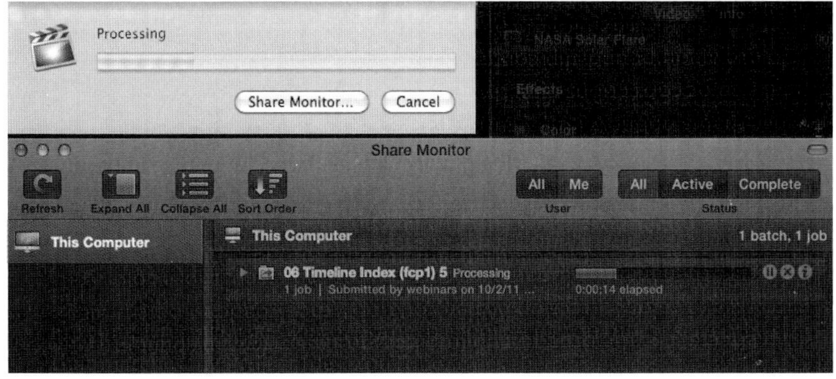

FIGURE 17.15 Click the Share Monitor button to display the Share Monitor, which shows the status of all background sharing and processing.

This opens the Share Monitor. On the left, click This Computer to monitor the tasks your computer is working on. At the top, be sure to select All for the User and Active for the Status, to see current jobs in process.

The three small buttons on the right of each active job allow you to pause, cancel, or get information on a job. Pausing is never a good idea, so just use these buttons to cancel a job that you started by mistake, or click the Get Info button to get technical insight on the current active task.

Summary

From planning your first Project to final export, this book has taken you through every step of crafting your vision with Final Cut Pro X. Together, we have covered a tremendous range of material to give you the security you need to tackle even large projects.

Video editing is a never-ending process of discovery. Learning new technology and more efficient ways to apply it is part of the challenge. But technology is only one side of the equation. The other is storytelling. Telling stories is as old as time—stories from hundreds of years ago still captivate us. Stories as new as tomorrow will introduce us to characters we want to learn more about.

Our role as editors is to balance the technology with the craft—to create powerful, compelling, visual stories that can change the world.

I can't wait to see what you create.

Keyboard Shortcut

Shortcut	What It Does
Command+E	Exports a high-quality QuickTime movie of the currently active Project

INDEX

A

Action safe, displaying, 235–236
alpha channels, 262, 281–282
animating using keyframes, 249–251, 268. *See also* keyframes
Aperture library, accessing, 89–90
append edit, performing, 34, 38, 122–125, 139
archiving. *See also* camera archives
  versus importing, 87
  long-term, 8
  memory cards, 70
  Projects and media, 13, 56–58
  space requirements, 87
aspect ratios, 295
audio. *See also* volume; waveforms
  adjusting, 34–35
  analysis on import, 190–191
  basics, 186–187
  creating music videos, 194
  detaching from video, 210, 228
  dual-channel mono, 200
  expanding from video, 189, 218
  human hearing, 186
  importing, 77–78
  keyboard shortcuts, 206
  letters F and S, 187
  loudness of, 188
  measuring, 188
  mixing, 52, 203–206
  mono, 190
  moving to picks, 140
  muting clips, 200–201
  pitch-shifted, 20
  polishing, 12
  recording for video, 187
  recording voice-overs, 201–202
  rules for, 204
  sample rates versus frequency, 187
  separating from video, 189
  skimming, 189
  soloing clips, 200–201
  sonic field, 190
  stereo, 190
  syncing double-system, 202–203
  toggling from video, 183
  toggling subframe display on/off, 210
  using Inspector with, 191–192
  viewing in clips, 189
  volume and gain, 188
  vowels versus consonants, 187
audio and video clips, syncing, 96
audio animation, displaying in Timeline, 268
audio clips
  auto-enhancing, 210
  collapsing, 210
  expanding, 210
  soloing and unsoloing, 163
audio edit points, selecting, 183
audio editing
  enabling, 139
  precision of, 203
audio enhancements, toggling display of, 210
audio levels
  adjusting, 35
  adjusting with mouse, 205–206
  displaying, 35
  drop by 6dB, 187
  maximum, 35
  relative and absolute, 35
audio meters
  displaying, 206
  resizing, 35
  toggling display on/off, 38, 210
  using, 188
audio Roles, exporting, 328
audio skimming, toggling on/off, 210
audio techniques, 192–198
audio transitions, applying, 228
audio volume, adjusting, 35
audio waveforms, displaying, 101, 103
audio-only
  editing, 210
  transitions, 219–221
auditions
  creating, 136–139
  finalizing, 140
  opening, 139
  previewing, 140
AVCHD (Native), storage and data transfer rate, 3
AVD-Intra 100, storage and data transfer rate, 3

B

background colors, making transparent, 281–288
background tasks, 29–30
  displaying, 22, 64, 96, 228, 268
  monitoring, 54
backgrounds
  colors, 283
  removing with Luma keys, 281–282
backtime edit, performing, 129–130, 139
Blade tool, using, 153, 164
Blend Modes, using, 264–265
Broadcast Safe effect, applying, 317–318
B-roll, creating, 36–37
Browsers
  locating, 89–90, 224
  selecting everything in, 320
Burns, Ken, 251, 255–257

C

camera archives. *See also* archiving
  creating, 58, 86–88
  using, 70
Camera Import window, displaying, 79
cameras. *See also* file-based camera; tape-based camera
  (H)DSLR, 90–92
  importing from, 96
  types of, 78
cards. *See* memory cards
Chroma keys, 281–288
clip audibility, toggling, 210
clip duration, changing, 140
clip effects. *See also* effects
  deleting and resetting, 284
  processing, 318
clip names
  hiding, 100
  toggling display in Event Browser, 116
clip skimmer, selecting, 301
clip speed, setting to normal, 297, 301
clip visibility, toggling, 210
clip volume, raising and lowering, 210
clips. *See also* compound clips; connected clips
  adding dissolve between, 36
  adding searchable notes to, 101
  arranging, 99
  converting into connected storylines, 183
  creating compound, 228
  deleting, 142–143
  deselecting, 142–143
  detaching, 189
  determining height of, 101
  disabling, 152, 163
  displaying, 98–103, 100, 116
  dragging, 93, 135
  enabling, 152, 163
  finding, 109, 111
  grouping, 99–100
  marking, 33, 96
  modifying duration of, 183
  moving, 140, 155–156, 210
  pasting effects into, 210
  pasting options, 147
  placement in editing process, 133
  playing, 124, 140
  previewing, 32–33
  removing ranges of, 154
  selecting, 96, 127, 139, 142–143, 301
  setting vertical height of, 23
  slowing down, 297
  soloing, 152, 210
  stacking, 262, 279, 283
  synchronizing, 210
  using ratings with, 104
  zooming into, 103
clock icon, purpose of, 30
codecs and formats, 75
color balance, turning on/off, 320
Color Board, 313–314, 320
color cast, fixing, 305–306
color correction, 12–13
  applying Looks, 304–305
  Balance Color, 305
  basic map, 311
  borrowing Looks, 307
  Broadcast Safe effect, 317–318
  Enhancement menu, 305–307
  hues, 314
  in Inspector, 313
  masks, 318–320
  Match Color, 306–307
  rules in, 311
  video scopes, 307–310
color grade and Look, creating, 13
colors
  adjusting, 316–317
  of icons, 19
  matching between clips, 306–307, 320
  removing, 311
Command Editor, displaying, 60, 64
Command key. *See* keyboard shortcuts
command set, listing, 63
compositing, 262–265
compound clips. *See also* clips
  breaking apart, 163
  creating, 148–150, 163, 228, 320
  deconstructing, 151
  fixed durations, 151
  navigating Timeline History, 151–152
  using for effects, 266–267
Compressor droplets, fixing, 18
computer monitors, using two, 26–27
connected clips. *See also* clips
  adding transitions to, 220
  editing into Timeline, 37
  trimming, 180
connected edit, performing, 38, 132–135, 139
connected storylines
  adding transitions to, 220
  converting clips to, 183
  creating, 228
  trimming, 181
  using, 135
connection display, toggling on/off, 23
connections, moving, 133, 140
consolidating Projects, 57–58
contextual menus, displaying, 30–31
Copy and Paste options, 146–147
copying
  Events, 42–43
  versus linking, 16
  media, 45, 67–68
  memory cards, 70–71
  Projects, 54
Crop controls, displaying, 268
Crop effect, using, 251, 253
Ctrl key. *See* keyboard shortcuts
cutaways, creating, 36–37
cuts, defined, 212, 166. *See also* trimming

D

date display, using with videotape, 99
Delete keys, using, 55
deleting
  clip effects, 284
  clips, 142–143
  End (Out) of clips, 96, 139
  Event render files, 46
  Events, 48
  folders, 55
  keyframes, 207
  keywords, 106–107, 116
  markers, 145, 163
  Project render files, 58–59
  Roles, 158–159
  Smart Collections, 109–112
  Start (In) of clips, 96
Dialogue Role, applying, 164
disk image, making for cards, 70
dissolve
  adding between clips, 36
  defined, 166, 212
distort effects, using, 257–258, 268
Dock, showing and hiding, 38
DPI (dots per inch) versus pixels, 93
drives
  backup, 4
  bit flux, 8
  boot, 4, 17
  connecting, 5, 7–8
  external, 5
  FireWire connection protocol, 5
  internal, 5
  media, 4
  requirements, 4
  storing, 8

drop shadows, 233, 242
duplicating Projects, 53–54

E

edit media, described, 67
edit points, using, 183
editing
append edit, 122–125
audio, 192–195
backtime edit, 129–130
connected edit, 132–135
creating auditions, 136–137
dragging clips from Finder, 135
insert edit, 125–127
overwrite edit, 128–129
preferences, 119–121
process, 32–36, 118
replace edit, 130–132
speeding up, 162
titles, 230
and trimming, 175
workflow, 8–13
edits
previewing, 36
replacing, 140
effects. *See also* clip effects
adding, 12
adjusting in Motion 5, 275–276
alpha channels, 262
animating using keyframes, 247–251
Blend Modes, 264–265
Broadcast Safe, 317–318
compositing, 262–265
corner pinning, 257–258
Crop, 251, 253
customization in Motion 5, 276
disabling, 284
distort, 257–258
drop shadows, 242
finding customized, 276
image degradation, 254
image stabilization, 258–259
Ken Burns, 251, 255–257
Luma keys, 262, 279–281
Opacity, 263
overview, 242–243
pan, 251
pasting, 243, 268
resetting for clips, 284
Rolling Shutter, 259–260
slo-mo, 299
Spatial Conform, 260–262
tilt, 251
Transform, 243–247
Trim, 251–253
using compound clips for, 266–267
zoom, 251
Effects Browsers, 23, 320
Effects Role, applying, 164
End (Out) of clips, 34, 105
deleting, 96, 139
jumping playhead to, 96
setting, 96, 123–124, 139
trimming to skimmer, 183
Event Browser
creating compound clips in, 149–150
defined, 40
displaying clips as filmstrips, 100
displaying, 21, 64
function of, 42
hiding clip names, 116
line colors, 113
showing clip names, 116
Switch, 101
using Roles in, 159
Event folders
defined, 40
managing, 18
moving, 17
moving files into, 44
using, 17
Event Library
contents of, 42
defined, 40
displaying and hiding, 21, 38
toggling display of, 64, 116
Event Manager X utility, 41–42
Event reference, changing to share Projects, 55–56
Event render files, deleting, 46
Events
accessing, 41
copying, 42–43
copying versus moving, 43
creating, 25–27, 38, 42, 96
defined, 17, 25, 40
deleting, 48
displaying, 98–103
grouping, 98
hiding, 48
linking Projects to, 31, 50
merging, 45
moving, 43, 46–47, 64
organizing media for, 43–44
placing in folders, 41
storing, 17, 40–41, 44
toggling display of, 21
tracking, 41
Events folder
accessing, 16
contents of, 25
exporting. *See also* Share menu
audio Roles, 328
high-quality master files, 323–324
hold frames, 294–295
QuickTime movies, 331
Roles, 324–329
XML files, 99, 329
Exposure panel, using pucks in, 314–315

F

fade handles, using to create transitions, 220
fading to black, 218
Favorites
displaying, 116
filtering, 104
finding in Events, 105
marking selected areas as, 116
file-based camera, using, 81–84. *See also* cameras
files
consolidating via merging, 46
importing, 88–89
importing from, 96
moving, 44
selecting, 28
Filter window, opening, 116
Final Cut Events folder, 40
Final Cut Pro 7, round-tripping, 18
Final Cut Pro X
hidden areas, 19
hiding, 38
interface, 19–25
starting, 18
system requirement, 2
website, 66
Final Cut Studio folder, contents of, 18
Find window, opening in Timeline, 164
Finder, dragging clips from, 135. *See also* Timeline Index
FireWire connection protocol, 5, 7
folders. *See also* media folders; Project folders; Projects folder
creating, 116
deleting, 55
hiding Projects in, 55
importing, 72–74
limitations of, 112
moving, 41
moving Projects to, 55
organizing Projects with, 54–55
revealing Projects in, 55
storing projects in, 24
font settings, 233–234
frame rate, deciding, 52

frames
converting to seconds, 214
moving between, 23
navigating, 183

G

gaps
creating, 155-156
inserting, 164
generators, using, 271-275. *See also* video clips
grayscale, adjusting, 313-315
green-screen keys, creating, 281-288
green-shoot, planning, 279

H

H.264, storage and data transfer rate, 3
Hand tool, using, 154, 164
handles, using, 53, 168, 212-213
hard drives. *See* drives
(H)DSLR cameras, 90-92, 259
hiding Projects, 55, 59
Histogram, using, 309, 320
hold frames, using 292-295, 301
Home Directory keyboard shortcut, 276

I

icons, colors of, 19
image degradation, 254
image stabilization, 258-259
images
compositing, 262-265
fitting into frames, 20
pixels versus DPI (dots per inch), 93
rotating, 246
scaling, 246
sizing and positioning, 243-247
iMovie Projects and Events, importing, 89
importing
versus archiving, 87
dragging files from Desktop, 93
files, 38, 78, 88-89
from (H)DSLR camera, 90-92
iMovie Projects and Events, 89
layered Photoshop files, 93
process of, 71
still images, 93-95
XML, 95, 99
importing media, 27-30. *See also* media
audio, 77-78
changing preferences, 78
copying files, 72
creating camera archive, 86-88
from file-based camera, 78-84
folders, 72-74
keywords, 72-73
optimizing media, 75
organizing, 72
setting preferences, 71-78
from tape-based camera, 85-86
transcoding, 75-76
video, 77
In point. *See* Start (In) of clips
Info Inspector, using, 113-115
insert edit, performing, 125-127, 139
inserts, creating, 36-37
Inspector
audio levels, 206
icon, 113
modifying keyframes in, 208-209
opening, 23
panning audio, 206
setting keyframes in, 208-209
Stabilization controls, 258
toggling display on/off, 210, 320
toggling open/closed, 116, 240, 268, 290
Transition, 223-224
using, 191-192
interlaced versus progressive, 51, 288, 294-295
iPhoto library, accessing, 89-90
iTunes library, accessing, 89-90

K

Ken Burns effect, using, 251, 255-257
Keyboard Highlight button, 61
keyboard shortcuts
get started editing, 38
managing events, projects, and shortcuts, 64
managing media, 96
organizing clips: ratings, keywords, and extended metadata,116
editing, 139-140
organizing edit, 163-164
trimming edit, 183
audio, 210
transitions, 228
titles and text, 240
built-in effects, 268
keying, 290
retiming, 301
color correction, 320
sharing and export, 332
keyframes. *See also* animating using keyframes
adding to animations, 268
adding to transitions, 227
adjusting in Timeline, 207-208
creating in Inspector, 249
defined, 106, 247
deleting, 207
jumping to, 250, 268
modifying in Inspector, 208-209
overview, 207
setting, 207-210
using to remove noises, 208
keys
adding masks, 288-290
Chroma, 281-288
interlaced footage, 288
Luma, 279-281
planning, 278-279
stacking clips, 279
keywords. *See also* Roles; Smart Collections
adding, 106-107
adding to keyboard shortcut, 116
applying to Events, 107
automatic, 106
changing, 107
deleting, 106-107, 116
displaying, 116
features, 106
finding in Timeline, 109
importing, 72
listing, 160
manual, 106
renaming, 108
storage of, 106
using to find clips, 109
viewing, 108-109

L

layouts, changing and returning to, 26
loop playback, toggling, 20
Luma keys, using, 262, 279-281

M

Magnetic Timeline, features, 147-148. *See also* Timeline
markers
accessing options for, 146
adding, 144, 163
converting to To-Dos, 145
deleting, 145, 163
described, 142
in FCP X versus FCP 7, 146

listing, 160
moving, 145
masks
adding, 288–289
versus mattes, 288
using for color correction, 318–320
master files, exporting, 323–324
match frame, explained, 193, 210
matching audio transition, applying, 217–218
media. *See also* importing media; proxy media
archiving, 56–58
copying, 67–68
defined, 40
file size, 45
management tips, 42
multiformat, 52
naming, 66
optimizing, 75
organizing, 43–44, 66
storing, 41, 44, 71
media folders, naming, 68–71. *See also* folders; Project folders; Projects folder
memory cards
archiving, 70
copying, 70–71
displaying contents of, 67
importing files from, 79
merging Events, 45–46
metadata, managing, 113–115
mixing, overview, 204–206, 209
monitors
calibrating, 27
using two, 26–27
mono clip, appearance of, 190
Motion 5
adjusting effects in, 275–276
adjusting generators in, 275–276
adjusting titles in, 275–276
Move controls, displaying, 268
movies
exporting QuickTime, 331
sizing still images for, 256
Music Browser, using, 89–90, 194–195
Music Role, applying, 164
music videos, creating, 194

N

network speed, requirement, 6
networks, using, 6
noises, removing with keyframes, 208

O

Opacity setting, using, 263
Option key. *See* keyboard shortcuts
Out point. *See* End (Out) of clips
output process, 322
overwrite edit, performing, 128–129, 139

P

panning audio, 197–198, 206
Paste and Copy options, 146–147
Photos Browser, using, 89–90
pixel aspect ratios, 295
pixels versus DPI (dots per inch), 93
Placeholder utility clip, using, 272–274
placeholders
inserting, 164
using with gaps, 155–156
playback preferences, 121–122
playhead
jumping to End of clip, 139
jumping to markers, 163
jumping to Start of clip, 139
locking in place, 140
position, 139
preventing from moving, 128
previewing around, 38
versus skimmer, 166
Position tool, using, 153, 163
Precision Editor
displaying and hiding, 183
jumping to frames, 172
keyboard shortcuts, 175
moving to edit points in, 173
opening, 222, 228
using, 170–174
Preferences window, opening, 64, 140, 228
progressive versus interlaced, 51
Project database, 48
Project folders, creating, 64. *See also* folders; Projects folder; media folders
Project Library, 23–24
contents of, 49
keyboard shortcut, 49
showing and hiding, 38
toggling between Timeline, 64
Project Properties, opening, 228
Projects
accessing, 41
archiving, 13, 56–58
consolidating, 57–58
copying, 54
creating, 30–31, 38, 49–52, 64, 96, 139
duplicates, 53–54
finding items in, 160
fitting into Timeline, 38, 163
hiding, 55, 59
linking to Events, 31, 50
making changes to, 275
moving, 54–55, 64
naming, 31
organizing with folders, 54–55
rendering, 228
revealing in folders, 55
sharing, 13, 55–56
storing, 17, 24, 44
tracking, 41
trashing, 59
Projects folder. *See also* folders; media folders
contents of, 17, 25
managing, 18
proxy media, accessing and creating, 75–76. *See also* media

Q

QuickTime movies, exporting, 331
quitting Final Cut Pro X, 38

R

radio script, creating, 32–33
RAID, using, 6–7, 68
Range tool, using, 127, 164
ranges, selecting, 140, 142–143, 153, 183
ratings, using, 103–106, 108, 111
Rejected clips and ratings, managing, 104, 116
render files, deleting, 46
rendering, 121
defined, 215
options, 216
Projects, 228
selections, 228, 268
Timeline, 268
tip, 216
replace edit, performing, 130–132
Reset button, using, 109
Retime Editor, toggling display of, 301
retiming
basics, 292
hold frames, 292–295
interlacing, 294–295
pixel aspect ratios, 295
speed changes, 296–298

retiming (*continued*)
  speed effects, 300
  speed ramps, 299
  speeds, 292
  variable speed changes, 298–299
  video quality settings, 297
RGB Parade, using, 310
ripple, defined, 166
ripple trim, performing, 171–172
Roles. *See also* keywords
  applying, 164
  applying and changing, 157–158
  creating custom, 158
  deleting, 158–159
  exporting, 324–329
  features of, 156
  modifying, 158–159
  using, 157, 159, 161–162
roll, defined, 166
roll edit, performing, 173
roll trim, performing, 175–176
Rolling Shutter, 259–260
round-tripping, getting to work, 18

S

saving changes, 32, 38
searches
  clearing, 109
  text versus keywords, 112
Select tool, using, 153, 163
Selection tool, selecting, 140
selections
  making, 142
  rendering, 228, 268
selects sequence, building, 150
sequences, number per Project, 31
Shapes utility clip, using, 272, 274
Share menu, options on, 329–331. *See also* exporting
sharing, 13, 55–56
  defined, 322
  monitoring, 331
Shift key. *See* keyboard shortcuts
shortcuts. *See* keyboard shortcuts
skimmer
  described, 19
  impact on edits, 128
  pitch-shifted audio, 20
  versus playhead, 166
  toggling on/off, 22, 38, 116, 139
  using with clips, 101
skin tones, color values for, 312
slide, defined, 166
slide edit, performing, 177–178
slip, defined, 166
slip edit, performing, 177
slo-mo effect, adding, 299
Smart Collections, using, 109–112, 116. *See also* keywords
snapping, toggling on/off, 139
soloing clips, 210
sonic field, defined, 190
sound bites, editing, 34–35
source media, using, 67, 69
split edits, using, 178–180
Start (In) of clips, 34, 105
  deleting, 96
  jumping playhead to, 96
  setting, 96, 123, 139
  trimming to skimmer, 183
stereo, explained, 190
still images, using, 93–95, 181–182, 256
storage, considering, 2–5
stories, overview, 10–11
storylines
  applying append edits to, 125
  applying insert edits to, 127
  applying overwrite edits to, 129
  benefits, 135
  breaking apart, 140
  types of, 118
surround mixes
  creating, 31, 209
  mixing audio to, 52
Switch, function of, 23

T

tape-based camera, importing media from, 85–86. *See also* cameras
tapeless media, 68
text
  adding, 12
  adding to titles, 238
  finding and replacing, 236–237
  font settings, 233–234
  manipulating, 232–233
  styles, 234
themes, creating, 270
thumbnails
  controlling contents of, 23
  displaying for clips, 103
timecode
  breaks, 86
  calculation of values, 156
  changing, 50
  displaying in Dashboard, 22
  explained, 22
  overview, 102–103
  preferences, 102
  setting starting, 31
  using to move clips, 156
  utility clip, 272, 274
Timeline. *See also* Magnetic Timeline
  audio animation, 268
  controls, 23
  creating Compound Clips in, 148–149
  described, 19
  elements, 49
  finding keywords in, 109
  fitting projects into, 38
  keyboard shortcut, 49
  modifying keyframes in, 207–208
  moving vertically in, 36
  navigating, 119
  opening Find window in, 164
  organizing with Roles, 161–162
  rendering, 268
  scaling, 23
  selecting everything in, 320
  setting keyframes in, 207–208
  toggling between Project Library, 64
  video animation, 268
  zooming into and out of, 163
Timeline History, navigating, 151–152, 163
Timeline Index, 23–24. *See also* Finder
  displaying, 116, 160
  features of, 159
  keyboard shortcut, 49, 109
  toggling display of, 64, 164
  using to find items, 160, 162
Title Role, applying, 164
Title safe, displaying, 235–236
titles
  adding corner locator to, 238
  adding lower-third name to, 238–239
  adding text to, 238
  adjusting in Motion 5, 275–276
  animating, 232
  Assembler, 232
  editing, 230
  font settings, 233–234
  length of display, 231
  number available, 232
  Push In, 237
  selecting, 232
Titles Browser, using, 230–231
To-Dos
  converting markers to, 145
  described, 142
  listing, 160
  using, 144–145
Tool palette, options in, 153–154

toolbar, described, 19
tools, switching, 153
trackless editor, explained, 118, 156–157
transcoding files, 3, 75–76
Transform controls, displaying, 268
Transform effects, 243–247
Transition Browser, 224–228
Transition Inspector, 223–224
Transitions
  adding, 11–12, 36
  adding keyframes to, 227
  adding multiple, 217
  animating, 226–227
  applying default, 38
  applying match audio, 217–218
  audio-only, 219–221
  background tasks, 214–217
  changing duration of, 218
  connected storylines, 220
  converting frames to seconds, 214
  creation of, 225
  cuts, 166, 212
  detaching clips, 222
  dissolves, 166, 212
  duplicating, 223
  expanding audio from video, 218
  fade handles, 220
  fading to black, 218
  handles, 212–213
  lack of out of sync indicator, 222
  multi-image, 227–228
  overview, 212
  Precision Editor, 222
  Project Properties, 215–217
  rendering, 214–217
  setting preferences, 213–214
  trimming clips under, 222–223
  video, 217–218
  video-only, 218–219
  wipes, 166, 212
Trash
  moving Events to, 46–47
  moving items into, 64
trashing projects, 59
Trim controls, displaying, 268
Trim effect, using, 251–253
Trim tool
  roll trim, 175–176
  selecting, 163, 183
  slide edit, 177–178
  slip edit, 177
  using, 153
trimming. *See also* cuts
  beginning of clips, 174
  clips under transitions, 222–223
  colors of clip edges, 171
  connected clips, 180
  connected storylines, 181
  dragging, 175
  and editing, 175
  endings of clips, 174
  error, 170
  handles, 168
  keyboard shortcuts, 178
  Precision Editor, 170–174
  purpose of, 167–168
  to range selection, 183
  ripple trim, 171–172
  roll edit, 173
  scene and problem, 169–170
  setting edit points, 172
  setting preferences, 168
  split edits, 178–180
  stills, 181–182
  stories, 11
  techniques, 174–175
  terminology, 166
  transitions, 166
  two-up display, 168, 172
two-up display, switching to, 168

U

Undo feature, using, 46–47
Utilities folder, opening, 38

V

Vectorscope
  toggling display of, 320
  using, 309–310
video
  detaching audio from, 228
  handles, 212–213
  importing, 77
  playing full-screen, 20
  separating audio from, 189
video and audio clips, syncing, 96
video animation, displaying in Timeline, 268
video clips, collapsing and expanding, 210. *See also* generators
video editing
  enabling, 139
  requirements, 2
video formats, 3
video properties, customizing, 50–51
video quality settings, 297
Video Role, applying, 164
video scopes, 307–310
video skimming, toggling on/off, 210
video transitions, applying, 217–218, 228
video-only transition, applying, 218–219
videotape, using date display with, 99
Viewer
  Background Tasks window, 22
  Dashboard, 22
  described, 19
  displaying full-screen, 36, 38
  displaying on two monitors, 27
  Effects Browsers, 23
  Event Browser, 21
  Event Library, 21
  features, 20–25
  Fit button, 20
  full-screen images, 21
  Inspector, 23
  moving between frames, 23
  playback buttons, 20–21
  Project Library, 23–24
  Project Timeline, 23
  Scale pop-up menu, 20
  scaling images, 20
  Switch, 23
  Timeline controls, 23
  Timeline Index, 23–24
  toggling loop playback, 20
  toolbar, 23
  zooming images, 20
  zooming in/out of, 268
voice-overs, recording, 201–202
volume, adjusting with menu, 206. *See also* audio

W

Waveform monitor, using, 308, 320
waveforms, viewing, 178–179, 187, 205. *See also* audio
white levels, managing, 312
wipes, defined, 166, 212

X

XML files
  exporting, 99, 329
  importing, 95, 99

Y

YouTube example, 330–331

Z

Zoom tool, using, 153, 164
zooming, 38, 268